THE STORY OF SPANISH

Also by Jean-Benoît Nadeau and Julie Barlow

The Story of French
Sixty Million Frenchmen Can't Be Wrong

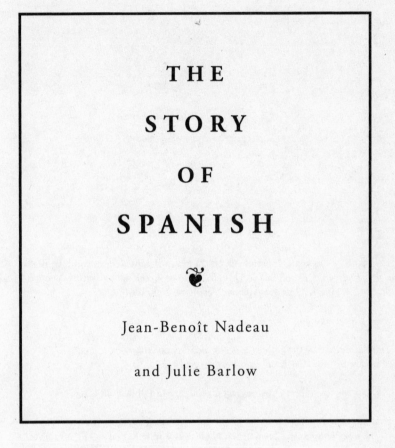

THE
STORY
OF
SPANISH

Jean-Benoît Nadeau

and Julie Barlow

ST. MARTIN'S PRESS ❧ NEW YORK

THE STORY OF SPANISH. Copyright © 2013 by Jean-Benoît Nadeau and Julie Barlow. All rights reserved. Printed in the United States of America. For information, address St. Martin's Press, 175 Fifth Avenue, New York, N.Y. 10010.

www.stmartins.com

Translations are by the authors unless otherwise noted.
Maps are by Julie Benoit unless otherwise credited.

Library of Congress Cataloging-in-Publication Data

Nadeau, Jean-Benoît.
   The story of Spanish / Jean-Benoit Nadeau and Julie Barlow. — First Edition.
      pages cm
   Includes bibliographical references and index.
   ISBN 978-0-312-65602-7 (hardcover)
   ISBN 978-1-250-02316-2 (e-book)
   1. Spanish language—History.   I. Barlow, Julie, 1968–   II. Title.
   PC4075.N33 2013
   460.9—dc23

                                                        2013002633

St. Martin's Press books may be purchased for educational, business, or promotional use. For information on bulk purchases, please contact Macmillan Corporate and Premium Sales Department at 1-800-221-7945, extension 5442, or write specialmarkets@macmillan.com.

First Edition: May 2013

10 9 8 7 6 5 4 3 2 1

Contents

Acknowledgments

We are thankful to a great number of people for aiding us in the research and writing of this book.

The list begins with our late agent, Ed Knappman, who passed away before he could read the manuscript. Ed, and his wife, Elizabeth, believed in *The Story of Spanish* when it was still a sketch on a restaurant place mat. Shortly before his death, Ed passed the baton to Roger Williams, our new agent, who has supported our work with skill and friendship.

Michael Flamini, our editor at St. Martin's Press, also believed in this project while it was still a collection of rough ideas. He was generous with his encouragement and guidance during the research and writing. We are also grateful to the team of editors, correctors, cover designers, publicists, marketers, salespeople, and more at St. Martin's Press, who crafted the finished product and got the book into our readers' hands (or their e-book reader). We would like to extend our thanks to our copy editor, Cynthia Merman. There are a lot of facts in this book and she truly scoured the manuscript.

Many more people also helped us make the book a reality. We thank Andrée Laurier of the Canada Council for the Arts as well as Brad Hector from the Canada-United States Fulbright Foundation. The financial backing of both organizations was vital to the book's development. We also are deeply grateful to Yvan Nadeau, our "guardian angel," as well as to our assistant and organizing genius, Veronica Louis, and to Tensy Cordoba, our patient and enthusiastic language coach.

In the Spanish-speaking world, key actors played an important role, starting with Darío Villanueva, secretary general of the Real

Academia Española (the Royal Academy of Spanish) and Humberto López Morales, director of the Asociación de Academias de la lengua española. We also address special thanks to Rosa Arbolí and Miguel Somovilla, who are, respectively, head librarian and head of communications at the Academia, for their enthusiastic support. Jose María Martínez, of the Instituto Cervantes, gave us a lot of his valuable time. And without the input of the Fundación Telefónica, we would have entirely overlooked the unprecedented study carried out to evaluate the economic value of Spanish. Professor José Antonio Alonso, director of the University of Madrid's Institute of International Studies in Alcalá de Henares, was very helpful in explaining it to us.

We gained early moral support and encouragement from Alejandra de la Paz, executive director of the Mexican Cultural Institute in Washington; as well as Guillermo Corral Van Damme, cultural industries policy director general of the Spanish Embassy in Washington; Javier Francisco Oterino Cuchí, cultural attaché at the Spanish embassy in Ottawa; and María Julia Rodríguez, who was cultural minister at the Canadian embassy of Argentina. The Arizona State University at Phoenix also gave useful institutional backing, including access to its library and databases. And Emily Spinelli, executive director of the American Association of Teachers of Spanish and Portuguese, opened a few more doors.

In Phoenix, Arizona, where we spent six months in 2010 as part of Julie's Fulbright grant, a number of people supplied precious help. First among them was Erik Lee, associate director of the North American Center for Transborder Studies at Arizona State University, who supplied us with a lot of good advice, insight, and help, and who in so doing became a good friend. We also thank NACTS director Rick Van Schoik and Sara Sonnenberg for welcoming us and helping us get the most out of our time at ASU, as well as Jaime Aguila for his advice.

In Phoenix, we owe a warm thank-you to Gantry York, organizer of the Phoenix Amigos Meetup Group, who oriented us through bilingual Phoenix and steered us toward some excellent sources for interviews. We were also fortunate to meet a rich variety of people at our daughters' school, notably Rona Johnson, Alicia Webber, Michelle Greenberg, and Irma García, who became a permanent resident of the United States shortly after we left Phoenix. And we are grateful to our neighbors in Tempe, Billy and Ashlee Miller, for helping us and our daughters feel at home.

We are also grateful to a number of friends who over the years helped us forge a personal connection to Spanish. Among those are Nuria and Claude Godcharles in Palo Alto and Celia Vara in Alicante, Spain, who opened our eyes to the reality of *La Movida*.

A Guide to Spanish Pronunciation

THERE ARE A LOT FEWER sounds in Spanish than in English. Almost all Spanish words adhere to the following pronunciation rules.

Vowels

In Spanish, each vowel is pronounced separately. *Auto* (car) has four sounds, one for each letter.

A sounds like the *a* in *far* but shorter.

E sounds like the *ay* in *play* when stressed—e.g., *médico* (doctor). If not stressed, it sounds more like the *e* in *bet*—e.g., *estudio* (study).

I sounds like the *e* in *be* but shorter.

O is the same as the *o* in *lock.*

U sounds like *oo* but shorter. Before most vowels, it becomes a semivowel that sounds like the *w* in *wall*—e.g., *fuego* (fire). *U* is always silent after *q*, as in *que*. After *g*, *u* is generally silent—e.g., *guerrilla*. But if *gu* is followed by a consonant, the *u* is pronounced—e.g., *gusto.*

Y; when used as a vowel, sounds like the *e* in *be* but shorter—e.g., *y* (and). When used as a semivowel, it sounds like the *y* in *yo-yo*—e.g., *hoy* (today).

Consonants

B, D, F, K, L, M, N, P, and *T:* are pronounced the same way as they are in English.

C in front of *a, o,* and *u* is pronounced like *k*—e.g., *canal*. In front of *e* and *i,* there are variations. In the Americas and some parts of Spain, *c* is pronounced like *s*. In northern Spain, *c* is pronounced like *th* in *path*.

Ch: Until 1994, this was a distinct letter (in the dictionary) but not anymore. It is pronounced *ch*.

G is complicated. In front of *e* and *i,* it sounds like a throaty *h*—e.g., *general*. In front of *a o,* or any consonant, it is hard—e.g., *gato* (cat). The special case is in front of *u*. Then it may sound like *gw*—e.g., *lengua* (language), or it is hard *g*—e.g., *guerrilla*. Or it may disappear into *wa*—e.g., *guardia* (guard).

H is always silent.

J is called *la jota*. It sounds like a very throaty *h*.

Ll: Until 1994, this was a distinct letter (in the dictionary) but not anymore. Depending on the location, it sounds like the *y* in *yo-yo* (e.g., *llama*) or the soft *j* of *measure* or *pleasure*. But in some dialects, it may sound like the *lli* in *million*.

Ñ is a distinct letter in the dictionary that falls between *n* and *o*. It sounds like the English *ng* of *sing*—e.g., *niño* (child).

Q is always pronounced like *k* and is always combined with a silent *u*.

R at the beginning of words or when appearing as *rr* sounds like a long trill. A single *r* anywhere else is almost always pronounced like a very short trill, or a single tap of the tongue.

S sounds like *s* except when it comes in front of *l, m,* and *d*. In those cases, it sounds like *z*.

V sounds like *b* but slightly softer.

W is reserved for foreign terms. It sounds like *w*. In Spain, it may sound like *b*—e.g., *wáter* (toilet).

X before a vowel sounds like *ks*. Before a consonant it sounds like *s*. But in Mexico, in place names with an *x*, it sounds like a throaty *h*—e.g., *México*.

Z in the Americas sounds like *s*. In northern Spain, it sounds like *th*.

Accents
The trema (¨) indicates that the letter *u* after *g* is pronounced, like *güiro* (gourd).

The acute accent (′) on vowels indicates peculiar cases of stressing (but not a different sound, as in French).

Spanish stressing rules are simple. Stress is always on the next to last vowel in words that end with a vowel or with *n* or *s*—in other words, the large majority of Spanish words. For words ending in any other consonant, like *merced* (market), the stress is on the last vowel. Words that follow the rule do not have accents.

For words that don't follow these rules, such as *médico* (doctor), *león* (lion), and *fácil* (easy), the accent shows where the stress is.

In some one-syllable words, the accent doesn't indicate any stress at all. It is used to differentiate homonyms, like *te* (objective case of you) and *té* (tea).

MAP I—SPAIN TODAY

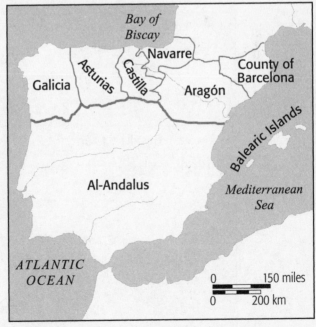

MAP 6—LATIN AMERICA TODAY

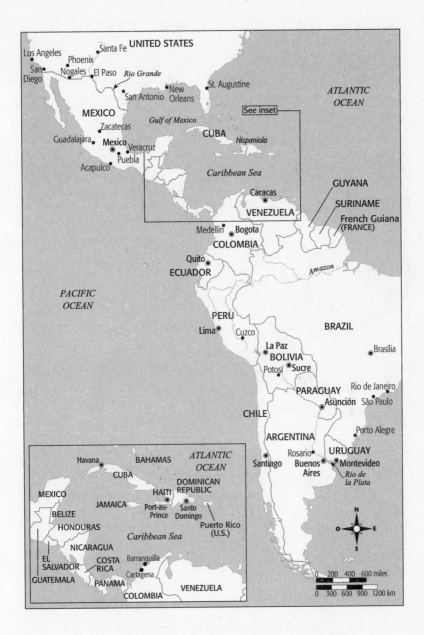

MAP 7—U.S. MINORITY POPULATION BY COUNTY (2010)

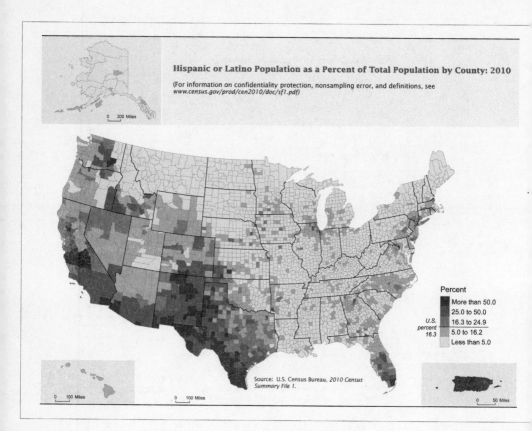

Hispanic or Latino Population as a Percent of Total Population by County: 2010

(For information on confidentiality protection, nonsampling error, and definitions, see
www.census.gov/prod/cen2010/doc/sf1.pdf)

Percent

- More than 50.0
- 25.0 to 50.0
- 16.3 to 24.9
- 5.0 to 16.2
- Less than 5.0

U.S. percent 16.3

Source: U.S. Census Bureau, *2010 Census Summary File 1.*

MAP 8—U.S. MINORITY POPULATION CHANGE BY COUNTY
(2000–2010)

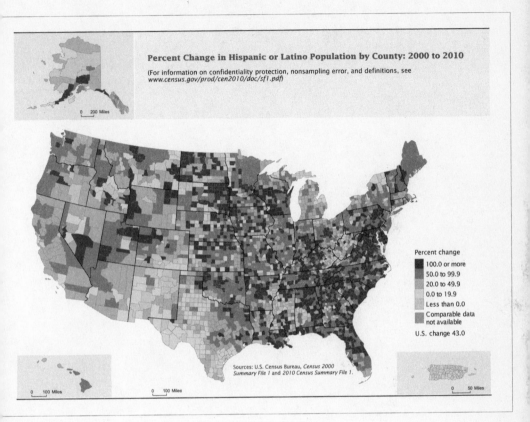

Percent Change in Hispanic or Latino Population by County: 2000 to 2010

(For information on confidentiality protection, nonsampling error, and definitions, see
www.census.gov/prod/cen2010/doc/sf1.pdf)

Percent change

- 100.0 or more
- 50.0 to 99.9
- 20.0 to 49.9
- 0.0 to 19.9
- Less than 0.0
- Comparable data not available

U.S. change 43.0

Sources: U.S. Census Bureau, *Census 2000
Summary File 1* and *2010 Census Summary File 1.*

0   200 Miles

0   100 Miles

0   100 Miles

0   50 Miles

Introduction

STROLLING THROUGH THE WALLED MEDIEVAL city of Toledo in the summer of 2012, we felt like we were in a gigantic open-air history museum. Every corner of the city gave us new insights into Spanish architecture, art, and archaeology, and spoke of the centuries of cultural interplay that forged them.

Indeed, modern Spain is the product of a succession of civilizations that occupied or dominated the Iberian Peninsula over the millennia: Celts, Phoenicians, and Romans were followed by German Visigoths, Arabs, French, and Castilians. As successive empires fought—and even destroyed—one another to gain control of the peninsula, Spain developed from the densely intertwined cultural layers each civilization left behind.

But one element of this story is particularly striking: none of the civilizations that dominated Spain completely erased the legacies of the ones that preceded it. Perhaps the most stunning physical example of this is the sixteenth-century cathedral of Córdoba. Known as the Mezquita-Catedral (Mosque-Cathedral), it consists of a Renaissance cathedral literally carved into the middle of a ninth-century mosque, which is still standing, its 856 columns encircling the cathedral like a forest. Spain is full of such medleys: in the San Román Church in Toledo, Visigoth-style arches face windows bordered in Arabic script. The walls of Seville's Real Alcázar palace—home to Christian kings since the Middle Ages—are covered with Arabic mosaics.

It was the same mind-boggling mesh of cultural influences that forged the Spanish language.

Spanish started out as a quirky, obscure dialect spoken by a remote tribe of cattle farmers in a northern strip of the peninsula. This tribe went on to become the Kingdom of Castile and León.

As the Castilians spread their influence throughout Spain, their language picked up vocabulary, ideas, and structures from the different cultures and societies the Castilians encountered—some of the most ancient texts in Old Spanish vernacular were written in Arabic script. Eventually, these influences blended into the language that would become Spanish. But even before Castilian had evolved into modern Spanish, the language left the shores of the peninsula and started acquiring new features from the civilizations of the New World. In the next centuries, this language spread so widely it would create a Spanish-speaking world ten times the size of Spain.

Today, Spanish is the world's second or third language with five hundred million speakers. Twenty-one countries use it officially, and Spanish has an important unofficial presence in a twenty-second, the United States. Yet Spanish is still evolving and changing, as the world where it is spoken changes.

It was the Spanish language itself that inspired us to write this book. Spanish is a cluster of contradictions. Over its history, it became—at once—one of the most organized and systematic tongues in history and a finely honed tool used to express disorder and passion. The tension of these conflicting impulses makes Spanish an irresistible topic for a couple of journalists looking for a good story.

Yet it took us a few decades to build up the courage to tackle the topic.

The first obstacle was a linguistic one: neither of us speaks Spanish as a native language. We were both attracted to Spanish starting in our student days at McGill University, but our first job was to learn one of Canada's official languages—English for Jean-Benoît and French for Julie. Still, we both studied Spanish at university and practiced it over the years on trips to Latin America and Spain.

Julie's initial interest in Spanish, which started in the mid-1980s, came from the fact that cold war politics and underdevelopment had made Latin America a top priority for human rights organizations. Years later, when she was studying Spanish in the city of Puebla, Mexico, she was ushered into the peculiar universe of Latin American *telenovelas* and learned about the addictive TV formula that is carrying Latin American productions to living rooms as far away as Croatia, Israel, and India.

Jean-Benoît's interest in Spanish was more down-to-earth—in fact, it was underground. In 1987, and again in 1990, he was part of an expedition of cave explorers who traveled to the remote sierra in the backwoods of the state of Puebla. The Mexican peasants he met there, like most of the campesinos of the Sierra Negra, spoke Spanish as a second language. Their mother tongue was Nahuatl, the language of the Aztecs, who were conquered almost five centuries earlier—and were supposedly wiped out.

These early experiences taught us that there was much more to the story of Spanish than conquistadores, revolutions, tango music, and great writers—important as all those are.

Then, years later, our professional experience gave us the tools we needed to write this book. In 2006, we published *The Story of French,* which explains how the French language evolved, became the language of a country, and then spread to almost every other country on the planet.

The origins of Spanish are similar to those of French. Both languages grew out of the Roman occupation of Western Europe and the "barbarian" invasions of Germanic tribes that followed Rome's decline. But before the Dark Ages ended, the two languages headed in radically different directions. French was heavily influenced by the language of its Germanic rulers, the Franks, whose dynasty would morph into France's monarchy. In Spain, the Germanic Visigoths ceded power to the Arabs, who, in turn, were unseated by Christian kings, punctuating the evolution of Spain's history with radical new influences.

Centuries later, the stories of French and Spanish diverged in another way. The French managed to spread their language across the entire globe. Although Spanish became the mother tongue of many more people, it never took root outside of the Americas.

Today, as an international language, Spanish has an entirely different personality from French. Twice as many people speak Spanish than French. But it is an official tongue in fewer countries than French—twenty-one, as opposed to thirty-six (sixty-three for English). In short, the status of an international language is not determined just by its number of speakers—although that helps.

There's another contradiction inherent in Spanish. It produced many global household concepts and names—tango, flamenco, Tex-Mex food, Gabriel García Márquez, Pedro Almodóvar, and Shakira are just some obvious examples. Yet as an international language, Spanish has always punched below its weight, particularly in science and technology. Sources differ on the numbers, but many American states produce more patents than the largest Spanish-speaking countries.

The best word to describe the approach we take to Spanish in this work is *biography*. We treat Spanish like a character, explaining how it grew up and who and what influenced it over the course of its long life.

As in *The Story of French*, a number of "sciences" shape the story, notably linguistics and statistics. But they are just part of the story. We did not set out to do a statistical survey of Spanish speakers or to write a book on linguistics. We believe that languages develop and spread not because of their inherent beauty but as a result of many factors. Spanish is not just a product of, but also a player in, history. As the French general Hubert Lyautey famously said to the French Academy in 1912, "A language is a dialect that possesses an army, a navy, and an air force." In our view, Lyautey's list should include politics and economics, demographics, visionary leaders, creators, and more.

The expression "empire on which the sun never sets" referred to

Spain before it did to Britain, and colonialism was definitely a major force carrying Spain beyond the shores of the Iberian Peninsula. Yet power alone—colonial or otherwise—does not explain how any language becomes international. Power is, in its essence, transient, and the links among power, language, and prestige can be subtle, or even contradictory. Three centuries of Spanish colonialism were not enough to turn Spanish into the main language in the most populous parts of the Spanish Empire, notably Mexico, Peru, Guatemala, Bolivia, Paraguay, and the Philippines. And then, it was the progressive *collapse* of the Spanish Empire that caused Spanish to spread in these areas.

Another word that describes our approach is *anthropological.* Anyone who learns a second language or becomes versed in a foreign culture enters a new world. Language is a universe its speakers inhabit, a mental frontier, just as important as ethnicity, religion, or ideology, and just as resilient to change. Language shapes how we organize our thoughts, our lives, and our nations—in short, our world. As we learned writing *The Story of French,* the mental universe shared by the speakers of any language has some enduring features yet it is constantly affected by political and economic change, technical innovation, and more.

So, while writing this book, we asked: What does it mean to be part of Spanish-speaking culture? What are the traits and features all its speakers share, and where did those come from?

The catalyst for this book actually came from a visit to Puebla in the spring of 2006, where we met a group of adult learners at a local Spanish-language school. They were all Americans from a variety of professions who had taken time off from their jobs to study Spanish. There was no reason to think they were anything but typical of an off-season student cohort at any Spanish school. And that got us wondering about the curious power of attraction of Spanish. In particular, what could possibly motivate people who spoke English—a language unanimously hailed to be the most powerful and important in the world—to invest all that time and energy in learning the language of a minority in their own country?

Six million Americans learn Spanish (more than all other languages combined) and an estimated fifteen million speak it with a degree of proficiency (this is not counting the thirty-seven million Hispanics who still speak the language). Americans' desire to speak Spanish is so ubiquitous today that few question it. Yet the phenomenon of Americans studying Spanish does not fit the laws that govern the spread of languages. Statistically, people are drawn to languages that will help them climb a socioeconomic ladder. They choose languages that will bring them power.

What is making Spanish so influential in the United States? Part of the answer lies in the language's quirky, vibrant, and accessible pop culture. This charisma gives Spanish a special kind of power in the United States, a singular quality that inspires many to learn Spanish. Spanish—literally—makes the world bigger.

This book is our attempt to explain where that world came from.

1. The Land of the Rabbits

THREE MILLENNIA AGO, WHEN ROME was still a swamp and Athens was barely strong enough to take on Troy, the Mediterranean world belonged to the Phoenicians, a civilization of master seafarers from the Middle East. Renowned for their mercantile prowess, the Phoenicians drummed up business as far north as Britain and Scandinavia and built trading ports all along the shores of North Africa.

It was during one of these construction phases, around 1200 BC, that the Phoenicians landed on the Iberian Peninsula.

The Phoenicians started settling the peninsula only around 800 BC. At the time, it was a sparsely populated land of dense forests and open plains teeming with wild boars, deer, wolves, and bears. Among the many novelties the Phoenicians discovered, one small mammal caught their attention. It was similar to a furry, tailless Middle Eastern creature with round ears that they called a hyrax, except this version had long ears and long legs, and multiplied at an astonishing pace.

The Phoenicians were evidently much impressed by these prolific little mammals. They named their new territory after them: *I-shepan-ha*, literally "land of hyraxes." Centuries later, the Romans Latinized this name to *Hispania*. And centuries after that, the name morphed into *España*.

In other words, Spain's names originally meant something like "land of the rabbits."

But the Iberian Peninsula had a long history of settlement long before the Phoenicians arrived. To get an idea of its historical layers, we traveled to the city of Burgos, the ancient capital of the Kingdom of Castile and León, in northern Spain. Located in the valley of the río Arlanzón, Burgos is still dominated by the old *castillo* (castle) built there twelve hundred years ago to defend settlers fleeing marauding Moors. But there had been people living around Burgos literally a million years before that.

From the ramparts of Burgos's Castillo, on top of the hill of San Miguel, we gazed down on a dense maze of tile roofs, a view dominated by the city's splendid Gothic cathedral. In the middle of the town is an enormous, futuristic glass structure, the Museo de la Evolución Humana (Museum of Human Evolution), which houses the finds of impressive archaeological digs carried out about ten miles from Burgos. One site, known as Atapuerca, produced some of the most impressive discoveries in European archaeology in the last thirty years.

Some of these discoveries forced historians to rewrite the story of the dawn of humanity. The oldest bones from Atapuerca are those of a man who died 1.2 million years ago. Previously, no one believed that humanity's ancestors had left Africa that early. Although archaeologists disagree about where the remnants fit in the evolutionary chain, their discovery indisputably makes Spain the European cradle of mankind. In addition to the 1.2-million-year-old *Homo antecessor*, archaeologists in the Burgos area found some Neanderthal remains dating from 60,000 BC, which would make them among the last of their kind. Recent dating of cave art in northern Spain has shown that it is ten thousand years older than similar finds in France.

They say that history is written by the conquerors, but this wasn't the case for the Phoenicians. That is probably because, although they settled in the southern Iberian Peninsula for eight hundred years, the Phoenicians never managed to pass their language on to its inhabitants.

The Romans, who landed on the Iberian Peninsula in the third century BC were the first to write down anything about the people who lived there. They recorded observations about the three principal ethnic groups they encountered: the Basques, the Iberians, and the Celts, none of whom had written anything about themselves beyond the names of their dead on gravestones.

Yet some of the words from the languages of pre-Roman Spain did find their way into modern Spanish.

The Basque language is believed to have evolved from a language used in Neolithic times. Today's Basque territory straddles the border of France and Spain, yet Spain has so many place names of Basque origin that historians believe that the Basques might once have occupied up to a third of the Iberian Peninsula. Among the civilizations the Romans conquered in Hispania, the Basques alone refused to give up their language. That language, Euskera, is still spoken today in both France and Spain, although it has been heavily influenced by Latin over the centuries.

Curiously, the Basques got their own name from the Celts, a tribe that migrated to the Iberian Peninsula around 2000 BC, and dubbed them *Vascos*, their name in Spanish to this day. The Celts spoke a group of related tongues similar to those spoken by the Celtic populations farther north, in France and Britain. These Celtic languages themselves originated in the same tongue that spawned Latin, a language linguists call Indo-European, spoken about eight thousand years ago in Turkey. Indo-European spawned Greek, Germanic, Celtic, and Sanskrit (a language of India), which all share some common vocabulary, like *papa* and *mama*.

In the southern part of the peninsula, the Romans discovered another tribe, called the Iberians. Again, the name came from a Celtic word *bier*, which meant river. *Bier* eventually morphed into *Ebro*, the name of Spain's main river. The Celts labeled the people living across the Ebro from them the Iberians, which just meant "the Riverians."

The Iberians, who were probably related to the Berbers in North Africa and had been on the peninsula for several thousand years before the Romans arrived, were the only native population in Iberia who had a written language. Unfortunately, almost no traces of the Iberian language survive and almost nothing is known about it, not even the name Iberians called themselves before the Celts named them.

In between the Iberians and Celts, the Romans discovered another group. The Romans seem to have run out of names by the time they discovered this people and just called them the *Celtiberians*.

Although most of what we know about these ancient civilizations comes from what the Romans wrote about them, the Romans didn't have much to say. This was a stark contrast to Gaul, where Julius Caesar wrote extensively about the Celtic civilization he conquered. Roman generals never recorded more than a few details about the people of the Iberian Peninsula, not to mention their languages. To decode Iberia's languages, historians have had to work from broken plates and tombstone engravings—not the most reliable sources, since ancient engravers wrote phonetically in ill-defined writing systems.

Nevertheless, many words from Iberia's original civilizations survived the centuries and are still part of modern Spanish. *Galápago* (turtle), *silo, puerco* (pig), *toro* (bull), *álamo* (poplar), and *salmón* (salmon) come from pre-Roman languages. Almost all the ancient words that made it into modern Spanish relate to material and agricultural life. *Barro* (mud), *charco* (puddle), *manteca* (fat, butter), and *perro* (dog) come from Celtic words, as do *camisa* (shirt), *cabaña* (shed), *carro* (cart), *cerveza* (beer), *cama* (bed), and *camino* (road).

The Basque language, Euskera, gave Spanish *izquierdo* (left). Basque probably contributed the rolled *rr* of Spanish: *pizarra* (slate), *chaparro* (oak), *zamarra* (sheepskin jacket), *narria* (flatbed truck), *cencerro* (cowbell), and *gabarra* (barge). All have a Basque origin.

But the story of Spanish really starts with Rome. The language the Romans brought to Hispania would survive other conquering empires as it evolved into a modern tongue. It would one day travel across the globe where it would grow to become the world's third language, spoken by five hundred million people in two dozen countries. It's amazing, then, to think that the Romans didn't really want to be on the Iberian Peninsula in the first place. The main reason they went was to defeat their rivals at the time—the Carthaginians, a powerful Phoenician colony based in today's Tunisia, which had grown to control the Mediterranean Sea by that time.

The Carthaginians were the catalyst that set the history of the Spanish language history into motion. In the third century BC, the Romans ran up against the Carthaginians while they were trying to consolidate their land power over the *Italian* peninsula. That sparked the First Punic War of 264–241 BC. The Second Punic War started a generation later, in 218 BC, when the Carthaginian prince Hannibal crossed the Pyrenees and the Alps with thirty-eight thousand men, eight thousand horses, and thirty-seven war elephants and attacked the Italian peninsula. While the elephants did not last long, Hannibal was a military genius who defeated one Roman army after the next. But when the Romans figured out that Hannibal was using the Iberian Peninsula as a base to rebuild his troops, they headed there and drove him back to Africa, in 201 BC.

The Romans established the province of Hispania in 197 BC. Hispania was their first overseas colony. (Rome had not yet conquered the land passage, which was the future province of Gaul.) By comparison, Gaul became a part of the empire 150 years later, and Dacia (the future Romania) 150 years after that. Though linguists debate the real effects of this on modern Spanish, one thing is certain: the Latin spoken in Hispania contained words that had actually disappeared in Rome by the time Rome started conquering its other territories. Relative to the other languages that grew out of Latin, Spanish, therefore, contains many words linguists label archaisms.

The Latin word *cansar* (to tire) was still being used when Rome began settling Hispania but disappeared 150 years later, when Caesar conquered Gaul. Spanish (and Portuguese) are the only Romance languages whose verb for "to tire" resembles *cansar*. The

Spanish word *cuyo* (of which, of whose) comes from a Latin word that slipped into Spanish with an identical form and meaning but was gone by the end of the first century BC in Rome, so no other Romance language acquired it. The Spanish word *además* (above all), from the Latin *demais,* had also disappeared from Latin by then. At the time of the conquest of Hispania, *querer* meant "to wish." The meaning later changed to "to seek." The Roman poet Terence, who wrote in second century BC, uses *querer* in the sense of to wish, a sense it still has in Spanish, whereas the French *quérir* means to seek. Other words in Spanish, such as *arena* (sand), *uva* (grape), *ciego* (blind), and *queso* (cheese), descend directly from this older version of street Latin that never took root in France or Romania.

The Spanish words *hablar* (to speak) and *preguntar* (to ask) also have their roots in this Vulgar Latin spoken when Hispania was conquered. They come from *fabulari* and *percontari* (in Rome, these would later change to *loqui* and *postulare*). And Spaniards say *mas* (more) instead of *plus* or *più* like the French and the Italians because the custom in 200 BC was still to say *magis* instead of *plus.*

Aside from their battles with the Carthaginians, the Romans were also drawn to the Iberian Peninsula by its silver. They weren't the first. Many empires had ventured onto the peninsula to conquer Tartessos, a kingdom located in a triangle between Seville, Cádiz, and Huelva. The Tartessians were the superstars of antiquity. By the time the Romans arrived there, they had been practicing intensive agriculture for some five thousand years and silver mining for two thousand years.

There are references to Tartessos in the works of the great Greek geographer Herodotus—not to mention in the Bible, where it is known as Tarsis—that describe its rich copper and silver mines and its bronze production. Much of Tartessos's mining wealth came from an area on the river then known as Luxia. Because its water was red and had a very high pH level, the river would later be known as río Tinto (Red River). And this is the origin of the name of the world's largest mining conglomerate, the Australo-British Rio Tinto plc, which got its start when it purchased the old Tartessian mines in 1873.

But silver or no silver, the Romans still had doubts about whether to stay in Hispania. They spoke of the peninsula as "outside" the civilized world.

Then when the Romans decided to conquer the interior of the peninsula, they got more than they had bargained for. As the Roman troops tried to subdue local inhabitants, the Iberians, Celts, and Celtiberians discovered a common penchant for guerrilla warfare and joined forces—a first. They launched surprise attacks by night, then blended into the scenery by day. The rigid structure of the Roman legion made it hard to win wars against these highly motivated rebels who had the home field advantage.

But if the Romans considered leaving Iberia to the rabbits, they changed their minds when they realized what would likely happen in their absence: the free Iberians would head north, join the Gauls, and throw a wrench in Rome's expansion plans in Gaul. There were other advantages to staying. In addition to silver, gold, and copper, the Iberian Peninsula was rich in wine, olive oil, and wood, commodities that were all beginning to run short back in Rome.

So the Romans fought on, advancing west and north across the peninsula, conquering one village at a time. The Romans didn't fully break the Iberians' resistance until 19 BC, when, two centuries after arriving on the peninsula, they subdued Cantabria. But they never totally got hold of that territory, which would always remain a core area of resistance in Spain.

For linguists, the great puzzle of the Roman conquest is how the Romans succeeded in doing what no one had done before them. The Phoenicians had controlled the Iberian Peninsula for eight hundred years, but beyond giving Hispania its name, they didn't leave a linguistic trace. The Greeks had established two trading posts in

Iberia around 500 BC, but again, their language disappeared with them.

The Romans managed to get the entire peninsula speaking Latin in about 250 years, even though they were fighting the Iberians the whole time.

How exactly did the Romans pull this off?

Not by force but by offering incentives. The Romans lured Iberians to Latin by tying it into the perks of city life, cities having always been their forte. As they advanced through Hispania, they built Augusta Emerita (Mérida), Hispalis (Seville), Italica (Itálica), Corduba (Córdoba), Toletum (Toledo), Caesaraugusta (Zaragoza), and Salmantica (Salamanca). The Romans connected these centers with splendid highways and linked the open cities of the sea to the closed villages of the mountains.

As they showcased the strengths of their civilization, the Romans conscripted the Iberian nobles to carry out the administrative work of running towns. Nobles were happy to do it, but there was one condition: they had to learn Latin. On the whole, the Iberian nobles complied. There were lots of advantages to learning Latin—notably, it improved communication with the Romans. Speaking Latin also boosted Iberians' status among their own countrymen. The Romans oiled the gears of the whole machine by offering to help build more cities and roads, and write laws and regulations—in other words, by creating more jobs for Latin speakers.

In short, the enterprising Iberians, Celts, and Celtiberians resigned themselves to the idea that learning Latin was the best way to prosper.

The Romans later used the same formula to spread Latin in Gaul, which Julius Caesar conquered in 51 BC, with equal success. Yet in Roman Britannia, which the Romans finished conquering in AD 77, the inhabitants never switched to Latin. Britannia's Celtic population was more uniform linguistically. In Gaul and

Hispania, where the populations did not have the same level of linguistic uniformity, the Latin language and culture became common bonds that united diverse groups.

In Hispania, Latin gradually progressed from the language of the upwardly mobile class to a common tongue across the peninsula. Everything suggests that the Celtic languages had died by the time the Roman Empire fell in the fifth century AD. The pre-Roman languages survived only in isolated areas like the extreme northwest (Galicia), where the Celtic tongue lasted until the seventh century. The only exception was, of course, the Basque land. Yet linguists today estimate that roughly half the Basque language consists of borrowings from Latin.

As the Romans slowly conquered the Iberian Peninsula from east to west, Latin absorbed new vocabulary along the way. About thirty of these Hispanicisms survived and became modern Spanish words, many even became part of mainstream Latin and were incorporated into the tongues of territories Rome later conquered. Pliny the Younger, a Roman magistrate and prolific letter writer who left behind many details of Roman life, claims *cuniculus* (rabbit) originated in Hispania (in modern Spanish, it's *conejo*). Other Latin words that probably originated in Hispania include *lancea* (in Spanish, *lanza,* in English, lance), *plumbum* (lead; hence *plomo*), and *minium* (a lead oxide). The Latin *gladius* (sword) came from an Iberian weapon that the Roman legions adopted as they fought their way through the countryside trying to subdue the rebellious Iberians.

By the close of the first millennium BC, Hispania was no longer a rebel territory of the Roman Empire. It was producing its own crop of thinkers and statesmen, including Seneca the Elder (54 BC–AD 39) and his son Seneca the Younger (4 BC–AD 65), the last great Stoic.

In the middle of the first century AD, Hispania even produced its first Roman emperor, Trajan (r. AD 98–117) and then Hadrian

(r. 117–138), the first Roman emperor who spoke the bourgeoning "native Latin" of Hispania.

It was Hadrian's language that would evolve into modern Spanish.

2. Vulgar Language

IN 2009, WE BOUGHT OUR six-year-old twins an illustrated Spanish-French dictionary. We were planning to move to Arizona for six months in 2010, and knew they would hear Spanish every day at their new school there.

Our girls had spent the first three years of their lives in Haiti speaking French Creole, a language whose vocabulary is estimated to be 80 percent French. So they picked up French quickly when they came to live in Quebec.

The effect was to make one of them, Erika, overconfident about language learning. When she learned that the Spanish word for arm is *brazo*—very close to *bras* in French—she thought she had discovered the Rosetta stone. Erika thought Spanish is just French with an *o* at the end of each word. "This is a *mano*," she said, adding *o* to the French word for hand, *main*. "That's a *porto*," she said, pointing to the door, which is *porte* in French, still close to the Spanish *puerta*.

The illusion lasted until she got to her head. "*Teto*," she announced (from the French *tête*), and we had to break the bad news to her that the Spanish word for head is *cabeza*. Yet all this did get us thinking: the relationship between Spanish and French is so obvious that even a six-year-old with hardly any reading ability can see it.

Many people who have mastered Spanish, French, or Italian know that speaking any one of them makes it much easier to decipher the others. The similarities in their vocabulary and grammatical structures are striking. Linguists have calculated that as much as 75 percent of the vocabulary of French and Spanish is common.

Of course, that's because French and Spanish both started out as Latin.

Yet what most people don't know is that the Latin that became Spanish was not the Classical Latin we still study today. Spanish evolved from a colloquial tongue that linguists call Vulgar Latin.

It's fair to say that Hadrian's Wall is more famous than Emperor Hadrian after whom it was named. The twelve-foot-high, seventy-three-mile-long wall crossing northern England was only one of the Roman emperor's many building feats. Born in the provincial town of Itálica, near present-day Seville, Hadrian was the second native of Hispania to become emperor. During his reign, from AD 117 to 138, Hadrian spent half his time abroad, traveling through his empire: Britannia, Germania, Egypt and North Africa, Anatolia (Turkey and the Black Sea area)—where he brought his team of builders with him.

But building wasn't all he was known for; Hadrian also went down in history for his speech. Like many young, upwardly mobile Roman citizens at the time, Hadrian was educated in Greek, not Latin. Hadrian had such a passion for Greek that his schoolmates nicknamed him Graeculus, "the Greekling"—but that came at a price. When Hadrian was twenty-five, he donned his first *toga praetexta* as a Roman quaestor (top civil servant) and made his first address to the Roman senate. According to the historian Aelius Spartianus, the senators heard his colloquial Latin and broke out laughing, and the future emperor decided to hire a tutor.

The problem was the quality of Hadrian's Latin. Having grown up in Spain, Hadrian communicated in the tongue common to all the Roman provinces: Vulgar Latin.

"Vulgar" here does not mean rude or obscene. The Latin word *vulgus* means "common people." When the Romans spoke of Hadrian's *sermo vulgaris,* they just meant common speech. (That's where the English *to vulgarize,* meaning "to popularize," comes from. It was only around the seventeenth century that *vulgar* came to mean "offensively coarse" in English.)

From the beginning of the Roman Empire until the ninth century, Vulgar Latin was the lingua franca from Hispania to Dacia (Romania), and from Napoli (Naples) to Londinum (London). Roman soldiers sent to conquer and occupy Europe spoke Vulgar Latin, or at least one variety of it—for there were many, even in Rome. Until the ninth century, Vulgar Latin speakers in all the Roman provinces could understand one another.

Linguists say that we "write in a language but speak in a dialect," meaning that there is big difference between how a language is written, in its standard form, and how it is spoken, colloquially. This is true of all languages and was the reason Vulgar Latin existed.

In short, the popular masses in the Roman Empire, including Hadrian, never spoke Classical Latin. *Classicus* means, literally, "first class" or "classy." It was the language of the educated, and it was hard to learn, even for them. Like German and Russian, Latin is a case language—each noun ends with a particular suffix (called a case) that indicates its function in the sentence. Latin sentences had no fixed word order because they didn't need it. People figured out the meaning of a sentence through the case endings. Whether you said *Marcus canem amat* or *Amat canem Marcus* or even *Canem Marcus amat*, you were saying "Marcus loves his dog."

This flexible word order made Classical Latin great for writing poetry but impractical for ordinary Roman citizens' day-to-day communication. Mastering the six cases required careful study and good reading skills, because you had to be schooled in Classical Latin in order to speak it. And as Hadrian learned, good pronunciation was even more critical. Latin speakers had to pronounce words precisely so listeners would recognize exactly the grammatical function of each word.

So it's not surprising that for daily business, the common folk in the Roman Empire, including traders and soldiers, adopted the easier-to-learn version of Latin.

Of course, languages are not static; they evolve constantly under new influences. Over the centuries, Roman subjects adapted colloquial Latin to their own needs, which made Vulgar Latin even more understandable and useful in day-to-day business. Speakers reduced the number of cases, added new features like articles and prepositions, made up new words, and established an unspoken rule that subject, verb, and object would always come roughly in the same order. They simplified the genders, reducing them from three (masculine, feminine, and neuter) to two, then added a dash of familiarity and humor to the whole mix to make Latin more down-to-earth. Curiously, for a number of centuries, people all over the Roman Empire made more or less the same changes to Vulgar Latin no matter where they lived.

Scholars today wish they knew more about Vulgar Latin, but there is not much evidence of it left, precisely because no one wrote it down. Linguists have been able to get glimpses of it from things like shopping lists, tombstone inscriptions, and notes scribbled in margins by writers, poets, and rhetoricians. The clergy used Vulgar Latin in some letters and sermons—not surprising, because the clergy had to make itself understood. A few authors, like the Roman playwrights Terence and Plautus (second century BC), tried to imitate the Vulgar Latin in their comedies, but since they used it for comic effect, no one knows if the writers were accurately depicting Vulgar Latin or grossly exaggerating it.

One of the best sources of Vulgar Latin words is Pompeii. When Mount Vesuvius erupted in AD 79, Pompeii and neighboring Herculaneum were buried under fifteen feet of ash, sheltering a wealth of shopping lists, diverse announcements, and not a few obscenities scribbled on walls of brothels from the abuses of time. (The engineer who first excavated the ruins of both cities, in 1738, was a Spanish captain, Rocque Joaquin de Alcubierre, who was working on a palace for the king of Naples, who also happened to be the king of Spain.)

Not surprisingly, scholars in the Roman Empire scorned Vulgar Latin (though they probably turned around and spoke it to their children and slaves in the same breath). Yet by the third or fourth century AD, Vulgar Latin was creeping into the written language.

We see this from the notes of Valerius Probus, a Roman grammarian who wrote a list of 227 "mistakes" commonly made in Latin, a document known as the *Appendix Probi*.

Probus would have been disappointed had he known the "mistakes" would interest future scholars more than his corrections. He inadvertently recorded 227 new words in Vulgar Latin for example:

CLASSICAL LATIN	VULGAR LATIN ("MISTAKE")	MEANING
alveus	albeus	barge
auris	oricla	ear
barbarus	barbar	foreigner, barbarian
bravium	brabium	reward
calida	calda	hot water
columna	colomna	column
digitus	dicitus	finger
masculus	masclus	male
mensa	mesa	table
nubes	nubs	cloud
numquam	numqua	never
oculus	oclus	eye
rivus	rius	river
speculum	speclum	mirror
tabula	tabla	board, plank

In fact, Valerius Probus may not even have written the text attributed to him. The earliest surviving copy of it was made in the eighth century, four centuries after he died. By then, it had probably been updated and corrected many times.

But the list is still considered crucial for understanding the phonetic development of Vulgar Latin. Classical Latin has five vowels; *a, e, i, o*, and *u* (written *v*), which were pronounced either as long on short vowels. Probus's text shows that Vulgar Latin speakers were fusing the long and short vowels. Since this meant the language lost some of its nuances, Vulgar Latin speakers created diphthongs, two adjacent vowels pronounced glidingly together as one sound (as, for example, in the word *sound*). That's how the Latin *tempus* became *tiempo* (time) and *porta* produced *puerta* (door). Diphthongs have been preserved in modern Spanish and Portuguese but not as much in other Latin languages.

Valerius Probus's list shows other changes that were under way and that would endure as features of modern Spanish. Speakers were dropping the middle unstressed vowels in words like *tabula* (table), which they pronounced *tabla*. The pronunciation of some consonants was also changing. The *m* at the end of words had become so soft that *numquam* (never) now sounded like *numqua* (Spanish: *nunca*).

The final *m* would eventually be dropped in Spanish. Words like *hominem, lucem, veritatem,* and *latronem* became *hombre* (man), *luz* (light), *verdad* (truth), and *ladron* (thief). The *v* in Latin was pronounced like a *w,* so *rivus* (river) sounded like *riwus* (closer to the Spanish *río).* The nasal *n* in the middle of words like *mensa* was dropped, producing *mesa* (table) in Spanish. In a feature now typical of Spanish, *v* was pronounced like *b,* so *taves* became *tabis* (corruption), *bravium* became *brabium* (reward), and *alveus* became *albeus* (barge).

Vulgar Latin speakers gave the language another interesting twist: they added a vowel (called an epenthetic vowel) to the beginning of names. This is how *sperare, spiritus,* and *spatha* acquired an *e* at the beginning, becoming *esperar* (to wait), *espíritu* (spirit), and *espada* (sword).

Simplifying had unintended consequences. Some changes in pronunciation made it impossible for Vulgar Latin speakers to understand whether words were subjects or objects. If *rosam* sounded like *rosa,* nothing made sense anymore.

Vulgar Latin speakers had to find new solutions. They established one of the fundamental features all Romance languages share—a fixed order of parts of speech: subject-verb-object. In Classical Latin, the sentence "Marcus is giving his father a book" is written *Marcus patri librum dat* (it could be written in any order without changing the meaning). But this was incomprehensible if the *i* of *patri* was not pronounced correctly, or if the *m* was removed. So Vulgar Latin speakers began saying *Marcus dat librum ad patrem* (it probably sounded more like *Marcu' dat libru' a' patre'*). Subject-verb-object—easy to understand who is doing what. Notice how close the Vulgar Latin is to modern Spanish: *Marcus está dando un libro a su padre* (Marcus is giving a book to his father).

To add nuance to their colloquial tongue, Vulgar Latin speakers invented definite and indefinite articles. As early as the middle of the last century BC, the Roman poet Catullus wrote about this new phenomenon. In Classical Latin, *illi* and *illa* meant *this* and *that*. Vulgar Latin speakers began to use them as definite articles, and eventually they became *el, la,* and *lo* in Spanish (the equivalent to English *the*). Using *unus* (the number 1), they introduced a further nuance with an indefinite article (equivalent to *a* in English), which in Spanish became *uno, una, unas,* and *unos*.

The inhabitants of Roman Hispania also combined prepositions and articles in order to convey different meanings. For instance, the Spanish words *después* (after) and *donde* (where) are combinations of Latin prepositions. *Después* comes from *de + ex + post. Donde* is simply *de + unde.* Romanians took it even further: they created the preposition *adineauri* (just recently), which is *ad + de + in + illa + hora* (hour). In Hispania, speakers created *ningulus* by combining *singulus* (one) and *nullus* (none). This is why Spaniards say *ninguno* (nobody).

One of the most uniform characteristics of today's Latin-based languages is the similar way they form adverbs: *rápidamente* (in Spanish), *rapidement* (French), *rapidamente* (Portuguese, Italian), *ràpidament* (Catalan). This is surprising because in Classical Latin there was no unified system for forming adverbs. The adverb for *absolutus* (complete) is *absolute,* but the adverb for *velox* (rapid) is *velociter.* For Vulgar Latin speakers, it was impossible to master the rules and exceptions. The way around this problem was to standardize the process by using a single suffix, *mens,* which means "in a mind": *absolumens* and *velocimens,* which mean literally "in a complete (or rapid) mind." And two thousand years later, all Spanish adverbs still abide to the old Vulgar Latin structure.

Vulgar Latin speakers also simplified verb conjugation. Due to sloppy pronunciation, people got confused between the future and conditional tenses. The common solution was to add the auxiliary verb *habere* (to have) after the main verb, which created *amara he, amara has, amara ha.* The verb endings of all Latin languages' future and conditional tenses are the corresponding conjugations of *habere* without the *h.*

The genius of a popular language is its familiarity and humor. Horses were prestigious animals in Hispania, and nobles called them by their Latin name, *aequus.* But Vulgar Latin speakers, making fun of the riders, started calling a horse a *caballus* (a beast of burden) instead, a joke that would produce the Spanish word *caballo* (horse). Like all slang, Vulgar Latin was often crude, as well as metaphorical. Leg in Classical Latin is *crus,* but people started referring to a leg as *perna* (ham), which became the Spanish *pierna.*

Diminutive terms are also typical of popular speech in all languages. The *Appendix Probi* shows that a couple of new diminutives were already developing in Vulgar Latin, like *auricula* (ear) and *rotela* (kneecap) to replace the proper *auris* and *rotula.* In Spanish, these diminutives produced *oreja* and *rodilla. Mane* (tomorrow) became *maneana*—very close to the well-known Spanish *mañana.*

But simplification was not always the rule as Vulgar Latin evolved into the Romance languages. In Hispania, Vulgar Latin speakers actually created two words for "to be." Classical Latin has only one verb for "to be," *esse,* which became *essere* in Vulgar Latin. But in Hispania, people created a second verb for "to be," *stare,* which had the sense of "to stand." This is why Spanish now has *ser* (to be, in essence) and *estar* (to be, in a state). *Estoy aquí* (I am here) is a state that can change. But *soy una mujer* (I am a woman) is an essence that will never change. This nuance is the first serious challenge in any beginner Spanish class.

Sometimes simplifications backfired. The reason Latin languages have both regular and irregular verbs is that Vulgar Latin speakers combined various verbs into one and combined conjugations in a haphazard way, not following any order. In Hispania, this happened with the two Latin verbs for "to go," *ire* and *vadere.* Hispanians made one verb, *ir,* but kept some of the conjugations from *ire* and others from *vadere.* The result is that when the Spanish verb *ir* is conjugated in the future tense, it uses the model from *ire* (*iré, irás, irá*). But when it is conjugated in the present, it uses the model of *vadere* (*voy, vas, va*).

Spanish did not always retain archaisms, and in some cases this differentiates it from other Latin-based languages. Spanish *hermano* (brother) came from the modern Vulgar Latin *germanus,* which had replaced the older *frater* (which the British and French both kept, producing *brother* and *frère*). And sometimes both Classical and Vulgar Latin terms produced two words in Spanish. "Beautiful," for instance, was said formally as *formosus,* which produced *hermoso.* But the more popular Latin *bellus* produced the Spanish *bello.*

After Rome lost its political hold over Western Europe in 476—and specifically over Hispania, in 404—Vulgar Latin survived and thrived. By the eighth century, it had evolved into a series of dialects known as Proto-Romances. Around that time, a monk in a monastery in northern France went to the trouble of writing vernacular translations of some thousand three hundred Classical Latin terms in the margin of his Bible. The times had evidently changed since the days of the *Appendix Probi* (whatever days those were exactly). In *Les Gloses de Reichenau,* the author doesn't consider words from Vulgar Latin "mistakes." He is simply translating Classical Latin into Vulgar Latin.

Here are some examples:

CLASSICAL LATIN	VULGAR LATIN	SPANISH	ENGLISH
canere	cantare	cantar	to sing
forum	mercatum	mercado	market
hiems	hibernus	invierno	winter
liberos	infans	infant, niño	prince, child
oppidis	civitatidus	ciudad	city
optis	meliores	mejor	best
ore	bucca	boca	mouth
vim	fortiam	fuerza	strength

The evolution of Vulgar Latin is all the more surprising since, when the Roman Empire fell, Hispania came under the control of Germans from the east. Yet strangely, the arrival of the Germanic tribes increased the hold of Vulgar Latin over the peninsula, just as Vulgar Latin was evolving into not one but a myriad of distinct tongues, each with its own separate territory.

Some of these tongues developed into regional languages still spoken in Spain today, while one among them would evolve into modern Spanish.

3. Waiting for the *Godos*

Some of the names of early kings of Spain sound strangely incongruous, as if they were pulled straight from the medieval folklore of Germany, rather than Spain: Reccared, Roderic, Athanagild, Leovigild, Seisebut, Chindasuinth, Recceswinth, and Wamba.

Yet given Spain's history, there's nothing strange about these names. In 507, a Germanic tribe, the Visigoths, took control of the Iberian Peninsula and ruled it for two centuries. Many common first names in Spanish today have Gothic origins, including Álvaro, Elvira, Fernando, Rodrigo, Gonzalo, Alfonso, and Ramiro. Gonzalo comes from Gundisalvus, whose root is *gunthis* (fight). Fernando is a combination of *frithu* (peace) and *nanth* (audacity).

The Visigoths were the last of the so-called barbarian tribes that moved into Western Europe when the Roman Empire collapsed at the end of the fifth century. In Latin, *barbarus* means "foreign." But most barbarians weren't invaders, at least not at first. They had been living in the Roman Empire, or were neighbors, since the first century, and most were partly or totally Romanized by the time they took power.

As a result of this intermixing, a number of Germanicisms entered Vulgar Latin before the barbarians even got to Hispania. The Germanic *suppa* (soup) became *sopa* in Spanish and *soupe* in French. *Bank* (bench) became *banco* in Spanish and *banc* in French. German was the source of Spanish words like *jabón* (soap), *guerra* (war), *guardia* (policeman), *yelmo* (helmet), and *embajada* (embassy). Other common terms include *rico* and *fresco* (rich and fresh). *Bandido* (bandit) came from the German *ban* (prohibition). *Compañero* and *compañía* (companion and company, respectively) are Latinizations of a Germanic concept, *galhaiba* (he who shares the bread).

At the end of the fourth century, the Roman Empire split between east and west. The Eastern Roman Empire, based in Constantinople (present-day Istanbul), was by far more solid than the Western. Predominantly Greek speaking, vigorously Christian, and prosperous, the East would continue operations as the Byzantine Empire for another ten centuries.

In the Western Empire, Germanic tribes flowed in to fill the power vacuum, either as refugees, marauders, or mercenaries for the Romans themselves. Although some of these tribes went north to Britannia and Gaul, many gravitated toward Hispania, the sun belt of the empire, which had lots of sparsely populated land up for grabs and where the weather was definitely fairer than in Britannia.

The Vandals, the Alans, and the Sueves started arriving in Hispania in AD 409. They moved in and divvied up the peninsula because there wasn't much stopping them. Hispania's Roman legions had blended into civilian life over the centuries and were long gone by this time. By 411, the Sueves and Vandals had settled in Galicia (the northwest), the Alans in Lusitania (the west), and the Vandals in Baetica (the south).

But the Romans weren't quite ready to give up. In a last-ditch effort to regain control over Spain, Rome hired the Visigoths, who had established their kingdom in Tolosa (Toulouse, France) to rout out the other German tribes. The Visigoth mercenaries did the job, virtually exterminating the Alans and chasing the Vandals across the Mediterranean into North Africa. Then they headed back to Gaul.

For nearly a century, Roman Hispania was divided between the Visigoths, who exerted some authority in the north, east, and south, and the Alans and Seuves, who controlled the northeast. In 507, the Franks routed the Visigoths from France, and the Visigoths moved south and set up their capital in Toledo; then, over the next 150 years, they pushed the other Germanic tribes out or conquered them.

There is very little evidence of the Visigoth presence in Toledo. Most of what remains—fragments of buildings and the odd engraving in Gothic characters—can be seen only behind glass display cabinets in museums. There are about a dozen churches throughout Spain that have characteristic Gothic horseshoe-style arches. Otherwise, almost everything the Visigoths built was destroyed by the empires that followed them.

Yet the Visigoths' intangible legacy was far more important: they left behind a powerful myth of a Golden Age of Christian rule that ended when most of Spain became part of the Muslim world. This myth would shape the destiny of Spain and the Spanish language.

During their actual reign, which only lasted two centuries, the Visigoths had very little impact on the language spoken there. For the most part, they let the "Roman" inhabitants of Hispania keep speaking Vulgar Latin. There simply weren't enough Visigoths—between one hundred thousand and two hundred thousand took refuge in Spain among four million Hispanians—to impose their German language. In addition, by the time they conquered Hispania, the Visigoths had been already doing business with the Romans for at least a century, so they spoke Latin. As a result, during the two centuries of Visigoth rule over Hispania, Latin remained the language of the administration, and all official documents were produced in Latin.

By the seventh century, the Gothic tongue was virtually extinct in Hispania. This was a marked contrast to the situation in France: the Frankish kings kept speaking Germanic until the end of the tenth century. Frankish heavily influenced French grammar, with the result that 10 percent of common French vocabulary is of Frankish origin.

Modern Spanish has almost no traces of Germanic languages. Spanish has only a few early Visigothic loans, including *espía* (spy), *ropa* (clothing), *sitio* (site). Later borrowings include *ataviar* (to adorn), *escanciar* (to pour wine), *ganso* (goose), and *tapa* (lid), probably the origin of the name for the Spanish dish *tapas*. There are many theories about how *tapas* came to refer to food. Some believe early *tapas* were slices of bread or cheese placed on top of drinks. The meaning of the word evolved from there. The other remnant of the Visigothic language is the Spanish suffix *-engo,* as in *abandengo* and *realengo* (belonging to the abbey or to the crown). It comes from the Germanic suffix *-ing,* in the sense of "belonging to." And, of course, Spanish kept many Visigothic names.

Beyond their small numbers, there was another reason the Visigoths had so little impact on the culture and language of Hispania: they were never popular rulers. The Goths forbade intermarriage and lived apart from the Romans. Visigothic kings were ruthless and constantly embroiled in rivalries. Every one of the thirty-three legitimate kings who ruled Visigothic between 507 and 711 was toppled by a usurper.

The Visigoths had another flaw, which adds a curious twist to the Christian Golden Age associated with their rule: although Christian, the Goths were actually heretics. Most of the inhabitants of the peninsula were Catholic by this point, but the Visigoths belonged to the Arian sect of Christianity, characterized by a belief, originating in Egypt, that Christ is subordinate to God. This rejection of the Trinity of God, Jesus, and the Holy Spirit made the Visigoths heretics in the eyes of their own Christian subjects.

Curiously, the Spanish term for the Visigoths, *godos,* would go on to have reactionary associations in Hispanic culture. In Colombia and Paraguay, it is a nickname for the Conservative Party. In Chile, it refers to someone from Spain. (Renaissance architects in Europe dubbed the architecture of the twelfth to fifteenth century "Gothic," a pejorative name for a style they looked down upon in favor of classical models.)

Despite their scant numbers, heretical faith, and the general bad opinion in which they were held, the Visigoths turned out to be important figures in the story of Spanish. They made their mark in two ways. First, they laid the groundwork for the incredible growth of Spanish by creating the myth of a unified, Christian Hispania.

Then, they actually contributed to unifying Spain by establishing a law code that would apply to the whole Iberian Peninsula.

Everywhere else in Western Europe, the former Roman provinces were fracturing; cities, ports, and roads were falling into disuse and communication lines were collapsing. This process of decay was considerably slower under the Visigoths, skilled warriors who progressively extended their domain over the peninsula.

Despite their unpopularity, the Visigoth rulers benefited from a peculiar advantage: they, and the local "Romans," were united against a common enemy, the Byzantine Empire, formerly the Eastern Roman Empire. The Byzantines were determined to reclaim control over the land Rome had lost 141 years earlier. They landed in Cartagena in 552 and carved themselves out a banana-shaped territory along the southern coast of the Iberian Peninsula. Nothing is left of this short-lived province today except the name, Spania. Such are the twists of history that the name of Spain turns out to be a Hellenism of a Latinism (Hispania) of the Phoenician name I-shepan-ha.

The threat of the Byzantine Empire motivated the Roman patricians of Hispania, and much of the population, to rally around the Visigothic Crown, heresies and all. This was mostly thanks to work of the two most famous personalities of Visigothic Hispania: Leander, and his younger brother Isidore, both of whom were appointed bishop of Seville. Both were also canonized—like a number of their siblings, including their brother Fulgentius and their sister Florentine.

Well-spoken and a brilliant writer, Leander was a true statesman as well as a deeply religious man. He understood that the Visigoths' heretical Arian faith was a political handicap, since it reduced the legitimacy of the Visigothic kings in the eyes of their Christian subjects. After being named bishop of Seville in 579, Leander converted the king's successor, Prince Hermenegild, to Catholicism. The king himself was not happy about Leander's initiative. He declared war on his son and exiled Leander to Byzantium. But Leander had the last word: he returned to Hispania three years later and converted the next prince in line to the throne, Reccared.

When Reccared inherited the Visigothic throne in 589, he made Catholicism the official religion of his kingdom. This new legitimacy allowed him to rally his Roman subjects to fight the Byzantines. It took thirty-five more years and six more kings to finally chase the last Byzantine soldier out of Hispania, but by 624, the peninsula was nominally united for the first time in two centuries.

When Leander died in 601, his brother Isidore, twenty-six years younger, succeeded him as bishop of Seville. Isidore of Seville is considered one of the greatest writers of the period, along with the Venerable Bede of England and Gregory of Tours of France. Among them, Isidore left the most substantial volume of writings. He wrote extensively on history, law, and theology, but also on language and culture. His most significant work, an encyclopedia called *Etymologiae,* was a massive work of 448 chapters in 20 volumes in which Isidore attempted to "account for all that was known." This work prompted the Vatican in 2005 to declare Isidore the patron saint of the Internet!

No other Christian thinker of the Middle Ages was as influential as Isidore. Until the invention of the printing press eight centuries later, his *Etymologiae* would be the second most read work, after the Bible. Historians regard him as the last philosopher of Antiquity or the last founding father of the church. And despite the fact that he was one of the most learned men of his age, numerous traces of Vulgar Latin were creeping into his writings, which he intended to be exemplary Classical Latin. Faustino Arévalo, a Jesuit who edited the Spanish version of the *Etymologiae* in 1763, counted no fewer than 1,640 "Spanish" terms in the Latin of Isidore of Seville, by which Arévalo meant Vulgar Latin terms that had made it into the Spanish spoken in the eighteenth century.

Since very few writings of the period survive, Isidore's voluminous output is important to show the stages of transformation of Vulgar Latin. It is all the more precious since Isidore wrote about language, including treatises on verbs and synonyms. A sizable part of his encyclopedia is devoted to etymology. To the modern reader, accustomed to scientific etymology, Isidore's attempts seem like pop etymology—for example, he affirms that *cattus* (cat) originated in the verb *cattare* (to see, to look). On the other hand, Isidore is right about the Spanish origin of the color *amarillo* (yellow).

As an erudite, Isidore was obsessed with preventing knowledge from being lost in the ruins of the Roman Empire. His encyclopedic work was an effort to protect and cultivate what was left of Rome, starting with culture and language. One of his great decisions as bishop was to call for the creation of bishopric schools that would provide formal teaching of Latin. As a result of Isidore's efforts, Latin—whether Classical or Vulgar—was taught longer in Spain than anywhere else in the former Western Roman Empire. This is another reason modern Spanish resembles Latin a lot more than French does.

Isidore also labored to create a unified set of laws for Hispania, which was a first in Europe. Isidore was a statesman obsessed with uniting Spain by means beyond the Christian faith. At the fourth Council of Toledo in 633, he went as far as preaching a famous formula: *rex, gens, patria*. Literally, this means "king, people, nation," but it carries the sense of "one king, one people, one nation." Isidore's point was that Romans and Visigoths had to merge into a single identity. The common link would be law. So Isidore spent his whole life compiling Roman law, a work he never finished.

Isidore did not have time to overhaul the law code before he died in 636. Less than seven years later, the next Visigothic king, Chindasuinth, created a coded legal system called the *Liber Iudicorum* or the *Lex Visigothorum,* better known by its later name, *Fuero Juzgo* (Charter of Justice).

Spain's Visigothic "law of the land" was a huge departure from the rest of Europe. The Barbarian invasions in Europe had introduced Germanic law into the former Roman Empire but didn't erase Roman law. The effect was that most of Western Europe had separate laws for "Barbarians" and for "Romans." In short, it was legal chaos. If a Visigoth killed a Roman, he was judged according to Visigothic law; if a Roman killed a Visigoth, he was judged according to Roman law. The system was both unjust and impractical—for starters, courts had no idea which system to use for the offspring of mixed marriages (which were outlawed in the first place).

Although the Visigothic nobility never really learned to respect their own laws, the Visigothic law code achieved three things that had a profound impact on later Spanish culture. First, Hispania became the only place in "barbarian" Europe where the same laws applied to all (theoretically). The *Fuero Juzgo,* which predates the English Magna Carta by five and a half centuries, is often cited as the foundation of representative government in Europe. The code proceeded from principles rather than customs, interdicts, and obligations.

Second, the *Fuero Juzgo* set a standard for Vulgar Latin. The best minds on the Iberian Peninsula would read and reread it for the next seven centuries.

Finally, constant reference to this important document implanted a "culture of language" in the peninsula based on orderliness and principles. The way a language is conceived tends to mirror the way the law of its speakers is organized. English-speaking countries use common law, a system based on customs, canon law, parliamentary writs, and royal decree. Common law does not proceed from a code or from principles, and English itself is a disorganized tongue that follows no code.

In Hispania, the clearly defined Visigothic code no doubt inspired a desire to organize the language in which it was written. This would manifest itself not only in the Kingdom of Castile but that of Portugal as well. As we will see in the coming chapters, the Christians—who were extremely busy fighting the Arabs as well as each other—codified their language as they expanded their hold on Iberia, beginning as early as the eleventh century, four or five centuries before the French or Italians tried to do the same thing.

Yet the most significant political impact of the Visigoths on Spanish was their legacy: the myth of a unified, Christian Visigothic Spain centered on Toledo. This idea of a Visigothic Golden Age was so resilient that in the twentieth century, during Franco's dictatorship, students were forced to memorize the names of Spain's thirty-three Gothic kings.

Of course, the Visigothic myth was just that, a myth. The Visigoths were never popular rulers, nor had they really unified the peninsula politically. Which is why, when Muslims from North Africa landed on the Iberian Peninsula and started taking control of Hispania, the locals hardly lifted a finger to resist them.

4. Almost Arabic

IN SEPTEMBER 2002, WE VISITED Tlemcen, Algeria, a university town of 150,000 people that was hosting a UNESCO conference on multi-lingualism. The conference attendees were the first group of visitors the town had hosted since the beginning of Algeria's decade-long civil war in 1990. Located some twenty-five miles from the Mediter-ranean, Tlemcen is an elegant city with a distinct French layout but Spanish flair. The hotels and public buildings, with their painted ceramic tiles and arched porticos, couldn't be more Andalusian.

Al-Andalus is 150 miles from Tlemcen, across the Mediterra-nean. Yet as we would see, the Andalusian influence in North Af-rica runs deep. On our first evening, we attended a dinner concert at a hotel called Les Zianides, where we sat at the table of a certain Dr. Muhammad Ben Amar, one of the conference's local organiz-ers. During the meal, a traditional North African orchestra played a *nuba,* an hour-long poem set to music. The style of the *nuba* music was completely foreign to us. Yet the sound of the crowd clapping their hands and snapping their fingers was familiar. "That's Andalusia!" Muhammad exclaimed, as if it was self-evident.

The city of Tlemcen actually provides a window on the inter-twined histories of North Africa and Spain. From the thirteenth to the fifteenth century, four kings of the Tlemcen-based Zianides dynasty were actually from Al-Andalus. The great Algerian Sufi mys-tic Sidi Boumediène—whose tomb is now a tourist attraction in Tlemcen—was born near Sevilla.

The history of Muslim Spain is the history of Islam itself.—Africa played a central role in it. After the Prophet Muhammad set off the Muslim campaign of conquest and conversion in the sev-enth century, Muslim armies moved west across North Africa. By the eighth century, they had settled in Morocco and began eying

Visigothic Spain, across the Mediterranean, as the next stage of their conquest.

One fine morning in April 711, a Moroccan general named Tariq ibn Ziyad set sail across the ten-mile-wide strait that separates Europe from Africa. Leading a small flotilla with five hundred troops and their mounts, Tariq landed near a tall cliff then known as the Pillars of Hercules (now Gibraltar). The name Gibraltar is a deformation of Jabal Tariq (or Mount Tariq)—in honor of Spain's first Arab conqueror.

The Muslim incursion into Hispania wasn't exactly a medieval version of D-day. Resources were tight. It took Tariq two months to ferry twelve thousand men to Spain in the four boats he had borrowed for the trip. On the other hand, the Muslims didn't face much resistance. The Visigoth kings—or, more precisely, some of the squabbling pretenders to the Visigoth throne—had actually welcomed the Muslims to Hispania to help them defeat their rivals.

But Tariq changed the plan. The Visigoths' squabbling had weakened them, so when Tariq got to the río Barbate, south of Cadíz, he turned on King Roderic's forces and wiped them out. No one even bothered to recover Roderic's body, which was left on the battlefield to rot.

The Visigoth reign in Iberia was over.

After the victory, Tariq's forces advanced into Iberia and conquered city after city, meeting little resistance. The Muslims took the Visigoth capital of Toledo, then seized the Roman city of Hispalia (today's Seville), then Saragossa. By the end of the summer, the Muslims had a firm grip on the peninsula. In 718, they set up their capital in Córdoba.

The Muslims entertained ideas of continuing north and conquering all of Europe. They even marched as far as present-day Poitiers, France. But in 732, they met their match in the Frankish military leader Charles Martel, who defeated them at the Battle of Poitiers. After that, the Moors decided to stick to the south: they settled for southern Spain, southern France, and Sicily.

In the north of the peninsula, a chain of small Christian kingdoms managed to hold their ground against Muslim raids for the
next three centuries. According to the historians W. Montgomery
Watt and Pierre Cachia, the Muslims were never especially committed to conquering the north of the peninsula, partly because they
didn't want to live in its cold, damp mountain climate. According
to the historian Philip K. Hitti, one Muslim judge in Toledo described northerners as "ill-mannered, dull-witted and foolish" and
attributed their defects to "lack of sun."

The Arab presence in the Iberian Peninsula would last eight centuries. It was a unique phenomenon in Western Europe. Spain and
Portugal are the only countries in Europe where Arab culture grew
and thrived as a native culture. The Arabic language would go on
to become so widely spoken in Spain that it almost displaced the
Roman dialects.

The Arabs called their new territory Al-Andalus. Theories abound
on the origins of the name. It is commonly believed to be a deformation of Vandalusia (land of the Vandals), named after the Germanic tribe that had fled the Visigoths and established a kingdom
in North Africa. But the Spanish philologist Alberto Porlan claims
that the name actually comes from a small islet near Gibraltar called
Chazirat Al-Andalus. According to yet another theory by the German historian Heinz Halm, Al-Andalus is a deformation of the
Visigothic *landa hlauts*, which refers to a Gothic system of land
distribution by lottery.

As for the Christians, they called the Muslim invaders *Moriscos*
(Moors), thinking they were from Mauritania. But even the use of
the word *Arab* was inaccurate. Like Tariq himself, most of the
Muslims who came to Spain from North Africa were not Arabs
but Berbers who spoke Tamazight.

The wide and lasting influence of Muslim culture in Spain is
surprising on one account. Few Moriscos actually settled in Al-
Andalus. Those who did were mostly single men. They married

local women and quickly blended into the population. In 756, there were only 60,000 Muslims living among four million "Romans." According to the linguist Antonio Alatorre, of the 200,000 Arabs living in Córdoba in 1311, only 500 were actually of "Arab" origin. The other 199,500 were Christian converts to Islam or Christians who had adopted Arab customs or language.

Until the eleventh century, Muslim rulers were tolerant of non-Muslims, requiring them only to pay a *jizya,* a form of head tax that amounted to a tribute from nonbelievers. Yet the practice of taxing nonbelievers encouraged assimilation as a tax-evasion strategy: Christians converted to Islam to avoid paying the tribute. That's how Guzman became Ben Qusman, García became Ibn Guarsiya, Martinez became Ibn Marandish, and Fernandez became Ibn Faranda.

Over the centuries, Al-Andalus spawned a mélange of religions, ethnicities, and languages, and with this a whole new set of words to describe new social realities. A large portion of the Christian population living under the Arab caliphates was called Mozarabic, from the Arabic *Musta'rab,* which means "Arabized." Despite their name—which suggests the opposite—Mozarabs spoke a form of Ibero-Romance, not Arabic. When a Mozarab converted to Islam, he was called *muladí,* from the Arabic *muwalladin* (the adopted ones). To most Spaniards today, *muladí* means "renegade."

Conversely, the Muslims who found themselves in Christian territory became known as *mudéjars,* from the Arabic *mudajjan,* meaning "those who were allowed to remain in Christian territories." Today *mudéjar* refers to the type of architecture common in northern Spain between the twelfth and sixteenth centuries, which combined elements of Gothic architecture with Arab techniques: brick and geometric motifs replaced stone and statues.

Yet in spite of their small numbers, the Arabs of Al-Andalus had a lot more success imposing their language and culture than either the Phoenicians or the Visigoths had centuries before them. Their success even rivaled that of the Romans. One reason for this was that the Roman population of the peninsula had never accepted the Visigoths as their own. Centuries after Visigoth reign ended, the Iberians still distinguished "Romans" from "Godos."

The Moriscos, on the other hand, brought a powerful, attractive civilization with them. The Christians were aware that Arab culture had a lot to offer. The Arabs knew about music notation and measures centuries before these were introduced to Christian Europe. They invented clocks and water catchment techniques—as demonstrated by the numerous Spanish terms for irrigation that are direct borrowings from Arabic, such as *atarjea* (duct), *acequia* (irrigation ditch), *aljibe* (cistern), *noria* (waterwheel), *arcaduz* (pipe), *zanja* (ditch), and *azud* (weir). The Arabs cultivated grapes and introduced rice, sugarcane, and saffron as well as apricots, peaches, pomegranates, and oranges. The Arabs grew exotic plants in botanical gardens and developed pharmacology.

Over the centuries of Muslim rule, Spain became an integral part of Muslim civilization, with its own string of accomplishments. Among other things, Muslim Spaniards were at the forefront of developments in astronomy, mathematics, chemistry, and agronomy.

There were obvious benefits to belonging to the Arab world. The reach of Arab culture was phenomenal. In the ninth century, Arab merchants were hawking their wares in China, Russia, and Africa. By the tenth century, the Arabs possessed a vast empire that stretched from Morocco to Central Asia, as far as the Punjab, covering six million square miles in all. The territories the Arabs conquered were ancient civilizations in their own right, so the Arabs cherry-picked the best of what each civilization had to offer, brought it home—and usually improved it.

Arab civilization continued to expand and develop. Arabs stumbled across papermaking in China, which they introduced in Spain in the twelfth century. From Spain it traveled into France. Paper, which was made from rags, old rope, and hemp, was much cheaper than papyrus, paper of strips of a bamboo, parchment, or vellum (strips of animal skin), so this discovery went a long way in facilitating the spread of Arab knowledge in Europe.

Advances in mathematics and the use of numerals were among the most dramatic accomplishments of Arab savants, many of whom were in Spain. Before the Arabs brought these to Europe, Europeans used Roman numerals, which were clumsy ($48 + 2 = 50$ being written XLVIII + II = L, for example). In India, the Arabs had come into contact with a totally new concept, zero, as well as a new method of writing numbers: what we now call Arabic numerals. The Arabs spent about two centuries figuring out how to use the zero to simplify calculations and mathematical operations.

The Arabs also excelled in medicine. The oldest treatise on ophthalmology was written in Arabic in the ninth century. *The Canon of Medicine,* by Ibn Sina (Avicenna) between 1010 and 1030 remained the standard medical textbook in Europe until 1650. In Spain, the Arabs had schools of pharmacy and certified physicians who wrote about smallpox and measles and knew how to cauterize wounds. They demonstrated how the blood circulates between the heart and the lungs and designed the first hospitals, called *himaristan,* including some that specialized in mental health, where they practiced music therapy.

Nowhere was the refinement and sophistication of the Muslim world more obvious than in Al-Andalus' capital, Córdoba. As early as the eighth century, the Arabs constructed a great *mezquita* (mosque), using stones left over from the Hispano-Roman basilica on whose site it was built. It was an architectural accomplishment beyond the reach of even the best Visigoth architects.

The mosque is standing today. When we entered it, we found ourselves in a mesmerizing forest of columns, some 856, each topped with a double arch of alternating brown and cream bricks. At the end of the fifteenth century, a number of the columns were cut away to make room for a Renaissance cathedral built, literally, in the middle of the mosque. But the surrounding mosque was preserved—and the whole complex is so vast we got lost in it, despite the fact that it forms a square. Though a marvel in itself, Córdoba's *mezquita* demonstrates how much Christians on the peninsula valued the great achievements of Muslim culture, even after they went on to oust the Muslims themselves.

By 1000, Córdoba had half a million inhabitants, twelve times more than Paris. It was the largest city of the Islamic world, larger even than Baghdad. The city had seven hundred mosques, seventy libraries, nine hundred baths, and miles of paved and lighted streets. As the historian Philip K. Hitti put it, "When the University of Oxford still looked upon bathing as a heathen custom, generations of Cordovan scientists had been enjoying baths in luxurious establishments."

Medieval Córdoba was a hub of intellectual activity. It had literary salons and universities that taught astronomy, mathematics, medicine, theology, and law. Scholars flocked there to study the works of great men of science and philosophy. The most famous philosopher of the Arab world, Ibn Rushd (Averroës), was born in Córdoba in 1126. He introduced the works of Aristotle, previously available only in Greek and Arabic, to Europe.

In the tenth century, while most of Europe's scholars were still counting on their fingers, Arab scholars in Córdoba were working on algebra (from *al-jabr*, meaning "reduction to the root"), and they recognized tangents and cotangents, as well as sine and cosine. One of the first Europeans to master Arabic numerals and arithmetic was the French philosopher and mathematician Gerbert d'Aurillac, who came to Spain around 965 (and who later became Pope Sylvester II). Following in his footsteps, European scholars flocked to the court of Toledo to copy the teachings of Al-Khwarizimi, whose name is the origin of *logarithm* and *algorithm*.

Ojalá (I hope so) is a common colloquial expression in Mexican Spanish. A casual interjection used in all sorts of situations, it originated as a deformation of the Arabic *wa sa llah* (God willing).

Whereas French was shaped by the contact between Vulgar Latin and Germanic, the language that most influenced the Latin vernaculars of the Iberian Peninsula was Arabic. Many other European languages also borrowed words with Arabic origins. In English *chemistry, scarlet, crimson,* and *tariff* are but a few examples. But modern Spanish absorbed a total of four thousand Arabic borrowings, or four times the average of European languages.

Aceite (olive oil) comes from the Arabic for olive, *al-zeitun*. A number of new words for colors entered Spanish vocabulary, like *azul* (blue) and *añil* (indigo). One famous Arabism, now the name of the United States' most famous prison, Alcatraz, means "sea eagle" in Arabic. And the world-famous cry of Spanish bullfighting *olé!* comes from the Arabic *wa llah,* meaning "by God."

Because so many other European languages were influenced by Arabic, it can be hard to pin down the exact origins of the Arabic words that entered Spanish—some, in fact, were adopted via other European tongues. But one distinctive feature of Spanish and Portuguese Arabisms provides a clue to their origins: the retention of the Arabic article *al*. Sicilians, who also lived with a long Arabic presence, adopted many Arabic words but left out the articles. The result: the Spanish word for cotton is *algodón* (from Arabic *al-qutun*), but in Italian it's *cotone*—derived from the same root but without the article. The Spanish *azúcar* (sugar) came from Arabic *al-sukkar,* whereas other languages adopted the Arabic noun without the article: *sugar* in English, *sucre* in French, and *zucchero* in Italian.

In 1602, Miguel Cervantes joked about this feature when Don Quixote explained to his sidekick, Sancho Panza: "This word, *albogues* [a type of clarinet], I'm telling you, is Moorish, just like all these words that begin in *al*, like *almohaza* [currycomb], *almorzar* [to breakfast], *alhombra* [the red one], *alguacil* [bailiff], *alhucema* [lavender], *almacén* [store], *alcancía* [box], and others like it."

Cervantes was right about all of them except *almorzar,* which comes from Latin. In fact, Spanish has many words starting with *al* that have nothing to do with Arabic: *alma* (soul), *alba* (dawn), *algo* (something), *alegre* (happy), *alegoría*, and *alerta*.

Given how common the Arabic borrowings with the article *al* were in Spanish, it's probably safe to assume that many European borrowings from Arabic, like *alchimia, alcohol, alkaline,* and *admiral,* entered through Spain. But no one actually knows for sure.

Borrowings are almost always a tribute to the novelties a specific culture produces and the areas in which that culture excels. Because the Arabs were great agronomists who mastered refined irrigation techniques, many Arabisms are words for edible plants, such as *arroz* (rice), *limón* (lemon), *zanahoria* (carrot), *jazmín* or *naranja* (orange). Another forte of Arab culture—public administration and military technology—supplied Spanish with the borrowings *barrio* (district of a town), *aduana* (customs), and *alcalde* (mayor).

Oddly, some of the Arabisms that found their way into Spanish were originally Latin words. The most famous is *alcázar* (fortress), which came from the Latin for castle (*castrum*). The Spanish word for tuna, *atún,* comes from *al-tun* in Arabic, which was a borrowing from the Latin *thunnus.*

The influence of Arabic was felt not only on vocabulary: Arabic also had a direct impact on the semantics of the Latin vernacular that developed in Spain. The Spanish word *hasta* (until) is a direct borrowing from Arabic (the Latin equivalent is *usque*). The well-known *hidalgo* (petty noble), who bore the brunt of the wars in the centuries to come, is the contraction of *hijo de algo* or *de alguien* (son of something or of somebody). This usage is a calque (or loan translation) of Arabic semantic, where *ibn* means "son." The linguist Antonio Alatorre also points out that *infante* (child of a king, prince) is another semantic Arabism.

Arabic displaced Latin as the language of prestige in Al-Andalus, and even among the Christian kingdoms in the north that remained outside Muslim reach. During Muslim rule, all treatises, as well as most law texts and contracts, were written in Arabic. It was the language of public administration, science, trade, military technology, and law.

Arabic was so prestigious that many Andalusian writers used Arab characters, rather than the Roman alphabet, to record their works, even when they wrote in Roman vernacular. The same thing happened in other parts of the Arab would: Persian, Urdu, Wolof, Malay, and Berber were written in Arabic script even though their oral form is not related to Arabic. The Spanish language has even retained a special term to describe this quirky writing system: *aljamía,* which comes from the Arabic word for "foreign." The result is that a large part of the body of Romance documents (poetry as well as contracts and wills) produced in Spain between the eighth and thirteenth centuries looks Arabic but sounds Romance when read out loud. This feature, unique in Western Europe, shows how deeply rooted Arab culture was in Spain.

It is possible that the Arabic influence forged one feature of modern Spanish (as well as Portuguese) that distinguishes it from other Romance tongues: its simplicity. Spanish is by far the most phonetic and most transparent of all Latin languages, including Italian. The Arabic spelling, which is remarkably systematic and phonetic, undoubtedly influenced the evolution of Spanish. The languages were in constant contact, after all. For centuries, Spanish scholars had the double duty of learning both Latin and Arabic, more so than any other scholars in Europe. When Spanish scholars gave the vernacular its modern form around the thirteenth century, it is hard to imagine how they could have avoided being influenced by the aesthetics of Arabic.

The Arabs' impact on place-names (for both cities and geography) in Spain was nothing less than remarkable, almost as great as that of the Romans. The most striking example is the former Roman camp of Caesar Augusta, which was first Arabized as Sarakusta and then, long after the Latin original had been forgotten, re-Hispanicized as Zaragoza. The name Seville went through a similar transformation: the Romans called it Hispalia, then the Arabs transformed it into Isbiliya, and this morphed as Sevilla.

On the long list of Arabic place-names in Spain, some of the most striking examples are Guadalquivir, from *wadi al-kabir* (Great River); Guadalajara, from *wadi al-hajara* (Stony River); and Madrid, from *al-magrit* (the Spring). The region south of Madrid made famous by the adventures of Don Quixote, la Mancha, got its name from the Arabic *al-mansha,* meaning "dry land" or "wilderness."

Many place-names in Spain even combine an Arabic word with an Arabicized Latin term, such as Guadalupe (*al-wadi* and *al-lupus,* meaning Wolf River) and Guadalcanal, which combines *al-wadi* (water) with *al-canal* (water canal).

The Arab footprint is obvious in Spain's architecture and also in cultural artifacts like flamenco and bullfighting, as well as poetry.

As we saw in Tlemcen, typical Andalusian music is the same on both sides of the Strait of Gibraltar. In Spain, in particular, people learn very young to *palmear* (clap) and to *chasquear* (snap fingers) in elaborate ways that are very common on the south shore of the Mediterranean, as we heard ourselves when we visited Tlemcen. Spaniards also use musical styles that most other Europeans have difficulty imitating. One variation of flamenco is *saeta,* a type of a cappella song sung during the processions of the Holy Week (preceding Easter) in Seville. This very emotional song, reminiscent of the call of the muezzin, is clearly Arabic in origin. It survived the centuries thanks to the Gypsies, who kept it alive.

Bullfighting is another Arab cultural borrowing. Nobody knows the exact origins of bullfighting. Apparently, there were more aurochs (large wild cattle, now extinct) on the Iberian Peninsula than anywhere else in Europe, and this surplus might have generated an old custom that predated even the arrival of the Romans. But the Arabs undoubtedly made two contributions to the art of bullfighting. They introduced new mounting techniques and the muleta, the cape originally meant to distract the bulls' attention so they wouldn't gore the horse.

Poetry—or rather, the love of poetry—is also an imprint of Arab culture in Spain. Since it is a sin in Islam to make images of God, believers were literally fixated on "the word." That led to the creation of a new form of visual art, Arabic calligraphy, central to the ornamentation of mosques. But it also channeled creative energy toward language. Arabic was a language of poetry even before it became the language of a religion, and poetry remained a revered art in Muslim Spain. This may explain why poets and playwrights are held in such high esteem in Spanish culture, not merely as members of the literati but also as popular figures. The Chilean poet Pablo Neruda, known for defending the common people, became famous throughout the Spanish-speaking world long before he won the Nobel Prize in Literature in 1971. In fact, he read his poems in front of whole stadiums.

Like the Visigoths before them, the Arabs in Spain would fall partly because of infighting among their own rulers. In the first decades of the eleventh century, when the caliphate of the Umayyad collapsed, Al-Andalus disintegrated into twenty or so petty kingdoms and principalities known as *taifas,* and these just kept on fighting. By this time, most of the Andalusian population spoke or understood Arabic, although they still probably spoke the Roman vernacular as well.

By the twelfth century, the caliphates and emirates were struggling to repel hordes of crusading Christians from the north. Yet curiously, even as the Arabs' territory shrank to the Emirate of Granada, or about half the size of today's region of Andalusia, Arab culture continued to grow for two more centuries. And the Arabic language was remarkably resilient. King Alfonso VIII of Castile (r. 1158–1214) minted currency with Arabic characters. In the new capital of Toledo, which the Christians conquered in 1085, the great King Fernando III (r. 1217–1252) had to force his notaries to write contracts in Castilian—they still preferred Arabic nearly 150 years after the Christians' conquest.

But the fundamental reason this book is *The Story of Spanish* and not *The Story of Arabic* is simply that after the Umayyad caliphate collapsed in 1031, Arab rule gradually lost its appeal to Christians. The two caliphates that followed, the Almoravids and the Almohads, were fundamentalist Muslims who were harsh and intolerant of Christians—a departure from earlier Arab rulers. Their very name is a summary of what was in store: Almoravid is from *Al-Murābiṭūn,* meaning "hermit," describing a type of devout soldier-monk; Almohad is from *al-Muwaḥḥidun,* meaning "the monotheists" or "the unitarians." Christians under their authority had to convert or leave.

In the end, many Christians converted, but many more fled to the Christian kingdoms in the north. There, they added manpower to the northern kingdoms, just as these kingdoms were gearing up to "reclaim" Spain from the Muslims.

This campaign, of course, would spread their language across the peninsula. But the question at this point, still unanswered, was: Which northern kingdom would spread its language?

5. The Curious Case of Castilian

ALMOST EVERYONE WHO LEARNS SPANISH as a second language faces the odd dilemma of being corrected about the very name of the language itself. No other European tongue has two names: some Spanish speakers call their language *español,* others call it *castellano.* And everyone seems to have a different reason for choosing one name over the other.

The root of the issue is the former dominion of Castile, the northern Christian kingdom that ended up leading the Christian *Reconquista* (Reconquest) of Spain.

Catalans, Basques, and Galicians are generally adamant about calling their tongue *castellano,* as this underlines the fact that their own languages are distinct from Spanish. Argentines use *castellano* to stress their independence from Spain. But Colombians use *español* to downplay the dominion of Castile and emphasize the equality of all Hispanics, united in language. Central Americans, Mexicans, and Caribbean Spanish speakers generally use *español,* but Salvadorans seem to prefer *castellano.*

The word Castilian generally evokes a sense of prestige, given its association with the powerful Kingdom of Castile, which is funny when you think about it, because at its origin, Castile was anything but prestigious.

We usually assume that major languages come from important places. But Spanish didn't originate in Spain's capital region, Madrid. The Roman vernacular that evolved into modern Spanish came from Burgos, the historical capital of Castile, now a small city famous as a meat-packaging center.

Castile began rather ingloriously, as a buffer zone between two other powerful kingdoms. When the Muslims conquered Spain in the eighth century, Christian Spain amounted to a strip of counties and kingdoms huddled along the Atlantic coast and the Pyrenees.

The leaders among these kingdoms were Asturias and Navarre. Located midway between the Pyrenees and the northwestern tip of the peninsula, Asturias has the kind of rugged terrain and wet, oceanic climate that makes aspiring invaders think twice. The Asturians were known for resisting everyone, including the Romans and the Visigoths. They would be the first to take on the Arabs. The first successful battle against the Reconquista was fought in the Asturian town of Covadonga by the last Visigothic king, Pelayo, in either 718 or 722 (sources disagree).

Navarre, northeast of Castile at the western foot of the Pyrenees, was the land of the Basques. Like the Asturians, the Basques were known for vigorously defending themselves, even from the Franks north of them, in Gaul. In 778, they defeated Charlemagne's nephew Roland in the mountain pass of Roncesvalles (Ronceveaux), a battle that inspired the *Song of Roland,* one of the oldest surviving works of French literature, although the unknown poet adapted the story as an epic battle between Christians and Saracens (as the French called the Moriscos) during the Crusades.

Asturias spawned a number of other kingdoms, including León and Portugal, which both started out as counties of Asturias before they grew into independent kingdoms. Navarre spawned Aragón. Catalonia, at the time, was a buffer kingdom of France, established to protect France from Muslim Spain.

During this period, each of Spain's northern kingdoms spoke a different variety of Ibero-Romance. The term "Romance" had appeared in eighth-century France, shortly after the Arab conquest of Spain. At the Council of Tours in 813, the clergy was encouraged to speak in the *rusticam romanam lenguam* (rustic Roman tongue). The fact that these learned bishops labeled the vernacular as Roman rather than Latin showed that the vernacular had evolved so far from Classical Latin that it needed a new label. (In the grammar of the time, Roman was written either *Romanans* or *Romanz,* which is why, in English, these Latin-based vernaculars are called "Romance" languages.)

Until roughly the turn of the first millennium, all the Romance dialects spoken in the peninsula were mutually intelligible. People from Galicia, León, Aragón, Catalonia, and Al-Andalus could hammer out a conversation between them with only few misunderstandings. For that matter, Iberians could easily understand the Romance spoken in the south of France. Jugglers, as the early French troubadours were called (their talents included juggling and poetry), circulated freely on both sides of the Pyrenees and entertained crowds and courts in any vernacular.

Given the power and prestige that came to be attached to its name, it's hard to grasp how modest Castile's early origins were. Castile in 800 was nothing more than a series of outposts built by Asturias and Navarre. (Castile graduated from county to kingdom only in the eleventh century.) And contrary to popular belief, the name Castile does not come from the formidable castles built there. In Latin vernacular, *castellum* meant "hill fort." These were the most outstanding features of Castile for centuries.

Some of the peculiarities of the language that would go on to become Modern Spanish can be traced back to the earliest days of Castile. Linguists describe the original dialect spoken in Castile as "very different" or even "abnormal" with respect to other Roman vernaculars spoken on the peninsula. That's because Old Castilian developed features that were absent from other Ibero-Romances.

Linguists are certain that one explanation for the Castilian "anomaly" is the influence of the Basque language from the neighboring Navarre. In the galaxy of Ibero-Romances, the Basque spoke a completely different, non-Latin language. The Basque influence is thought to explain at least one striking feature of early

Castilian: the disappearance of *f* at the beginning of hundreds of words. Old Basque did not have an *f* sound. Castilian was the only Romance language to transform the *f* of the Latin *filius* (son) into *h,* producing *hijo.* Portuguese, French, and Italian kept the *f* and say *filho, fils,* and *figlio.*

As the following examples show, the list of *f*-deprived Latinates in Castilian is remarkably long compared to French and Italian:

ENGLISH	LATIN	SPANISH	FRENCH	ITALIAN	PORTUGUESE
ant	formica	**hormigas**	fourmi	formica	formiga
to do	facere	**hacer**	faire	fare	fazer
hunger	fames	**hambre**	faim	fame	fome
iron	ferrum	**hierro**	fer	ferro	ferro
leaf	folium	**hoja**	feuille	foglia	folha
oven	fumus	**horno**	four	forno	forno

Basque probably influenced Castilian in another way. In the Basque language, the pronunciation of consonants tends to shift from generation to generation, but vowel pronunciations remain very stable (the opposite of English). Sure enough, Castilian consonants changed in ways distinct from other Hispano-Romance dialects:

ENGLISH	LATIN	GALICIAN/ PORTU- GUESE	LEONESE	ARRA- GONESE	CATALAN	MOZARA- BIC	CASTILIAN
brother	germanus	irmão	giermano	girmo	girmá	yermano	hermano
flour	farina	farinha	farina	farina	farinal	farina	harina
January	januarius	janeiro	genero	genero	giner	yenair	enero
night	noctem	noite	nueite	nuci	nit	nohte	noche
woman	mulier	muller, mulher	muyer	muller	muller	mulleres	mujer

The influx of immigrants to Castile also explains many of the language's peculiarities.

The first documents that use the name Castile were written by Mozarabic Christians who had fled Muslim rule to settle in the north around the year 800. During the first century of the Arab period, Castile was repopulated by these refugees, as well as soldiers and shepherds from Asturias, León, and Navarre. According to the linguist Ralph Penny, the arrival of so many speakers of different dialects meant that people began speaking a koiné, a common language built on the features that all the dialects shared, and stripped of some of the nuances of each. In other words, early immigration simplified the dialect but added a twist. As a result of the Basque influence, the early Castilian speakers tended to blend their Romances in ways that made Castilian more distinct.

When we visited Burgos and its splendid Gothic-style cathedral, one of the most well preserved in Europe, we met two types of travelers: smartly dressed tourists wielding cameras, mostly from Spain, and visitors hoisting backpacks, almost all French. In the two days we spent in Burgos, at least a dozen French hikers asked us if we knew "the Way."

The Way of St. James, or the Camino de Santiago, is a pilgrimage route to the shrine of Santiago de Compostela, built over what's believed to be the tomb of St. James, discovered around AD 820. A challenging five-hundred-mile trek across rugged territory in northern Spain, the route winds from Basque country to the westernmost tip of the peninsula. For twelve centuries, millions of pilgrims have walked the Camino. In 2010, 135,000 hikers made the trek. Most of them momentarily lost their way when they stopped in Burgos.

But that's nothing new. Starting in the ninth century, thousands of pilgrims passed through Castile on their way to the Compostela. Ultimately, this influx would set off the transformation of what was an obscure northern march into a kingdom that controlled most of the Iberian Peninsula—and one that would spread its dialect across the peninsula.

In other words, Castile owes much of its early political ascendency to the French, who were responsible for developing the Camino de Santiago. The story of French involvement in northern Spain began in 795, when the Holy Roman Emperor Charlemagne, also known as Charles I of France, created seventeen buffer counties between France and Spain, along the Pyrenees between Navarre and the Mediterranean Sea. His main motivation was to block the Saracens—as the French called the Moors—from moving north. Charlemagne called these counties the Marca Hispánica, or Spanish "March." (The word refers to "frontier" or "buffer zone," not "marching.") They would go on to become the kingdoms of Aragón and Catalonia. (The tiny country of Andorra, about three times the size of the District of Columbia, is a remnant of the marches, as is the little-known Spanish enclave of Llívia on the French side of the border.)

French interest did not stretch beyond the marches until 813, the year the alleged burial site of the apostle St. James was discovered in Compostela, Galicia. The shrine, originally called Sanctus Jacobus, became Santi-Iago, then Santiago de Compostela (which means "field of the stars"). After its discovery, devout European Christians looking for pilgrimage sites realized that it was a lot easier to cross the Pyrenees than to voyage all the way to the Holy Land. They started flocking to Santiago de Compostela.

The sudden influx of foreigners, mostly French, boosted the self-confidence of Spain's northern Christian kingdoms, which had suffered from being on the outskirts of the Christian world. The shrine in Compostela turned the northern kingdoms into a destination. French kings started to marry their offspring to princes and princesses of Spain's north.

French culture was so influential that Iberians changed their script from Visigothic characters to the more compact French Carolingian script. The Spanish—including the Arabs in the south—also adopted the French feudal system, with its shared system of legal and military obligations for vassals and lords. French pilgrims came with merchants and *juglares* (jugglers), as the early troubadours were known.

The task of rendering sounds into writing is difficult, especially since all languages have more sounds than letters. The French added entirely new spellings. Previously, a Castilian notary who wrote the name pronounced *Sánchez* could have spelled it *Sangiz* or *Sanggeç*. After the French, spelling was rationalized into *Sánchez*.

Many French borrowings introduced into Catalan also spilled over into Castilian: *mesón* (from *maison,* house), *vianda* (from *viande,* meat), *corajé* (from *courage,* courage), *jamón* (from *jambon,* ham), *monje* (monk), *linaje* (lineage), *homenaje* (homage), *mensaje* (message), *duc* or *duque* (duke), *hostal* (hotel, inn).

The French even shaped the very name by which Spaniards called themselves and their language: *español.* Before the French, it would never have occurred to the inhabitants of Galicia, Navarre, Castile, or León that they had anything in common. It was the southern French, who spoke Occitan, also known as langue d'oc, who threw all the Iberians into the same basket and dubbed them *espaínol* or *españón,* a deformation of the Latin *Hispaniolus.* Linguists are certain of the French origin of the term because of the way the words evolved. The form *espainol* or *españon* is, simply put, more characteristic of old French than old Castilian or any of the Romance dialects spoken south of the Pyrenees. Although the French used this catchword for all the people of all the fringe kingdoms in the north of Spain, it took the Spanish three more centuries to adopt the name.

The French also introduced religious zeal, which would have an enormous impact on the Castilians. In the early Middle Ages, the French were the most fanatically religious people in Europe, practicing a deep, almost mystical form of Christianity. As pilgrims began flocking from Bayonne to Santiago de Compostela, the French built cathedrals, churches, and monasteries along the road. Some of these Romanesque-style buildings are still standing.

Gradually, through the increased contact, the French transmitted their religious fervor to the Spanish. The French introduced Cluniac monasticism, with its orthodox Roman liturgy and rites: the first Cluniac monastery was built by king Sancho of Navarre in 1022. The French also introduced soldier-monks to Spain, the most famous being the Knights Templars. The Templars then spawned a series of Spanish military religious orders (whose original purpose was to protect pilgrims) such as the Order of Santiago and the Order of Calatrava.

The French shaped the nature of the Spanish Reconquista from the outset. Before the arrival of the French, Christians and Arabs skirmished, but the battles were really just land grabs. The French gave the Spanish a religious motive for fighting the Arabs, imbuing the Spanish with the notion of holy warfare against the enemies of the church. Churchmen then added a political angle to the religious quest by propagating the myth that Spain had once been a "unified and indivisible" Visigothic kingdom.

All of this would justify a centuries-long campaign to "reconquer" Spain from the Muslim "occupiers." The idea that the Muslims had stolen their kingdom gave northerners a common enemy and a moral claim for fighting the Muslims: they were getting back what was theirs. Although Santiago is still Spain's patron saint, he was known in medieval Spain as Santiago Matamoros, St. James the Moor-Slayer.

In the eleventh century, the stakes of fighting the Muslims got even higher as the "Reconquista" (reconquest) took on the dimension of a quasi Crusade against the Moors to liberate the town of Barbastro, near Huesca. That summer, soldiers from Burgundy,

Normandy, and Aquitaine, along with some Italians, joined in the Iberian fight against the Moors.

That the Castilian tongue came to dominate the other dialects in Spain over the next centuries was mostly because the once-obscure Kingdom of Castile took the lead in the Reconquista.

6. The Kings' Speech

HISTORIANS STILL DON'T UNDERSTAND EXACTLY how the once-obscure County of Castile grew from a collection of outposts into the leader of the Reconquista and the dominant power of the peninsula. Some attribute Castile's success to its Visigothic heritage. Others argue that Castile it was the closest to Andalusian centers like Toledo and Córdoba. One adjective that frequently appears in descriptions of the early counts of Castile is *orgulloso* (proud) and some historians speculate that this character trait might partly explain Castile's remarkable success in leading—and completing—the Reconquista.

Whatever drove them, Castilian kings progressively won wars and built alliances with their Christian rivals and against the Moors, and gradually tightened their grip over the peninsula. The influence of the kings of Castile grew as Castilians colonized the depopulated Al-Andalus. In the process, the Castilian language either pushed aside or overpowered most of the other Ibero-Romance dialects spoken in Spain.

The Spanish Reconquista would last almost eight centuries. The half dozen Christian kingdoms in the north spent as much time fighting each other as they did fighting the Moriscos. The twelfth-century French troubadour Pierre Vidal complained that the kings of northern Spain had forgotten the Moriscos were their enemies. (In fact, the terms *Morisco* and *Arab* were misnomers, as most were converted Christians.)

Yet there was a reason the Christian kingdoms were at each other's throats: one of the biggest stakes of the Reconquista was deciding which of Spain's northern kingdoms would dominate the Iberian Peninsula.

As a consequence of such jockeying, the progress of Castilian was not straightforward.

Languages generally acquire prestige when their speakers gain political clout. Yet strangely, as Castilian, the language of increasingly powerful kings and larger numbers of people, spread, its reputation continued to lag. For centuries, Castilian remained a strictly oral tongue. Even native Castilian speakers considered it rough and crude, no better than a peasant's lingo, and erudite speakers resisted using it to write.

For anyone interested in plunging into a visual (albeit, heavily romanticized) experience of Spain's Reconquista, it's hard to beat the 1961 epic film *El Cid*. Set in the chaos and conflict of the period—starring the breathtaking young Sophia Loren alongside Charlton Heston—the film is a sumptuous historical re-creation of medieval Spain, complete with castles overlooking the Mediterranean, thousands of extras on horseback, and sword fighting on tawny beaches. The overall effect is dazzling, even fifty years after the film was shot.

The narrator solemnly introduces El Cid as a valiant warrior who did nothing less than unite Muslims and Christians in Spain. The problem is that the story—of ambition, exile, revenge, rivalry, and reckless military scheming—is as hard to summarize as the period itself. El Cid surmounts countless obstacles while reaching his destiny. He is set up by some rivals in the king's court. Then he seeks to restore his honor. Along the way, he turns his own wife against him, gets banished from his kingdom, and shifts allegiances back and forth between Muslims and Christians.

El Cid was a real character in Spanish history. Born Rodrigo Díaz de Vivar in Burgos around 1043, he became a Christian general and was sent into exile for seven years either because he stole some booty owed to the king or his rivals successfully slandered him—the actual reason has never been established. During this exile, he fought for the Emirate of Zaragoza as a mercenary general. His wife, Jimena, was the niece of the king of Castile. After reconciling with the king, El Cid carved up his own personal fiefdom in Valencia, where he died in battle in 1099 from an arrow in the eye.

One of the few established facts about El Cid was his nickname: El Cid Campeador. It came from the Latin *campi doctor,* meaning "master of the military arts" or "champion." The Moriscos, whom El Cid both fought and led, called him Al-sayyid (lord or master). The Arabic term was then Hispanicized into El Cid. He must have been one good fighter to have earned such monikers in both Latin *and* Arabic.

After he died, El Cid spawned a literary cycle that survived for centuries, culminating with *El Poema del Mio Cid* (The Song of My Cid). This 3,735-verse epic is, for the Spanish-speaking world, the equivalent of *Beowulf* or the *Chanson de Roland.*

The origins of the text are as obscure as the story itself is confusing. The Spanish philologist Ramón Menéndez Pidal, the first scholar to study the poem from a historical perspective, established that the original was probably written in 1140. An "Abbot Peter" signed the first written copy in 1207, but the only surviving copy dates from the fourteenth century.

Although it is hailed as the first piece of literature written in Castilian, *El Poema del Mio Cid* wasn't written at all at the outset. Like all literature of *jugleria,* the *Poema* began as an oral tradition, and was only later transcribed. When it was written down, according to the Mexican scholar Antonio Alatorre, it was probably written in Aragonese, not Castlilian, which might explain why some of the rhymes in the poem don't work in the later Castilian version.

Like *El Poema del Mio Cid,* the earliest texts in the history of Castilian weren't actually written in Castilian. The first written examples of vernacular Ibero-Romance were the *Gloss of San Millán de la Cogolla* and the *Gloss of Silos.* Glosses were basically monks' notes. Since parchment was expensive and rare, monks scribbled in the margins of already written parchment. These glosses, dated around 980, each come from neighboring monasteries near Burgos, in San Millán and Silos.

Yet while both were composed *in* Castile, the glossers actually wrote in the Aragonese language. The reason: native Castilians still didn't think their dialect was fit for writing.

Even in the eleventh century, no one was yet writing poetry in Castilian. In the middle of the twelfth century, the Galician chronicler of King Alfonso VII declared that Castilian had the subtlety of *atables* (small drums). Until the thirteenth century, Castilian was regarded as a crude, rugged, ugly, uncultured language not suitable for poetry, religious writing, or even contracts, for that matter. Poets of the period wrote in Mozarabic, Aragonese, or Galician-Portuguese.

Written texts started to appear in Castilian only after 1200. A significant figure of the time was a Castilian deacon named Gonzalo de Berceo (1190–1264), who wrote an important body of original religious poems in Castilian. This was a first, and he had to borrow vocabulary from oral languages and from the songs of the jugglers. *El Poema del mio Cid* was transcribed into Castilian around 1200, when the prospects of Castilian were improving, both socially and geographically.

One surprising feature of *El Poema del mio Cid* is how easy it is for modern readers to understand it, once they get over the hurdle of Gothic characters and different writing conventions. A text in Old French of the same period is much more difficult for a modern reader—and Old English is even harder. That's because, compared to other Romance languages, Old Castilian became a literary language relatively late in its evolution, so by the time writers began using it, Castilian had had the time to evolve to a form close to its modern Spanish, as the following excerpt shows:

Meçio mio Çid los hombros e engrameo la tiesta,
¡Albriçia, Albar Fañez, ca echados somos de tierra!

Mio Çid Ruy Diaz por Burgos entraba,
En su compaña, sesaenta pendones; exienlo ver mugieres y varones:
Burgueses y burguesas por las finiestras son
Plorando de los ojos, ¡tanto habian el dolor!
De las sus bocas todos decian una razon:
¡Dios que buen vasallo! ¡Si hobiese buen Señor!

My Cid shrugged his shoulders and shook his head,
"Good news, Álvar Fáñez, for we are banished from this land!"
My Cid Ruy Díaz entered Burgos,
In his company sixty pennons, women and men came out to
see him:
Burghers, men and women, are at their windows,
Weeping from their eyes, they felt such sorrow
From their mouths all said one thing:
"God, what a good vassal, if he had a good lord!"

There were some differences in pronunciation between the Castilian of *El Cid* and modern Spanish. The *h* was not silent but pronounced as it is in English. The *g* and the *j* were pronounced *di,* so *gente* (people) sounded like *diente* and *consejo* (advice) was more like *consedio.* Today, *g* and *j* sound more like the Scottish *ch* in *loch.* The *ç,* a consonant that has since disappeared, was pronounced *ts.* So El Cid sounded like El *Tsid. Çerca* (close) was pronounced *tserca.* Still, on the whole, a modern reader can make it out.

The reputation of Castilian slowly improved as the Castilians made their way south over the next two centuries. The watershed victory for the Castilians was the conquest of Toledo in 1085. The city was a brilliant Arabic, Jewish, and Christian cultural center, almost on a par with Córdoba. It became the capital of New Castile in 1087.

This conquest of Toledo was not only the key to controlling the center of the peninsula. It also defined the Reconquista, since

Toledo was, of course, the original Visigoth capital. Recapturing it was highly symbolic and added a moral luster to the Reconquista, which Castilian propaganda then exploited to its fullest.

Though the Castilians would get a lot of mileage out of the myth that they were fighting the Reconquista to bring back Visigothic Spain, the idea was disingenuous, to say the least. Prior to the Reconquista, the Castilians had built their identity on rejecting everything Visigothic. The Leonese, Castile's rivals, had embraced their Visigoth heritage but the Castilians scorned the Visigoths and rejected their law code. Around the middle of the tenth century, the Castilians went as far as burning all the copies of the Visigothic law left in Burgos. They came up with their own law code, called the *albedrío* (which now means "fancy" or "free will" but at the time referred to a system of arbitration based on local custom). It was only after the king of Castile took Toledo, then united his kingdom with León, that Castile accepted and then embraced its Visigothic "heritage," including Visigothic law.

When Castile marched into al-Andalus, it encountered buffer territories that were sparsely populated and open to colonization. The Castilians redistributed that land to members of the nobility and military as payment for their services. For the benefit of soldiers, the Crown divided the no-man's-land into large *ranchos:* the word comes from *ranchear,* "to settle down," originally from the French *se ranger.* Because this land was relatively empty, the victors adopted a totally new mode of production: ranching and open-range cattle grazing. La Mancha and Extremadura became open-range land.

The invention of open-range ranching did create new problems. Since all animals were loose, it was difficult to determine what stock belonged to whom. And because large herds had to be moved between north and south through cultivated lands, stock holders and farmers came into conflict. Spain invented a number of solutions to these problems, including *cañadas* (grazing and migratory routes), as well as branding. This new mode of production put Spain in a position to trade wool with England, and wool became Spain's main export for centuries.

Oddly enough, conquistadores faced the same situation in the Americas two centuries later, and Spain quickly transplanted ranching to the New World.

Although the Castilianization of Spain proceeded at a much slower pace than the Reconquista, it did drive out other Ibero-Romances, starting with its first victim, Mozarabic. In fact, it's probably more accurate to describe the disappearance of Mozarabic as a collapse. It had been by far the most widely spoken of Ibero-Romance varieties. Then, between the thirteenth and fifteenth centuries, it became practically extinct. The reason for its disappearance is somewhat of a mystery but probably has to do with the rise of fundamentalist Muslim emirates that forced Christians either to convert or flee to the Christian kingdoms of the north, where they blended in the local parlance.

Mozarabic ended up having very little influence on Castilian—it had more of an impact on Leonese. Nevertheless, several Spanish words, including *gazpacho, muchacho* (boy, guy), and *semilla* (seeds), originate in Mozarabic. It was sometimes written in Roman letters and other times in Arabic.

In 1948, the Hungarian Jewish professor Samuel Miklos Stern caused a stir when he took a fresh look at the *jarchas* (from the Arabic *kharjas*), the final refrain in a type of Arabic poetry called *muwashshahs*. *Muwashshahs* were made of five stanzas alternating with five or six refrains. The last one was the *jarcha*. *Jarchas* were always sung in the local vernacular. Until then, Western Romanists had long ignored *jarchas* because they assumed that since they looked Arabic, they were Arabic. But Stern was an Arabist, and he realized that when read aloud, the *jarchas* did not sound Arabic at all but Romance. His conclusion: *jarchas* from Spain were transliterations of Mozarabic.

Stern knew because when he transcribed the Arabic script into Roman letters, he was in front of something that resembled Romance. And indeed, a verse like *"gryd bš y yrmn lš km"* is just an Arabic rendition of the Mozarabic: *"Garyd vos, ey yermanellas"* (Tell me, little sisters). This line in Mozarabic is quite close to the modern Spanish: *"Decid, vosotras, ay, hermanillas."*

According to the linguist Ralph Penny, the rapid penetration of Castilian into new territories was one more factor explaining why modern Spanish has a relatively simple sound system (phonology) and simple structure (morphology). So many new speakers of Castilian came into contact with one another so suddenly that they had to keep it simple. He writes: "Both the phonology and the morphology of the modern language [Spanish] are notably simpler than those of most other varieties of Romance, and perhaps offer fewer contrasts than any other variety at all. This relative simplicity has been caused by the repeated dialect mixing which has occurred among central Hispano-Romance varieties, from the beginning of the Christian Reconquista of the Peninsula onwards."

One of the great turning points of the Reconquista was the Battle of Las Navas de Tolosa, when Castilian King Alfonso VIII, allied with his rivals the kings of Navarre, Portugal, and Aragón, defeated a combined army of Muslims from Spain and North Africa. It was one of the greatest battles of the Middle Ages, during which some 100,000 Arabs and 2,000 Christians were killed.

But Alfonso's nephew, Fernando III (r. 1217–1252), was the true great figure of the Reconquista, which he more or less finished off. What sets Fernando apart from other kings is that he fought the Moriscos rather than other Christian kingdoms. Starting with Úbeda (1235), Fernando toppled one Muslim emirate after another: Córdoba in 1236, Jaén in 1246, Seville in 1248 after a siege lasting sixteen months, and finally Cádiz in 1250.

Fernando also benefited from a dramatically bigger war chest than his predecessors. Under his reign, Castile and its old rival

León were definitively united in 1230. With the resources of both kingdoms at his disposal, he effectively doubled his budget to fight the Moriscos.

By the middle of the thirteenth century, the only thing left of Muslim Spain was the Emirate of Granada, which amounted to about half of present-day Andalusia. It remained a vassal state of Castile and paid tribute in gold to Castile for two more centuries. The borders of Portugal and Aragón were more or less fixed. Castile held three-quarters of the peninsula.

Thus, the linguistic map of Spain was redrawn: León was squeezed into a narrow corridor between Castile and Portugal. Aragón was limited to a triangle in the northeast, on the Mediterranean. And Castile became a huge wedge down the center of the peninsula.

Yet in spite of his military victories, Fernando left his heir with a colossal challenge. When Fernando's son, Alfonso X, succeeded him on the Castilian throne in 1252, he inherited more territory than any other Spanish king had controlled since the Visigoths six centuries earlier. But his kingdom was as diverse as it was expansive. There was little binding together the inhabitants of the recently conquered territories. It was occupied by *mudéjares, muladí,* Christians and Jews, who neither spoke a common tongue nor worshipped the same God.

Although not the warrior his father was, Alfonso understood that his subjects needed more than a king to keep them together. They needed a common language. The problem was, Castilian was still fighting an uphill battle to become a reputable tongue.

Alfonso X would change that.

7. The Prince of Language Buffs

THE EASTERN AND WESTERN WALLS of the U.S. Capitol's Chamber of the House of Representatives are decorated with twenty-three relief portraits of famous historical lawgivers who inspired American legislators. It's kind of a curious collection. There are more French faces (including Napoleon's) than British, more Muslim kings than popes, and more great figures of antiquity than actual Americans (which include only George Mason's and Thomas Jefferson's).

One of the portraits, the face of a handsome bearded medieval king, framed in laurels, doesn't really fit any category.

The enigmatic character is Alfonso X, who was king of Castile from 1252 to 1284. Castilian though he was, King Alfonso X actually had a more direct impact on American law than some of the more obscure characters on the wall. Alfonso X codified the *Siete Partidas* (Seven Parts), which remained the basis of the Spanish legal system until the nineteenth century. When the United States annexed what is now the American Southwest from Mexico in 1848, old Spanish deeds, oaths, and contracts were recognized by American courts and Alfonso X's *Siete Partidas* became a foundation law of the United States.

Alfonso X would make tremendous contributions to the story of Spanish. Yet he certainly did not go down in history as one of Spain's great kings. Alfonso X was an ambitious imperialist who spent his reign dilapidating Spain's royal treasury to finance far-fetched schemes like invading Morocco, or trying to get himself crowned Holy Roman emperor, neither of which came to fruition. His fiscal policy was so misguided that he ended up setting off major rebellions throughout his kingdom, first, of the *mudéjares* in 1264, then of the entire Castilian nobility in 1272. When Alfonso finally departed from this world, he left his kingdom on the verge of a civil war.

Yet in one way, Alfonso X did as much to unify Spain as had his father, the great Fernando III. Alfonso X devoted all his talents and energy to achieving a single objective: improving the reputation of the Spanish language. It was his one project that proved a resounding success.

Though by Alfonso X's time the reputation of Castilian was improving, few poets were willing to use it for literary production, or for writing anything more refined than a contract—and poets were the arbiters of taste in the Middle Ages. Fernando III had done his bit to promote Castilian by ordering his chancery to write official documents in it. Yet at the end of Fernando's reign, Castile was still multilingual. Fernando's own tombstone was testimony to this: it bore inscriptions in four languages: Latin, Arabic, Hebrew, and Castilian.

Even a king can't force people to use a language they're not interested in and Alfonso X knew it. To get his subjects to adopt Castilian, he had to make it more prestigious. And there was only one way to do that: by making Castilian a vehicle of culture, on par with Greek and Latin.

Despite his shortcomings as a statesman, Alfonso X was unmatched in his erudition. He came by this both by inclination and through education. Although he spent much of his childhood in Galicia, Alfonso's mother spoon-fed him the Arab classics available in Toledo, the intellectual jewel of Europe. Known as the *cabeza de Europa* (head of Europe), Toledo had attracted renowned twelfth-century European scholars like the English Daniel of Morley and the Italian translator Gerard of Cremona, both of whom traveled to Toledo to study ancient Greek and Arabic texts there.

To transform Castilian into a prestigious tongue, Alfonso worked with what he had—literally.

During his thirty-two-year reign, Alfonso earned the title El

Sabio (translated as "the Wise" although it literally means "the Savant"). He orchestrated the production of his brain trust like a giant conductor. He determined what books would be written or translated, assigned the work, then edited and improved language or style. He went as far as saying what illustrations should be included in manuscripts. There is a lot of dispute, still to this day, about what Alfonso actually wrote himself and what he had commissioned. According to Alfonso's biographer Joseph O'Callaghan, the king would have described himself an "active general editor" rather than author.

Many scholars consider Alfonso the precursor of the humanist movement in Europe, which encouraged the recovery and study of lost classics. Whatever the case, Toledo was full of important Latin, Greek, and Arabic works, and Alfonso spent his life translating as many of them as possible into Castilian. Before he became king, Alfonso translated two Arab classics himself: *El Libro de Calila e Dimna* (anecdotes and moral tales for the use of kings) and *El Lapidario* (a book on magic). In the prologue to *El Lapidario,* published in 1250, he explains that he translated it from Arabic into Castilian so people could "have a better understanding of it, and could approve of it."

Many authors wrongly credit Alfonso with creating Toledo's famous Escuela de traductores (School of Translation). In fact, the school was nearly a century old when Alfonso was born. Its real creator was Raimundo, archbishop of Toledo from 1126 to 1151. Many classics that had been forgotten in Europe and often survived only in their Arabic translation had been made available to Christian Europe after the taking of Toledo in 1085. Thanks to Raimundo, Jewish, Arab, and Christian scholars systematically translated them into Latin or Castilian or both.

But even by Alfonso's time, Toledo still had plenty of works left to translate. And thanks to the diverse cultural heritage of Toledo, the king also had a good supply of Arab, Jewish, and Christian scholars and translators at his disposal. Under Alfonso's supervision, they produced, literally, a tidal wave of Castilian translations on all manner of subjects—from magic and law to astronomical tables. They produced the *Libro de los juegos* (Book of Games), which included a description of a novel Persian game called *ajedrez* (chess). It is fascinating to read the thirteenth-century description of a game that had not yet been Europeanized, with moves like *jaque mate* (checkmate), itself an Arabicization of *shâh mâtâ,* meaning "kill the shah."

Yet during his lifetime, it was Alfonso's scientific work that brought him the most renown in Europe. Like his Arab predecessors in Toledo, Alfonso was fascinated with astronomy and astrology. His most famous accomplishment was the *Alfonsine Tables,* which calculated the position of the moon, sun, and planets with respect to stars. For the next three centuries, these remained the most popular astronomical tables in Europe. Everyone used them, even Nicolaus Copernicus, the first European astronomer to claim that Earth was not the center of the universe. Alfonso also commissioned a translation of the *Libro del saber de astronomía* (Book of Astronomical Knowledge), a collection of thirteen Arabic scientific treatises from the ninth to the twelfth century.

Alfonso X's range of interest had almost no limits: he worked on everything from history and astronomy to poetry and science. He produced the *Estoria de España* and the *Crónica General,* histories of Spain and of the world. The former alone has an astounding 1,135 chapters. To write it, Alfonso X drew on the Bible, Saint Augustine's commentary, Pliny the Elder, Ovid, French authors, and even Arab historians like ibn-Wasif and el Bacrí. The very title *Estoria de España* also demonstrates eloquently how much progress the French idea of an "España" had made in the peninsula.

In terms of the language itself, Alfonso's two most influential works were his law code, the *Siete Partidas,* and his *Primera Crónica General* (History of the World), both of which would be read by generations of scholars and lawyers. The *Siete Partidas,* known in its time as the *Book of Laws,* would be particularly influential. Alfonso's father had translated the Latin *Fuero Juzgo* into Castilian in the early thirteenth century, but Alfonso went much farther by recompiling laws and standardizing them, something that had not been done for six centuries. In just nine years, between 1256 and 1265, his appointed team of experts in law and philosophy produced seven books dealing with the church, canon law, marriage, inheritance, crimes, and commerce.

As a result of this program, Castilian gained a degree of prestige it had never known. Alfonso managed to replace texts in Arabic, Hebrew, Galician, and Aragonese with Castilian, and even substituted Castilian for Latin as a language of history, science, and jurisprudence.

Alfonso X was the first medieval king in Europe to put his vernacular language to broad and spectacular use. He was also the first to recognize that vernacular languages needed rules.

A prince among language buffs, El Sabio was centuries ahead of most of Europe's other crowned heads in forging language policy and three centuries ahead of the Italian and the French in standardizing the grammar and spelling of a vernacular tongue. During his reign, Castilian went from having great differences in spelling from one text to the next to having almost no differences. His influence was so profound that Alfonso X is sometimes referred to as Spain's first "academician," even though the Spanish language academy wasn't founded until four centuries after his death. Most of Alfonso's standards remained in place until the sixteenth century.

Alfonso's language policy was that any documents produced by his chancery, any translation made by his scholars, any scientific work written by astronomers or legists under his patronage had to meet impeccable writing standards and be understandable to readers. He himself was an indefatigable editor, constantly taking collaborators to task for sloppy writing and copying. His works are full of notes with definitions of Latin or Greek words scribbled in the margins in Castilian. His ideas evolved considerably, and in the later years of his reign he even called for retranslations of some of his earlier translations.

There were no dictionaries or grammars to speak of at the time: Alfonso forged the standards of Castilian while creating his entire body of work. The material his chancery produced stood as the model for correct usage. It was a work in progress. His earlier works include many words borrowed from Aragonese and Occitan as well as Arabic, Latin, and French. The first 116 chapters of his *Primera Crónica General* (which predate 1270) contain a number of archaisms, such as amalgamated pronouns, like *nimbla* for *ni me la* and *quemblo* for *que me lo*. There were also some verb contractions, like *Té* for *Te he* (I have you). These archaisms would disappear from later chapters.

As time went on, he changed his approach. He either Castilianized the borrowings (by hiding them in Castilian-sounding words) or opted for bona fide Castilian terms. He dropped the Arabic terms for latitude and longitude and replaced them with the Castilian *ladeza* and *longueza*.

Castilian syntax also became more sophisticated during his rule, which allowed writers to express nuances. In early Castilian, sentences were short and simple, and subordinate clauses were rare. During the thirteenth century, largely as a result of Alfonso's intellectual pursuits, sentences became longer, with more conjunctions, pronouns, and time markers.

On this particular point, Alfonso X might have been too successful. Spanish prose came to be characterized by very long and windy paragraphs stocked with adjectives and subordinate clauses. Spanish-language writers often seemed to be trying hard to avoid the appearance of being direct.

People who learn Spanish after speaking English, or even French, are often struck by how much more phonetic and systematic Spanish appears to be. The roots of this feature can be traced back to Alfonso X. At the time of his reign, some Spanish writers were still using the Arabic alphabet to render Spanish dialects. And even within the Roman alphabet, there was a lot of variation.

Alfonso X set out to put order in Spanish spelling, which he rationalized to a degree. The writers, grammarians, and lexicographers of many languages were faced with the same choice at the time of whether to make the spelling of words conform to their original, Latin form—even if the actual pronunciation of the word had changed—or to adapt spellings to be consistent with their pronunciation. In most European languages, writers and grammarians took the phonetic route and created spelling systems that moved away from etymological roots. There were two resounding exceptions: French and English, whose scholars and clerics relished obfuscated spellings that didn't reflect pronunciation. They simply could not resist the temptation of showing off their erudition in Latin, even when they were writing in vernacular.

Under the influence of Alfonso, Castilian went the other way. It maintained its phonetic form even if that meant reducing the number of sounds to fit what was available from the Roman alphabet. Spanish has never been perfectly phonetic: *b* and *v* sound the same, as do *c* and *z*. And Alfonso had to acknowledge that new letters or groupings of letters were necessary—such as *rr*, *ñ*, *ç*, *gu*, and *ll*—in order to render some sounds that were common in Spanish but nonexistent in Latin.

One more factor that pushed Spanish spelling in such a different direction, particularly from that of French and English, was the background of Alfonso X's writing brain trust. In France, as in England, writers (including translators) were clerics or Latin trained. In either case, they resisted their vernaculars. Latin was the language of prestige, period. When French clerics did write in Françoys, they constantly tried to Latinize it to give it a luster of legitimacy and prestige.

The situation in Castile was completely different. Castile had two languages of prestige: Latin and Arabic. Thanks to five centuries of Muslim presence in Spain, the writers, translators, and scribes who worked in Alfonso's court were not dominated by clerics or Latin-trained scholars: they included many non-Christians and, notably, a large number of Jewish scholars.

Jews had arrived in Spain in Roman times and had endured persecution under the Visigoths—some of the writings of St. Isidore, for instance, were rabidly anti-Semitic. As a result, they welcomed Arab rule, which was relatively tolerant, at least at first. When this tolerance was erased by the fundamentalist dynasties, Jews switched their loyalty to the Christian kings.

Jewish translators were known for their language skills in Latin, Arabic, Greek, and Hebrew. They also welcomed Castilian as a language of learning. Promoting Castilian actually allowed them to undermine the Catholic church by displacing Latin, the liturgical language and language of teaching (though in Spain, Arabic competed for this status). Alfonso X and the Jews had different reasons to promote Castilian, but they concurred on the result, and they succeeded.

Alfonso X welcomed Jewish scholars to his court and provided generous patronage to them to translate classical Arabic and Hebrew sources. He even freed them and their descendants from paying taxes, although like his father he required Jews to wear a yellow-and-red badge.

But Alfonso's program of rationalization didn't work perfectly; there were lots of exceptions. As a result of Latin's influence, he still used *u* for *v* and *i* for *j*—so the modern *viejo* could be spelled *vieio*, *uiejo*, and *uieio*. *Huvo* (I had) was spelled *uvo* or *ruo*. There was some variation between *t* and *d* as final consonants—*voluntat* or *voluntad* (will). And he never managed to define whether the verb endings for the imperfect tense (also called the past continuous in English) would be *ía* or *íe*, as in *tenía* or *teníe* (I was holding). Usage did settle to *tenía* in the years to come.

Yet overall, Alfonso X made Spanish spelling better reflect pronunciation. By controlling his production, he was able to set a standard for Spanish that would remain in place for centuries. The regularity of the spelling and grammar in the *Poema del Cid*— generally believed to have been copied in the fourteenth century— shows that Alfonso's standardization efforts bore fruit.

When Alfonso X embarked on his ambitious program, he called Castilian "Our Latin" with the intention of instilling Castile's vernacular with the same prestige as Latin—a long shot at the time. Then, during the 1270s, he went even farther, describing his language policy as *castellano drecho* ("right" or "straight" Castilian). This meant that his writers had to strive to use a "pure," correct Castilian devoid of foreign influence, namely, French.

His ideas spread.

The great Mexican philologist Antonio Alatorre called the spirit with which Alfonso imbued the language *conciencia linguistica* (linguistic awareness). With Alfonso X as a model, writers had to consciously try to conform to the correct way of writing. In the absence of any reference book, Alfonso's doctrine of *castellano drecho* was the drive and the model.

This idea of correctness, which is usually associated with French and with language "purism," is in fact central to Spanish culture and much more ancient. In Spanish, correctness is less a quest for purity—as in French—than a desire to use language in an exemplary manner. Even though today, as a result of mass media, the populist trend is as strong in Spanish as it is in English, native speakers of Spanish expect public discourse to be a model, to set an example. Even the uneducated expect to be addressed with a certain elevation in language use, as a mark of respect.

All languages are driven by usage, the result of billions of exchanges between millions of individuals. Usage is shaped by jokes, interjections, contracts, plays, poems, and more. But in all languages, some key individuals play a more central role, and Alfonso X played that role for Castilian. His influence was already evident in the work of other writers of his generation. His nephew, the poet Don Juan Manuel, closely supervised the work of copyists to make sure that they did not introduce mistakes or "improve" on his work. This sort of care was unheard of before Alfonso X.

A good example of this sense of correctness was the effort of Castilian writers who worked to reverse a linguistic trend in the thirteenth and fourteenth centuries. In all languages, speakers tend to erode and cut words. Under the influence of French, Spaniards had begun to leave off final vowels. They said and wrote *yot recib* instead of *yo té recibe* (I receive you), *nief* instead of *nieve* (snow), *trist* instead of *triste* (sad). During the last eight years of his life, Alfonso X worked to restore *castellano drecho* and bring back the vowels that were being dropped. This could have been just a fad, if all writers of Castilians had not followed his lead, but by the fourteenth century, they had stopped truncating words and reverted to previous spellings. This reversal of the erosion of Castilian speaks volumes about the existence and the effectiveness of the "linguistic conscience" of Spanish.

In spite of Alfonso's intellectual and linguistic achievements, there was one field in which the king changed little: poetry.

One of Alfonso X's most famous works is a set of 420 religious poems titled *Cantigas de Santa María* (Songs of Saint Mary). Accompanied by no fewer than forty miniatures and abundant musical notations, the *Cantigas* praise the grace and miracles of the Virgin Mary. According to the king, the poems were endowed with some miraculous healing power: after Alfonso X fell ill in 1277, he claimed to have been cured after the *Cantigas* were laid on his chest.

Yet, curiously, the poems were written in Galician, not Castilian. Historians suspect that a cleric named Airas Nunes actually wrote them, although Alfonso knew Galician, having spent much of his childhood in Galicia. It was all very well to develop Castilian prose, but even Alfonso was still loath to write poetry in Castilian. He was probably unaware of the body of work of his contemporary, Gonzalo de Berceo, the first poet to write poetry in Castilian.

The reason Alfonso was so untypically averse to in using Castilian for poetry was that during his reign the prestige of Galician was still unmatched—in fact, it was bolstered by the powerful Crown of Portugal.

8. The World According to Portugal

BETWEEN THE TWELFTH AND SIXTEENTH centuries, Portugal managed to completely escape the control of the increasingly powerful Kingdom of Castile. This had momentous consequences for the story of Spanish: nearly a sixth of the territory of the peninsula was left outside the grasp of Castile. Later the jockeying for influence between Portugal and Spain went on to trigger a naval race over control of the Atlantic that, in turn, set European colonialism in motion. Today's maps of Spanish- and Portuguese-speaking countries are the result of this competition.

Portuguese and Spanish are separate languages, but no other international tongues are as close. For centuries, Portuguese had almost exactly the same story as Spanish. Throughout antiquity and until about 1200, Portugal was colonized by the same empires as the rest of the Iberian Peninsula. The only difference was that those empires—the Carthaginians, Celts, Romans, Barbarians, and Arabs—got to Portugal later. The local Celts in Portugal called themselves Lusitanii; the Romans called their province Lusitania. And that's why borrowings from Portuguese are called "Lusitanisms," and not "Portuguisms."

Portugal's geography is more or less the same as Spain's; there's no natural barrier such as a mountain range or river that separates the two countries. In the Middle Ages, there was no real linguistic barrier between them either. The inhabitants of Lusitania, like everyone else in the northwest of the peninsula, spoke Galician or, more exactly, Galician-Portuguese—since Galician and Portuguese were identical for centuries. And until about the eleventh century, Galician was not regarded as a different language from Castilian. Castilian and Galician were both considered dialects of the same language group, Romance.

During the Reconquista, as the increasingly powerful Kingdom of Castile worked its way down the Iberian Peninsula capturing territory, Portugal managed to dodge its grasp. In 1128, Portugal proclaimed itself a kingdom. By this time, the Portuguese were already carving out a distinct identity, which included language. In 1249, Portugal conquered Algarve in the south and effectively concluded its own side of the Reconquista.

Things began to change later that century. In 1290, the remarkable Portuguese king Diniz I (r. 1279–1325) declared Portuguese the exclusive language of secular government, and relegated Latin to church use only.

To some extent, Diniz had language regulation in his blood: he was the grandson of King Alfonso X of Castile. Like his grandfather, he was scholarly by nature. A poet and troubadour, Diniz wrote—or edited—several books on topics ranging from administration to hunting and science, and wrote poetry in Galician-Portuguese.

After Diniz made Portuguese an official language, Portuguese and Spanish went their own ways, evolving separately. In Portuguese, some consonants disappeared—Castilians say *Alfonso* and *Juan* while Portuguese say *Afonso* and *João*. The pronunciation of sibilant vowels like *s* and *z* shifted to *sh* and *zh* (soft *j*). Portuguese speakers also developed a tendency to swallow whole syllables—the Spanish *caliente* (hot) became *quente* in Portuguese.

In *Empire of the Words*, Nicholas Ostler offers a good illustration of the differences:

English	Will you give me hot eggs and bread?
Spanish	¿Me haces el favor de darme huevos calientes y pan?
Portuguese	Faz favor de darme ovos quentes e pão?

Linguists have calculated that Spanish and Portuguese have a "lexical correspondence" of 90 percent, which means that nine words out of ten are the same, even if the spelling is different. Portuguese is no more different from Spanish than are Galician or Catalan—some even say less so. The difference is a political one: the territories of Galicia, Catalonia, and Aragón became part of the story of Spanish because Castile took control of them. In the long run, Portugal managed to keep Castile at bay.

The question of whether Portuguese and Spanish are mutually comprehensible depends on whom you ask. Educated Portuguese speakers generally say they understand Spanish, but even well-educated Spanish speakers tend to say they can't understand Portuguese.

The difference has nothing to do with language as such and everything to do with perceived hierarchy, the product of centuries of political domination of Spain over Portugal.

As we have seen, the Castilian language was considered a backward tongue well into the Middle Ages. In the thirteenth century, even King Alfonso X, the great promoter of Castilian, preferred Galician for writing poetry. It took another two centuries for Castilian to really establish itself as a prestigious literary language. From that point forward, Castilians looked down on Portuguese speakers, along with anyone who spoke the other languages of the peninsula, whether Basque, Catalan, Galician, or others.

The Castilian superiority complex is one reason Spanish contains fewer borrowings from Portuguese than from either French or Italian. Old Castilian borrowed a number of Portuguese words from lyrical poetry—which was a forte of Gallician-Portuguese until the fourteenth century—but most of those disappeared with time. The relatively few Lusitanisms left in Spanish include *regañar* (to tell off), *mermelada* (marmelade), *caramelo* (caramel), and *zorro/zorra* (fox).

Yet Castilian borrowed heavily from Portuguese in one area: words that had anything to do with the shipping business, navigation, the sea, or geography. Castilian adopted *vigía* (lookout), *virar* (to tack), *estela* (wake of a ship), *tanque* (water tank). From the sea it took *albatros, callao* (pebble beach), *marejada* (swell), *monzón* (monsoon), *tifón* (typhoon), *acantilado* (cliff), and *cachalote* (sperm whale). From geography and exotic destinations, the list is almost endless: *mosquito, banana, volcán* (volcano), *bambú, ananás* (pineapple), *mandarín* (Mandarin).

That reason is that it was Portugal, not Spain, that led the pack of European kingdoms aspiring to dominate Atlantic exploration. It's surprising to think that tiny Portugal was once a preeminent sea power. But, actually, it had no competition. Portugal initiated major sea exploration two centuries before other Western European powers did and blazed the trail for everyone else, including Spain.

Some scholars have attributed Portugal's head start to the fact that it has such a long Atlantic coastline, but it probably had more to do with foreign policy. King Diniz I surpassed his Castilian grandfather in one way: he was a skilled policy maker and one of the most remarkable European kings of the Middle Ages. At a time when most of Europe's monarchs were squandering their resources on wars with other European powers, Diniz set out to reorganize his country's economy instead. He built castles, monasteries, and new towns, and improved farming techniques by creating schools of agriculture, earning himself the sobriquet El rei lavrador (the farmer king).

Diniz made another decision that would shape the fate of the Portuguese language: he shifted Portugal's attention from the Mediterranean to the Atlantic Ocean. This new focus put Portugal on the path to developing naval technology, discovering sea routes, and establishing a maritime empire before anyone else.

To finance the naval program, Diniz reopened Portugal's old silver, copper, and tin mines. In doing so, he attracted interest from England, always short on precious metals. In 1294, Diniz hammered out a commercial treaty with England that granted Portuguese traders the right to land in English ports. The original idea was to build a navy to fight Moorish raiders prowling Portugal's shores. Diniz planted whole pine forests to make sure he'd have enough wood to build his ships, then he created maritime insurance funds to make sea ventures more appealing to ambitious merchants and adventurers.

Diniz's passion for his navy didn't die with him. Portugal's princes, kings, and aristocrats kept developing merchant fleet and sea business for centuries. At the end of the fourteenth century, during the Hundred Year War with France, England even came to Portugal looking for assistance with naval warfare. England's enemy, France, was allied with Castile. The Castilian navy—well developed by this point—was taking a toll on English trade. Because of its strategic position, Portugal could block any Castilian fleet trying to move north. And Portugal had the naval know-how to do just that. In 1386, England and Portugal signed an alliance that is still in effect today.

But this was nothing compared to Portugal's next move.

Food aficionados might be surprised to learn that tempura, the Japanese basic method for frying, comes from a Portuguese word. Portuguese traders and missionaries brought it to Japan when they landed in Nagasaki in 1543. The word's origin is not clear: it might come from the Portuguese *temperar* (to cook or to season), or *tempero* (cooking), or *têmporas* (meatless days in the Catholic religion). For that matter, Japanese has many other Lusitanisms, including *karuta* (playing cards, from *cartas de juego*), *pan* (bread, from Portuguese *pão*), *arukōru* (from *álcool*), and *karpa* (cape, from *capa*). Some words, like *manto* (cloak), *kappu* (cup), and *shabon* (soap), are almost identical in pronunciation to the original Portuguese.

It shouldn't seem odd to find Portuguese borrowings in Japanese. At its height, the Portuguese overseas empire included Brazil, India, most of the African coast, and most of the coast of Far East Asia, including Japan. Even the name Labrador is a deformation of the name of Portuguese explorer João Fernandes Lavrador, who sighted the shore of the northern peninsula in 1498. In fact, the only two places Portuguese mariners did not reach were Australia and Antarctica—and they might have gotten there but didn't return alive to tell the tale.

Portugal owed its giant leap as a sea power to several key technical advances it made in shipbuilding and celestial navigation in the fifteenth century. Some of these seem amazingly simple in retrospect. The first breakthrough came between 1410 and 1440, when the Portuguese created a new sort of ship out of a fisherman's boat: the *carabela* (caravel). It was an improved version of an Arab boat called the *qarib* or *carib* (probably the origin of the name *carabela*), and featured a central rudder, up to four masts, and triangular sail. Relatively small, 50 to 160 tons, it could sail against the wind—which previously only galleys could do. The caravel's shallow keel made it equally suitable for coastal and fluvial navigation. What's more, because it ran on wind power, the caravel required much less manpower, only fifteen to twenty-five sailors as opposed to three hundred on a standard galley. But they soon developed a larger version that could carry fifty men, which they called a *nau* (carrack).

Cartography was another Portuguese forte. As exploration expanded, the Portuguese Crown started requiring captains and navigators to report their findings on Portolan charts, realistic representations of harbors and shores. At the end of the fifteenth century, this evolved into the *Padrão Real* (royal register), a centralized record of Portugal's naval discoveries that was considered a state secret and carefully hidden from spies (who found it anyway).

Portuguese sailors also experimented with sailing techniques. Contrary currents and winds made return trips along the coast of Africa difficult. The Portuguese solved the problem with one bold move: they sailed caravels about five hundred miles away from the African shore, in the open sea, where they could catch a western current and trade wind that would bring them directly back to Lisbon. This technique was called *volta do mar* (return from the sea). Before the Portuguese, nobody had dared to do it.

But *volta do mar* had a catch. With ships sailing for weeks at a time in the middle of what seemed to be nowhere, sailors needed new navigation techniques to figure out where they were. Once again, Portugal was able to solve this thanks to the scientific legacy of the Arabs. In particular, the Portuguese turned to the stars, reviving some old Arab astronomical science, using the *Stella Maris* (sea star, or Pole star) and the astrolabe (star finder) to determine their latitude. As the Portuguese traveled south, they lost sight of the Pole star, so they figured out how to find their bearings using the elevation of the sun. In the southern hemisphere, they discovered the southern equivalent of the Pole star, a constellation called the Southern Cross.

These advantages gave Portugal a seventy-year lead in seafaring over Castile and a nearly two-century lead over the English and the French.

Meanwhile, the Portuguese got even more ambitious. In the fifteenth century, they invaded North Africa, a daring move that the king of Castile had not been able to pull off. In 1415, a mighty Portuguese fleet of two hundred ships carrying twenty thousand soldiers crossed the Strait of Gibraltar and took the fortress of Ceuta. That conquest set off a glorious era of Portuguese expansion in all directions. Over the next 120 years, the Portuguese claimed the entire Moroccan shore as their own, capturing Tangiers and Anafé (Casablanca). By the end of the fifteenth century, the Portuguese had explored and mapped eight thousand miles of African coast.

As early as the 1420s, the Portuguese had established colonies in Madeira and the Azores. By the end of the century, they also controlled Cape Verde, which included the islands of São Tomé and Principe. The remaining important islands, the Canary archipelago, belonged to Spain.

The prime mover in all these exploits was a Portuguese prince, Henrique. Although he never became king, Henrique (1394–1460) became more famous than his father, King João I, and most Portuguese kings after him. Known to historians as Henry the Navigator, Henrique actually sailed only once, to Ceuta in 1415. He earned the nickname because he sponsored, or personally mandated, a third of the Portuguese expeditions to Africa that took place during his lifetime. Between 1444 and 1446—Henrique's peak—this amounted to more than thirty expeditions.

Henrique wasn't driven by a quest for knowledge or a thirst for discovery. He was after gold. In Ceuta, he saw gold arriving on trans-Saharan caravans that had started out on the coast of West Africa. When he returned to Portugal, he set about organizing expeditions that would bypass these caravans and get to the gold sources. For years his countrymen laughed at his idea—until 1441, when a ship full of gold dust and slaves arrived from Guinea. That made Henrique a public hero overnight.

By 1450, the Portuguese had converted Madeira into sugarcane plantations, which would eventually overtake Cyprus as Europe's main source of sugar—*melaza* (molasses) is from the Portuguese *melaço*. Good wines also started flowing out of Madeira. Two generations before the discovery of the Americas, Portugal had also developed a slave trade and slaving industry, including the first slave market in 1441. The Portuguese made the whole hideous commerce easier by tapping into existing African slave markets instead of carrying out raids themselves. By 1445, they were selling a thousand slaves a year.

It was the Portuguese who developed the African slave trade and defined the vocabulary of slaving. Spanish, like English, adopted a great number of Portuguese terms, starting with *negro* (black) and *mulatto* (which originally meant a mule, a cross between a horse and a donkey). The Spanish *criollo* (Creole) is a deformation of the Portuguese *crioulo*, which referred to a slave born in captivity, as opposed to an *escravo* (Portuguese for slave). *Crioulo*, in turn, comes from the Portuguese *cria* (a servant raised in his master's house). Eventually, Spanish speakers would adopt the word *criollo* to refer to any "Spanish people born in the colonies" (the expression was derogatory). In English, Creole took many more meanings: it can refer to a descendant of a French or Spanish settler, a mulatto of French or Spanish descent, a dialect of Spanish or French, or a Louisiana pidgin spoken by Afro-Americans, derived from English, French, Portuguese, and Spanish.

By the time of Henrique's death in 1460, Portugal had built the framework for overseas colonial expansion that would serve as the blueprint for all other European countries' colonial undertakings— notably, Spain's. In 1481, King João II upped the ante by switching the focus of exploration from gold to spices. The reason was that the Turks had captured Constantinople twenty-eight years earlier, putting an end to the Byzantine Empire. This completely disrupted trade routes to and from India. Genoese and Venetian traders, who had a monopoly in spices, jacked their prices higher than the price of gold because supplies diminished. João figured that his navy was good enough to find a way to solve this problem, by sailing around Africa to get to the Indian Ocean. Then Portugal could trade directly with India. So João began sending expeditions to look for the route around Africa, if there was one.

Portugal's interest in finding a new route to India was what brought an enterprising Genoese explorer by the name of Christopher Columbus to court. Columbus had been working in the wine and sugar trade of Madeira for some time. He had even married into the Portuguese nobility and he spoke Portuguese. In 1485, he approached King João with a novel scheme: forget about rounding Africa and instead sail west to India.

King João listened with a friendly ear, then handed Columbus's plans to a committee of experts to be evaluated. Contrary to the contemporary legend that everyone in Columbus's time believed the world was flat, most mariners actually knew that Earth was round, especially the avant-garde Portuguese. Thanks to their Arab heritage, the Portuguese used trigonometry and algebra to calculate the size of Earth with surprising accuracy. King João's experts could see that there was something amiss in Columbus's plan:

Columbus was claiming that India was only twenty-five hundred miles west of Portugal, but the Portuguese knew the real distance west was five times that. They also knew that no caravel could carry enough food and water to make the trip Columbus was proposing. So they sent Columbus on his way.

In 1488, Columbus returned to talk João about his project again. But before he got a chance to make his pitch, the king learned that there was a safer route to India than the one Columbus was proposing: the Portuguese sailor Bartholomeu Dias had succeeded in rounding the Cape of Good Hope at the southern tip of Africa. Columbus had missed his chance at getting Portuguese support.

And Portugal missed out on discovering the Americas.

Portugal's bad luck would be good news for Spain and for the Spanish language.

9. Fourteen Ninety-two

1492 WAS A BIG YEAR in the history of Spanish, and not just because it was the year Columbus accidentally discovered America. Columbus sailed away on August 3, 1492. Just five days prior to his departure, the Edict of Expulsion of the Jews came into force in Spain, prohibiting Spanish Jews who had not converted to Christianity from remaining in the kingdom. In a matter of months, one hundred thousand Spanish Jews fled Spain, creating a diaspora of Spanish speakers in Europe, North Africa, and the Ottoman Empire. But that wasn't all. Seven months prior to that, on January 2, 1492, the last Moorish stronghold in Spain, Granada, surrendered to the Spanish monarchs.

All these events had a momentous impact on the future of Spanish. The capitulation of Granada established the dominion of Castile, and of the Castilian tongue over the peninsula. The expulsion of the Jews created the first mass migration of Spanish speakers outside Spain. And the discovery of the Americas triggered an even larger migration and spawned a Spanish-speaking overseas empire the likes of which had never before been seen.

There was one common link among all the events of 1492: Spain's "Catholic" monarchs, Isabel I *la Católica* (1451–1504), the queen of Castile, and Fernando II *el Católico* (1452–1516), the king of Aragón.

The actual marriage of Isabel and Fernando, in 1469, was just one episode in the ongoing game of alliances between European dynasties. Curiously, it was Isabel's idea to marry the king of Aragón, not her family's. She had even refused a number of advantageous unions, including an offer from the king of Portugal, so she could marry Fernando, who was her cousin. Because of their consanguinity, Isabel and Fernando needed the pope's permission to get married, but they swiftly obtained it. Then she fled to marry Fernando in secret.

The elopement would eventually unite the Crowns of Castile and Aragón, and create the Kingdom of Spain, but a number of things had to happen first. Fernando, the oldest son of the king of Aragón, was next in line to the throne of Aragón. But for Isabel, becoming queen of Castile was a long shot. She was the half sister of the king, Enrique IV (also called the Impotent). It was Enrique's daughter, Juana, who was the rightful heir. But since Juana's mother had had a "very friendly" relationship with a certain Castilian noble, Juana was suspected of being illegitimate. Moreover, Juana was already the wife of the king of Portugal, and many Castilian nobles feared a takeover by the rich and powerful Portugal. King Enrique IV's death in 1474 triggered the four-year War of the Castilian Succession between Isabel and Juana, who also dragged France and Portugal into the standoff.

Ultimately, Isabel prevailed. In 1479, Juana was declared persona non grata in Castile. The same year, as luck would have it, Fernando's father died, making him king of Aragón. The Crowns of Castile and Aragón were automatically united.

The union sparked unprecedented hope in the peninsula. In the cathedral of Toledo, there is a special chapel devoted to the "new" monarchs. One wall is covered by a large caramel-colored tapestry with the Castilian crest in the middle and the words "*Tanto monta*" woven on each side. This was a short version of the motto Isabel and Fernando assumed for their union: *Tanto monta, monta tanto, Isabel como Fernando* (It's one and the same, Isabel the same as Fernando). Territorially speaking, it truly was a union of equals. Though Castile y León was bigger than Aragón, the Crown of Aragón brought a lot to the table: it was a naval power that had dominion over Sardinia, the south of Italy, and a large portion of Greece.

Yet in a number of ways, Isabel and Fernando ran their own kingdoms separately. Each monarch had a separate foreign policy— Fernando took care of Italian and papal affairs, and Isabel was responsible for overseas exploration. This is one reason Isabel is held in so much higher esteem than is Fernando in the Americas, even today. Isabel also conducted a number of reforms: she pulled Castile out of debt and made an effort to reduce crime by creating Europe's first organized police force, the Santa Hermandad (Holy Brotherhood), a rural militia of informal groups of vigilantes that already stood watch in various parts of the kingdom. Nicknamed *mangas verdes* (green sleeves) because of their uniforms, the Santa Hermandad was known for arriving late on the crime scene. To this day, the Spanish use the ironic expression *"¡A buenas horas, mangas verdes!"*—meaning "It's about time!" or "too late!"

Isabel and Fernando were the first monarchs to refer to their joint kingdoms as a single political entity and the first rulers to generalize the use of the name España. Two centuries earlier, Alfonso X had used the old French label in the title of his *Estoria de España,* but he was still the king of Castile and León. The new monarchs went a notch further, designating both the language and culture of their realm as *español,* a catchall name they chose deliberately to emphasize their subjects' shared common identity. (The English used the same trick two centuries later when they conquered Wales, Ireland, and Scotland and called their new territory Britain. The difference, of course, was that the British never changed the name of their language to British: the British still speak English.)

Though in many ways they ran their kingdoms separately, Isabel and Fernando were nevertheless determined to unite them in spirit—literally. They could have chosen language as a tool, as Alfonso X had. Instead, they chose religion. The Catholic monarchs, as they would come to be known, promoted orthodox Catholicism and rallied their kingdom around two projects: wrapping up the Reconquista and kicking off the Spanish Inquisition.

Spain was fertile ground for a state-organized plan of religious persecution. Under previous empires, whether Arab or Christian, religious coexistence had never been peaceful. Even during the reigns of Christian kings who officially tolerated Jews and Muslims, the populations saw things differently. In June 1391, a huge wave of massacres resulted in the deaths of fifty thousand Jews. That's why, during the next century, an estimated two hundred thousand Jews converted or said they did and became *nuevo cristianos* (new Christians). But converting to Christianity did not spell the end of troubles for former Jews.

At a time when religion trumped national identity, Isabel and Fernando feared that too many Jews and Muslims would weaken a Spanish-Catholic Crown. The original Inquisition was created in the twelfth century by the Roman Catholic church to fight heretics in France. In 1478, Spain's monarchs applied to the pope for permission to create their own Inquisition, a religious tribunal with the mandate of rooting out false converts. The pope agreed almost immediately. In 1480, Spain got its first Grand Inquisitor. (When it started, the Spanish Inquisition was not about rooting out Protestantism. The Protestant movement started only thirty-nine years *after* the Inquisition was created, when Martin Luther nailed his famous 95 theses on the door of a church in Wittenberg, Germany.)

Contrary to the famous line in the *Monty Python* sketch, the Spanish Inquisition was never "fanatically devoted to the pope." Rather, it was the exclusive tool of the Spanish Crown, directed, at least initially, toward conversos, not Jews. It turned out to be a political coup that set Spain apart from all the crowns of Europe. For the previous five centuries, Europe's monarchs had been struggling to gain political control over the church in their countries. Spain's monarchs were the only ones who pulled this off.

The Spanish Inquisition began by persecuting conversos, not Muslims, mostly because Jews were an easier target—Muslims constituted large minorities around Seville and Valencia (and in Granada, obviously). But originally, the Inquisition wasn't mandated to persecute actual Jews. It focused strictly on so-called Marranos (secret, or crypto-Jews) who allegedly "pretended" to be Christians but practiced their rites in secret. Indeed, many families

of converted Jews did keep up Jewish traditions like lighting can-
dles on Fridays, baking unleavened bread, keeping the Sabbath,
and even inscribing tombstones in Hebrew. (Some of these rites
survived twenty generations and can be observed today as far away
as New Mexico.) Unfortunately, those traditions made it easy for
inquisitors to locate them: even the absence of smoke from chimneys
on a Saturday could be cited as proof that a family was Marrano.
("Did it not prove that they observed Sabbath?")

Tomás de Torquemada, inquisitor general from 1483 to 1498,
would change this. The organizational genius of the Spanish Inquisition, his name has gone down in history as synonymous with
intolerance and cruelty. Torquemada never flinched from his mission. While he was in charge, an estimated two thousand Spanish
"heretics" were burned at the stake. Countless others were "questioned," tortured, and forced to do some form of harsh public penance, like bearing heavy crosses.

Torquemada wasn't satisfied with just burning or torturing un-
repentant Marranos. Before him, the Inquisition had no authority
to arrest and try unconverted Jews or Muslims. Torquemada argued that Spain's unconverted Jews were helping the conversos
escape the Inquisition and that Spain had to find a way to get rid
of Jews, period. Torquemada pleaded his case incessantly to Queen
Isabel, either to send Jews into exile or force them to convert.

For ten years, Isabel and Fernando resisted the idea of expelling
Spain's Jews for the simple reason that they couldn't afford to.
Since 1482, Isabela and Fernando had been trying to conquer the
last Emirate of Granada and kick the Nasrid Dynasty out of Spain.
Although their religious fanaticism was sincere, the real motive for
this war was to unite the kingdom against a common enemy. The
plot worked: fighting the Moors kept the Castilian and Aragónese
nobility from infighting. But as the monarchs discovered, taking
Granada was no walk in the park. Although the Emirate of Granada
was much smaller even than the Kingdom of Aragón, it was well
protected behind the natural barrier of Sierra Nevada (the Snowy

Mountains). Granada could afford to defend itself: it was an important trade center whose population was constantly bolstered by the inflow of Muslim refugees from the rest of the peninsula and it maintained strong ties with the Zianid kingdom in Tlemcen (today's Algeria).

The Granada War lasted ten years. It was a long, grinding, costly affair. The only way they could finance it was with the tax revenues from Spain's prosperous urban class, of which Jewish merchants, tradesmen, scholars, and financiers formed an important part. But circumstances were about to change. After the formal surrender of Granada on January 2, 1492, Isabel and Fernando no longer needed the Jews to finance their war, so Torquemada's wish came true. Within a few weeks, Isabel and Fernando decided to expel the unconverted Jews from Spain. In February, the Crown wrote the Edict of Expulsion and it was ratified at the end of March. It gave the Jews exactly four months to leave the country—or convert.

Of all the events of 1492 that affected the Spanish language, the expulsion of the Jews was the most immediate and dramatic. It is impossible to know exactly how many Jews went into exile. Most scholars agree on the figure of one hundred thousand, though studies range from as many as eight hundred thousand to as few as forty thousand. This massive exodus created large colonies of Spanish-speaking Sephardic Jews from Istanbul to Manchester, from Morocco to Sarajevo (*Sephardic* comes from the Hebrew word for Spain, *Sefara*). They went to Turkey, North Africa, Italy, the Netherlands, France, and the Balkans. The single largest contingent—twenty-three thousand by some estimates—went to Portugal. But Portugal soon started its own inquisition, in 1536, and the Portuguese Jews (many of whom were Spanish) were forced to flee to the colonies and Western Europe.

For generations, even centuries, Spanish Jews maintained their language, which was called Judeo-Spanish, Judezmo, Judio, Sefardi,

Spanyol, Spagnol, Spañol, Haketia, or Ladino, depending on where they lived. The two most common names, used interchangeably, are Judeo-Spanish and Ladino, but to complicate things further, many speakers of Ladino refer to their language simply as "Spanish."

No matter where it was spoken, Ladino remained close to Spanish. About 60 percent of the basic vocabulary is Castilian (the rest is mostly Turkisms, Hebrewisms, and Arabisms). Because Judeo-Spanish speakers moved away from Spain before the great transformation of Castilian pronunciation in the sixteenth century, Ladino actually sounds more like Galician-Portuguese than modern Castilian—native speakers of Spanish would say it sounds like a version of Spanish that predates Cervantes. The spelling, however, evolved toward an even more phonetic version of Spanish. For instance, the Spanish *corazón* (heart) is *korason* in Ladino.

In 1496, the pope declared Isabel and Fernando *Los Reyes Católicos* (the Catholic monarchs). Their unification strategy had worked. The Spanish Inquisition, along with the taking of Granada, kindled a new idea in Spain: religion and nation were one.

At the time, no one foresaw the social and economic side effects of this policy. The expulsion of the Jews sent shock waves throughout Spain, not because of the cruelty it entailed—times were cruel anyway—but because it stripped Spain of 2 percent of its inhabitants, most of whom were urban, educated, and affluent. At a time when Europe's economy was shifting from agrarian to industrial, Spain could not afford this loss. The effect was compounded by the fact that after the Jews, the Inquisition attacked the Muslim population. In 1501, Spanish Muslims were forbidden to practice their religious rites. A century later, Spain had expelled about five hundred thousand Muslims.

This brings to roughly four hundred thousand the total number of non-Catholic Spanish exiled from Spain between 1492 and 1608, almost twice the number of Spaniards who migrated to the Americas during the same period. For any country, this migration would have represented an enormous loss. It was all the more so for a country a third the size of France.

Yet the expulsion of the Jews and of the Moriscos had a revolutionary effect on the Spanish language. For the first time, Spanish spread beyond the peninsula. Dozens of Spanish-speaking Sephardic communities took root in the Ottoman Empire, the Balkans, and Northern Europe. In the Mediterranean, Spanish became a trade language, a status it never had enjoyed before due to the domination of Genoa and Venice. Ladino became so common in the Ottoman Empire that people mused, "Castilians spoke the Jewish language."

The influence of Ladino was even greater in the Portuguese and Dutch empires. In the Dutch colonies of the West Indies, the language of Portuguese-Jewish planters (many of whom were Judeo-Spanish) was one of the most likely sources of Papiamentu, the Creole that developed there. Many historians have marveled at how Portuguese remained the trade language in the East Indies long after the Dutch and the English started divvying up the Portuguese trade empire in 1663. They credit the survival of Portuguese to "Dutch pragmatism," but it probably had more to do with the fact that there were Ladino-speaking middlemen throughout the Dutch empire, which stretched all the way to Indonesia.

When countries force the most educated members of their society into exile, other countries reap the rewards. The expulsion of the Jews from Spain bore this out. Many Sephardic Jews and their families rose to great prominence elsewhere. Among the celebrities were the British prime minister Benjamin Disraeli (in office 1868, 1874–1880); the Dutch philosopher Baruch Spinoza (1632–1677), one of the most important thinkers of the early modern period; the Italian painter Amadeo Modigliani (1884–1920). In 1776, the well-known New York rabbi Gershom Mendes Seixas (1745–1816) rallied American Jews behind the insurgency: this earned them equal status in the new republic, an idea revolutionaries in France would imitate fifteen years later. In the United States, prominent

Sephardic Jews include the Supreme Court justice Benjamin Cardozo, the poet Emma Lazarus, and the actor Hank Azaria. Names in British history include the boxing champion Daniel Mendoza, the financier and philanthropist Moses Montefiore, and the political economist David Ricardo. In France, Prime Minister Pierre Mendès-France, the bankers Émile and Isaac Pereire, and the philosopher Jacques Derrida were Sephardic Jews.

But the Holocaust drove Judeo-Spanish to the brink of extinction. In the Balkans and Greece, the Ladino language made Sephardic Jews easily identifiable. The one exception was Bulgaria where, thanks to intense anti-Nazi sentiment and several heroic individuals, fifty thousand Sephardic Jews survived. Author Sandy Tolan visited Bulgaria to research his best-selling book, *The Lemon Tree: An Arab, a Jew, and the Heart of the Middle East,* the story of a friendship that develops between a Palestinian returning to Israel in 1967 and the Jewish woman now living in his family's former house. To research his central character, a Sephardic Jew originally from Bulgaria, Tolan interviewed Bulgarian Ladinos in Sofia in 2003. Tolan, who speaks Spanish, reported that "many words and pronunciations were different but we could understand each other." At the time, there was still a Club Ladino in Sofia that met on Tuesday evenings to reminisce and share poems and proverbs in Ladino.

In North Africa, French colonialism and the creation of the Alliance Israelite Universelle (precursor of the Alliance Française) eroded the existence of Judeo-Spanish by contributing to the assimilation of Sephardic Jews to French. Today, the largest Sephardic communities are in Israel (which has 1.1 to 1.5 million Sephardic Jews) and France (which has about 350,000). But the largest Ladino-speaking community is in Israel, with about 100,000 speakers.

Over the centuries following the expulsion of the Jews from Spain, Ladino speakers could have bolstered Spanish as a European language, the same way French Huguenots carried their tongue throughout Europe after the 1685 revocation of the Edict of Nantes (which ended toleration of Protestants in France) with the support of a cohort of antirevolutionaries a century later.

But that didn't happen because the other million Spaniards who left the motherland also left the continent. The New World was where the next chapters of the story of Spanish would unfold.

10. New Turf

IT'S PROBABLY FAIR TO SAY Christopher Columbus was as skilled at sales as he was at sailing—at any rate, he was as fanatically determined in both areas. Columbus spent nine years traveling from the court of one European monarch to another, trying to convince one of them to finance his "Enterprise of the Indies." The king of Portugal turned him down twice. The monarchs of France, England, and Spain also sent him packing.

But Columbus wouldn't take no for an answer.

Fortunately for him, political changes in Spain suddenly transformed what sounded like a far-fetched plan into an appealing proposal and now Spain's Catholic monarchs were inclined to support him. Before 1492, the Spanish couldn't even have considered exploring the Atlantic. They couldn't afford it, being trapped in a costly war against the last Muslim emirate in Granada. When the war ended that year, Spain's sights turned to the sea and it boosted its budget for naval affairs.

Columbus had supporters helping make his case on the inside. Luis de Santángel, the crown's treasurer and a famous converso, told the monarchs that Columbus's expedition would cost them less than a weeklong party at court. Diego de Deza, a Dominican friar and tutor of the Infante, promised that the expedition would enable them to convert hordes of Asian pagans.

Isabel and Fernando bought both arguments. They named Columbus admiral of the ocean sea, viceroy of yet-to-be-reached India, and governor of the yet-to-be-discovered lands, gave him the honorary title of *don*, and sent him on his way with a promise that he could keep a 10 percent cut of whatever riches he found. It was a generous offer on paper. In reality, the monarchs really weren't expecting Columbus to find anything, or even make it back alive.

Columbus set sail from the port of Palos on August 3, 1492, in command of a small fleet of three ships, the *Niña,* the *Pinta*, and the *Santa María,* with a total of ninety men on board. After a short stopover in the Canary Islands, he sailed full west with the trade winds. Luck was on his side. For thirty-five days straight, he sailed into the sunset under blue skies with the wind at his back.

Not everyone on the trip was willing to trust his luck. Columbus's men were nervous about their chances of returning and became mutinous. On October 10, Columbus promised that if they didn't find land within three days, he'd turn back. Two days later, at 2 A.M., his watchman spotted land. October 12, just before lunch, Columbus set a wet foot on the island of Guanahaní, Bahamas, which he renamed San Salvador.

On this first visit to "India," Columbus discovered the islands of Cuba and *La Española* (Hispaniola). The voyage was a huge linguistic challenge. The islanders, whom he called Indios, spoke dialects of either Cariban or Arawak. But Columbus had expected to hear the languages Marco Polo and other explorers had described in their accounts of their voyages to India. With that in mind, he had brought along interpreters for Latin, Greek, Arabic, and Aramaic. (It wasn't as silly as it sounds. Five years later, when the Portuguese Vasco da Gama actually found the eastern route to India, the first Indian "natives" he met in the port of Calicut were Arab merchants from Tunis, who spoke Arabic and Italian.)

The more Columbus explored, the more new languages he encountered. At least, 600 languages were spoken in the New World, from 125 different language families, and all were unknown to Europeans. That was because the New World had had no contact with Eurasia for at least twelve thousand years. Unlike other voyagers before him, Columbus had no way of communicating with the new populations he met.

According to the great scholar Humberto López Morales, it took two full weeks before Columbus recorded the first Native American word in his log journal: *canoa* (canoe). Columbus had been hearing the word for two weeks by that time. He had originally called it an *almadía,* an Arabism meaning, "raft." Yet the *canoa* was actually a dugout. So, being a sailor, Columbus noted the difference and introduced the native term. He alternated between using *almadía* and *canoa* for six more weeks, before *almadía* disappeared from his log.

López Morales also noticed that Columbus, while searching for names for the new things he saw, constantly vacillated between native and Castilian terms. Where Castilian words seemed sufficient, he used them. Otherwise, he and his men adopted a native term. Rope beds were so different from regular beds that Columbus quickly recorded the new word *hamaca* (hammock) for them and never used *cama* (bed). On the other hand, he persisted in calling the locals Indios two months after he had recorded the name Caribe (Caribbean). Although Columbus dropped the term Indios before returning to Spain, for some reason the label stuck.

Aside from *canoa* and *hamaca,* Columbus recorded relatively few local terms in his diary: *ajes* (a tuber), *cacique* (chief), *cazabe* (manioc bread), *nitaine* (a member of the nobility), *aji* (pepper), *tiburón* (shark), *bohío* (hut), *Cuba, Caribe.* When he returned to Spain, he still hadn't found words to describe the strange "dry leaves" he'd see natives smoking, the "fires" they burned, or the "lizards" he encountered—*tobacco, barbacoa* (barbecue), and *iguana* were introduced later.

Columbus's obsession with riches is obvious from the number of words for gold he recorded—*tuob, caona, noçay,* and *guanín.* This fixation on gold, India, and China set Columbus and his less-than-fluent interpreters on more than a few wild-goose chases. When Columbus heard there might be gold in *Cubanacan* (mid-Cuba), he thought his interpreter was saying *El Gran Can* (the Great Khan). He sent a scholar, Luis de Torres, accompanied by a sailor, Rodrigo de Jerez, to verify. The sailor was uniquely unqualified: his only credential was that he had once met an African king in Guinea. Equipped with Latin passports and letters of support,

the two ambassadors roamed from village to village for days without finding a khan, either great or small. But they met lots of locals
smoking "rolls of leaves." Jerez returned from America as Europe's
first tobacco addict, and the Spanish Inquisition, not known for its
open-mindedness, jailed him for sorcery for seven years.

In an attempt to solve his communication problems for his next
voyage, Columbus kidnapped a dozen locals with the plan of turning them into interpreters. Columbus wildly underestimated the
task he was assigning them. The "interpreters" not only had to
learn Spanish. To be useful, they also had to learn all sorts of other
American dialects and languages. By Columbus's second voyage, in
October 1493, the surviving captives managed to teach some European interpreters basic Taíno, a dialect of Arawak, but finding
good interpreters would remain one of the main stumbling blocks
of early explorations for twenty years.

We know very little about the people Columbus encountered on
his expeditions for the simple reason that most of them died from
the biological shock the Europeans set off in the New World. The
natives of America had no immunity to smallpox, influenza, ty-
phus, or diphtheria, all endemic to Europe. Of those who survived,
many died victims of the atrocious encomienda system of forced
labor Europeans introduced.

The scale of this infectious shock was unprecedented and has
never been equaled. Estimates put the original population of the
Americas in the range of 50 to 100 million. Experts believe that
disease wiped out as much as 95 percent of this population within
decades. By 1650, there were only 10.5 million people left in the
Americas, including the settlers. By 1514, disease and slavery reduced the Taíno population on the island of La Española from one
million to twenty-two thousand adults and three thousand children. A century later, they were gone. It would be the same story
everywhere else. These horrendous statistics dwarf the death toll
of the Black Death, which killed off a third of Europeans in the

fourteenth century. Many of their languages—the main competitors to Spanish—died with them.

Spanish technological superiority, of course, only amplified the biological shock. The Aztecs called the first horses they saw "big dogs." Because seafaring techniques, steel, and the horse were all unknown in the Americas, the conquistadores (conquerors) were able in the 1520s to conquer societies including the Aztecs and the Incas, who were richer and more populous than Spain itself. European colonial powers held on to this technical superiority for the next 250 years, until the Comanche Indians mastered the use of horses in the southwest United States. For that matter, in the three places where the Spaniards had the hardest time imposing their rule (the interior of Argentina, Guatemala, and north of the Rio Grande), the locals had either developed some immunity to Eurasians' diseases or had mastered horse warfare.

During the first century of Spanish colonization, 250,000 Spaniards went to the Americas, and another 500,000 followed in the seventeenth century. The number, relatively small compared to the native population, raises the question of how Spanish ever became the main language of the continent. It wasn't because the Spanish were adamant about teaching Spanish. Spanish spread because most of the native population was wiped out within decades of Columbus's arrival, and half the six hundred known native languages of the Americas disappeared with them. Simply put, Spanish had little competition.

The situation was different in Asia, where the arrival of Europeans did not provoke a biological shock. (Nor did it in Africa, for that matter.) Europeans' technical advantage was never as strong in Asia as it was in the Americas. According to scholar Nicholas Ostler, this is the main reason that the Spanish failed to impose their language in the Philippines. Similarly, the impact of Portuguese culture and language remained shallow in their Asian and African trade empires, though it was profound in Brazil.

The massive epidemics were a double-edged sword. On one

hand, the annihilation of Native Americans made it easy for the Spanish to impose their rule. When Pizarro reached Peru in 1532, a smallpox epidemic had already devastated the Inca Empire in 1528 and led to a civil war. But the epidemics also left Spaniards with no native labor to exploit. And that was the whole point of settling the New World in the first place. Lamenting this conundrum, the Spanish even developed a saying: *"Sin Indios, no hay Indias"* (Without Indians, there can't be any Indies).

Columbus's first voyage was slightly disappointing. He proved he could reach "India" from the West in five weeks, but he came back nearly empty-handed. He found neither the Great Khan nor much in the way of gold or spices. Still, Isabel and Fernando sent him on a second expedition.

And that's how Spain and Portugal ended up drawing the linguistic map of the Americas.

Spain had given Portugal a monopoly on Atlantic sea exploration in 1479 with the Treaty of Alcáçovas. At the time of Columbus's voyages, this treaty was still in force. Now the Spanish monarchs knew they needed to renegotiate. Their solution? They approached the pope and convinced him to write a bull (a formal papal pronouncement) giving Spain the right to explore in the Atlantic. As luck would have it, the new pope (Alexander VI), elected eight days after Columbus's departure, was their old friend, Alejandro Borja, previously bishop of Valencia, who had supported their consanguine marriage and rallied the Castilian nobility behind Isabel's bid for the Castilian crown.

The pope's bull granted Castile a monopoly over all explorations west of the Azores. In return, all the Spanish Crown had to do was promise to evangelize the natives.

Portugal, of course, was furious and refused to recognize the bull. So while Columbus set off on his second voyage, Castile kept negotiating with Portugal. In the town of Tordesillas, Portugal managed to get the line separating its territory pushed back 370 leagues (1,000 miles) west of the Cape Verde islands. This included the eastern tip of what is now Brazil.

Spain and Portugal signed the Treaty of Tordesillas in 1494. The linguistic map of the Americas today pretty much corresponds to the lines of the treaty: Portugal got Brazil and Spain got everything south of the Rio Grande. By the time France, England, and Holland began to establish overseas colonies, the Spanish language was firmly established in its core areas.

Like the second, third, and fourth moon landings, interest in Columbus's second, third, and fourth voyages to the West Indies declined. Columbus undertook his second voyage in October 1493 with seventeen ships and twelve hundred men (still no women), including seven hundred colonists but returned with nothing to show for it. That only fueled the growing criticism of him in Spain. Rumors spread that he and his two brothers had turned into despotic rulers in La Española. Columbus's persistent claims that the ever-elusive India was on the other side also began to raise questions about his ability.

In 1499, Isabel and Fernando started wondering whether Columbus wasn't too much of a one-man show. They doubted that he alone could find the passage to India, especially since the Portuguese were multiplying exploration voyages. So while Columbus was away on his third voyage, the monarchs sponsored a new group of explorers to find the *tierra firme* (the continent). The ships were commanded by Alonso de Ojeda, Pedro Alonso Niño, Diego de Lepe, Vicente Yañez Pinzón, Rodrigo de Bastidas and, finally, Amerigo Vespucci.

It's curious to see Columbus's (supposed) burial site today in the cathedral of Seville—a raised coffin carried on the shoulders of four kings. Columbus died rich, but he certainly wasn't considered a national hero, let alone by kings. By 1500, his reputation had suffered so much that he was put on trial in Spain for his "despotic and tyrannical" governance of La Española: he was jailed for six weeks and lost his titles. Although he was allowed to make a fourth voyage two years later, his glory days were over.

What happened with the next generation of explorers explains why this new continent is called America and not Columbia (in honor of Columbus). Off the coast of Brazil, the Italian explorer Amerigo Vespucci understood that he had reached a new continent, and not India. A cartographer, merchant, and navigator, Vespucci had sailed three times to the Americas, alternately under the authority of Portugal and Castile. He also correctly deduced that if this continent was not India, there had to be an unknown ocean on the other side of it that *led* to India.

Vespucci became famous in Europe when he published two accounts of the "new" continent in 1502 and 1504. Cartographers soon began proposing names for it. The Castilians favored *Indias* or *Gran Tierra del Sur* (Great Southern Land). The Portuguese preferred *Vera Cruz* (True Cross) or *Terra Santa Cruz* (Land of the Holy Cross). Other cartographers pushed for *Tierra del Brasil* (Land of Brazil), *Tierra de Loros* (Land of Parrots), *Nueva India* (New India), and *Nuevo Mundo* (New World). The last label, the title of Vespucci's first account, was the one that stuck.

But in a curious twist of fate, a continent discovered by mistake acquired its name thanks to another mistake. Vespucci's writings had traveled to a small town in France's Vosges Mountains called Saint-Dié, where a cartographer named Martin Waldseemüller was so thrilled about them that he published *Cosmographiae Introductio* (Introduction to Cosmography) in 1507. The book included a map of the New World that drew the lines of the new continent's eastern shore with surprising accuracy. Waldseemüller called the new continent *America* in honor of his source: Amerigo Vespucci. In 1513, when Waldseemüller learned that Christopher Columbus was the true discoverer of the New World, the cartographer tried to reverse his decision. In subsequent editions of his book, he called it *Terra Incognita*.

But the first edition of his map had already sold one thousand copies. The name America was out there, and it would stick.

11. The Accidental Grammarian

WHEN ISABEL WAS VISITING SALAMANCA with her traveling court, a certain Andalusian scholar named Antonio de Nebrija decided to take advantage of the visit to present to the queen an early version of an unusual project he was working on: a Spanish grammar. The queen was not impressed. "What's the use of it?" she reportedly asked.

Most erudite Spaniards of the fifteenth century would have understood her puzzlement. In fact, many would have laughed at the idea that Castilian even *had* a grammar. In their minds, only scholarly languages like Latin or Greek had a grammar.

In a way, at least at that time, they were right.

Until Nebrija wrote his grammar, no one had bothered even to define what the nouns and verbs of Castilian were, let alone describe the rules that governed their use. The same was true of all European vernaculars at the time. A number of scholars had produced specialized grammars, lexicons, and spelling guides targeted to specific fields such as poetry or notary work. French scholars had penned a learning guide for members of the English court. In the thirteenth century, Uc Faidit had written a grammar of Provençal.

But none of these even came close to what Nebrija was working on. Nebrija understood that vernacular tongues had a grammatical structure, and that to be useful and thrive, their grammar needed to be defined. With his *Gramática de la lengua Castellana*, he became the first European to record and thoroughly systematize the grammar of a vernacular tongue.

Early in his career, Nebrija had distinguished himself mostly as a teacher of Latin: everything in his life had steered him away from Castilian. Born Antonio Martínez de Cala y Jarava between 1441 and 1444, near Seville, Nebrija adopted the name of his home-town, Nebrixa, now spelled Lebrija. He studied in Salamanca before traveling to Italy to complete his education at the University of Bologna. In Italy, he fell under the spell of the international humanist movement, which promoted the revival of classic literature in Latin and Greek and went as far as Latinizing his own name as Antonius Nebrissensis, after the fashion of the humanists.

Little more is known about the man himself. One historian described him as ill-tempered, another as unfaithful in matrimony. Only one thing is certain: Nebrija was inhumanly energetic. Like Alfonso X, the scholar is often described as Spain's first "academician," even though he lived two hundred years before Spain got a language academy. But in fact, he was an academy all by himself.

When Nebrija returned to Salamanca after studying in Italy, he was already a renowned Latinist whose knowledge surpassed that of even the most literate Castilians. Nebrija brought home the new science of philology—combining the study of literature with history and linguistics. Then he quickly settled on his new mission: to completely revamp Latin teaching in Spain, a reform he felt vital if Spaniards were to benefit from the humanist movement, whose lingua franca was a Latin of the highest standards.

Latin teaching in Spain was in a sorry state at the time, and Nebrija set out to raise the standards by his own example. His teaching methods were so rigorous that many doctors, theologians, jurists, and scholars who had unwittingly built careers on botchy Latin turned against him. Some of Nebrija's foes were so resentful they tried to drag him in front of the Inquisition, accusing him of heresy.

Yet Nebrija soldiered on. In 1481, he published one of the great literary successes of the European Renaissance: a grammar of Latin called *Introductiones latinae*. It would be reprinted seventy times during his lifetime and remained the Spanish reference book for Latin teaching until 1770.

Nebrija didn't stop with the *Introductiones*. One of his protectors, a Dominican friar named Hernando de Talavera, who was confessor and counselor to the queen, suggested that Nebrija translate the grammar into Spanish so that more Spaniards could read it. Nebrija took his advice and in 1488 published a new edition of *Introductiones* that included some comparison between Latin and Castilian. The work included a basic translation dictionary.

This was Nebrija's first step toward standardizing Castilian.

The first translation of his Latin grammar was a revelation. It exposed a very basic problem that had escaped everyone else's notice: Castilian had a grammar, as did all languages, but it was completely undefined. Before this, no one had even bothered to write a comprehensive dictionary to translate Latin into Castilian, or vice versa.

Nebrija knew the time had come to codify Castilian grammar. Thanks to the legacy of the thirteenth-century King Alfonso X, whose court had been a veritable factory of literary production of all kinds, Castilians were producing massive amounts of poetry, prose, plays, and chronicles by Nebrija's time. Literary production had become particularly abundant after the 1450s. But this boom in Castilian writing had a curious side effect: it highlighted Castilian's shortcomings and, more specifically, made Castilian's lack of standardized grammar and spelling rules glaringly obvious. When the printing press arrived in Spain in 1472, the need for consistent grammar rules became even more urgent. In the absence of a dictionary, printed works become the reference of a language. Before the printing press, copyists produced manuscripts one at a time, so the grammar or spelling inconsistencies in these works showed only once. But when printers began producing hundreds, or even thousands of copies of documents, more people were exposed to grammatical and spelling errors, and those errors challenged the standards, which were still ill defined.

Since the time of Alfonso X, the reading public for Castilian had increased dramatically. In fact, Castilian was quickly wiping out the other written vernaculars on the peninsula. Castilian had even invaded poetry, previously the exclusive turf of Galician-Portuguese. Its influence had reduced Leonese to the status of a rustic language: playwrights used it in their works for the dialogue of shepherds and villains. Even Aragonese was disappearing: in 1528, the playwright Jaime de Huete would apologize for including Aragonisms in his plays.

Castilian was also changing rapidly. First, its pronouns were taking new forms. The plural pronouns *vos* (you) and *nos* (we) were in the process of being transformed by the addition of *otros* (others). This led authors to produce the forms that are current today: *vosotros* and *nosotros*, which literally have the sense of "you all" and "we all." *Ustedes* is the contraction of *uuestra mercedes* (your graces); *usted* is the same abbreviation in the singular. This formal form was generalized the same way *you* took precedence over *thou* in English (historically, *you* was formal and *thou* was informal).

The suffix *-illo* had by this time morphed into *-ito*, *-cito*, and even *-tico*, and was creating a whole new category of diminutives that are still common in colloquial Spanish today: *disgusto* (disgust) becomes *disgustillo* (a slight disgust), *poco* (a little) becomes *poquito* (a wee bit), and *pobre* (poor) is morphed into a *probrecito* (poor little thing). (Costa Ricans are known as "Ticos" in the Spanish-speaking world because of their custom of using the suffix *-tico* instead of *-ito* or *-cito*: they say *hermanitico* instead of *hermanito* for "little brother.")

The Italian Renaissance was in full swing in Nebrija's time, so people were introducing hundreds of Italianisms into Castilian, including *bonanza* (fair wind, prosperity), *corsario* (corsair), *novela* (novel), *piloto* (pilot). As humanism became more fashionable, literate Castilians tried to add chic to Castilian by introducing Latin words, phrases, and syntax. The Latin trend affected the written style of Castilian: writers began separating adjectives from nouns and putting two, three, or four unrelated terms in between. Writers also took to displaying their knowledge by multiplying synonyms, a fashion to which even Nebrija himself succumbed in the prologue to his grammar:

> *Cuando bien comigo* pienso *mui esclarecida Reina: y* pongo delante los ojos *el antigüedad de todas las cosas: que para nuestra* recordación *e* memoria *quedaron escriptas: una cosa* hallo *y* saco *por conclusión mui cierta (. . .)*

> If you *thought* like me, my enlightened Queen, and *considered with your eyes* the antiquity of all things which have been left into writing for our *record* and *memory*, there is one conclusion I *found out* and *drew* with certainty (. . .)

In 1492, Nebrija published both a first grammar of Castilian and a dictionary, the *Lexicon hoc est Dictionarium ex sermone latino in hispaniensem.*

He was actually not the first scholar to write a dictionary of Castilian. Two years earlier, Alfonso de Palencia had published the *Uniuersale Compendium Vocabulorum,* which supplied Castilian translations of Latin words. But Nebrija's Latin-to-Castilian dictionary, with thirty thousand entries, set a new standard. And Nebrija kept raising the bar. Three years later, he added a volume to the dictionary, this time with Castilian-to-Latin translations, which included the first Native American word: *canoa* (canoe). Though Nebrija embraced the rule of one entry per line, and categorized each term as noun, adjective, verb, or adverb, the work was far from what we would call a dictionary today: it didn't include full definitions, and the words were sometimes classified in alphabetical order, sometimes according to etymology.

Yet in spite of its shortcomings and limitations, Nebrija's dictionary shaped the development of Spanish lexicography for centuries. In 1500 it was translated into French, as *Vocabularius.* Though it was eventually eclipsed by the work of the French lexicographer

François Estienne, who published two French-Latin dictionaries in 1539, Nebrija's work did inspire the early French lexicographers César Oudin and Jean Nicot.

Nebrija's choices consolidated what Alfonso had begun two hundred years earlier and shaped the development of the Spanish language for centuries to come. Nebrija reinforced some of the fundamental characteristics of Spanish, including a strong tendency toward phonetic—rather than etymological—spelling.

Like all great grammarians and lexicographers, Nebrija determined the written standards for Castilian by referring to common usage. Even from its earliest origins, Castilian had always tended toward simplicity, no doubt a result of the multiple instances of leveling the language went through during the population shifts that took place during the Reconquista. Like Alfonso, Nebrija embraced this quality. In the introduction of the *Gramática,* he stated his goal as "*adecuar la escritura a la pronunciación*" (to conform writing with pronunciation).

Again, following Alfonso's precedent, Nebrija jettisoned Latinized spellings.

Some Castilian scholars were still writing *fablar, facer,* and *fijo,* which were etymologically correct, even though Castilians pronounced them *hablar* (to speak), *hacer* (to do, to make), and *hijo* (son). (In the *Poema del mio Cid,* these words appear with an *f,* even if oral Castilian had never pronounced the *f.*) Sticking to Latin etymology would have been a common choice for a grammarian of his time, but Nebrija bucked this trend. He noticed that some writers had started to replace silent *f*'s with *h*'s and decided to systematize the practice.

Yet the letter *h* was an issue of its own. A Latin inheritance, it was sometimes silent, sometimes pronounced, as in English. Nebrija decided to keep the *h* in spelling but only if it was actually pronounced (again, much like in English). Most Spanish grammars written after Nebrija did the same.

One of Nebrija's great contributions was to distinguish between the letters *u* and *v,* and *i* and *j,* which nobody had done before. *U* and *j* do not exist in the Classical Latin alphabet. They had begun to appear in Castilian centuries earlier as a fancy way to write *v* and *i.* Nebrija realized that these graphic innovations could actually make Castilian clearer, but only if he assigned specific sounds to them. So he did.

Nebrija was the first to develop terminology for verb tenses: he called them *passado* (simple past), *venidero* (future), *acabado* (perfect), *no acabado* (imperfect), *mas que acabado* (pluperfect). It would take four more centuries for another grammarian, the Venezuelan scholar Andrés Bello, in the nineteenth century, to follow Nebrija's path and organize the verb system of Spanish.

More globally, Nebrija also introduced two notions that became the foundation of Spanish speakers' attitude toward their language: *buen uso* (good usage) and *fijeza* (fixedness, or stability in the sense of standardization).

In the case of *buen uso,* Nebrija was, again, perpetuating the work of Alfonso. Two centuries earlier, the king had established *buen uso*—he called it *castellano drecho*—as the "ethic" of Castilian. It summed up his quest, and that of all the copyists he employed, to find a middle ground where language rules would follow good taste. After Nebrija embraced it, the idea would become influential not just in Spain but also abroad. In France it spawned the notion of *bon usage,* which became the foundation of the French ethic of language purism.

Nebrija also established the idea of *fijeza,* or "setting" a language. Previously, the idea that a language could be "pure" or "classical" had applied only to Latin; Nebrija was the first to apply it to a vernacular. The idea caught on, especially outside Spain. In 1583, the Florentines created the first language academy, the Accademia della Crusca, which produced a dictionary twenty-nine years later, 120 years after Nebrija. *Crusca* means bran, the part of wheat that is discarded. The academy took this name because its mission was to clean up the language (i.e., discard the bran). In 1635, the French followed suit and created the French Academy.

It is an understatement to say that Nebrija devoted his life to standardizing Spanish. He was about fifty-one when he published his grammar and his dictionary in 1492. Over the next twenty years, he added ten thousand words, and he didn't stop there. At age seventy-five, in 1517, Nebrija set another precedent in the story of Spanish when he published his *Reglas de la Orthographía en la lengua castellana* (a book of spelling and pronunciation). Like his grammar and his dictionary, the *Reglas de la Orthographía* was a spin-off of his original Latin grammar. *Reglas de Orthographía* became an instant hit and inspired a long series of similar works.

The *Orthographía* (or *ortografía* in its modern spelling) is a genre unique to Spanish culture and alien to English and French speakers. An *ortografía* is the closest thing one can get to a sixteenth-century tape recorder. It explains how each phoneme in Spanish sounds and shows how each sound is written. In short, an *ortografía* sets out the rules for spelling, pronunciation, and punctuation so that speakers can transcribe what they hear and sound out what they read.

Nebrija's *Orthographía* was an ingenious and original idea that spawned an entirely new genre of Spanish reference works. After Nebrija, a new *ortografía* appeared in Spanish every fifteen years or so, up to the present. In 2010, the Real Academia Española (Spain's official language academy) published an eight-hundred-page *ortografía*.

Nebrija's *Reglas de Orthographía* arrived in the nick of time, just when the Crown of Castile was putting the overseas colonial expansion into overdrive. Scholars often wonder at the unity of correct pronunciation and grammar among countries as varied as Spain, Mexico, Paraguay, and Ecuador. Nebrija is the reason. The fact that he codified spelling prevented Spanish from exploding into a myriad of dialects after the Spanish Empire spread across the globe.

Strangely, during his lifetime, Nebrija's Castilian grammar was less successful than his other works. On one hand, this can be explained by the fact that grammars simply never sell as well as dictionaries, mainly because vocabulary changes faster than do the structures of a language (dictionaries have to be revised more frequently to remain useful). But another factor accounted for the relative unpopularity of Nebrija's grammar: he was ahead of his time. Even educated Castilians had difficulty swallowing the idea that Castilian *had* a grammar. (By the time the idea sank in, the Spanish language had evolved so much that Nebrija's work was obsolete.)

One last factor that might explain the modest success of the grammar was Nebrija himself. He never managed to conquer his inner Latinist. When he wrote his grammar, Nebrija believed that Castilian was on a downhill slope. At best, he thought the grammar would stall its inevitable decadence. In his dedication to the queen in the grammar's prologue, Nebrija promised to "*limpiar, fijarla en su alcanzado esplendor*" (clean, stabilize [Castilian] in its broken splendor)—the decisive word here being "broken."

Nebrija's bleak assessment of Castilian's prospects probably didn't help Isabel overcome her earlier doubts about the utility of a Castilian grammar. That might be why, in the *Gramática*'s prologue, Nebrija pitched the work as a tool of foreign policy. On the fifth line of the prologue, he writes, "*Language has always been the companion of empire and has followed it in such a way that they have jointly begun, grown, and flourished . . .*" Farther down, he explains, "*After your Highness has put the barbarians and the nations of foreign tongues under her yoke, upon your victory, these will need to receive your laws, those that a conqueror imposes to the vanquished, and with those laws our language. Then, my Grammar shall assist in the knowledge of these laws, like we needed to learn the grammar of Latin to learn Latin.*"

Looking back, Nebrija's words sound prophetic, but only in retrospect. He wrote the prologue in August 1492, just after Christopher Columbus had set sail for India. Yet Nebrija wasn't referring to an empire in the New World, because no one yet suspected its existence. The empire to which he alluded was the one Spain's monarchs dreamed of establishing over the Mediterranean world, all the way to Jerusalem, and maybe even to India—Isabel and Fernando were never short on ambition.

So while Nebrija was the first thinker in Europe to conceive of language as a political tool, he was mistaken about the trajectory of Castilian. Language is rarely the instrument of empires. It follows empires, and even then, not always. Nebrija did not have to look far for examples. Of all the empires that had controlled the Iberian Peninsula—including the Carthaginians, the Romans, the Visigoths, and the Arabs—only one imperial language had taken root: Latin.

When Nebrija died in 1522, around the age of eighty-one, all his predictions about Spanish were proving wrong. Far from declining, the Castilian language was reaching new literary heights. Though Spanish would become the language of an empire, it wasn't the empire he'd imagined.

12. A Loss for Words

THE STORY OF how Hernán Cortés conquered Mexico's Aztec Empire is one of obstinate greed, veering on lunacy. Cortés had been in Cuba since 1511, working as secretary to the governor. In November 1518, disobeying the orders of the governor, Cortés sailed away to the mainland of Yucatán with a fleet of 11 ships carrying 110 sailors, 518 foot soldiers, 16 horsemen, 13 gunners, 32 crossbowmen, 13 harquebusiers, and 200 native and African support troops. Cortés also had 32 horses, 13 guns, 10 large-caliber cannons, and 11 small cannons with him.

This wasn't much to conquer an empire of twenty million people, and Cortés knew it. Yet when he decided to take on the Aztecs a year later, Cortés was so confident in his victory he ordered his soldiers to sail nine of his eleven ships into the sand. (Contrary to popular belief, he never burned them.) What explained this confidence?

Cortés had a couple of secret weapons. One was smallpox. The other was language.

Back when Columbus began exploring the New World, the linguistic divide between the Old World and the New World was twelve thousand years old. Not a single person could bridge the gap. Three decades later, when Cortés set out to conquer the Aztecs, this linguistic divide had been bridged. Cortés had two willing interpreters to help him talk his way into the heart of the Aztec Empire.

Language was so critical to the conquistadores' plans that they developed different terms for interpreters: *lenguaraces* (polyglots), *farautes* (heralds), *trujamanes* (interpreters), and the more specialized *naguatlatos* (interpreters of the Aztec language). Six months before he took on the Aztecs, Cortés stopped in Yucatán. He already had a Mayan interpreter, Melchorejo, who had been captured by another conquistador on a previous trip. Through the interpreter, Cortés got wind of *barbudos* (bearded men) living among the Mayas. Cortés suspected that these were stranded Spaniards and sent out messengers to find them. One of the *barbudos* answered the call: Gerónimo de Aguilar, a Franciscan friar who had been shipwrecked eight years earlier and was enslaved by the Mayas, during which time he had learned their language. Aguilar agreed to work for Cortés, a good thing because Melchorejo had run away by that time.

Cortés got another break a month later when he arrived in Tabasco, Mexico, and the local king offered him twenty female slaves. One of the slaves, a beautiful woman with an aristocratic background, seemed particularly intelligent. Her name was Malíntzin (an honorific title). She spoke Mayan and Nahuatl (the Aztec language). Sure enough, she became Cortés's second interpreter, counselor, and mistress, and a controversial figure who went down in Mexican history as La Malinche or Doña Marina (she is also known by the very vulgar *La Chingada*, literally, "the prostitute").

With Malíntzin and Aguilar, Hernán Cortés had a team of interpreters who were as precious as all his horses, cannons, and guns put together. Through their voices, Cortés learned about the Aztec Empire and its wealth. Thanks to La Malinche, he figured out which of the native confederations resented Aztec rule, and he made alliances with them. By August 1519, Cortés had put together a force of thirteen thousand Totonac allies (from the Caribbean coast) and three thousand Tlaxcalan warriors (Nahua Indians) to march with him to the Aztec capital of Tenochtitlán. In 1519, Cortés deftly used his interpreters to gather intelligence to fool Moctezuma, detain him in his own palace, negotiate a ransom, and then arrange his death at the hands of his own subjects.

The Aztec Empire was a multinational, multilingual empire in which Zapotecs, Mixtecs, Tarascans, Otomi, Huastecs, and Totonacs all understood Nahuatl. Its subjects had to provide corps of *nauatlato* (interpreters). When Cortés first landed, two of the officials of the Totonac territory who met them were Nahuatl speakers.

The conquest of Mexico inaugurated a gigantic campaign of aggression that completely changed the map of the Spanish language. In a matter of eleven years, Spain seized control of the continent's two largest and most powerful empires: the Aztec and Inca, which covered less than 10 percent of the continent but represented 40 percent of its population.

The conquest of the Americas was far from organized. Though the Real y Supremo Consejo de Indias (Royal and Supreme Council of the Indies) in Madrid had laid out a plan, the Spanish crown could not afford to send armies overseas to execute it. Spain had neither the ships to carry soldiers nor the local population base in the Americas to feed them once they got there. Spain's largest colony, Cuba, which had three thousand Spaniards after twenty years of colonization, was barely self-sufficient.

In the end, the whole operation was left up to a handful of rapacious entrepreneurs, operating with scant military forces. On his third expedition, Francisco Pizarro took on the entire Inca Empire with a mere 160 men and 60 horses.

Christopher Columbus's constant invocation of Marco Polo's cities of gold clearly whetted Spain's appetite to carry on exploring. In 1517, the governor of Cuba began sending conquistadores to Mexico's Yucatán and to Central America. (The admiral ship of the first gold convoy that left Hispaniola in 1502 was named *El Dorado*.) Hidalgos (the lower rung of nobility) were a dime a dozen in Spain and had had no battles to fight since the fall of Granada. Spain cashed in their restless energy and made them conquistadores. According to the Peruvian historian Julio R. Villanueva Sotomayor, hidalgos constituted 30 percent of all conquistadores in the New World. Cortés was one of these.

Francisco Pizarro, Cortés's second cousin, conquered the Inca Empire roughly the same way Cortés conquered the Aztecs. Pizarro had been present in the New World since 1502. He became mayor of the newly founded city of Panama in 1519. In Panama, he heard about a rich empire to the south. With his associate, Diego de Almagro, Pizarro made two forays south to scout out the situation. To prepare, Pizarro also read Cortés's accounts of the conquest. When he was ready to launch his conquest of Peru, he followed Cortés's recipe to the letter, landing in Peru with half a dozen Quechua interpreters, talking his way to the heart of the empire—and then striking.

But there was one difference in Pizarro's case. After his second scouting expedition to Peru in 1528, he left behind the smallpox virus. By the time he actually attacked the Inca Empire in 1532, a major epidemic had killed the Great Inca and triggered a civil war.

Although they shrouded themselves in a varnish of legality, the conquistadores were an unruly and insubordinate bunch. At the very best, they paid lip service to the Church and the Crown, and generally they spent as much time fighting each other as they did the Incas or the Aztecs. During the wars of conquest, more Spaniards were killed by other Spaniards than by natives. After conquering Peru by slaughtering an army of eighty thousand Incas and then capturing their emperor—whom he had strangled after receiving a ransom of six tons of gold—Pizarro had to fight off other Spaniards trying to get a piece of the action. He was eventually assassinated by Spaniards.

Still, these ruthless, gold-obsessed quasi mercenaries allowed Spain to sweep through the Caribbean, Mexico, and Central America and across the Andes. In 1500, Columbus had claimed 40,000 square miles for Castile. By 1515, Spain's possessions had grown to 200,000 square miles. By 1540, the lands claimed reached 2 million square miles, and by 1600 another 400,000 square miles were added to that. By 1550, the map of the whole continent was pretty much what it is today. Lima and Mexico were capitals of the two viceroyalties. Panama, Cartagena, Asunción, Buenos Aires, and Santiago were exactly where they are today. By 1740, the Spaniards had explored or surveyed most of the 7.7 million square miles they claimed.

Outside of the Aztec and Inca empires, which were the jackpots for Spain, there was comparatively little gold. This absence of gold had been well documented by three of the strangest expeditions that ever took place: those of Cabeza de Vaca, Hernando de Soto, and Francisco Vázquez de Coronado.

The first one was certainly the most bizarre. It began in Florida in 1527 headed by Pánfilo de Narváez, with six hundred men. The story was told by one of the four survivors, Álvar Núñez Cabeza de Vaca, who was found eight years later . . . on the Pacific coast!

Narváez's force had already been reduced by half, by arrows and fevers, when it tried to escape Florida on five primitive *barcas*. Stranded on the Texas coast, the last four castaways tried to survive either as slaves, merchants, or medicine men. In the end, they walked west across the Sonora desert and down the Sea of Cortés (California Bay), where they came across a party of Spaniards. Cabeza de Vaca's *La Relación* (The Report) reads like a surprising work of ethnographic observation, although some of his hearsay sparked the legend of the Seven Cities of Gold, allegedly to the north of Mexico.

This legend led Francisco Vázquez de Coronado to mount an expedition with 440 men and 1,300 horses, as well as 500 head of cattle as a walking food supply. His guide was a French Franciscan monk, Marcos de Niza, who claimed to have seen the Seven Cities of Gold—he even wrote a book about it. They did find the mythical Cíbola, which was no city of gold but a brown adobe pueblo. On the grounds of even more shady intelligence, Coronado's men pushed all the way to eastern Kansas, but the whole affair was a dismal failure.

Had Coronado moved just a few hundred miles farther east, he would have crossed paths with yet another Spaniard, Hernando de Soto, who had left from Florida three years earlier with 620 men. De Soto's guide was a fifth survivor of the ill-fated expedition of

Pánfilo de Narváez, who had been detained twelve years by Florida natives. De Soto followed a very strange M-shaped course over three thousand miles, before crossing the Mississippi—where he died in 1542. By then, the surviving members of his expedition were convinced that there was no gold to be had and attempted an escape by cutting across Texas, before backtracking and sailing down the Mississippi and eventually to Mexico.

These three voyages had phenomenal ethnographic interest, but the failure to find gold in the north was what mattered to the Spaniards. For the next two generations, the initiative to colonize the territory, starting with Florida, would fall on Havana, which half-heartedly attempted to make one big Cuba out of it by building plantations.

Spain created the first permanent European settlement in the continental United States at St. Augustine, Florida, in 1565 and half a dozen more in the following decades. It established Jesuit orders in Virginia's Chesapeake Bay in 1570. The first Thanksgiving was celebrated in St. Augustine in 1565, fifty-six years before the Pilgrims celebrated it in 1621.

In spite of Antonio de Nebrija's assertion in 1492 that the Castilian tongue had reached its full maturity, the Spanish were at a loss for words when they explored the New World. Cortés was flabbergasted by the 430 temples he encountered when he entered the imperial capital of Tenochtitlán in 1520. The best word he could come up with to describe them was *mezquitas* (mosques). When the Spaniards didn't have words handy to name the new realities they were encountering, they adopted native terms. The most famous case: a new fruit called *xitomatl* (tomato). A drink, *xocolatl*, became *chocolate*. The Spaniards came across novel staples like *aguacate* (avocado), *cacahuete* (peanut), *chayote, mole,* and *nopal*—a variety of edible cactus that was so important in the Mexican diet it would one day figure on the national flag.

Many of these foods remain basic staples of Mexican cuisine to this day and are eaten worldwide. Others, like *tamales* and *atole* (a beverage made from corn meal mush), remain popular in Mexico, although less known abroad.

In Peru, conquistadores discovered staples of the Inca Empire like *kinua* (quinoa), and delicacies like *cuy* (guinea pig). They also discovered practical items like *caucho* (rubber), *llamas*, and *koka* (coca leaves), which the natives used for curing altitude sickness.

And then there was the curious case of *barbacoa* (barbecue), a cooking technique Spaniards encountered in the islands that used smoking branches. The word itself is Taíno, but shortly after the conquest it became a popular way of cooking meat in Mexico. In fact, it's an early example of fusion food that combined Arawak technique, European meats, and Mexican flavors.

Although Americanisms entered Spanish from all corners of the conquered territories, the bulk, like *barbacoa,* came from the Caribbean. For the first twenty-five years after the discovery of America, the Spanish presence was limited to the Caribbean is- lands, Lesser Antilles, and sections of the coast. As they spread out, the Spaniards reused the words they had adopted or coined in the Caribbean, transposing them on new discoveries on the continent. This was particularly the case in Mexico and Peru. According to Professor Humberto López Morales, of the sixty-nine Taíno terms used in Spanish chronicles, sixty-three described realities outside the Caribbean. In comparison, only thirty-nine of the ninety-five Nahuatl terms in the chronicles came to apply to realities outside Mexico. And only eight out of twenty-four Quechua terms were used to describe things outside the Inca zone.

The preponderance use of Caribbean terms holds true today. Although Nahuatl was a bigger and more influential culture than that of the Taínos, few Nahuatl words are used outside Mexico, while many Caribbean words entered Spanish and spread from there into other European languages. The Aztecs had two Nahuatl words for corn, a plant that originated in Mexico and was the di- etary foundation of the Aztec Empire: *centli* and *tlaulli*. But the

Spaniards adopted the Taíno word *maíz*. The words *mamey* (an ever-green tree), *yucca*, and *papaya* come from Taíno and Carib. Even the Peruvian staple *patata* is a compromise between the Taíno *batata* (sweet potato) and the Quechua *papa*. The Caribbean terms *manatí* (manatee) and *güiro* (gourd) gained prevalence, although other na-tive civilizations had different words for them. Yet Spanish did adopt a new suffix from Nahuatl: *-iche*, which comes from *-itzin*.

According to Humberto López Morales, only 683 of the 88,000 words in the dictionary of the *Real Academia Española* (or less than 1 percent) originate in Native American languages. Although thousands of words from native languages are still used locally in South and Central America, almost all of the native borrowings that made it into standard Spanish come from five languages: Ar-awak (mainly the Taíno dialect), Caribe, Quechua, Nahuatl, and Tupí-Guaraní. When the conquistadores got to the Southern Cone (the area south of the Tropic of Capricorn—Argentina, Chile, Uru-guay, and Paraguay), they borrowed only a handful of words from Tupí-Guaraní, the dominant native tongue there, including *jag-uar, petunia, maraca*, and *tapioca*.

The Spanish also used native words for place-names. The Ori-noco River, named by Columbus in 1498, is inspired by the Guarauno word for "a place to row." Panama may mean *abundance of fish* or *butterflies* in the Cueva language—nobody knows for sure because it was extinct by 1535, all the speakers having been exter-minated by the Spanish colonizers. Peru's name is the Spanish de-formation of the name of a local ruler of Panama, Birú. In Nueva España, Cortés chose to rename the capital Mexico, alluding to the tribe at the origin of the Aztec Empire, the Mexican people. The number of large cities and states with native names is notice-ably higher in Mexico than anywhere else, but this is more the re-sult of the political choices of the Mexican state since independence than a trend from colonial times.

Generally, when it came to naming places, the Spanish fell back on their own language and cultural references. Columbus, for instance, had a mystical inclination toward Christian names like El Salvador. La Florida is a reference to the Spanish name for Easter, *la Pascua florida* (literally, flowery Easter). Some Spanish place-names are simple cut-and-paste borrowings from Spain, like Nueva Granada (future Colombia), Nueva España (Mexico), and Guadalajara.

Other Spanish place-names were physical descriptions of what the Spanish saw before them: Costa Rica (Rich Coast), Honduras (a good anchorage), río de la Plata (River of Silver), and Cabo cañaveral (Cape Canaveral), in reference to a dense thicket of cane vegetation; *caña* is sugarcane). Other names reflect the trials of exploration: during Pizarro's second expedition in 1528, he left behind Puerto deseado (Desired Port), Puerto del hambre (Port of Hunger), and Puerto quemado (Burned Port). When Diego de Nicuesa found a bay along the Panama coast and yelled *"Paremos aquí, en nombre de Díos"* (Let's stop here, in the name of God), the settlement was appropriately named Nombre de Díos.

Other names were inspired by myths. After hearing about a tribe of fierce female warriors who had defeated his men on the río Santa María de la mar dulce, King Charles V changed the river's name to Amazonas (Amazon), a reference to Greek mythology. The Antillas (the lesser Caribbean islands) were named after a land from a medieval Portuguese legend. California was a reference to an obscure novel of chivalry written around 1500 about a Queen Calafia, ruler of a kingdom of black Amazons.

Although the conquistadores did find gold and other riches like gems and pearls, few of them hit pay dirt in the New World, contrary to their expectations. The gold mines they found in the West Indies were exhausted within a couple of years. In 1532, even Hernán Cortés decided to give up searching for gold and fell back on ranching on his encomienda in Oaxaca.

But in 1546, everything changed. The Spanish discovered two phenomenally rich silver lodes in Potosí, Bolivia, and Zacatecas,

Mexico. By the end of that century, 330,000 pounds of gold and 7.5 million pounds of silver reached Spain from the Americas. The total haul was worth between $1 and $10 trillion in today's money, an enormous amount for a small, predominantly agrarian society. (To compare: Spain's annual GDP today is $1.4 trillion.)

The Potosí and Zacatecas mines produced millions of coins of unparalleled purity, of which two became famous: the *doblón* (doubloon), so-called because it was worth two gold *escudos,* and the silver *real de a 8* (which had the value of 8 *reales*). In the English world, the *real de a 8* became known as the Spanish dollar (from the German thaler) or the piece of eight. The piece of eight did more than supply the signature line of Long John Silver's parrot in *Treasure Island* (who cried, "Pieces of eight!"). Spanish silver made Spain the richest country in Europe. It flowed into Europe and as far as the Ottoman Empire and China. Until the nineteenth century, the Spanish colonies would produce 70 percent of the world's supply of precious metals.

The Spanish Crown also made a killing out of other resources, including *cochinilla* (carmine), a dye extracted from the cochineal, an insect that lives off Mexico's national cactus. The dye, highly valued by the Aztecs, kick-started a prosperous dye and tanning industry in Spain, and carmine remained Mexico's most important export after silver until the end of the nineteenth century.

Some American commodities eventually caught the fancy of Europeans like indigo (a dye), cocoa, guano (a fertilizer and ingredient for gunpowder), rubber, and tobacco. Other commodities that became famous Latin American exports, like sugar, coffee, bananas and cattle, had to be imported before becoming the foundation of gigantic fortunes there. Sugar and cattle, in particular, had a profound impact on the story of Spanish. In particular, sugar brought millions of people, mostly slaves, to the Spanish-speaking world to work on plantations.

13. The Canary Effect

SEVILLE'S HISTORICAL CENTER CONCENTRATES the pillars of Spain's Renaissance society in a remarkably succinct manner. In ten minutes, one can stroll from the Andalusian capital's cathedral—the biggest Gothic cathedral in the world—to its sprawling Real Alcázar, or royal palace—where Christopher Columbus negotiated the terms of his voyage to the "Indies" with Spain's Catholic monarchs.

Wedged between them is a beautiful Renaissance building, built in the sixteenth century with one objective: to get merchants out of the cathedral, where they had the bad habit of doing business. From merchants' exchange, the building's function evolved over the centuries of Spain's colonial empire until 1785, when it acquired its permanent vocation as the Archivo de Indias (Archive of the Indies).

Today the archive houses every official document handled by Spain's colonial bureaucracy during the conquest and settlement of the Americas. Scholars and history buffs can plow through forty-three thousand volumes containing eighty million pages and eight thousand drawings and maps, enough documents to cover more than five miles of shelves. There is everything from Miguel de Cervantes's application for a job in the Indies (he was turned down) to the deeds from settlements in Upper California and account books for the *quinto real* (royal fifth), a 20 percent tax the Crown collected on all precious metals that arrived from the New World.

In the archives, a researcher with a knack for deciphering sixteenth-century handwriting and decoding seventeenth-century red tape would be able to learn almost anything about how the Spanish settled the New World. The Archivo de Indias contains names of treasure ships sunk in the last decade of the sixteenth century, descriptions of diving techniques used to recover their treasures, Columbus's journal notes from his fourth voyage, details from the first sighting of the Galápagos islands, notes on the languages spoken on any Philippines island, and all the native words that appeared in the correspondence between Spain and the New World.

In the 1960s, Peter Boyd-Bowman, a linguist at the State University of New York at Buffalo, decided to plunge into the archive in the hopes of answering a question that had been nagging linguists for decades: Why exactly does American Spanish have such a strong Andalusian flavor?

Spain's Casa de Contratación (House of Trade, which controlled all commercial activities overseas) kept good records, because the Spanish Inquisition demanded that all Spanish settlers be bona fide Catholics, not Jews, Muslims, or Protestants. Boyd-Bowman was the first to compile statistics, taken from the *libros de pasajeros* (passenger lists), about the profession and place of birth of passengers.

The raw numbers Boyd-Bowman compiled seemed to verify what linguists had assumed all along, that most New World settlers came from southern Spain, particularly Andalusia and Extremadura. According to the records, there were sixty-four thousand Spanish settlers from 1499 to 1579 and more than half the registered settlers in the first eighty years of colonization came from the south of Spain. The proportion of southern Spanish among the conquistadores was roughly the same: Cortés, Hernando de Soto (who explored North America), Vasco Núñez de Balboa (who discovered the Pacific), Álvar Núñez Cabeza de Vaca (who made a land journey to the interior of the continent) all came from the south.

On further inspection, Boyd-Bowman concluded that the number of Spanish settlers who traveled to the New World was probably four times higher than what the official statistics said, since many clandestine or illegal immigrants were smuggled to the New World on Spanish or foreign ships.

Indeed, compared to all other European colonial powers at the time, Spaniards immigrated massively to the Americas. It is estimated that a quarter of a million Spaniards went to the New World in the sixteenth century, and another half million in the next, for a total of 750,000. By the end of the seventeenth century, Spain had sent seventy-five times more people to the New World than France did, even though France's population was four times Spain's. England's performance also paled in comparison to Spain's—150,000 colonists to the thirteen colonies. What's more, Spain continued to send even more settlers and immigrants to the Americas throughout the eighteenth and nineteenth centuries.

Columbus's discovery set into motion a migration in numbers and proportions that had not been seen since Roman times. Where language was concerned, the migrations produced the same result as those of Rome, but on a bigger scale: Spanish became the language of a continent. (As in the case of Latin, subsequent events would push and pull the language in different directions. For Spanish, these would be the forced migrations from both Africa and Europe, and the reorganization of the entire New World economy.)

The transportation system Spanish settlers used to travel to the New World also reinforced the Andalusian influence in the Americas. No matter where the settlers came from, they all departed from the port of Seville. They were steeped in the Andalusian accent for at least three months, sometimes up to a year, while waiting for a ship. The ship's first stop was the Canaries, where the speech was heavily Andalusian, then settlers spent five to twelve weeks sailing with Andalusian sailors. When they arrived in Havana, the accent was Andalusian again, and they usually spent at least several weeks there before shipping elsewhere.

Centuries later, Latin American Spanish has retained distinct Andalusian features. The main one is so well known in Spanish that it has its own name—*seseo*. This refers to the Andalusian pronounciation of *c* and *z* as *s* rather than as *th*. In central and northern Spain, Zaragoza is pronounced "Tharagotha" instead of "Sara-gosa," as it's pronounced in the Americas.

The *yeísmo* is another prominent Andalusian feature of Latin American Spanish. This is the habit of pronouncing the letter *ll* like the *y* in *yo-yo*. In places where speakers use *yeísmo*, *halla* (I find) sounds like *haya* (I had). The *yeísmo* is the norm in the Americas, except in Colombia and some parts of South America. It is also used in many parts of Spain. Elsewhere, *ll* is pronounced as soft *j*, rendered by *zh* in English, which is pronounced like *s* in "mea-sure."

(No one knows exactly why the *seseo* or the *yeísmo* appeared in Spain. Linguists have determined that over the course of the six-teenth century, they came to characterize more or less regional ac-cents that separated Andalusia from the north of Spain. Some linguists think that they have their origin in the Mozarabic dialect widely spoken throughout the south of Spain, but it's difficult to determine because this dialect vanished after the Reconquista.)

Yet, since the Spanish spoken in Spain was still changing at the outset of colonization, it doesn't really make sense to talk of the "Andalusian influence" on American Spanish. For example, the *voseo*—the name for the practice, common in Central America, Argentina, Chile, and Uruguay, of addressing people *vos* rather *tú*—completely disappeared from Spain during this period, re-placed by *tú*, a practice called *tuteo*.

Nor was Andalusian Spanish in any way transplanted intact to the colonies. On the contrary, continuous waves of immigrants brought their idiosyncrasies and continued to influence the lan-guage in the New World. It took centuries for New World cities to grow enough to be able to absorb newly arrived immigrants with-out being linguistically influenced by them in turn. Even by the eighteenth century, only Havana, Mexico, and Lima had more than 50,000 inhabitants: Buenos Aires had only 20,000; Caracas had 19,000; Quito had 25,000; Santiago de Chile, 28,000; and

Montevideo, 10,000. If 5,000 or 10,000 people passed through these cities every decade—entirely possible because they were main ports of entry serving vast provinces—it was enough to profoundly affect the local way of speaking.

Some linguists have theorized that there are actually two types of Spanish in the Americas: "lowland" Spanish (near the coastline) influenced by Andalusia, and "highland" Spanish (in the mountains) influenced by the Madrid Standard spoken by colonial authorities. According to this theory, lowland speakers (in Cuba, Puerto Rico, Dominican Republic, Panama, coastal Venezuela, and Colombia) swallow the s: *estás* (you are) comes out as *ehtah*. But other linguists have found so many exceptions that they believe this generalization is meaningless.

At any rate, the huge scale of Spanish migration explains why the influence of native languages on Spanish is relatively shallow, accounting for less than 1 percent of the vocabulary in General Spanish today. In the sixteenth century, writers vacillated between calling peppers the Taíno *ají* or the Nahuatl *chili*. By the next century, they were using the European word *pimiento*—even if pepper aficionados still distinguish among *ají, chili*, and dozens of other types like *jalapeño* and *pasilla*. Many more Americanisms followed the same path to obscurity. Chroniclers of the fifteenth and sixteenth centuries spoke of the Taíno *alcabuco* (mountain), but their successors switched back to *monte*.

Most settlers arrived after native populations had already been wiped out by slaughter or epidemics. In the Caribbean islands, native cultures were nearly extinct fifty years after Columbus. Many nativisms died with their speakers. In the islands, the early Spanish colonists called the new type of fowl they discovered *guanaxa* (turkey, from Carib). The word was abandoned for the Castilian *pavo* (peacock), in spite of the scant resemblance between the two birds. Some words disappeared from standard Spanish but remained in use as regionalisms: Cubans still say *guanajo* (turkey) while Mexicans prefer *guajolote*.

Some local terms were adopted quite late, perhaps because it just took time for colonists to realize they really were facing new realities. *Sabana* (savannah) and *puma* replaced the Castilian *llanura* and *tigre*. By 1550, after enduring a great many *tormentas* (thunderstorms) and *temporales* (heavy rainfalls), colonists realized that the Taíno *huracán* was something altogether different and deserved its own name.

Oddly, a number of nativisms that disappeared from Spanish usage remained common in other European languages, like *caiman* and *buccaneer* in English. French also retained a number: *pirogue* (dugout, from Carib *piragua*), *caoutchouc* (rubber, from Quechua *caucho*), *ananas* (pineapple, from Tupí-Guaraní), and *maringouin* (mosquito, from Tupí-Guaraní).

Like the explorers before them, migrants to the Americas invented new vocabulary to describe the novelties they encountered. The process started in ports, where travelers, mostly from Spain's cities, saw their first ship—a caravel in the early years, or by the middle of the sixteenth century a *galeón* (galleon). This new type of ship was designed to transport huge cargoes of supplies while defending itself against pirates or privateers. The galleon was typically five times larger than the caravel. The so-called Manila Galleon, which sailed the route between Manila and Acapulco, was twenty times bigger than a caravel.

Most galleons traveled in mandatory *flotas de Indias* (the so-called Spanish treasure fleets consisting of seventeen ships). These were necessary for self-protection. The English, French, and Dutch during the sixteenth century carried out a policy of looting. There was an entire subculture of *filibusteros* (freebooters, or pirates of the West Indies), *corsarios* (privateers, acting under license of their government), and *bucaneros* who carried out the various forms of piracy. Piracy and looting was a big business at a time when one hundred ships brought back a total of two hundred thousand pounds of silver per year. El Draque—the Spanish nickname for Sir Francis Drake—set the record in 1579 when he returned with enough silver and gold to match half of the English queen's annual income.

These high stakes are perhaps the reason the Spanish put a lot of energy into solving problems particular to the colonies or to naval affairs. The Spanish soldier, painter, musician, and inventor Jerónomio de Ayanz y Beaumont made history in 1604 when he patented a steam-powered pump to drain mines 150 years before the Industrial Revolution. As manager of the empire's 550 mines, this genius of logistics had forty-eight other patents for various inventions, including a new design for a compass, pumps to drain sunken ships, high-precision scales "that could weigh the leg of a fly," an arch structure for dams, and even a diving suit. Another contemporary, Blasco de Garay, introduced the paddle wheel (to replicate oars) and tested many diving apparatuses including techniques for generating light underwater and desalinating seawater.

But another development in this period did nothing less than completely reconfigure the society and physical geography of the entire Caribbean: that was sugar, which Columbus introduced in Hispaniola on his second voyage in 1493. The prototype sugar plantation was developed by the Portuguese on the island of Madeira in the first half of the fifteenth century. It quickly turned into the world's first global commodity.

The development of the plantation system had a tremendous impact on the Americas, transforming entire economies and even the ecology of some islands. *Ingenios* (sugar mills) were built and run by *mayordomos* (superindendents); *mandadores* (administrators) gave orders to *tacheros* (workers) who ran the *tacho* (sugar evaporator); and markets had to be found for the different types of sugar: *rubio, moreno,* or *negro* (light brown, dark brown, or raw sugar). (Following the same route as sugar, coffee and bananas built on the same basic plantation structure supplanted sugar as main exports of the Caribbean in the nineteenth and twentieth centuries.)

But growing sugar required more labor than the islands' dwindling native population could supply. In 1513, the Spanish established a triangular trade with Africa that brought millions of slaves to the Caribbean. By 1575, Cuba alone had ten thousand African slaves. By the time the last shipload of slaves arrived in Havana in 1870, three million of the fifteen million African slaves who had been traded across the Atlantic had come to a Spanish colony.

Slave masters in the period also developed a baffling series of names to describe racial subcategories, starting with *negros* and *mulatos*, and splintering into *tercerón* (one-third black), *cuarterón* (quadroon), *quinterón* (one-fifth black), *zambo* (native father and African mother), *chino* (the opposite), and *pardo* (mixing all races).

African slaves had a phenomenal impact on music in the Americas. According to the artist and professor Michael D. Harris, West African slaves brought to the Americas timbales and bongos, the call-and-response melodic form ostinato (a motif that is persistently repeated) and, more important, rhythm. In "Art of the African Diaspora," Harris writes, "West Africa, along with Southeast Asia, has the most complex rhythmic structure of traditional music found anywhere in the world. Everywhere African and European music styles mixed, the results were similar." In Brazil this mélange spawned samba; in Haiti, *mereng*, in Cuba, *habanera*, and in the southern United States, blues and tap dancing.

Africanisms seeped into the Spanish language, but few endured. The most famous are *bongó*, *samba*, *mambo*, *conga* (a drum and an dance), and *ñame* (yam)—all of which entered other languages as well. However, Africanisms are much more present in the regional Spanish spoken by Cubans and Puerto Ricans—there are 131 Africanisms in Puerto Rican Spanish alone.

Some Africanisms have acquired a multiplicity of meanings depending on the country where they are used. *Congo* is a good example. In northern Colombia, *congo* refers to a dance and dance partners. It describes yet another type of dance in Cuba, Ecuador,

Nicaragua, and the Dominican Republic. In Paraguay, *congo* is either a carnival dance or the dancer. In Venezuela, it's a type of pig; in Guatemala, a wasp. In Costa Rica and Nicaragua, it refers to a monkey. To a Puerto Rican alone, it may mean a black man, a fetish, a tobacco leaf, and a banana. As an adjective, Argentines use it in reference to a rooster. Venezuelans use it to qualify a person who is small and fat. To young Puerto Ricans, it means "praiseworthy," while Paraguayans use it to describe someone who is easy to take advantage of.

Julie grew up in a small town in southern Ontario next door to a Dutch family who originated from Curaçao, a former Dutch colony in the Caribbean. During her childhood, she occasionally heard snippets of a language that sounded to her a bit like Spanish coming from next door. In fact, this "Spanish" was Papiamentu, a Creole language.

Spoken by most inhabitants of Curaçao, Aruba, and Bonnaire, Papiamentu is possibly Spanish based, and possibly Portuguese based. But it is hard to determine because sixteenth-century Spanish and Portuguese were very close anyway. Papimentu mixes Portuguese and Spanish interspersed with Dutch, English, and Italian. Its name comes from the Portuguese *papear* (to chat, to talk), but no one knows for sure where the language originated. It might have grown out of the Portuguese-African pidgin used in slave trading posts on the west coast of Africa, but it also could have originated in the Judeo-Portuguese or Judeo-Spanish spoken by the Sephardic plantation owners throughout the Dutch colonial empire. The Papiamentu words *danki* (thank you) and *djus* (juice) have no relation to Spanish or Portuguese. However, the Papiamentu *bon dia* (good day) is a lot closer to the Portuguese *bom dia* than the Spanish *buenos días,* while *pan* (bread) is identical to Spanish. And as for the typical Papiamentu question *Kon ta bai?* (How are you?), it looks like a mix of Portuguese (*Como vais?*) and Spanish (*¿Cómo te va?*).

Oddly, even though Africanisms entered the Spanish in the colonies, this never produced Spanish-based Creoles on a large scale, like it did in French-speaking Caribbean colonies. Spanish Creoles exist in small pockets, but they are far less numerous than even English, Dutch, and Portuguese Creoles. One reason may be that Spanish colonies introduced African slaves much more progressively, and spread them over a greater number of colonies, than did the English or, above all, the French. On the Spanish side of the island of Hispaniola, slaves were only slightly more numerous than the colonists, whereas on the French side—today's Haiti—there were almost twenty-five times more slaves, a total of seven hundred thousand among thirty thousand Europeans.

The Spanish colonial reality created a geographic vocabulary that is still integral to the worldview of most Spanish speakers. *América* designates the entire continent, not just the United States. The word is never used in the plural (this was a British custom; they created the category to distinguish Spanish colonies from the thirteen colonies, which was America to them). Consequently, *Americano* designated any colonial living in America. As Americans gained influence throughout the nineteenth century, the Spanish began speaking of "Hispano-America" but *Americano* remains common. Citizens of the United States are *Estadounidenses* (United Statesians). Mexicans call the Rio Grande the río Bravo or río Bravo del Norte. The Gulf of California is el mar de Cortés (the Sea of Cortés). And the Mexican continuation of the Rockies is the Sierra Madre.

The Spanish colonial empire spawned a myriad of new titles and labels for the social, political, and racial structures that it was built on. Like the racial categories of the Caribbean, these terms were sometimes disconcertingly specialized. In 1587, in Cartagena de la Indias, Colombia, the writer Miguel Hidalgo used the word *indiano* for the first time. He wasn't referring to natives (*indios*) but to Spanish who had returned from the West Indies after making their fortune in the New World, a special type of *nuevo rico* (nouveau riche).

The Spanish who remained in the New World had two names: *peninsulares* (born in the peninsula) and *criollo* (Creole, born in the colony). This latter word comes from the Portuguese *crioulo,* originally referring to a slave born in the house of his master. While it retained this specialized meaning in Spanish slaving, it also came to describe any Spaniard born outside Spain.

But the criollos were quickly outnumbered by an entirely new social group: the *mestizos* (mixed race). It was the mestizos who turned Spanish into a native language of the Americas.

Mestizos were the product of a simple fact: Spain sent few women to the New World before 1600. Until 1519, less than 5 percent of migrants were women. In 1542, Mexico had 2,335 *españoles puros* (pure Spanish), but only 217 of them were women. The proportion of women didn't jump until 1560, when it reached about 28.5 percent of settlers. The number of male and female colonists did not become equal for two centuries.

So for at least three generations, Spanish men took mostly native women as wives, mistresses, concubines, or victims. Cortés, Pizarro, Almagro, Pedro de Alvarado, Belalcázar, Garcilaso de la Vega all set the example. Francisco de Aguirre, who was involved in the conquest of Peru, Bolivia, Chile, and Argentina, boasted fifty mestizo children. By 1650, half of Mexico City's population was mestizo. This process of *mestizaje* (miscegenation) was characteristic of Spanish colonialism and very different from what went on in English colonies. Although it was initially discouraged, the Spanish Crown approved of it as early as 1503 when it figured out it was an efficient tool for converting natives, Hispanicizing them, and getting colonists to settle down.

This enthusiasm for the *Nueva Raza* (new race) is distinctive to Spanish colonialism. Yet at the same time, Spanish colonial society was characterized by widespread racial oppression, which materialized in a system of *castas* (castes) that assigned ranks to all ethnic groups. Mestizos had higher status than Indians, something like a free person of color in the American Old South.

And above them were the criollos, who were one step below *peninsulares*.

Mestizos made important intellectual contributions to early colonial Spain. Fernando de Alva Ixtlilxóchitl, a mestizo writer famous for his histories of the Toltecs and of the Chichimecas, became governor of Texcoco in 1612 and Tlalmanalco the next year. On the other hand, Garcilaso de la Vega, a distinguished Peruvian mestizo writer who produced the first account of the history of Peru before Pizarro, ended up seeking political refuge in Spain but was forbidden to marry there on the basis that, as a mestizo, he was *gente sin razón* (a person without reason).

The etymology of Spanish vocabulary illustrates the inhumanity of the Spanish caste system. *Mestizo*, like *mulato*, comes from the horse trade. *Mulato* can be traced back to *mulo* (mule), and *mestizo*, from *mezclan*, means mixed as opposed to purebred. The son or daughter of a *mestizo* and a Spanish woman was called a *castizo* (meaning a very prolific animal). A *chamizo* was the son of a *castizo* and a *mestiza*. A *cholo* or *coyote* was the child of a *mestizo* and an Indian. The level of detail in this system of categories is dehumanizing. A Spanish and a *mulato* produced a *morisco* even if they had no relations with Moors, and a *mulato* with a native begat a *zambo*. Other terms, such as *lobo* (wolf), *chino* (Chinese), *cambujo*, *albarazado*, *zambazo*, and *jíbaro*, described further combinations of Spanish, *mulatos*, and natives . . . and the list goes on. Some of those old colonial terms have currency today: a *cholo* now describes a Chicano gangster in the Los Angeles area. Jíbaro refers to a Puerto Rican peasant.

The mestizos, and more generally the process of *mestizaje*, accelerated Hispanicization in the New World. Contrary to the rest of the population, who spoke only native languages, most mestizos were at least partly bilingual. By 1650, they accounted for a quarter of Mexico's population of 1.5 million and half of the population of the capital city. As their numbers grew, the proportion of Spanish speakers grew too.

The other thing the mestizos did was weaken the encomienda system.

The encomienda (estate) was introduced in Hispaniola in 1503 and became the basic land-grant scheme for all the Americas for the rest of the sixteenth century. The word derives from the verb *encomendar* (to trust or entrust). Designated *encomenderos* were given a chunk of land and full rights to exploit natives to work it and to administer justice. They could do anything they wanted with the land—ranch, farm, mine, cut lumber, or grow sugar. Most *encomenderos* were conquistadores or Aztec or Inca notables. La Malinche and the daughters of Moctezuma were granted large encomiendas. In return, the *encomenderos* were obliged to provide natives with protection, justice, and religious instruction—none of which were distributed generously.

The encomienda had a disastrous effect on the native populations of the Americas: millions of people were forcibly displaced to work on them and were decimated by disease in the process. By the time the Spanish Crown passed a set of better laws to protect natives, in 1542, the encomienda system was beginning to crack. The church was horrified by the conditions of quasi slavery natives were subjected to. Eventually, *encomenderos* had trouble finding workers, since their system was killing off the Indian population.

Ultimately, by encouraging more mixed marriages, the system defeated itself. The labor rules of the encomienda system applied only to natives, excluding mestizos, who were considered a different "race." To spare their children from this punishing regime, natives sought mixed-race unions.

Spain saw the writing on the wall, so to exploit the growing mestizo population, it invented a new labor system. At the beginning of the seventeenth century, the encomiendas morphed into the nominally more acceptable hacienda (derived from the verb *hacer,* to make) system. The main difference was that the *patrón* or *hacendado* was the owner of the estate, not just the grantee. Technically, the people working for him were wageworkers, not forced labor, but the difference was mostly semantic since most people had no other possibility for employment. Haciendas began to spread throughout Spain's colonies, side by side with the estancias (ranches) of the plains of the río de la Plata, and the smaller versions of them, fincas, in Central America and the Caribbean.

The slow collapse of the encomienda system was not just the result of economics. It also happened because the Spanish Church was competing with the Crown for the loyalty of Native Americans. And this race for the natives' souls would shape the spread of Spanish in the New World.

14. The Missionary Position

AMONG MEXICO'S ARCHITECTURAL ATTRACTIONS, the basilica of Nuestra Señora de Guadalupe (Our Lady of Guadalupe) in Mexico City doesn't hold a candle to other wonders. The massive Pyramid of the Sun in Teotihuacán, the Temple of Palenque in the jungle of Chiapas, and the gigantic murals Diego Rivera painted in Mexico's National Palace are far more impressive. Built in the 1970s, the stadium-like circular basilica is a modern structure that is more functional than inspirational.

Yet, as the site of an astonishing human spectacle, nothing else in Mexico compares.

Every year, on December the 11 and 12, millions of Latin Americans arrive at the basilica in *camiónes* (buses) or packed into two-ton trucks with dashboards, hoods, roofs, and bumpers festooned with garlands and statues of the Virgin. In the days leading up to this event, it's normal to see peasants walking and cycling with five-foot-tall images of the Guadalupe strapped to their backs—or more shocking, pilgrims with blood streaming down their legs, not because of traffic accidents but because they crawled along the gigantic boulevard leading up to the basilica on their hands and knees.

In 2009, a whopping 6.1 million visitors came to the basilica to pay their respects to the Queen of Mexico, the Patron Saint of the Americas—that is, the Virgin Mary.

This holiday is the apex of the nonstop veneration of the Virgin Mary that occurs inside the church all year. Each of its ten thousand seats offers a view of the basilica's pièce de résistance, a painting of the Virgin, roughly six by four feet in size, that hangs a few feet above the altar. According to tradition, this image was miraculously left on the *tilma* (apron) of Chichimeca peasant Juan Diego in 1531. The *tilma* now hangs in the basilica, protected by bulletproof glass—two centuries ago, in 1790, someone threw bleach on it (after which the image allegedly reconstituted itself by miracle). Then in 1921 it was bombed. This is why visitors are shuttled along two moving walkways in front of it and not allowed to linger for too long.

The image is a perfect symbol of the religious syncretism so typical of Latin American Catholicism. The actual likeness of the Virgin is believed to have been inspired by an Aztec goddess, Tonanzin, whose temple was on the same Tepeyac Hill where Diego saw the apparition. At any rate, her features seem deliberately chosen to appeal to native Americans. She is brown—she is often called *la morenita* (the little brown one)—and dressed in blue and green, colors associated with the Aztec divinities for celestial objects and earth. The rays of light framing her are in the form of *maguey* (agave cactus) leaves, which was the main ingredient of the pulque, a ritual spirit of the Atzecs. Although there was a Lady of Guadalupe in Extremadura who inspired a cult between the fourteenth and the sixteenth centuries, the Mexican Guadalupe comes from the Hispanicization of the Virgin's own name for herself. To Juan Diego, she allegedly referred to herself as Coatlaxopeuh, which means "the one who crushes the snake" in Nahuatl.

And powerful she is.

The Mexican Nobel laureate in literature Octavio Paz went as far as saying that, after experimenting with politics for two centuries, the only things the Mexican people still had faith in were the Virgin of Guadalupe and the National Lottery. Veneration for the Guadalupe is believed to have prompted no fewer than five million Native Americans to convert to Christianity before 1536, only five years after her appearance.

The Catholic church would go on to be so successful in Latin America that its center of gravity shifted from Europe to the Americas. The Mexican revolutionaries of 1810 put the Virgin's image on their flags. A century later, during the Mexican Revolution, she marched at the head of Emiliano Zapata's troops. One José

Miguel Fernández y Félix even changed his name to Guadalupe Victoria before he became the first president of Mexico (1824–1829). Pope John Paul II visited the shrine of Nuestra Señora de Guadalupe on his first trip abroad, in 1979. Juan Diego, who was canonized in 2002, was the first native of the Americas to become a saint. The ceremony attracted twelve million people to its worldwide gatherings.

The fact that the Virgin allegedly spoke to Juan Diego in Nahuatl might be the result of a curious decision made by the Catholic church. In the centuries following the conquest, the church actually promoted native languages over Spanish, a policy that stalled the progress of Spanish in the Americas for 250 years.

The reason the Spanish were pragmatists. To consolidate their hold on the Americas, they built on what was already there. After conquering the Inca and Aztec empires, Spain decided to use Nahuatl and Quechua, as well as Guaraní in the less populous Southern Cone, as the lingua francas with which the Spanish missionaries, conquistadores, traders, and administrators would communicate with the natives and mestizos. In fact, it was the existence of these widely spoken languages, which the Spanish dubbed *lenguas generales* (auxiliary languages), that allowed Spain to establish its empire quickly over such a vast territory. ("Pure-blood" natives amounted to 99 percent of the population on the continent in 1590s, and was still 55 percent in 1810.) The Caribbean islands were an exception to this policy, but that's mainly because their native cultures were virtually extinct by 1550: there were no native languages for the church to fall back on.

On the continent, the Aztec and Inca empires were so enormous that even after 70 to 95 percent of their populations were wiped out by epidemics, there were still between one and four million natives in Mexico alone.

In short there was nothing inevitable about the spread of Spanish on the continent. Two centuries after the conquest, Spanish was still in a fragile position. And there was nothing really surprising in that. Empires don't always succeed in making the inhabitants of a conquered territory adopt their tongue. In Spain, only the Romans managed to do so. Although the Arabs were present in Spain for eight centuries and ruled most of the peninsula for four centuries, they only weakened the grasp of Romance, at best. After the Portuguese lost most of their East Indies to the Dutch in 1680, the Dutch were never able to impose their language and Portuguese remained the lingua franca in most of the colonies.

Place-names in Central America amply demonstrate how influential Nahuatl was. Even though Guatemala was predominantly Maya, the name Guatemala come from the Nahuatl word *cuauhtitlán,* meaning "between the trees." In southern Mexico, it is common to find place-names that end with the suffix *-tenango,* a deformation of the Nahuatl *tenan-co* (in the citadel of). Huehuetenango means "citadel of the ancients," Momostenango means "citadel of the chapel," Chichicastenango means "citadel of the bitter nettle."

In Peru, the Quechua tongue was so robust it continued to make progress after the Spanish conquest. When Pizarro arrived in 1532, the Inca Empire was in the process of switching its imperial language from Aymara to Quechua, a change that had begun because of Inca conquests a century earlier. After the Spanish chose Quechua as the *lengua general,* it spread south with new mining settlements to Bolivia and as far as Córdoba in Argentina. By the eighteenth century, even the criollo landed class of Peru had embraced Quechua as a symbol of their political legitimacy.

In the New World, the Catholic church, which amounted to a vast administrative machine charged with the objective of saving souls, turned out to be one of the most important forces spreading the *lenguas generales.*

By the sixteenth century, the Spanish were the most militant and proselytizing Christians in Europe. In Spanish eyes, the conquest of the Americas was part two of the Reconquista. According to the papal bull of 1493, converting natives was the supreme objective of the Spanish Empire (gold was an unstated supreme objective). Since language was primarily considered a means to this end, the job of teaching languages naturally fell to the missionaries.

Like colonial administrators, Spain's missionaries were pragmatists. They knew it was impossible to teach Spanish to all Native Americans. In 1552, there were only 802 friars working among millions of pagans in Mexico. So the Spanish Crown and the missionaries simply decided to learn the native languages and preach in them. The idea was more paternalistic than progressive. Many missionaries believed that American Indians were too stupid to learn Spanish.

A number of key Spanish missionaries showed no particular attachment to the Spanish language. Some famous missionaries of the Spanish colonial empire weren't even Spanish, including the Austrian Eusebio Kino (Kühn) and the Flemish missionary Pieter van der Moere, famous for organizing the first (bilingual) school for sons of native nobles.

The policy of teaching in native languages did not stifle the burgeoning intellectual activity of Spain's missionaries. If anything, it fed it, by sparking an enormous demand for grammars, dictionaries, and native-language versions of prayer books. This is probably why Mexico got its first printing press in the 1530s, decades before Madrid. The grammars of native languages were all modeled on Antonio de Nebrija's famous *Introductiones latinae*. By the end of the nineteenth century, 1,188 books had been written in 369 of the 473 known native languages.

During the sixteenth century, Mexico spawned an impressive body of Nahuatl literature, including plays, histories, and psalms. The intellectual giant was the missionary Bernardino de Sahagún. In 1529, Sahagún started interviewing survivors of the conquest about their civilization, who told him about life before Cortés. He went on to compile a twelve-volume *Historia General de las cosas de Nueva España* (General History of Things of New Spain), known as the *Florentine Codex*, because it is in an archive in Florence. Sahagún is rightly regarded as the father of modern ethnography. His documentation of the culture, worldview, rites, economy, and social organization of the people is considered among the greatest intellectual accomplishments of all time. Written in Nahuatl and Spanish, this twenty-four-hundred-page ethnographic encyclopedia of Aztec life also included two thousand images.

In Peru, around the same time, Fray Domingo de Santo Tómas wrote the first grammar of Quechua, *Grammatica o arte de la lengua general de los indios de los Reynos del Perú* (Grammar or Art of the General Tongue of the Natives of the Kingdoms of Peru). His goal was to demonstrate that the natives spoke a language of civilization and were not, as many believed, intellectually inferior to Europeans. In a few instances, Santo Tómas turned the European arguments on their head: he quotes one chieftain who claimed he was "getting closer to being a Christian, since he had learned to swear to God, play cards, and steal."

Syncretism is a fascinating feature of religion in the Americas, particularly in Mexico. Aside from the Guadalupe herself, the best example is Mexico's national fall holiday on November 1 and 2, *el Día de los muertos*. Mexicans celebrate by leaving *calaveras* (sugar skulls) and other *ofrendas* (offerings) of flowers, *pulque*, and *pan de muerto* in cemeteries.

This kind of religious syncretism, still thriving in Mexico, is key to understanding how the church became so popular all over Latin America. The clergy won droves of native followers by tolerating pagan customs and communicating in local languages. Whereas the Inquisition demanded strict orthodoxy in Spain, the church in the colonies welcomed native rites and customs as long as they didn't contradict doctrine.

On New Year's Eve, 1987, Jean-Benoît saw a good example of a Mexican syncretic custom in a large *municipio* (town) called San Sebastián Tlacotepec de Porfirio Diaz, in a remote area of the State of Puebla. The custom is called *La Chispa*. After mass, locals walked from house to house with a scarecrow figure of a grandfather (symbolizing the old year) filled with firecrackers. Children dressed like skeletons and witches trailed behind the procession asking for alms. Then the scarecrow was tied to a palm tree on the *zócalo* (plaza) and set on fire, provoking a chain reaction of explosions.

The church also won followers simply by defending and protecting the native population. Spanish missionaries were men of their time who tolerated levels of violence that would be referred to law enforcers today. But the missionaries weren't heartless. Many denounced abuses of natives by conquistadores. The Spanish king gave the first bishop of Mexico, Fray Juan de Zumárraga, the title Protector of the Indians.

The most famous protector of the Indians was Bartolomé de Las Casas, author of one of the most celebrated works of his time, the *Brevísima relación de la destrucción de las Indias* (A Short Account of the Destruction of the Indies), published in 1552. Las Casas was no saint himself. He came to Hispanionala as an eighteen-year-old conquistador and was granted an encomienda for his efforts. In 1510, he became the first priest ordained in the colonies, but he still defended the encomienda system. (Because of this stance, Dominican friars, who condemned slavery, denied him confession.) Las Casas continued to accumulate encomiendas until 1514, when he had an epiphany, publicly renounced his property, and began to preach against the system. In 1542 he persuaded the Spanish king to pass the *nuevas leyes* (new laws), limiting the amount of violence slave owners could inflict on their slaves. It took him another decade to get around to rejecting the enslavement of natives, period, and unfortunately he waited until he was on his deathbed to try to extend the same rights—limited as they were—to Africans.

Las Casas's *Brevísima* went on to become a classic of liberal arts education. Yet his denunciation of abuses against the natives was more of a pamphlet than a full account of what went on in the *Indias.* It is based partly on events Las Casas witnessed, but relies heavily on secondhand sources. While there is no denying the atrocities committed by conquistadores and *encomenderos,* one of

Bartolemé de Las Casas's central theses is flawed: the worst of the genocide against natives was committed not by men but by disease, the transmission of which was generally unintentional, at least in the beginning—which is no excuse for the abuse. Las Casas was probably aware of this, but as a propagandist, he deliberately conflated the epidemic and the atrocities to drive home his point. His work also had an adverse effect: Protestant Europe embraced it as anti-Catholic and anti-Spanish propaganda, despite the fact that the Spanish Crown was making honorable efforts to correct wrongs with respect to natives, and that the English were about to repeat the same mistakes.

Like the church, Spain's colonial administration did little to promote the Spanish language, at first. In 1503, *Las Instrucciones reales* (the Royal Instructions) ordered that all indigenous children be brought to towns and taught to read and write—in Latin. The administration slowly changed its tune and started to promote Spanish in the next decades. In 1533, the Crown printed twelve thousand *cartillas* (booklets) to help Mexican natives learn *castellano*.

Teaching was the clergy's job, and missionaries wanted to stick to the *lenguas generales*. In 1550, the clergy openly resisted the Crown's *Real Cédula* (Royal Decree) stating that natives should be taught Spanish. The same year, Fray Rodrigo de la Cruz asked Charles V to order all Indians to learn the Mexican (Nahuatl) language, which he described as "an extremely elegant language, already spoken by many in every village."

In 1596, King Felipe II tried to get the church to teach natives in Spanish. But facing resistance, the king reduced his demands to making a teacher of Spanish *available* for anyone who *wanted* to learn Spanish. The clergy made sure there would not be too much demand. They were simply protecting their own turf. By using native languages, the clergy had exclusivity over natives' souls: they positioned themselves as the sole intermediaries between natives and the outside world, which allowed them to "shelter" natives from the dangerous ideas of Protestants and the French philosophers.

* * *

Despite the progress of the *lenguas generales*—mostly at the expense of other native languages—Spanish in the colonies had one thing going for it: it was widely spoken in the cities.

In the end, Spanish spread in the Americas the same way French spread in France. Originally a language of northern cities, French became the official language of France in 1539, then slowly spread south through urban power centers. But it took centuries to become a common tongue. French was spoken widely throughout the country only after the French government introduced mass education in the nineteenth century.

The same thing happened with Spanish in the Americas. Spanish had taken root on the Caribbean islands and among the urban classes and mestizos on the continent. It was a language of prestige, influence, and social promotion spoken mainly by the personnel and demimonde of the Spanish viceroyalties—the viceroy, governor, *corregidores* (magistrates), captains, civil servants, clerics, literati, and courtesans. (Like French, Spanish spread outside these confined circles only once the authorities got serious about teaching, in the eighteenth and nineteenth centuries.)

The New World cities of the sixteenth century were impressive. Mexico became the seat of a cathedral in 1527 and it got its own university in 1551. Lima had a university in 1555 and a theater by 1602. By 1550, there were already seven printers in Mexico City (there were still none in Madrid by this time). In 1722, Mexico started the first Spanish-language newspaper in the colonies, *Gazeta de Mexico*. This was followed quickly by papers in Guatemala, Lima, and Buenos Aires. European travelers in the 1600s compared Mexico City to Paris, Rome, and London.

In 1593, one of the great writers of the time, the Spanish poet Bernardo de Balbuena, wrote about Mexico City's conversations, games, receptions, hunting and garden parties, picnics and evening balls, concerts, visits, races, promenades, "a new comedy every day," fashion, carriages, women's headdresses, jewels. In manner of speech, the *novohispanos* (New Spainers) had the reputation of being more polite, delicate, and rhetorical than the *peninsulares*.

The greatest literary figure of the Latin American colonial era was probably the criolla poet Sor (sister) Juana Inés de la Cruz, who even gained a following in Spain during her lifetime. In 1662, at age eleven, she pleaded with her mother to dress her as a boy so that she could study at the university. Once there, her knowledge of astronomy and mathematics proved so phenomenal that she was invited to the viceregal court. After becoming a nun, she collected more than four thousand books, as well as papers, pens, and musical instruments. But she was an emancipated character who argued for the education of women and condemned the double standards that punished prostitutes more harshly than their clients. This led her to open conflict with religious authorities, for which she had to do penance. In 1693, she sold all her books and stopped writing. She died of plague—compounded by a broken heart—two years later, at age forty-three.

Yet while the urbane centers of New Spain were taking off, in the territories the Spanish called El Norte, a completely new Spanish language culture was taking shape around missions and ranches.

15. Moving *Norte*

AFTER HIGHWAY I-19 PASSES TUCSON, Arizona, then curves to the west, the San Xavier del Bac Mission literally pops out of the desert. A sprawling white complex built in the trademark earthquake-proof Mexican colonial style, the mission is a startling sight amid saguaro cactuses.

We were surprised to stumble on its Moorish dome and white bell towers, neatly tended cactus gardens, majestic sand-colored façade, and massive mesquite wood doors in the Arizona desert. The interior of the church has been described as a "Baroque vision of heaven." Entirely renovated starting in the 1990s, it is painted in deep red, gold, and blue tones and decorated with some fifty statues of saints.

Even in the midst of such splendor, you can attend a calf-roping competition on any Sunday afternoon in the corral next door. The first time we visited this place, almost everyone competing was either Native American or mestizo. This shouldn't have been a surprise. Ranching was an established way of life in Mexico and the U.S. Southwest long before the founding of Jamestown in 1607.

We actually "discovered" Mexico's cowboy culture in 1990 when we were traveling in Mexico's Sierra Negra, 150 miles southeast of Mexico City. In the hamlet of Tepepa de Zaragoza, we met Don Eligio Gergue, a local patriarch who introduced himself as a ranchero. He had some twenty head of Texas longhorns. At the time, we thought he was a strange cultural transplant. Only years later did we realize that ranching culture *comes* from Mexico. Texas longhorns were descendants of Andalusian cattle, which had been imported to the Americas a mere ninety miles from the village where he was standing.

The origins of ranching date to the Middle Ages, when Castilians,

Basques, Galicians, Aragonese, and Leonese began free-range sheep and cattle grazing. Spain organized these territories under an owners' guild called a *mesta*, then exported the concept, along with ranching techniques, when exploration of the Americas began. Six months after Cortés captured Mexico City, a conquistador named Gregorio de Villalobos landed several head of Andalusian cattle near Tampico.

Mexico's geography, which shares many features of Spain's, turned out to be ideal for cattle raising. By 1580, there were sixty-two ranching encomiendas around Veracruz, with a total of 150,000 heads of cattle. Within decades of the conquest, Mexican *vaqueros* (literally, "cowers"), mostly mestizos or natives, developed their own cattle-ranching techniques. They invented the *lazo* (lasso) technique. Once the steer was roped in, the vaquero swiftly twisted his rope around the saddle horn. This name of the technique, *da la vuelta* (give it a turn), eventually morphed into English *dallying* or *dally roping.*

The western saddle called the Spanish saddle in the American West until the beginning of the twentieth century—was originally called a *silla vaquera mexicana* (Mexican cowboy saddle). An adaptation of a Spanish war saddle, *la jineta,* it has a lower center of gravity, longer stirrups for a better knee grip, and a high conical saddle horn, all designed to simplify cattle roping (before the saddle horn, vaqueros tied ropes to their horse's tail).

David Dary, in *Cowboy Culture: A Saga of Five Centuries,* explains how the clothing of the Mexican vaquero grew out of the ranching environment. Vaqueros spent long periods living in remote grazing grounds, so they made shirts and pants from the material they had on hand: cowhide. They developed *chaparreras* (chaps), *chaquetas* (jackets), and *botas* (wrapped leather leggings). They also turned *espuelas* (spurs) into an emblem of cowboy culture. In old Spain, spurs were the prerogative of horsemen, who enjoyed a rather exclusive status. In Mexico, where cowboys worked all day on horses, even cowhands wore spurs with *rodajas* (rowels, also called jingle bobs). So the quintessentially jingling sound of a cowboy's stride, an archetype of the sound track of cinematic Westerns, is, in fact, Mexican.

By 1529, Spanish authorities in the Americas had established a Spanish-inspired body to regulate stockholders, called Mesta. The Mexican Mesta published the first catalog of *marcas* (brands) used to differentiate cattle in the western hemisphere; it included Cortés's brand, which consisted of three Latin crosses. (This was how "branding" arrived in the Americas.) Every year, Mesta members organized a *rodeo* (from *rodear,* to surround or encircle), to "round up" all the heads of cattle, brand them, and accustom them to human presence. By 1537, the Mesta system had spread throughout New Spain. Anyone with more than twenty head of cattle had to join it.

By 1562, there was already a ranching aristocracy in place in Nueva Vizcaya, the first province of New Spain. Ranchers lived in town and ran their ranches as absentee owners via powerful *estancieros* (overseers). In David Dary's account, by the 1570s Mexico had herds of up to 130,000 head. In fact, the herds got so big that meat became a by-product of the *matanzas* (slaughters); ranchers raised stock mostly for tallow (for candle making) and hides, which were thriving businesses.

Naturally, such prosperity attracted thieves. Chichimeca Indians began raiding, as did roaming bands of vaqueros, and later *bandidos,* armed with breastplates, harquebuses, scythes, and *desjarretaderas* (hamstring knives). To protect ranches and missions, Spain created fortified bases called presidios. From 1577 to the beginning of the nineteenth century, ranchos and presidios became the basis for settlement in the Mexican frontier.

Although each area developed its own folklore, ranching forged a common link across Spain's empire. Ancient Spanish ranching techniques were adopted—and adapted—all over the American continent and took slightly different forms, spawning different vocabulary, from place to place. Argentines call cowboys *gauchos;*

Peruvians, *chaláns;* Ecuadorians, *chagras;* Venezuelans and Colombians, *llaneros;* and Chileans, *huasos.*

Spain used ranching and plantations to settle the vast goldless territories north of Mexico City and Cuba. The first Spanish settlement in this area—the future United States—was a fort, St. Augustine, Florida, founded in 1565, surrounded by a few small plantations. But in the arid plateaus north of Mexico, plantations were futile because of lack of water, so the Spanish fell back on ranching. Ranching solved a lot of problems: mostly it made it possible for the vast territories that lacked roads or navigable waterways to be self-sufficient. The Spaniards had a solid grasp of the northern landscape by that time and were developing vocabulary to describe the geographic realities of the continent. Many essential terms come from Spanish, including *cañon* (canyon), *chaparral, mesa,* and *tornado.* Other words, such as *mesquite,* are Hispanicized native terms.

The Spaniards also adopted native practices, like making *ramadas,* which means "branches" and refers to a small shelter, typical of the Sonora desert, made of branches with a roof but no walls. They are made out of steel and concrete today, but are still ubiquitous in the Southwest, particularly in Arizona, where they cover children's playgrounds, bleachers, patios, picnic tables, and cars.

Hundreds of Native American groups would acquire Spanish or Hispanicized names, including the Comanche, Apache, Navajo, Maricopa, Mohave, Pecos, Jumano, Wichita, and Pima. And many Indian leaders took Spanish names, like Apache chiefs Geronimo and Cochise, as well as Navajo chief Manuelito and Cahuilla chief Adam Castillo.

Confident that the Spanish could implant ranching in the north, the king of Spain ordered Juan de Oñate, known as the "last conquistador," to start colonizing it. In 1598, Oñate forded the río Bravo del Norte (Rio Grande) at El Paso, claimed all the territory north as Nuevo Mexico, and declared it open for settlement. Farther north, up the valley of the río Bravo del Norte,

Oñate encountered a series of *adobe pueblos* (villages) with large, settled populations of Indians from various ethnic groups. With this population base to build on, Oñate started founding missions and ranches, including Santa Fe.

So it's no surprise that five American states have Spanish names: Florida, California, Nevada, Colorado, Montana. And four more—Texas, New Mexico, Utah, and Arizona—have Hispanicized Indian names. The oldest written records of U.S. history—mission charters, contracts, deeds, oaths, diplomas, and correspondence—were written in Spanish by conquistadores and missionaries, notaries, *alcaldes* (mayors), *empresarios* (entrepreneurs), and *soldados* (soldiers).

Spanish colonialism generated a peculiar Spanish frontier culture that, for many generations, was the only unifying link from Texas to California.

Once Spain's missions and presidios were established, ranching helped the Spanish convert natives into settlers. Missions concentrated scattered populations and transformed natives from nomadic hunters into sedentary farmers. As David Dary explains, missionaries deliberately got natives to develop a taste for beefsteak and horsemeat, then for European clothing and blankets. They taught them Spanish and selected the strongest and most capable among them to handle horses and cattle.

Arizona's San Xavier del Bac Mission followed this to the letter. The mission was established by the dynamic Jesuit Father Eusebio Kino, who was born in the Tyrol. Kino arrived in the O'odham village of Wa:k in 1692 (the name was later deformed into el Bac), inhabited by Pima Indians, seminomads who left every fall to go hunting. A skilled rancher himself, Father Kino managed to convert the Pimas into cattlemen. Most of the twenty-four ranching missions he founded in Baja California and in the Sonora desert—with a total of seventy thousand head of cattle—still exist today as missions or towns.

San Xavier is still standing thanks to the Presidio (fort) of San

Agustín del Tucsón, from O'odham *Chuk Shon,* meaning "spring at the base of the black mountain." Since ranching was such good business, missions were subject to raids by rival tribes or rustlers. To defend the missions, ranches, and their flock from Apache, the Spanish built a chain of nineteen presidios from California to Louisiana.

The mastery of the horse—an animal extinct on the continent for nine thousand years—gave the conquistadores their key technological edge over the native populations, and the Spanish did their best to keep horsemanship a military secret as long as possible. The Spanish explorer Francisco Vázquez de Coronado was partly responsible for letting the secret out of the bag and turning the natives into effective horsemen. Coronado brought hundreds of horses with him in his 1540 expedition in search of the Seven Cities of Gold, which took him as far as Kansas. Many of the horses broke loose on the return trip, later multiplying into millions of animals that went on to change the lives of hundreds of Indian bands and tribes. The Apaches, in particular, became excellent horsemen, which would soon spell trouble for the Spaniards.

The most important setback in the settlement of the north occurred in 1680 with the so-called Pueblo Uprising, when all the pueblo Indians in Nuevo Mexico rebelled under the leadership of a chief named Popé. The ensuing massacres forced the Spaniards to evacuate Santa Fe and fall back on El Paso. But worse, after the uprising, hundreds of domesticated horses fell into the hands of a little-known tribe called the Comanche.

The Comanche went down in history books as reckless raiders, but the historian Pekka Hämäläinen argues in *Comanche Empire* that, on the contrary, over a relatively short period in the eighteenth century, the Comanche combined horsemanship, diplomacy, and trade skills to build a very effective empire. Before the advent of automatic guns, Comanches could shoot twelve arrows in the time it took a Spaniard to load a musket. The Comanche and Apache resistance was so effective that it nearly ended colonization efforts

in Texas and most of northern Mexico. To this day, Texans call a
full moon a Comanche moon, a tribute to the horsemen's remarkable mobility in the cover of night.

The Spaniards were slow to colonize Texas. In 1686, the Spanish captain Alonso de León and the Franciscan father Damián
Massanet traveled east to verify progress of the French, who were
moving into the west bank of the Mississippi, which was Spanish
territory. In what would become East Texas, León and Massanet
were greeted by friendly Caddos. The Indians repeated the word
chechas (friendly, allies) and the Spanish soon named the new territory Tejas. But not all the Indians in Texas were friendly. It took
the Spanish four decades to build a dozen missions there. In 1825,
there were fewer than four thousand Mexicans in Texas. The new
Mexican government outsourced the business of settlement to
twenty-three *empresarios*, who solved the problem. By 1834 there
were ten times more inhabitants, including seventy-eight hundred
Mexicans.

In addition to native hostility, the colonization of Texas and
Nuevo Mexico was slowed by politics and economics. The colonies
were under the authority of backward provinces whose governors
had other priorities. The economics of the Spanish colonies was
based also on mercantilism, which didn't help their development.
Colonists had to purchase supplies from authorized Spanish merchants, who sold them through official channels at a high price, a
monopoly system that made life expensive.

When Americans began arriving in Texas at the beginning of the
nineteenth century, they encountered a totally unfamiliar mode of
agriculture. Free-range cattle raising was nonexistent in the East,
where farmers raised small herds behind fences on midsize farms.
Early Americans in Texas were in awe of the Mexican vaqueros'
mastery of roping techniques. For that matter, it was easy to spot old
Texans from the East: they were often missing a thumb or two, lost
while they were learning how to *da la vuelta*. It took a deft hand to
lasso a bucking steer and attach it to a saddle horn.

Colonial Spain had an easier time settling in Alta (Upper) California, where natives didn't have horses. The Spanish were spurred to act by the fear that the British and the Russians would beat them to the Pacific. On the other hand, the Spaniards enjoyed an advantage, having mastered the terrain.

In 1769, a Franciscan mission was established at San Diego as a base for colonization of coastal California. In all, Franciscans founded twenty-one missions in California, all linked by the Camino real (Royal Road).

Naturally, because of numerous contacts with ranchers and vaqueros, ranching vocabulary in American English borrowed heavily from Spanish. Some words are immediately recognizable: lasso, rodeo, corral, bronco, and pinto. Many more are only modified slightly: mustang, stampede, buckeroo, chap, cinch, and jacket, which come from *mesteño, estampida, vaquero, chaparreras, cincho,* and *chaqueta.* Some Spanish terms are almost totally corrupted: *jáquima* (halter), *mecate* (horsehair rope), *cuarta* (small whip), *jacal* (wooden hut) morphed into hackamore, McCarty, quirt, and shack. *Caballerango* (groom) somehow turned into *wrangler.* And one of the most curious is the ten-gallon cowboy hat, which of course never contained ten gallons: the word comes from the Spanish *tan galán,* meaning "so handsome"!

The dollar—name, symbol, and all—is another legacy of the Spanish empire in the United States. "Spanish dollars" were used as currency in the thirteen colonies starting in the 1690s. And it was no wonder: gold and silver extracted from Mexican and Bolivian mines had been flooding the monetary systems in Europe, the Arab world, and as far as China since 1546. Until the middle of the nineteenth century, Spanish dollars were the foundation of the world's monetary system.

The name *dollar* (from the German *taler*) is a vestige of the time when the Spanish Empire included not just swaths of the Americas but also whole sections of Europe. Spanish dollars, having gained wide currency in the thirteen colonies through trade, served as the model for the creation of the U.S. dollar in 1792. The Spanish dollar would remain legal tender in the United States until 1857.

Even the dollar sign—the $—is a product of the United States' Spanish heritage. There are two explanations for the origins of the symbol. Either it is a condensed version of the abbreviation for *peso*: p^s, or it is a symbolic rendition of a section of herald of the crown of Castile, stamped on the backside of each Spanish dollar. The $'s straight line would represent the pillar on the right-hand side while the S shape is a stylized version of a banner twirled around the pillar. In either case, specialists agree that it's the dollar that took the *peso* sign. The Spanish dollar connection is also the origin of the custom of striking currency initials with a bar to indicate a currency, like ¢, £, ¥, and €.

Naturally, when a bunch of stockbrokers began trading in a room on Wall Street in 1792, they traded in Spanish dollars—what else? Traditions die hard, and the Spanish dollar remained the currency of reference at the New York Stock Exchange for 205 years. That's why the NYSE expressed fractions of dollars in eighths—as in "piece of eight"—rather than cents. This oddity lasted until the exchange finally adopted the decimal system and was done with the piece of eight, in 1997.

But long before the Spanish dollar made fortunes for Wall Street, the New World wealth created a golden age in Spain, the likes of which had not been seen in Europe since the glory days of the Roman Empire.

16. Golden Age

WE OFTEN WONDERED WHY ENGLISH, French, and Spanish speakers spell and pronounce the name of Miguel de Cervantes's masterpiece, *Don Quixote,* three different ways. English speakers pronounce *Quixote* more or less as Spanish speakers do, but spell it with an *x*, whereas the Spanish spell it *Don Quijote.* In French, the famous hidalgo's name is both spelled and pronounced differently: it's *Don Quichotte,* pronounced with a soft *sh* sound.

What explains the differences? In the seventeenth century, when Cervantes published his two-volume work, Spanish spelling and pronunciation were shifting radically. The English, French, and Spanish just stopped the clock at different times. The English stuck to the way *Quixote* was spelled when the first volume was published in 1605. The Spanish updated the *x* to a *j* in accordance with the spelling changes that happened after Cervantes's death in 1616. And the French continued to pronounce *Don Quixote* as it was pronounced early in the century—when *x* in Spanish sounded like *sh*—but decided to spell it phonetically, which resulted in *Quichotte.*

The sixteenth and seventeenth centuries were the last period of major pronunciation and spelling shifts in Spanish. But unlike earlier periods in the development of the language, modern linguists have enormous stocks of raw material with which to study exactly what was going on. Spanish writers produced a mountain of plays, poetry, and prose works—including *Don Quixote,* considered the world's first novel—not to mention the paperwork of colonial bureaucracy and the mass of intercontinental written correspondence.

The sixteenth and seventeenth centuries, known as Spain's golden age, were a groundbreaking period for Spanish literature. The expression *Siglo de Oro* (Golden Century) was first coined in the eighteenth century by the Spanish writer Luis José Velázquez de Velasco out of nostalgia. He described this as an era when "good poetry would flourish along with other good letters."

Yet the Siglo de Oro really should have been called the Silver Age, for that was the metal that fueled Spain's cultural output. The tremendous outflow of silver from the mines of Zacatecas and Potosí made Spain the richest and most powerful country in Europe. Their coffers overflowing with New World riches, Spain's kings, the Hapsburgs, turned themselves into the world's most generous patrons of the arts.

Curiously, though, none of the renowned figures of seventeenth-century Spain—Cervantes, or the painters El Greco or Velázquez—thought there was anything golden about those times. New World riches did not trickle down to all members of Spanish society. Cervantes, for one, never managed to secure the regular patronage of a noble.

It's probably more accurate to describe Spain in the sixteenth and seventeenth centuries as an Age of Flux. For the first time in twelve hundred years, the Spanish weren't fighting each other and the country was at relative peace. Still, daily life was a challenge. The Crown was exhausting its finances warring with every other power in Europe as well as colonizing the Americas. Most ordinary citizens were victims of hunger, banditry, epidemics, and riots.

The population of Spain was also increasing rapidly. During this time, it doubled to reach eight or nine million. But the country also experienced unprecedented population movements. One person in eight left the country during the same period, a total of more than 1.4 million Spaniards: 750,000 immigrated to the Americas, while a half million Muslims were expelled in 1609, following 100,000 Jews in 1492.

Spain's golden era was a direct product of its cities. To this day, Spaniards are famous for injecting energy and color into city life, but the tradition started centuries ago. In Madrid, the streets are crowded with pedestrians and passersby. Hordes of pedestrians from all walks of life transport themselves by foot well into the night. The same is true in Burgos, Alicante, or any Spanish city: the streets are packed with people conversing, connecting, and unwinding.

Streets in Spain have always been venues of some kind of show. In sixteenth-century Seville, Madrid, and Valladolid, streets were a dirty mess from which human and animal corpses were removed daily. But they were also the scene of permanent shows—markets, *autos* (religious plays), festivals, and processions of *penitentes* (religious penitents) in hooded robes. From time to time, the king would declare a public fiesta, a *corrida* (bull run, from *correr,* to run). Madrid's Plaza Mayor was famous for corridas during which *mata-toros* (bull killers) on horseback pierced bulls with javelins, to the joy of screaming crowds.

Spain had always had a strong urban culture. People fleeing the Reconquista had sought refuge in its walled cities. By the seventeenth century, Valladolid, Barcelona, Zaragoza, Valencia, Santiago de Compostela—but above all, Seville—were bustling with activity that mixed rich and poor, nobles and commoners in close quarters. With 150,000 inhabitants, Seville was Spain's largest city—and its richest: it was the control center of New World settlement and the funnel through which the riches from the Americas poured into Spain.

But cities were changing. Seville was quickly being surpassed by the booming new capital, Madrid. A town of only fifteen thousand at the time of Columbus's first voyage, Madrid's population matched Seville's by the seventeenth century.

It was in the swirling urban melting pots of Spain's cities that Spanish evolved from a medieval tongue into a modern language.

Because so much was written in the sixteenth and seventeenth centuries, it is relatively easy to isolate the thousands of little changes that gave the Spanish language its modern spelling and phonetics. Linguists can see what words rhymed by looking at the poetry of the time. They can also guess at pronunciations by some of the spelling mistakes. Since people tend to write words the way they sound, writers' errors left strong clues as to how words sounded.

Many students of Spanish in the United States and France are drawn to the language because of its usefulness, combined with its relative simplicity. Spanish is easy for English and French speakers to learn because its spelling rules are largely (though not completely) systematic and its spelling is strongly phonetic. As we have seen, the roots of this simplicity go back to the Old Castile, when the re-population of New Castile during the Reconquista brought together large numbers of people who spoke different dialects. These migrants voluntarily simplified their ways of speaking so they could communicate with each other. The defining work of King Alfonso X in the thirteenth century, and of Antonio de Nebrija two centuries later, codified and reinforced this fundamental characteristic of Spanish.

Nevertheless, over the sixteenth and seventeenth centuries, a number of sounds in Spanish disappeared, like *sh* (represented by *x*), The *ts* sound (written *ç*), soft *z* (written *s*), *v, di* (written *g*), and *ds* (written *z*) also disappeared. At the same time, a number of sounds from regional varieties of Spanish—particularly Old Castilian—spread, including the guttural *h* (written *j*), soft *h* (written *g*), and *th* (written *c* or *z*).

Some of the changes happened suddenly. The writer Benito Arias Montano reported that in 1560, speakers of Andalusian Spanish pronounced the *s* differently from *z* and *c* (both of which they pronounced, like speakers in Old Castile and Toledo, *th*). But just twenty years later, Andalusians switched to *seseo,* pronouncing all these sounds indistinguishably as *s.*

Hundreds of doctoral theses would not be enough to unravel the chaos of shifting pronunciation in the period. As pronunciation changed, writers were sent scrambling for new spellings. The new *x* sound was exactly the same as the one familiar to northerners and rendered with a *j*. Writers didn't know when to use *x* or *j*. The two letters were actually used interchangeably until writers began to reserve the *x* for the *ks* sound in Greek- or Latin-derived terms.

In Spain, writers and lexicographers were fairly thorough when it came to changing *x* to *j*. They were less so in Mexico, where the spelling of place-names like Mexico, Texas, and Oaxaca were not updated. The Mexicans kept the *x* pronounced *sh*, because of its importance in Nahuatl. In fact, the Nahuatl influence in Mexico warded off pronunciation changes that were taking place in Spain. During the seventeenth century, Spanish pronunciation morphed into the harsher MeHico and TeHas. But Mexicans retained the Nahuatl pronunciations *Meshico* and *Teshas*. In the United States, *Chicano* is a remnant of the period when Texicanos was pronounced *Teshicanos*—in English, this morphed into *Chicanos*.

The pronunciation changes did not gain instant acceptance in Spain: some even provoked linguistic mudslinging between northerners and southerners. Castilians regarded the Andalusian custom of pronouncing *ll* like *y* as a *vulgarismo andaluz despreciable* (despicable Andalusian vulgarism). Conversely, Andalusians declared the northern custom of pronouncing *v* like *b* repulsive. But the acrimony didn't endure. Both groups ended up adopting both of these pronunciations over the course of the century.

Given the enormous shifts in spelling and pronunciation going on in seventeenth-century Spain, it's worth wondering why Spanish spelling didn't become as inconsistent as English spelling—English pronunciation was shifting during the period as well. The reason was, quite simply, that the Spanish, inheritors of a well-established normative language tradition, sought order.

In the sixteenth and seventeenth centuries, Spain produced many grammars, dictionaries, and *ortografías* in the tradition of Antonio de Nebrija's work. But the rapidly shifting sound system explains, at least partly, why Spanish speakers developed such a penchant for spelling guides.

Following in the footsteps of Nebrija, a number of grammarians published influential *ortografías*, starting with Alejo Venegas, in 1531, whose *Tractado de orthographía y accentos en las tres lenguas principales* (Treaty of Spelling and Accents in the Three Main Languages) compared Spanish to Latin, Greek, and Hebrew.

The great dictionary of the period was Sebastián de Covarrubias's (1539–1613) *Tesoro de la lengua castellana o española,* published in 1611. It was the first dictionary to describe Castilian entirely *in* Castilian, and the first monolingual dictionary in Europe. (Six years earlier, Jean Nicot had published a similar work in French in which only 80 percent of the definitions were written in French, the other 20 percent in Latin.) His definitions have none of the clinical neatness of a modern dictionary. They are full of notes, including songs, comments, and personal anecdotes. Covarrubias's *Tesoro* did have shortcomings, though. He was in his sixties when he started it. Conscious that his years were numbered, he cut corners to speed things up, with the result that his definitions got shorter starting at the letter *d.* Still, this was the best work in the 220 years between Nebrija's dictionary and the founding of Spain's Real Academia de la lengua a century later, in 1713. It included 17,000 entries, with 2,200 added in a supplement in 1612.

Some sixteenth-century grammarians sought to make Spanish absolutely phonetic, but the initiatives never took root. The author Gonzalo Correas, who signed his works "Korreas," wrote two books, in 1627 and 1630, calling for Spanish to become fully phonetic. He proposed turning both the hard *c* and *q* into *k,* and turning both the soft *c* and *z* into *s.* These recommendations were part of his magnum opus *Ortografía Kastellana, nueva i perfeta,* but no one followed them until two centuries later, when the Venezuelan grammarian Andrés Bello made similar suggestions.

Oddly, although Spanish phonetics shifted, the grammar

changed little. One of the few changes concerned articles. The feminine definite article *la* had been established for a long time, but for the masculine equivalent, speakers hesitated among *el, le,* and *lo*. In the seventeenth century they finally settled on *el*. However, Spanish has kept the peculiarity of retaining the neutral article *lo*. It refers to an idea in the abstract, like *lo mejor que* (the best that) or in the sense of "the business about," as in *lo de la huelga de mineros* (the business about the miners' strike).

Few people in Siglo de Oro Spain could afford to own their own reference works, so they looked to poems, novellas and, more important, plays for models of the new writing standards. The Spanish golden age produced an enormous quantity of great poetry, prose, and dialogue, and this gave a huge push to the standardization of the language.

Theater was the supreme literary genre that bridged all social classes in sixteenth-century Spain. People pushed through crowds for an hour to get a standing spot from which they could watch a play. The actual theaters were often no more than canvases slung between two houses; people who lived nearby rented their balconies to women or the gentry. Madrid had dozens of daily performances, usually with packed houses. Plays were one-performance shows where actors went on stage having barely learned their lines. The tremendous appetite for theater forced playwrights to be prolific: a playwright who had not written one hundred plays was thought to lack inspiration.

The creative genius of the period was Félix Lope de Vega (1562–1635), who wrote a staggering eighteen hundred plays and three thousand sonnets, or three times what prolific writers like Balzac, Dickens, Tolstoy, and Galdós ever produced. It's hard to fathom how anyone could be so productive, especially since Lope de Vega spent parts of his life as a soldier and experimenting with the priesthood (which did not prevent him from fathering fifteen children from his two wives and five other women). Cervantes called him a *Monstruo de la Naturaleza* (Monster of Nature).

A contemporary of Shakespeare, Lope de Vega is regarded as one of the inventors of modern theater as we know it. The subjects of his plays ran the gamut, from the creation of the world to the life of shepherds in mythical Arcadia to the life of St. Isidore to the voyages of Columbus to the death of Francis Drake to the love life of common folk. Like Shakespeare, Lope de Vega was among the first playwrights to create characters with psychological depth, structured dialogue, and appropriate costumes—before that, anything went. Yet unlike Shakespeare, he mixed comedy and tragedy in a single play, and ignored classical conventions like the unity of action, time, and place. Whereas medieval plays were always static, Lope de Vega was all about movement, even transporting characters back and forth across the ocean.

The three recurrent themes of Lope de Vega's plays are love, faith, and honor. While love and faith were common themes in all European theater, honor was a peculiarity of Spanish theater. In fact, it plays the same role as the Fates in Greek tragedy: honor pushes heroes to do things they don't necessarily want to do, to the point of killing someone who attacked your honor, even if it's a friend or a son.

Of all the writers of the Siglo de Oro, Pedro Calderón de la Barca (1600–1681) explored the theme of honor to its fullest in the two hundred lyric poems, comedies, and dramatic pieces he wrote over his career. Calderón, known for perfecting the "cape-and-sword" plays, explores the theme of honor in its most abhorrent forms. Unlike Lope de Vega, he was a highbrow aristocrat who refused to cater to the public's taste for action—to him, action was secondary to the exploration of psychological depths. His work inspired the French playwright Pierre Corneille's famous play *Le Cid* and the German romantics, who rediscovered Calderón in the nineteenth century and worshipped him as Shakespeare's equal—a bit of a stretch. Still, Calderón was the last great Baroque playwright and writer, and his death in 1681—which left a void that took two centuries to fill—is generally the date historians use as the end of the Siglo de Oro.

Along with theater, Spanish writers broke ground in prose, which was quickly becoming the most popular type of writing among the general public and even among the learned. This fondness for prose, peculiar to Spain in the period, probably grew from the influence of Oriental stories translated into Latin and Spanish in the previous centuries.

The most popular prose genre was the novella, in particular the *libros de caballería* (chivalric novellas). Inspired by French epics, chivalric romances were common in Europe but wildly popular in Spain. *Amadis de Gaula*, a smash hit by Garci Rodríguez de Montalvo in 1508, sparked the vogue. The three-book work tells the story of Prince Amadis of Gaul, abandoned at birth on a boat, then raised by Scottish knights. It recounts the adventures and setbacks of the knight as he searches for his origins. Montalvo's story was so successful that it inspired a wave of knight-errantry tales in Spain.

The other popular sub-genre in Spain was the sentimental romance. Its prototype was *Tragicomedia de Calisto y Melibea*. The work, published by Fernando de Rojas in 1499, reads like a long dialogue. Until 1634, 109 editions of *La Celestina* appeared, and it was translated into Italian, German, French, and English. The book is better known by its nickname of *La Calestina*, after a secondary character, Celestina, who concocts a scheme that allows the protagonist, Calisto, to talk to his beloved Melibea. The plan seems to be working until Calisto falls from a ladder while trying to scale her garden wall and dies from head wounds. Grief stricken, Melibea hurls herself from a tower. Sound familiar? Some scholars speculate that Shakespeare might have borrowed elements for his *Romeo and Juliet*.

In reaction to the ever-popular chivalric and sentimental genres, Spanish writers began to experiment with antiheroes and forged the decidedly anti-idealistic genre of *picaresque* novels (from *pícaro*, rogue or rascal). These were satirical episodic tales about characters pulling themselves out of misery via decidedly unchivalric means. The first novella of the genre, published in 1554, was *La vida de Lazarillo de Tormes y de sus fortunas y adversidades* (The Life of Lazarillo de Tormes and of his Fortunes and Adversities). It was published anonymously, no doubt because it was packed with heresies. Mateo Alemán's 1599 *Vida del pícaro Guzmán de Alfarache* (Life of the Rogue Guzmán de Alfarache) was the first to feature the word *pícaro* in it. Tremendously popular, it was imitated instantly, then quickly translated into other European languages.

The *pícaro* was not just a literary invention. Golden age Spain was rife with such characters. Often a former student or soldier, the *pícaro* was a cynical, amoral, and antisocial ruffian who lived on the fringes of society among vagrants and scoundrels, beggars and swindlers, professional thieves and hired killers, common assassins and impoverished hidalgos. The theme is already present in *La Celestina,* where the title character is a brothel keeper. Most picaresque plots revolve around cheats and prostitutes, living in a general climate of hypocrisy, who are trying to escape their binds by cutting deals with complacent husbands and corrupt magistrates.

The influence of the picaresque novel (the expression was coined only in 1815) on Spanish and world literature was enormous. The genre inspired all the antihero literature and films of the twentieth century. Among non-Spanish classics, the genre influenced Alain-René Lesage's *Gil Blas* and Henry Fielding's *Tom Jones,* not to mention the plots of the first six novels of Dickens, which are all driven by the themes of hunger and poverty—vintage picaresque. The *Ocean's Eleven* (as well as *Twelve* and *Thirteen*) films are contemporary cinematic renditions of the picaresque genre.

The picaresque no doubt appealed to its readers because it reflected the reality of city life, which was far from golden, and criticized the Christian or chivalric ideals. Not every Spaniard got a share of New World gold, and many of the conquistadores who did were glorified scoundrels. In Seville, a business city where African slaves outnumbered hidalgos, people made fortunes one week and fell into misery the next. Sevillians loaded ships destined for the New World with wine, oil, soap, ceramic tiles, cloth, and mercury, and unloaded gold, silver, sugar, and rawhides from the returning ships. Madrid's streets were cluttered with beggars who ate at the soup kitchens of monasteries. People gathered to hear gossip at the *mentideros* (lie parlors)—a pun between *mendigar* (to beg) and *mentir* (to lie). At the most celebrated *mentidero,* just behind Madrid's Plaza Mayor on the steps of the monastery of San Felipe el Real, people gathered to talk about the wars in the Netherlands or what was going on in the king's bed.

In Carlos Fuentes's words, picaresque novels proved "that all views of life, the low as well as the high, can fascinate and that a realistic representation of life, even if it portrays the ugly, the grotesque, the unpleasant, the crude and the repulsive can be made appealing."

And then, in a category all his own, was Miguel de Cervantes Saavedra with his *El Ingenioso hidalgo Don Quixote de la Mancha* (The Ingenious Hidalgo Don Quixote de la Mancha), one of the world's most widely read and translated books. Cervantes was the first writer to fuse the chivalric novel and the picaresque, probably because he struggled all his life to avoid falling into the dregs of Spanish society, where his bad luck perpetually threatened to lead him. Given his ongoing financial struggles, this son of a failed surgeon, born in 1547, ended up living a surprisingly long life—he died in Madrid in 1616 at age sixty-eight.

Miguel de Cervantes's life was an incredible series of misadventures and reversals of fortune. His occupations ranged from valet, soldier, slave, and prisoner to tax collector, poet, playwright, and novelist. As an active soldier, he took part in the epic naval Battle of Lepanto in 1571, where he lost the use of his left hand. He was captured a few years later by Algerian corsairs and lived five years as a slave until his family came up with the money for the ransom. As a tax collector, he was sued for embezzlement—he was always on the verge of personal bankruptcy—which earned him five years in a Seville jail.

Cervantes composed a good quantity of poetry at the beginning of his career, but he would have more success in drama. Surprisingly, he never managed to secure royal patronage, even though he spent years hanging around the king's court in Madrid vying for it. His efforts probably failed because he refused to flatter the nobles. His grating sense of humor, and the fact that some of his works were censored, probably didn't help his cause.

Cervantes began composing *Don Quixote* while he was in jail. The story was of Alonso Quixano, a retired gentleman from an unnamed village in La Mancha. Quixano is so obsessed with books of chivalry that when he looks at his old mare, he sees a battle horse instead. A plain farm girl becomes an elegant, desirable lady, and an inn is transformed into a castle. After being "knighted" by the innkeeper, Don Quixote sets off with his "squire," his faithful sidekick Sancho Panza, who tries to bring him down to earth. Their adventures begin when Don Quixote attacks windmills that he imagines are ferocious giants. Don Quixote's imagination also transforms subsequent encounters with a prostitute, a goatherd, a soldier, a priest, an escaped convict, and a scorned lover into episodes of a chivalrous, but pointless, quest. When the story draws to an end, this eternal dreamer, defeated and trampled, returns to his village, renounces knight-errantry, and announces his intention to retire as a shepherd.

Although *Don Quixote* is regarded as the world's first modern novel, contemporary readers usually find it a difficult read—like most "classics." Like *Moby-Dick,* the best-known scenes constitute only about sixty pages of the entire work. Most of its 668 pages are filled with disjointed tall tales where the levity of the work is a bit elusive, arising as it does from pure exaggeration and verbosity, as well as Sancho Panza's comments.

Don Quixote is important as a work of social commentary on

Golden Age Spain. Don Quixote himself is a hidalgo, a member of the lowest rung of the nobility. Exempted from direct taxation, immune from debtor prison, forbidden to work, hidalgos had pedigree but no means. So the only thing they could really trade in was their honor. This is obvious in Don Quixote's penchant for intervening violently in matters that do not concern him, as well as his disinclination to pay off debts, a tendency that frequently lands him and Sancho in a fix. Yet Don Quixote fights and suffers for his knightly ideals as he attempts to right the wrongs of the world, protect the weak and oppressed, and bring about what he calls the "Golden Age."

As Carlos Fuentes puts it, Miguel de Cervantes's work dug into much deeper themes than honor. Through what appears to be an innocent satire on the novels of chivalry, Cervantes creates a world of multiple points of view. In short, *Don Quixote* is about uncertainty and doubt.

And in that sense, Cervantes foretold exactly where Spain was heading.

17. Sunset on Spanish

WHILE GREAT BRITAIN WAS COLONIZING Africa and Asia in the nineteenth century, the British famously dubbed their colonial possessions "the empire on which the sun never sets." But the expression was already two centuries old by that time. It had been coined by a Spanish priest, Fray Francisco de Ugalde, who wrote about *el imperio en el que nunca se pone el sol* in the 1520s.

The empire he was referring to was, of course, Spain's.

In Ugalde's day, under Charles V (r. 1516–1556), Spain had taken possession of the New World colonies, the Low Countries, Burgundy, Austria, and southern Italy. This empire didn't yet span the globe, but it would soon. Charles's son, Felipe II (r. 1556–1598), colonized the Philippines and annexed Portugal—which added one more empire to his own, including India, Japan, and most of Africa's west coast.

In the two centuries the Hapsburgs ruled Spain, Spanish not only spread across the planet; it also got as close as it ever would to being Europe's lingua franca.

In April 1536, Charles introduced Spanish as a diplomatic tongue when he addressed the pope, a group of cardinals, and some French and Venetian ambassadors, on a visit to Rome. Charles's choice had nothing to do with linguistic preferences—the king was born and raised in Ghent, and learned Spanish only when he took the Spanish Crown, at the insistence of the Castilian Cortes Generales (parliament). When he addressed the pope in Spanish, Charles made a political statement: Spain was rising as a European power, and its language was rising with it.

The sixteenth and seventeenth centuries held a lot of promise for both Spain and its language. Spanish culture, literature, habits, and customs were revered in France, Flanders, Austria, Bohemia,

Germany, England, Sweden, and beyond. Spanish poetry flourished among Italy's high society. Italians hailed Spanish manners
as the best in Europe.

Because of this sway, most European languages borrowed heavily from Spanish over the period. Even though Britain and Holland considered Catholic Spain their archenemy, their languages
absorbed Spanish words. A number of Spanish borrowings in English came from New World novelties (cigar, mosquito, tomato,
barbecue, alligator); many more described habits and customs of
the Spaniards themselves, such as booby (from *bobo*), castanets
(from *castañeta*), grandee (from *grande*), desperado, escapade, guitar, jade, lime, oregano, parade, peccadillo (small sin, from *pecado*),
piccaninny (from *pequeño*), plaza, poncho, punctilio, sherry (from
jerez), siesta, and vigilante. Many military and technological borrowings also entered English, like bandoleer (from *bandolera*), com-
rade (from *camarada*), cask (from *casco*), cargo, embargo, flotilla,
jennet (from *jínete*), and stockade (from *estacada*).

Not surprisingly, French absorbed more Spanish words than
did any other European language: since the ninth century, large
numbers of French and Spanish had been regularly crossing the
border into each other's countries, even during the Wars of Religion. The French words *désinvolte* (casual, via Italian), *bravoure*
(bravery), *grandiose, fanfaron* (boastful), *matamore* (braggart), and
jonquille (daffodil) all come from Spanish. The French even adopted the cedilla (*ç, cédille*), which became the French diacritical
mark indicating that a *c* should be pronounced like *s*, though curiously, this happened just as the cedilla was disappearing from
Spanish. The famous French ethic of language purism was built on
a concept originally from Spain: the French adopted the Spanish
idea of *buen uso* (good usage) defined by Antonio de Nebrija.

Spanish literature was read all over Europe. Original works
were published in Spanish in Milan, Venice, Lyons, Paris, Rouen,
Antwerp, and Amsterdam. Translators, interpreters, and teachers
were in constant demand. The teaching of Spanish as a foreign

language reached its peak, especially in France, where it became a veritable cottage industry. To this day, more French people study Spanish as a second language than all other Europeans combined.

The popularity of Spanish spawned a series of translation dictionaries of European languages, the closest thing anyone had to learning guides at the time. In 1591, the English grammarian Richard Percyval published his famous *Bibliotheca Hispanica, Containing a Grammar, with a Dictionarie in Spanish, English and Latine*. In 1597 in Paris, César Oudin (royal professor of Spanish) wrote *Grammaire espagnole*, which continued to be reprinted until 1913. Oudin was as passionate as he was knowledgeable about Spanish, and carried on a life-long rivalry with the Spanish grammarian Ambrosio de Salazar. The 1611, *Tesoro de la lengua* by Covarrubias quickly inspired translation dictionaries in French, English, and Italian—César Oudin's *Thresor de deux langues française et spagnole* and the English Hispanist John Minsheu's *Ductor in linguas* (Guide into Tongues).

While the fortunes of Spain rose, Spain's Hapsburg kings were also planting the seeds of decline.

Charles V, the preeminent Spanish king of the sixteenth century, was long-lived, intelligent, and a visionary. When he came to power in 1516, he changed the motto of the Spanish Crown from *Nec plus ultra* (in Latin, meaning "Nothing further beyond") to *Plus ultra* (meaning "Further beyond"). Charles knew that Spain's future was in America. His goal was to shift Spain's focus from the Mediterranean basin to the Atlantic Ocean. He even made the first plan to dig a canal across the Isthmus of Panama.

But things soon went awry. In 1520, Charles inherited the crown of the Holy Roman Empire. That dragged him back into European affairs just when Europe was about to be engulfed in the Wars of Religion. Spain continued to acquire new territories in Europe—including Bohemia and Hungary—but neglected its American territories. Charles tried to avoid a train wreck: he knew that Spain couldn't hang on to the Americas if it overextended itself in Europe. So before he abdicated, he downsized the European empire by handing over some of his eastern territories, including Austria, to a lesser branch of the Hapsburg dynasty.

Unfortunately, his successor wasn't as farsighted. Spain's next king, Felipe II, was as intelligent as his father but had his sights set squarely on Europe. He inaugurated his reign by building the first professional army in Europe, hiring 100,000 paid soldiers, then beefing up Spain's naval fleets. His objective: protect Spain from the rising Ottoman Empire, defeat Protestantism, and make Spain the hegemonic power in Europe, no less.

In 1571, Felipe II took on the Turks. He put Spain at the head of a massive fleet of the Holy League that had 68,000 Christians manning 212 galleys armed with 1,815 guns. The Christian army attacked the Ottoman fleet off the coast of Greece in Lepanto and sent thirty thousand Turks to the bottom of the ocean, giving Spain—and Christians—supremacy over the Mediterranean for the first time in ten centuries.

Felipe II then tried to strengthen Spain's position in Europe by marrying foreign queens. His first bride was the Catholic Mary I of England, whom he married in 1554, offering her as a wedding gift the world's largest pearl, the thirty-one-carat La Peregrina, discovered in Panama decades earlier. (Richard Burton would one day offer it to Elizabeth Taylor as a Valentine's Day gift.) But when Bloody Mary—so named for her treatment of dissenters—died in 1558, Felipe's plan to oversee English affairs died with her. The king never managed to keep up good relations with England after that, and from 1585 to 1604, Spain and England were at war.

This war brought Spain more humiliations, notably the sinking of Spain's Great Armada, during Felipe II's attempt to invade England. The battle wasn't a glorious one, mainly because it didn't happen. Spain had sent 130 ships to the port of Gravelines, in northern France, to embark thirty thousand Flemish soldiers for the landing in England. Spain was embroiled in a series of naval skirmishes with British ships, but it was a storm that sank 90 percent of the Spanish ships, drowning twenty thousand sailors.

In short, after scooping up gobs of European territory in the sixteenth century, Spain experienced a series of setbacks in the seventeenth. One of the most severe was the loss of Portugal in 1640, just sixty years after Spain had annexed it.

Spain's kings were a big part of the problem: they suffered from inbreeding. Even Charles had shown signs of it. He had epilepsy and an overdeveloped jaw that complicated chewing his food to the point that he usually ate alone. But he perpetuated the royal policy of heirs marrying their cousins, strengthening alliances at the price of weakening the royal line.

Things had gotten much worse by the time of Felipe II's successors, particularly Charles II (1665–1700), the last member of the Hapsburg line, who was feeble-minded and whose tongue was so oversized he had difficulty closing his mouth. Nature has a way of stopping such indignities: Charles failed to produce an heir. But this brought about the 1701–1714 War of the Spanish Succession, between the Hapsburg and Bourbon dynasties, which sent Spain to new diplomatic lows in Europe.

By the eighteenth century, Spain had lost all hope of becoming the supreme power of Europe. And when Spain declined, so did the prospect *of Spanish* as a European lingua franca.

Spain was the spiritual center of the Counterreformation during the violent Wars of Religions that pitted Catholic and Protestant Europe against each other from 1524 to 1648. So, not surprisingly, British and Dutch history has tended to vilify and demonize characters like Charles V and especially his son Felipe II, and then project that interpretation onto all Spaniards.

As a matter of fact, the persistent use of the word *Spaniard,* with the strong negative undertone all English words ending in -*ard* carry, attests to this age-old discrimination. *Spaniard* comes from Old French *Espaignart,* yet the French have long since adopted the neutral *Espagnol.* The Italians, the Germans, and the Portuguese use neutral terms in their languages, but in English, the noun *Spanish* applies to a group or the nationality while a Spanish individual is a *Spaniard.* A number of Protestant countries maintain the same distinction, including the Dutch, who use the *Spanjaarden* rather than *Spaanse,* and the Swedes, who use *Spanjorer.*

This word reflects the abundance of prejudices about Spain and Spaniards in English-speaking and Protestant cultures. Three and a half centuries after the Wars of Religion, these prejudices blended into others, including a negative perception of Mexicans. Spanish nationalist historians in the early twentieth century summarized the whole school of Hispanophobia as *leyenda negra* (black legend).

On the other hand, religious orthodoxy really did handicap Spain and hasten its decline. The Inquisition was a doubled-edged sword. While it gave the Spanish Crown stupendous political and social control over its population and fostered a vibrant form of mystical Catholicism in Spain, it stymied the intellectual advances that the humanist movement was bringing to the rest of Europe. During the reigns of the Hapsburgs, the religious zealotry that had once fueled the Reconquista isolated Spain from the intellectual progress that was happening everywhere else in Europe.

Nothing illustrates the link between Spain and the Catholic faith quite like the Escorial palace that Felipe II built outside of Madrid. From the outset, the building was intended to be both a palace and an abbey, to celebrate Felipe's victory over the French in Saint-Quentin in 1557. But the Escorial is no Versailles. It has none of the white walls, brightly lit halls, mirrors, and abundant gold ornamentation of the famous French palace. Its gray stone walls are thick, and its rooms are dark. With the exception of a fabulous library and several beautiful frescoes and tapestries, the overall mood of the palace is austere.

The design was deliberate. Unlike Versailles, the Escorial was not built for pleasure or as a showcase for a monarchy's splendor. It was built to demonstrate the unity of the Spanish Crown and the

Catholic faith. The king and the queen's apartments were designed to communicate directly with the abbey's enormous basilica so the monarchs could listen to mass nonstop, if they so pleased.

There is no doubt that religious sentiment in Spain during the Hapsburg era was genuine, intense, and mystical. Spaniards' faith is manifested in the works of seventeenth-century painters like El Greco. Madrid's Prado Museum, as well as thousands of churches throughout Spain and the Americas, displays row upon row of intense religious paintings that depict saints shedding tears and Christ figures dripping with blood, their knees and elbows scraped to the bone.

Spain's spiritual elite of the period swarmed to monastic life, joining new religious orders such as the Jesuits, Carmelites, and Augustinians. In 1625, there were nine thousand monasteries in Spain, and as many convents. In a population of eight million, two hundred thousand Spaniards were members of the clergy—twice as many Spaniards as there were in Felipe II's army.

But it was not just the fervor that set Spain apart from the rest of Europe: Spain was the only country in Europe that actually controlled the religion its inhabitants practiced. Spain had achieved this, of course, by getting the pope to authorize a national Inquisition, which he did in 1478.

The Inquisition turned religion into public theater. By the seventeenth century, the number of "proven" miracles had doubled, encouraged by the creation of *cofradías* and *hermandades* (brotherhoods), whose hooded adherents marched in hundreds of religious processions. The chief purpose of the brotherhoods was to demonstrate penance or piety, but processions were also organized to pray for rain, or for the rain to stop.

And the Inquisition was remarkably effective. The mere thought of being brought before it was enough to keep Spaniards in line—in fact, during the forty-four years of Felipe IV's reign, only thirty heretics were actually burned.

But the Inquisition went too far. During the four centuries it was in force, it turned Spain into a hub of racial and intellectual rectitude, and eroded Spanish culture, diminishing the prospects of the Spanish language in the process.

The Inquisition's policy of converting or expelling Jews and Muslims produced a crippling mentality of *limpieza de sangre* (purity of blood) in Spain. Proof of pedigree became so important that the Spanish ended up resisting all innovation to the point of dismissing talented thinkers and creators. The painter Diego Velázquez (one of the stars of the Prado) spent his life proving his purity of blood and *limpieza de oficio* (purity of trade). In such a climate, even conversos were doubted, which fostered even more orthodoxy. People were suspected of being *novo cristianos* (new Christians) five, six, or even seven generations after their families converted.

It was not Spain's intense Catholic belief per se that impeded intellectual developments. The Order of the Jesuits, for instance, was founded specifically to promote education. It was established in Paris in 1534 by a group of seven theology students—including five Spanish priests—and run by a Spaniard of Basque origin, Ignatius de Loyola. The goal of the order was to foster leadership in both the church and the secular world. The Jesuits made an impressive number of intellectual achievements. Famous members of the order include Honoré Fabri (1607–1688), who furthered studies in probabilistic mathematics, Athanasius Kircher (1601–1680), who discovered microbes, Alexandre de Rhodes (1591–1660), who created the modern version of Vietnamese writing, and later, Georges Lemaître (1894–1966), who developed the big bang theory.

At the beginning of the Hapsburg dynasty, the Spanish were interested in intellectual progress of all kinds. There had been great enthusiasm for universities. Saragossa attracted students from Aragón. Valencia specialized in medicine. Castile had universities in Salamanca and Valladolid that specialized in Roman and Spanish law. Charles V himself had admired Erasmus (1466–1536), a luminary of the European Renaissance who promoted humanism

and argued for church reform. Felipe II made the library the centerpiece of the Escorial, because he wanted to create a spiritual and
intellectual center for the Counterreformation.

But religious orthodoxy resulted in authorities clamping down
on free thought and teaching. In a way, a language is a key that
opens the wonders of another culture. And the more wonders, the
more people want the key. Sixteenth- and seventeenth-century
Spanish was losing its usefulness because Spain was cutting itself
off from, rather than participating in, new intellectual developments. In 1559, the Grand Inquisitor Fernando de Valdés not only
created an index of forbidden books but went as far as forbidding
Spaniards from leaving Spain to study elsewhere. In doing so, he
effectively shut Spain out of the Renaissance and the early phase of
the Enlightenment. Erasmus's books were banned in Spain after
Luther's Reformation. Cervantes does not even dare allude to what
he owes to Erasmus, although the "prince of humanists" is believed
to have been one of the great Spanish writer's foremost influences.

Ultimately, this self-inflicted isolation handicapped Spain.
While Isaac Newton was developing his theory of gravitation and
René Descartes was inventing analytic geometry, university professors in Spain were punching and kicking each other in fights over
whether or not Adam remained incomplete when God removed
one of his ribs.

Starting in 1557, the Hapsburgs also progressively drained Spain's
royal coffers. Nothing was too grandiose for them. Austere as they
are, the Escorial palace and abbey are big enough to hold both
Versailles and Buckingham Palace. The Hapsburgs didn't have a
cash flow problem. During the collective reigns of the Hapsburg
kings, millions of pieces of eight and doubloons flowed into Spain.
The kings could procure anything silver could buy—and ignore all
financial considerations. Felipe II, for instance, chose Madrid as
Spain's capital even though it is not located on a river and required
supplies to be shipped by mule. Thanks to the incredible means at

his disposal, he was able to build the enormous Escorial in a mere twenty-one years and finish by 1584.

But strangely, Spain ended up defaulting on loans every twenty years or so over the course of the Hapsburg dynasty. Why? Spain had too much of a good thing. The gold and silver that flowed into Spain from the New World ended up almost ruining the Spanish economy.

During Felipe II's forty-four-year reign, prices rose by 500 percent. This made foreign goods extremely cheap and destroyed well-established local industries. In Toledo, the number of textile factories dropped from hundreds in 1596 to a mere fifteen by 1646. In Burgos, the raw wool industry collapsed. Spain's middle class took to investing in *juros* (government bonds) instead of businesses. Peasants had no money to invest in equipment, so yields fell, forcing people to survive on rye bread, cheese, and onions (as well as olives in Andalusia).

Smuggling became rampant in the colonies, where settlers sought to buy cheaper British, Dutch, and French goods. That further fueled the downward spiral of Spain's economy. The Crown owed most of the New World's gold and silver to bankers and creditors even before it left Havana. But because the silver kept flowing in, the Hapsburgs kept spending it.

Public finances were complicated by the fact that the Spanish Crown ran a huge administration in a loosely tied country. Kingdoms like Aragón, Valencia, and Galicia, nominally under the Castilian Crown, hardly paid taxes. Castilians bore the brunt of taxation. Under Felipe II's reign alone, taxes increased by 430 percent while average income increased by only 80 percent.

In the last half of the seventeenth century, Spain lost its preeminence, piece by piece, as its European territory was whittled away. In 1640 it lost both the Low Countries and Portugal, then in 1659 it lost a number of Catalan provinces. Spain also forfeited territory to France in the humiliating peace treaty of 1660.

In short, the Hapsburg kings ended up squandering all the

cultural prestige and the capital of sympathy they had built. They fought more wars than they could pay for, emptying Spain's royal coffers in the process, and then threw their weight behind a brand of religious fundamentalism that stunted intellectual breakthroughs in Spanish, isolating the Spanish from the developments happening in Europe.

Yet amazingly, despite these blunders, the Spanish Empire didn't explode. At the end of the Hapsburg dynasty, during the second half of the eighteenth century, Spain controlled 7.7 million square miles of territory, or forty times more land than the territory of Spain itself.

So even though the sun was setting on Spain, the destiny of the Spanish language was just beginning to unfold.

18. The Bourbon Identity

"BE A GOOD SPANIARD, my son . . . but don't forget you were born in France."

With those parting words, King Louis XIV of France sent his seventeen-year old grandson, Philippe, off to become king of Spain in 1700. The last Hapsburg king in Spain hadn't produced an heir, and the young French prince had the strongest claim to the Spanish throne. So Philippe went to Spain, became Felipe V, and ushered in a century of Bourbon kings.

The Bourbon dynasty did not start out smoothly. Britain, the Netherlands, and Austria favored the Hapsburg pretender to the Spanish Crown. The dispute pitted European powers against each other for thirteen years in what came to be called the War of the Spanish Succession (1701–1714).

But the war didn't stop Felipe V from reorganizing Spain. The Crown of Castile had been running both its state and empire loosely before he arrived. After redecorating an entire wing of the Escorial palace in the style of Versailles, Felipe really got down to work. His objective was to turn Spain into a modern nation-state and strengthen Spain's grip on its colonies, starting with some centralization. In other words, he wanted to run Spain as if it were France.

A good Frenchman, Felipe understood exactly how language could help him. He knew that Castilian had to be *the* language of administration, in both Spain and the colonies. That wasn't yet the case in either place. Although Galician and Basque were now mainly rural, colloquial languages, Aragonese and Catalan were the languages of autonomous kingdoms and still rivaled Castilian. The Aragonese and Catalonians had even sided against the Bourbons during the War of the Spanish Succession.

Between 1707 and 1716, Felipe worked to extinguish both of

these tongues. He passed a series of *Decretos de Nueva Planta* (Decrees of Reorganization) that outlawed Aragonese and Catalan as administrative languages and forbade their teaching. He then abolished the *fueros* (charters) that granted special privileges to cities, reducing the political clout of each. With Aragon and Catalonia stripped of their capacity for self-rule, their languages declined. Felipe ousted local officials and replaced them with Castilian-speaking civil servants from Madrid.

Felipe didn't invent this technique for erasing nonofficial languages. French kings had been using language as a political instrument for more than a century. The French Academy, established in 1635, was a tool for, among other things, consolidating the position of French in France. In 1713, Felipe created a Spanish-language academy, the Real Academia Española, modeled directly on the French Academy.

King Felipe then used a similar approach to eradicate the native languages in Spanish America. During the seventeenth century, when Spain was in economic and social decline, it had neglected its colonies and more or less left them to fend for themselves. As a result, criollos filled the power vacuum, taking the best jobs for themselves and developing their own little colonial aristocracy. Felipe knew that the criollos' power threatened Spain's grip on its colonies. So in 1718, he passed the *Leyes de India* (India Laws), which subjected all people in the Americas to Castilian law, not local law. Spain then started appointing *peninsulares* to replace criollos in administrative and executive positions in the colonies. The criollos resented the move and developed derogatory terms for *peninsulares,* like *gachupines* in Mexico (pretentious hidalgos), *chapetónes* in Peru (clumsy beginners), *maturrangos* in Buenos Aires (bad horsemen), and *godo* (Goth) in Chile.

This power play had the desired consequence: it diminished the *lenguas generales.* The new colonial officials who arrived from Madrid neither knew the native languages that had been used to communicate with the native population for the last two centuries nor cared to learn them. Nahuatl, Quechua, and Guaraní quickly declined.

Only the church continued to protect native languages. But even among clerics, attitudes were changing. A growing minority in the Catholic hierarchy believed that native languages were doing more harm than good. Indeed, training clergy in native languages had always been an enormous drain on colonial resources. What's more, as important as *lenguas generales* had been, not all the natives in the Americas understood them, or wanted to—Nahuatl, for instance, was the old imperial language of the Aztecs. Mayas, Tarascans, and Zapotecs preferred their own tongues over it and opted to speak Spanish rather than Nahuatl.

So clerics started reconsidering their position on *lenguas generales*. Things changed definitively with the arrival of Francisco de Lorenzana y Butrón. Appointed archbishop of Mexico in 1766, Lorenzana was an exemplary, enlightened Jesuit-trained bishop, but above all, a *regalista* (royalist). He decided it was time to dispense with *lenguas generales* once and for all. The year after Lorenzana was appointed, the Spanish Crown made the momentous decision to expel the Jesuit Order from the Spanish Empire (Lorenzana himself was not part of the order).

The move had more to do with Spain than the colonies per se. The Crown had been looking for ways to reduce the power of Spain's nobility. Instead of attacking the whole aristocracy, the king made examples of the Jesuits. They were not numerous, so they were relatively easy prey. Why the Jesuits, among all religious orders in the Spanish Empire? In a way, the Jesuits were victims of their own success. Being effective missionaries, they had developed a power network of their own that made the Spanish Crown nervous. In Paraguay, Jesuits ran forty semi-independent *reducciones* (missions) with up to a hundred and fifty thousand believers, where no one spoke Spanish, no one was enslaved, and no money changed hands—they ran on barter. Scholars called the Jesuit period between 1607 and 1767 the "last outpost of utopia in the New World."

In 1767, the Crown simply outlawed them. Thousands of Jesuits were expelled from the New World, destroying the Jesuits' power network and freeing property and cattle that Spain could either keep or redistribute to supporters.

Yet that also left Spain with a dilemma. In Mexico alone, 682 priests had to be replaced overnight. Since the Jesuits had spent years learning local languages, it was impossible to replace them quickly.

The only way around the problem was to have clergy stop learning native languages. Spain did the obvious: it followed Lorenzana's recommendations and terminated the *lenguas generales* policy. Clerics were instructed to preach in Castilian. Both the viceroy of Mexico and the Council of the Indies rejected the idea, but Lorenzana was determined. So he took the issue to the king.

Charles III (r. 1759–1788) was the third Bourbon king. He was both a reformer and a despot who saw things pretty much the way his predecessors had. Like many monarchs of the century, he was intrigued by the reformist ideas of *la Ilustración* (the Enlightenment)— or at least some of them. Though he was lukewarm about the political philosophy of the French *philosophes*, Charles thought he could put progressive Enlightenment ideas to use to get better returns or, as he put it, "bring my royal revenues to their proper level."

Until then, the Spanish Crown had stated, halfheartedly, that the natives should be taught Spanish, but all decrees to that effect had been watered down or ignored. Three-quarters of the inhabitants of the Americas were rural natives who spoke their own languages. In fact, Castilian appointees who ventured outside Mexico City and administrative cities reported being struck by how decidedly *not* Spanish New Spain was.

Charles decided to change that. On April 16, 1770, he published the *Real Cédula* (Royal Summons), the full title of which is a perfect summary of what was in store. It read as follows: *Real Cédula para que se destierren los diferentes idiomas que se usan en estos dominios, y solo se hable el castellano* (Royal Summons for doing away with the different languages spoken in these domains, so that only Castilian be spoken).

Archbishop Lorenzana applied the directive *al pie de la letra* (to the letter) in Mexico. Starting in 1782, the Spanish Crown paid to train civil and religious authorities in Castilian. Spanish started gaining ground in the colonies, more or less by default. As Nicholas Ostler explains in *Empires of the Word*, "[The] Indians' use of their own languages was simply wished away, as the Spanish authorities increasingly addressed them in Spanish willy-nilly. All official support for education in the indigenous languages came to be withdrawn; professorial chairs in the universities were discontinued; books written in them ceased to be published. Courts in Mexico ceased to entertain pleas written in Nahuatl." By the end of the eighteenth century, written Nahuatl, Quechua, and Guaraní had disappeared.

But Charles's *Cédula* had one unexpected result. As colonial authorities started communicating exclusively in Spanish, contacts between Castilian and native languages increased. As linguists know, more bilingualism means more borrowings between languages, and sure enough, the Spanish spoken in the Americas began absorbing more native vocabulary during this period.

We met a Spanish instructor in Puebla, Mexico, Claudia Moreno, who was passionate about literature and culture and liked to begin her classes with articles about the particularities of Mexican Spanish—specifically, the many words Mexican Spanish borrows from indigenous languages. Some are current and some have gone out of style, but they include *tacuche* (a man's suit, from the Tarascan word for "fabric"), *guango* (meaning "loose," as in clothes, from *guanoche*), *tepache* (a drink, whose name comes from *tepamani*, meaning "to thicken"), and *charal* (a thin person, but literally a type of elongated fish that lives in volcanic lakes). Nahuatl has been the main source of borrowings in Mexican Spanish, but many more native languages produced regionalisms like *huarache* or *guarache* (a type of sandal or an oval-shaped tortilla, from Tarasco), which is used a lot, even in the United States. Literally thousands of such terms, adopted long after the *Conquista,* are used in the varieties of Spanish spoken in the Americas today.

According to the Puerto Rican linguist Humberto López Morales, two-thirds of the native terms that entered the Spanish language were adopted during the eighteenth century. (The same phenomenon took place in France, in the nineteenth century, when Paris introduced universal schooling. Most of the population of France at the time spoke a regional language. As a result, the French were very bilingual for two or three generations, during which time hundreds of dialectal words entered mainstream French.)

Spain was always much more committed to its colonies in the Americas than was Britain or France. Spain held on to its empire in its entirety for a total of 320 years, after which several territories remained Spanish possessions for another seventy years, until 1898. France and Britain's empires did not remain intact nearly as long, since they had to deal with the catastrophic loss of New France and the thirteen colonies, respectively.

Yet if it hadn't been for the Bourbons, Spain's empire would probably have ended a century earlier. The Bourbons carried out a number of key reforms that consolidated the empire. They united Spain's various fleets under a single *armada* (navy), fortified more ports in the New World, then got rid of the *Flotas de Indias* (Spanish treasure fleet) and replaced them with regular lines of register ships, to facilitate trade. Trade between Spain and its colonies increased 700 percent over the course of the eighteenth century.

The Bourbons also boosted trade *between* Spain's colonies. They removed the *Casa de Contratación*'s monopoly on trade in 1778, and then eliminated the *casa* altogether a year later. This did wonders for out-of-the-way centers like Buenos Aires and Caracas, whose development had been hampered by the fact that they were run by a remote viceroyalty on the other side of the Andes, in Peru. The Bourbons also created new viceroyalties. In 1718 they founded New Granada and established its capital in Santa Fe de Bogotá (now Bogotá). The viceroyalty included the territories of present-day Venezuela, Colombia, Panama, and Ecuador. In 1776, the Bourbons created the viceroyalty of the Río de la Plata, which ruled over the entire Southern Cone (minus Chile) from Buenos Aires. In Spanish America, the population was increasing, cities were expanding, and the colonies were producing more minerals, growing more agricultural produce, and raising more livestock.

Back in Spain, the Bourbons set out to improve and modernize agriculture, industry, commerce, and the arts and sciences, following the prescriptions of Enlightenment thinkers. After establishing the Spanish language academy in 1713, they created an academy of medicine and natural science in 1734, and of fine arts in 1744 (Real Academia de Bellas Artes de San Fernando). They established economic societies—the ancestors of today's chambers of commerce. To improve agriculture, they encouraged German and Swiss Catholic immigrants to settle the southwest of Spain.

The last years of the eighteenth century were good ones. Spain made peace with Britain in 1783, and a decade of economic prosperity followed. Thanks to increased mercury production (essential to the refinement of silver), Spain had all the pieces of eight and doubloons it needed to buy what it could not produce at home.

That said, over the eighteenth century Spain lost and regained vast expenses of the Americas. It was a period of colonial horse trading. The 1750 Treaty of Madrid gave Portugal control over the entire Amazon River basin. Spain and Portugal then traded colonies south of Brazil. Portugal gave away its colony of Sacramento (now Uruguay) and Spain gave Portugal seven Guaraní missions in the upper Uruguay River. Spain and Portugal then joined forces to defeat the Jesuit-supported Guaraní (this episode in history inspired the film *The Mission*). Yet even after the Jesuits were expelled, Guaraní remained so strong that 80 percent of the population of today's Paraguay is bilingual, which is an exception on the continent.

Spain was at war with Britain and showed it could still rule the waves, at least some of the time. Spain lost Gibraltar in 1704 and spent the rest of the century challenging British naval supremacy. In 1747, during the siege of Cartagena de las Indias, Spain inflicted one of Britain's worse naval defeats, sinking 53 of Britain's 183 warships, killing 18,000 men.

The Spanish colonial empire was still holding its own. In 1763, at the end of the Seven Years War—when Britain, Spain, and France dragged most of the other major powers into a war sparked by competition over colonial empires—Spain laid hands on most of Louisiana. The British gained Florida but gave it back to Spain in 1783, as repayment for Spain supporting the insurgents in the thirteen colonies.

Britain was on the rise and the British trade empire continued pumping Spanish dollars out of the Spanish Empire and bringing them back to Britain. The Spanish Crown reacted by developing trade within its own empire and barring English—and soon American—merchant ships. Even when Spain managed to resist smuggling and keep its trade monopolies in place, Spanish dollars flowed to London, which effectively built the financial center of Europe on Spanish pieces of eight.

In Spain, only the northeast and the north managed to enter the Industrial Revolution while the rest of Spain was stifled by outmoded mercantilist policies. Thanks to the presence of lignite (a type of coal), Barcelona rose as a center of textiles in the second half of the eighteenth century. At the other end of the Pyrenees, Bilbao, the main center of the Basque country, put its rich iron ore deposits to use. Barcelona and Bilbao became the centers of Spain's industrial revolution, and the only national alternatives to Britain, the leader in producing manufactured goods. This early start in industrialization is the root of both cities' prosperity, particularly Barcelona's.

But this transformation probably came too late to save an empire that was running its course. Spanish colonial rule could be best described as enlightened despotism: there was no democracy, and dissent was brutally repressed. In Peru, a mestizo who called himself Túpac Amaru II and claimed to be a descendant of the Inca ruler Túpac Amaru, started a rebellion against Spanish authorities that spread to the Southern Cone, inspiring another Bolivian leader, Túpac Katari. Túpac Amaru II himself was quartered in a public execution, and the repression following his revolt in 1780 resulted in the deaths of 100,000 Indians. Túpac Amaru's inability to control the violence of his troops also led the criollos of Peru to side with the Crown against the natives. This pattern was repeated in every native revolt on the continent.

In the end, the idea of expelling the Jesuits in order to extinguish their sway in the colonies backfired. It was the Jesuits who had brought the reformist spirit of the Bourbons to Spanish America. The Jesuits were the continent's most enlightened clergy, who taught a liberal curriculum and "served the Spanish American élites a big dose of Descartes and Leibniz," as Carlos Fuentes wrote. In the colonies, their expulsion was felt as a terrible loss.

Ultimately, though, more than the failed rebellions in Peru and Colombia, the growing sense of criollo identity in Spain's colonies, as well as alienation from Spanish authority, fueled revolutionary spirit. By the time Spain's colonies had their own power networks and were developing their own identity, some exiled Jesuits were criollos themselves. Many ended up in Rome, and once there, they wrote about the new American identity they had developed. These writings are among the earliest reflections on a distinctly American social identity, different from that of Spain.

So in a curious twist of history, some of the earliest accounts of life in Latin America ended up being written in Italian by exiled Jesuits—like the work of one of the foremost Jesuit scholars, the

Mexican-born Francisco Xavier Clavijero, who wrote the *Ancient History of Mexico*, and the Chilean Jesuit Juan Ignacio Molina, who wrote two essays on the natural and civic history of Chile in 1782 and 1787, respectively.

In short, the Bourbons' policies had mixed results. While the Bourbons undoubtedly strengthened the position of the Spanish language in the colonies, ultimately their reign fueled the creation of a strong new Spanish American identity.

This new identity was about to—literally—revolutionize the Spanish-speaking world.

19. The Secret Lives of Language Academies

LANGUAGE ACADEMIES MATTER TO PEOPLE—AT least that's what Miguel Somovilla realized when he started working as the director of communications for Spain's Real Academia Española (Royal Academy of Spanish). A journalist, Somovilla was familiar with the history of Spain's language academy and understood its importance to Spain's literary classes, but had no idea ordinary people were interested in it.

That realization struck Somovilla in 2012, when he opened up the Academy to the public for the first time. The building, designed by the architect Miguel Aguado de la Sierra and inaugurated in 1894, is a splendid brick-and-stone neoclassical edifice across the street from the Prado in Madrid's elegant museums quarter. Its rooms and halls are adorned with lush tapestries, thick carpets, ornate furniture, and crystal lamps. Its libraries contain 120,000 books including precious ancient editions of works of Cervantes and Lope de Vega, which are stacked to the ceiling behind glass doors. It's worth seeing for its own sake.

Yet until 2012, only Spain's *académicos* (academicians) and the occasional VIP had set foot inside the building. That September, Somovilla opened the Real Academia for Madrid's annual *Noche en blanco* (White Night) festival, an all-night open-doors event. He was expecting a couple hundred visitors. Instead, three hundred people lined up in front of the Academia two hours before opening. Personnel stopped counting visitors after the first two thousand. "I had no idea people cared so much about what the Academia has done and what it represents," Somovilla said. "It was a complete revelation to me."

There is a widespread misconception in the English-speaking world that only France has a language academy. That's probably because the French have always excelled at branding their academy—and their language. Yet the French Academy, founded in 1635, was not the first of its kind. It just became the most influential, capitalizing partly on the growing influence of France and French culture. Today, most languages of large nations—including Mandarin and Hindi—have an academy, institute, office, or official committee that sets standards of use. Even small languages like Catalan, Basque, and Galician have their own regulating bodies. One of the most successful is the Academy of the Hebrew Language, located in a small pavilion in Jerusalem. It perpetuates the work of Eliezer Ben-Yehuda, who revived Hebrew as a spoken language at the end of the nineteenth century.

Effective language academies don't arbitrarily invent words, or make up rules. Nor do they force people to speak a particular way. An academy's job is to set standards of usage. And it does this, first, by listening to the people who speak it. More than police, academies act as referees. Their members listen to the different, often contradictory ways languages are used and decide which are the best. Then they recommend usages—they do not legislate. Academies generally try to make choices speakers will like. Otherwise, no one listens to them, and their work becomes futile.

Although the Real Academia Española is not as well known as the Académie française, its academics always understood the nature of their job better than their French counterparts did. It would go on to be one of the best, most effective language academies on the planet.

When Spain created the Real Academia Española in 1713, it was pretty much the last European power to do so—the Swedes, Danes, Prussians, and Russians all had academies by that time. Yet the Academia immediately distinguished itself. The reason was simple: it worked well. That was probably because Spain had a well-established tradition of language correction before it created an academy. King Alfonso X, Antonio de Nebrija, and their countless followers and imitators were de facto *académicos*. The Academia would just perpetuate their work.

The origins of Spain's language academy are similar to those of France's. The French Academy grew out of gatherings of poets that were common in the seventeenth century. In 1635, France's powerful Cardinal Richelieu simply selected one of them and made it into the country's official language academy. At that time, the ideal of language purism was growing in France. Richelieu took it upon himself to make it official. He declared that the academy would "cleanse" French and make it clear, precise, and comprehensible.

Eighty years after the founding of the French Academy, Spain had some four dozen protoacademies. Most were short-lived *tertulias,* literary societies with a varnish of formality, where writers and poets met to discuss their work. (Hernán Cortés hosted his own academy when he lived in Andalusia between 1541 and 1547.) Members of these clubs were assigned humorous monikers like Silencio (silence), Miedo (fear), Relapso (relapsed), and Lluvia (rain).

Following in Richelieu's footsteps, the Spanish noble Juan Manuel María de la Aurora Fernández Pacheco Acuña Girón y Portocarrero (1650–1726)—the eighth Marquis of Villena, for short—decided to follow the French example and create a bona fide language academy. The Marquis of Villena was a general and diplomat, and a favorite of King Felipe V. He was a *mayordomo* (steward of the king), making him one of the highest-ranking noblemen of the kingdom. Villena was also one of the most learned men of his time, who owned a fantastic library.

Villena, like the founders of most European academies, used the French Academy as a model—yet in many ways, the French Academy represented the competition. In the eighteenth century, Spanish had to contend with the fact that French and Latin were the preeminent languages of culture. Latin was still the language of instruction in Spain's universities, and it was hard to blame scholars for choosing it over Spanish. In 1713, Spanish had little more than a few half-baked grammars and out-of-date dictionaries to offer. Latin had a full toolbox of works. (It would take another century for the Spanish Crown to reform higher education and order universities in Spain to teach in Spanish.)

Outside the universities, Spanish was fighting a losing battle with French, which had been influential in Spain since the eighth century. French culture by now reigned supreme in Europe, where France led the nascent *Ilustración*. French speakers had at their disposal a complete and of up-to-date body of reference works, including dictionaries and grammars. And French was in vogue in Spain, like it was everywhere—Spanish courtesans even spoke French among themselves.

In a way, Villena decided to fight the French with French, emulating the French Academy. On August 3, 1713, he selected one of Spain's existing groups of literati and made it into an academy "like the French one." He handed his own library over to serve as the core of an *academia* library. Villena had no difficulty convincing King Felipe to rubber-stamp his project, and the king gave it his approval in October 1714. Being French, Felipe loved the idea of linguistic purity. Since he was still trying to get his kingdom to speak Castilian, the Real Academia Española served his purposes by adding a varnish of prestige to Spanish, making it more attractive.

The Real Academia quickly surpassed the French Academy, if not in reputation at least in effectiveness. Notably, Villena and his company managed to avoid some of the errors the French had made. Richelieu had entrusted the job of purifying French to authors, and authors are not necessarily good lexicographers. From the start, the members of the French Academy passively resisted their mandate to write a dictionary; for a group formed to promote the highest levels of literary expression, the task struck them as overly mechanical. And their negative attitude never really changed. *Le Diction-naire de l'Académie française* has always been considered mediocre and was used only outside France, where it offered foreigners access to France's highly normative, virtually nonexistent—but much idealized—"court language." To this day, French academicians yearn to be the very literary club they started out as.

The first *académicos* in Spain—a mix of authors, literati, and thinkers—were happy to write a dictionary. They had been selected for that purpose. (The Academia's membership eventually grew to twenty-three *académicos*, or one per letter, since the Spanish alphabet had no *j, u,* or *w* then. There are now forty-six.) The Academia's original motto was *aprueba y reprueba* (approve and reprove). After Felipe granted it official status, the motto was updated at the suggestion of the Spanish noble José Solís y Gante to *limpia, fija y da esplendor* (to clean, set, and give splendor), echoing the program King Alfonso X had carried out in the thirteenth century. The Academia's official mission was defined as "to cultivate and determine the purity and elegance of our Spanish language."

Villena and his colleagues quickly got to work on the dictionary. One of the founding members of the Academia, the great historian Andrés González de Barcia, came to the first meeting with a plan and models for a dictionary: he brought the third edition (1691) of the dictionary of the Accademia della Crusca, in Tuscany, and a 1611 dictionary, *Tesoro de la lengua castellana o española* (Thesaurus of the Castilian or Spanish Language), written by Sebastián de Covarrubias. Among the Spanish dictionaries published in the 221 years between Nebrija and the founding of the Academia, Covaburrias's was the best.

From the outset, the *académicos* prided themselves on working in a collective spirit toward a clearly defined goal. The first *académicos* worked fast, though unfortunately not fast enough for Villena, who died one year before the first volume of the *Diccionario de la lengua castellana* appeared in 1726. The sixth, and last, volume was published in 1739. It fit all the requirements of what we now consider a dictionary: it was impersonal in tone, and its entries all had the same structure: words were shown in different forms, by gender or number, then labeled by part of speech. (In contrast, Covarrubias included his personal opinions or observations in his definitions.)

Since it included quotes from hundreds of Spanish authors, including Cervantes, Lope de Vega, and Calderón de la Barca, the dictionary came to be known as the *Diccionario de autoridades* (Dictionary of Authority).

The *Diccionario de autoridades* offered thorough word definitions. In contrast, the definitions in the French Academy's dictionary were terse. *Man* was defined simply as an *animal raisonnable* (animal with reason), and *woman* as *la femelle de l'homme* (the female of man). The Academia's definition for man was more thorough:

> *Rational animal, that stands straight up, with two legs and two arms, and with its eyes set on Heavens. It is sociable, provident, astute, retentive, full of reason and good advice. It is a creation, which God made of his own hands in his image and resemblance. The word comes from the Latin* homo, *with the same meaning: and even if the true sense applies to either* man *or* woman, *the term in Castilian applies primarily to the male. In Old Castilian, the form was* home. *Fray Luis de Granada,* Symbolo de la Fé, *part 1, chap. 21:* "The Divine Providence raised men above ground, and made them tall and straight, so that they could look into Heaven and come into the knowledge of God." *Cosme Gómez de Tejada,* Leon Prodigioso, *part 1, apologo 22:* "Man is a physical compound, rational in body and soul." *(our translation)*

But the *Diccionario de autoridades* did have some drawbacks. For one, the vocabulary it contained was limited to "court language" and omitted colloquialisms as well as trade and scientific terms. It excluded most technological vocabulary (though it had lots of terms for religion, showing Spain's ongoing resistance to the Enlightenment). There were also very few descriptions of grammar. Those included were copied from Latin—the *académicos* seemed to assume that all grammars followed the same pattern as Latin logic, even though Nebrija had demonstrated the contrary two centuries earlier. The style and tone of the articles were inconsistent because each *académico* wrote his part his own way.

Much of the work of writing a dictionary consists of choosing between alternative spellings. The *académicos* decided that the letters *c* and *z* would be pronounced *th*. They made the letters *u* and *v* represent different sounds and suppressed the letters *ç* and *ss,* which were common in Old Castilian but obsolete by this time. In some cases, the *académicos* hung on to Greek and Latin etymologies; for instance, they kept the *th* of *theatro,* the *ch* of *patriarcha*, and the *ph* of *orthographía*. And in several cases, they reverted to Latin etymology, writing *doctor* and *perfecto* instead of *dotor* and *perfeto* (Italian academicians dropped the Latin etymology and spelled them *dottore* and *perfetto*).

But the *académicos* didn't retire after producing the *Diccionario de autoridades*. For the next forty years, two more works would absorb most of their energy: an *Orthographía* and a *Gramática*.

The *Orthographía,* published in 1741, was where the academy showed its true reforming spirit and its influence. It was written in the spirit of Nebrija's dictum that Spanish speakers "should strive to write as we pronounce and pronounce as we write." Like the *Diccionario,* the *Orthographía* had models. Antonio de Nebrija had published his *Orthographía* in 1517, following which one Spanish scholar after another published an *ortographía* of uneven quality every fifteen years or so. The academy's *Orthographía* went on to be its most influential work: it was small and practical, and the *académicos* updated it frequently. In the time it took the Academia to produce a new version of the *Autoridades*, it produced six new versions of the *Orthographía*. By the seventh edition, spelling had been reformed to the point that *Orthographía* had become *Ortografía*. The Academia still reedits its original *Ortografía* to this day.

The job of a good academy is to figure out what people want, and the Real Academía Española did that well. In the next decades, the Academy dropped entire sections of etymological spelling— *theatro* became *teatro*, *elephante* became *elefante*, and *patriarcha* became *patriarca*. *Philosophia* was cut down to *filosofía*, and *chímica* (chemistry) became *química*. Few contested the spelling reforms proposed in the *Ortografía*, and they became universal in a matter of years.

In 1803, the *Ortografía* gave each of the letters *x, j*, and *g*—used interchangeably for centuries—its own turf. The *ks* sound was represented by *x*; the harsher guttural *h* was represented by *j*, while the softer, hissing sound became *g*. That same year, the sounds *ch* and *ñ* were defined as letters in their own right. As the linguist Antonio Alatorre writes, the universal adoption of these new spelling standards across the Spanish-speaking world demonstrated that Spanish writers were conscious that they needed to respect the same rules and norms of Spanish no matter where they lived.

But the reforming spirit didn't turn Spanish into a fully phonetic tongue. Far from it. The letter *c*, for instance, still may represent a hard *c*, as in *cama* (bed), or a soft velar *th* as in *cero* (zero). The same sound *th,* can be represented either by the letter *c* or the letter *z*. And in Latin America, these two letters are pronounced exactly like *s*.

Why didn't the Academia go all the way and make Spanish truly phonetic? Probably because, like the French Academy, it knew that if the reforms it proposed were too radical, the literati wouldn't embrace them. So the Academia made compromises.

The work on the *Ortografía* also helped systematize a practice that has become characteristic of Spanish: hiding borrowings. Throughout the Spanish-speaking world, speakers Hispanicize words spontaneously. *Baseball* becomes *béisbol* and *computer* becomes *computador*. Other borrowings, notably from French, go through the same Hispanicization process: *ordinateur* (computer) was turned into *ordenador*. Whenever a French borrowing looks Spanish, as in the case of *avión* (aircraft), it is simply adopted, more or less the way it is written in French. Or it goes through the same Hispanicization process as the French *vent d'aval* (off-sea wind), which became *vendaval* in Spanish.

The custom of Hispanicization became characteristic of Spanglish, which quickly transposes English words into Spanish-looking equivalents—like *Unaited Esteits* (United States).

This reflex has its roots in the eighteenth-century Spanish ideology of *casticismo* or *purismo*. Though some scholars draw nuances between these terms, they amount to the same thing: rejecting neologisms or borrowings that mix foreign voices or strange turns of phrase. This was in no way exclusive to Spanish culture: the French and the English did exactly the same thing in the same period to make their languages look more genuinely Gallic and Germanic, respectively. But Spain's Academia embraced the practice from the outset. The *Ortografía* encouraged it, and still does. By providing rules on the proper Spanish way to render sounds, it gives writers tools to spontaneously Hispanicize foreign borrowings in ways that all other Spanish speakers accept. According to the rules of the *Ortografía,* the verb *to watch* will spontaneously become *wachear* or *guachear* in Spanglish.

Yet despite its influence, the recommendations of the *Ortografía* occasionally spark debates among Spanish speakers. In 2010, the eight-hundred-page *Nueva Ortografía* recommended changing the names of half a dozen letters, including *y, b,* and *v. Y* used to be called *i griega,* and the Academia recommended changing this to *yé. B,* formerly known as *b larga,* was changed to *be,* and *v* was changed to *uve* (before that it was *b baja* or *corta*). The changes seem to be taking root now, but they were polemical at the time, and the Academia was surprised by the flak it got for recommending them.

The *Ortografía* also tackled punctuation. In the 1754 edition, it recommended the use of reverted question marks and exclamation marks: ¿, ¡. In Spanish, it is customary to put the mark at the beginning of the phrase that is being emphasized. "Do you like tea?" reads "¿Te gusta el té?" and "Finish your tea!" reads "¡Termine tu té!"

This can be very useful in long paragraphs, all the more so because simple statements and questions in Spanish have the same word order: "You like tea" and "Do you like tea?" are both "Te gusta el té," with or without question marks. In fact, one reason Spanish paragraphs and sentences can afford to be much longer than in English partly owes to this ingenious punctuation system.

The reverse punctuation had been used for 150 years before the founding of the Academia, but it was the Academy that determined the proper usage, deciding, for instance, not to mark a whole sentence but only the phrase that contained the actual question or exclamation, for example: "Pedro, ¿te gusta el té?" or "Pobrecito, ¡termine tu té!" The whole Hispanic world has followed these prescriptions, although single question and exclamation marks are becoming more frequent with the increased use of keyboards.

The Spanish Academy's *Gramática* (Grammar), printed in 1771, also helped unify and standardize Spanish. The *Gramática* was one of the Academia's great successes. Writers had long been waiting for a reference work that would resolve the discrepancies in Spanish grammar. Due to popular demand, the *Gramática* was reprinted just three months after its publication. Twenty-five years later, the Academia was already working on its fourth edition.

Like the *Diccionario,* the *Gramática* was inspired by, and modeled on, precedents, but in this case, the models were Spanish. Since 1492, a number of authors had followed in the footsteps of Antonio de Nebrija and produced comprehensive Spanish grammars, including Juan de Valdés's *Diálogo de la Lengua* (Dialogue on the language, 1535), Andrés Flórez's *Arte para bien leer y escribir* (The art of reading and writing well, 1552), and Martín Cordero's, *La manera de escribir en castellano* (The way to write in Castilian, 1556). These works really amounted to how-to guides rather than formal grammars. Cristóbal de Villalón's *Gramática castellana* (Castilian grammar, 1558) was closer to a true grammar, but it still focused on practical problems. The Academia's grammar turned out to be such a success that it became the universal standard of the language for generations and was reedited, with slight modifications, for two centuries.

During the 1770s, the Academia experienced a serious crisis: the huge success of the *Ortografía* and the *Gramática* were draining all the Academia's energy and preventing the members from working on a new edition of the *Diccionario de autoridades*. At seven thousand eight hundred pages, the *Diccionario* was bulky and costly to print. Yet since this dictionary was the Academia's original raison d'être, the *académicos* knew they had to find a way to update it, but the sheer volume made this an almost impossible task. Instead, they decided to publish a kind of *autoridades* "light" that defined words with a few illustrative examples but without references to authorities. Presented in one volume instead of six, this dictionary was cheaper and easier to use.

The *académicos* themselves almost dismissed the new *Diccionario de la lengua Castellana* as a quick fix, until, to everyone's surprise, it turned out to be a resounding success—the biggest yet. Once again, the Academy had given the public exactly what it wanted. In 1793, the Academia stopped working on the *Diccionario de autoridades* altogether, and the new short dictionary became the standard.

The success of the Academia did not put an end to other scholars' efforts. In 1786, the Jesuit priest Esteban de Terreros y Pando published the landmark *Diccionario castellano con las voces de ciencias y artes y sus correspondientes en las tres lenguas francesa, latina e italiana* (Castilian dictionary with terms from science and art and their correponding terms in French, Latin, and Italian). One of the most important thinkers of the eighteenth century, Terreros y Pando (1707–1780) was the first lexicographer to provide a complete terminology for technology in Spanish, with each term translated into the other three languages. In other words, it compensated for the Real Academía's failure to include real-life vocabulary. To get a real picture of eighteenth-century Spanish, contemporary linguists use his work as well as that of the Real Academia.

Today, Spain's *académicos* work to continuously update the dictionary, letter by letter. They meet every week in the *Sala de Juntas* (plenary meeting room) of the Real Academia Española, a curiously dark room where each member takes a seat at a specially designed round table equipped with built-in microphones and a shelf for reference materials. Over the years, the Academia has succeeded where the French Academy failed (and still does): it managed to produce a new edition of its dictionary every decade, an impressive rate considering that the work is carried by out in plenary committees. These editions have not been of even quality and have rarely kept up with the times, but they have provided a universal reference for Spanish writers everywhere. As Darío Villanueva, secretary of the Academia, said, "When people identify us as members of the Real academia española, they ask us questions, make comments, and offer criticism. They really take this to heart."

It's a happy conclusion to a situation that could have ended much differently. At the time the Real Academia was enjoying its early successes, the Spanish Empire was about to explode, a situation that could easily have split the Spanish language into dozens of different dialects.

20. Riding the Tiger

IN 1999, VENEZUELAN PRESIDENT HUGO Chávez officially renamed his country the Bolivarian Republic of Venezuela. The
move underlined the fact that Venezuela had just joined the club of
Latin American nations that embraced *bolivarianismo,* or socialism
inspired by the life and works of the nineteenth-century revolutionary Simón Bolívar, who would come to be known as *El Libertador*
(the Liberator). A soldier, writer, and thinker, Bolívar was a larger-
than-life character who liberated half a dozen countries from Spanish rule. His charisma, drive, and determination inspire revolutionary
longings to this day, but the legend of El Libertador has always
overshadowed his inglorious end. Chávez no doubt omitted men-
tioning the fact that Bolívar turned into a dictator and that Venezuelans emptied chamber pots on his head as they chased him out
of the country in 1830.

Today, there are entire books consisting exclusively of the rallying
calls Bolívar coined while liberating Colombia, Peru, Venezuela,
Ecuador, Panama, and the country that took his name, Bolivia.
They include *La Patria es la América* (Our nation is America), *¡Unión!
¡Unión! ¡O la anarquía os devorará!* (Union! Union! Or anarchy will
devour us!), *No somos indios ni europeos, sino una especie media*
(We're neither Indian nor European, but a race in between), *El arte
de vencer se aprende en las derrotas* (The art of victory is taught by
defeat), and *La guerra a muerte* (Fight to the death).

Perhaps thanks to his way with words, Bolívar became the best
known of the Latin American revolutionaries who transformed
Spain's four viceroyalties into seventeen independent countries by
the beginning of the twentieth century. By 1830, the Philippines,
Puerto Rico, and Cuba were the only remnants of Spain's colonial
empire, and Spain would lose these, in one fell stroke, sixty-eight

years later, and Panama remained a province of Colombia until 1903.

But paradoxically, Spain's loss turned out to be a fantastic boon for the Spanish language, since each new Spanish-speaking country offered a capital city as well as a unique vision, policies, and culture that would help further disseminate Spanish.

The Latin American independence movement actually began stirring in the late eighteenth century, when colonials started seeing themselves as members of new cultures, whether they were Mexican, Peruvian, Chilean, or other. Bolstered by these new identities, the elite class of criollos began demanding reforms from Spain, ranging from more taxing powers, freedom of press, land reform, and universal male suffrage to free enterprise and a constitutional monarchy.

These reforms all fell short of a demand for independence. That's because the vast majority of criollos were stakeholders in the colonial bureaucracy. They didn't question the legitimacy of the Crown per se—at first.

Bolívar (1783–1830) grew up in this proreform atmosphere in eighteenth-century Venezuela. As one could guess from his full name—Simón José Antonio de la Santísima Trinidad Bolívar y Palacios Ponte y Blanco—Bolívar entered the world as a full-fledged member of the criollo aristocracy. His family, of Basque origins, had made its fortune ranching, running slave plantations, and mining in Venezuela. Bolívar's reformist sympathies radicalized under foreign influence, especially when he lived in France, from 1804 to 1806.

But before Bolívar became El Libertador, another revolutionary figure set the Latin American independence movement in motion: *El Precursor* (the Precursor), Francisco de Miranda.

Like Bolívar, Miranda was born into Venezuela's criollo elite. The son of wealthy merchants, Miranda (1750–1816) grew up believing in the legitimacy of the Spanish Crown. He became a captain of the Spanish army at age twenty-one, but he ended up in jail a decade later, accused of acting against the orders of a superior officer. Locked behind bars, Miranda began questioning the nature and legitimacy of Spain's absolutist power.

After being released from jail, Miranda traveled to London, where his growing anti-Spanish sentiment found fertile ground and radicalized. At the time, both Britain and France were looking for ways to undercut the Spanish. By 1790, Miranda was conspiring with the British to help Venezuela gain independence from Spain. Miranda then fought as a general in the French Revolution, starting in 1791. (Miranda is the only American whose name is included on the Arc de Triomphe.) By 1806, Miranda was leading an attack on colonial Venezuela, waving a Venezuelan flag he had designed himself.

Miranda's hope was that Spain's colonies would one day be united in a vast federation of territories stretching from Cape Horn to el Norte, throughout the continent—in the Hispanic worldview, South, Central, and North America have always been a single entity called *América*. He envisioned this federation as a single country led by a hereditary ruler he called the "Inca," in honor of the great Inca Empire. Miranda's preferred name for the federation, Colombia, was originally coined by English poet and lexicographer Samuel Johnson for a female allegory of Britain's thirteen colonies. The idea caught on among Spanish American revolutionaries, who also pictured Spain's former colonies united under the umbrella of a Gran Colombia.

Though the French Revolution inspired both Miranda and Bolívar, it was the Haitian revolution that really sparked revolutionary sentiment in Spain's colonies. The slaves and Indians living in Spain's colonies were equally inspired by the violent liberation struggle Toussaint Louverture led on the island of Saint-Domingue, causing the criollos to fear insurrection. In addition to Haiti, Tupac Amaru II's rebellion in Peru in 1779–1781 had shown the criollos that if the underclass rose against Spain, it could also rise against them. Among his many famous phrases, Bolívar coined "riding the tiger," meaning that if the criollos failed to master this powerful underclass, they would be devoured by it. Indeed, most criollos feared what they called *pardocracía* (mestizocracy)—a word coined in Venezuela.

Napoleon proved to be another catalyst to revolution in Latin America. When he lost the 1805 battle of Trafalgar, off the coast of Spain, he literally dragged Spain's navy down with him. Spain lost eleven of its fifteen ships. With Spain's navy now incapable of defending sea routes, colonial centers were left to their own devices. The resulting economic crisis aggravated social discontent and increased desires for autonomy there.

Napoleon then added fuel to the fire. In 1808, he invaded Spain and plopped his brother Joseph on the Spanish throne. The Spanish suddenly found themselves fighting for their *own* independence in Europe, and the colonies were left utterly to their own devices. To fill the power vacuum, local *juntas* (councils) started popping up across the Spanish Empire. Rebellion broke out almost everywhere as loyalists rallied to fight the insurgents who were calling for independence.

Such calls for independence—called *gritos*—resounded throughout Spanish America. Mexico's *Grito de Dolores* (Cry of Dolores) is still commemorated every September 15. On that day, in 1810, Miguel Hidalgo, a parish priest of the town of Dolores, rang his church bell and called for independence and sedition against the Spanish Crown. Each year, Mexican presidents reenact *el Grito* by solemnly ringing Hidalgo's bell and calling out the names of Mexican heroes.

The first round of rebellions went nowhere. Most criollos remained royalists, and with well-trained armies at their disposal, they managed to quell most of the rebellions by 1812. The situation quickly stabilized. Using the threat of rebellion, the royalists then wrung concessions from Spain, forcing it to adopt a liberal constitution that granted the colonies some self-rule. That temporarily satisfied even the rebels.

But everything changed when Spain's new king, Fernando VII, took the throne in 1814. He promptly threw out Spain's new constitution and canceled the reforms the royalists had wrested from Spain. Alienated criollos everywhere realized that reform was futile. Independence was unavoidable. Criollos rebelled and Spain's empire started collapsing, first on the fringes, with Venezuela and Argentina, later in the core areas of Mexico and Peru.

The fall of Peru was the combined work of Bolívar, who arrived from the north, and another liberator, the Argentine José de San Martín, who had liberated the Southern Cone countries, including Chile. The last battle of the wars of independence was fought in 1824 in Ayacucho, Upper Peru (now Bolivia). By 1825, Spain had lost everything except the Philippines, Cuba, and Puerto Rico.

But independence was only one step toward forming new countries in Latin America. Between 1820 and 1870, Spain's former viceroyalties splintered into new countries, and most of the continent fought over their new borders.

Bolívar created Gran Colombia in 1825. In 1831, a year after his death, the union fell apart and splintered into the provinces of Venezuela, Colombia, and Ecuador, which became countries of their own. In the Southern Cone, the United Provinces of Río de la Plata was split among Bolivia, Uruguay, and Argentina. Between 1865 and 1870, Paraguay fought territorial wars with Argentina, Brazil, and Bolivia. Chile and Peru conquered Bolivian territory and cut off the country's access to the sea. Colombia and Venezuela, Ecuador and Peru, and all the countries of Central America also ended up in border disputes with each other. Between 1838 and 1841, the runaway Federal Republic of Central America dissolved into Nicaragua, Costa Rica, Honduras, El Salvador, and Guatemala.

Not even Mexico avoided border battles. Mexico got its formal independence in 1821, but by 1841 it had splintered into seven different entities. One of these was Texas. But the Texas settlers got exasperated with Mexico's unstable rule and called for independence of their own. After a brief war, Texas declared its independence in 1836, but Mexico never recognized it.

Far from the rallying cries of his early days, Bolívar finished his life uttering bitter testimonials of failure: *De lo heroico a lo ridículo no hay más que un paso* (From heroism to ridicule, there's only a step), and from his deathbed, *Los tres gran majaderos de la historia hemos sido Jesucristo, Don Quijote . . . y yo* (The three great idiots of history have been Jesus Christ, Don Quixote . . . and I).

Most new nations in Latin America kept the names they had acquired as Spanish colonies. But some, including Argentina, experimented with different names. Argentine was originally a nickname for the high society of Buenos Aires, poking fun at their attachment to French culture (*argent* means silver in French; the Spanish word is *plata*). Argentina then popped up among the various names the state experimented with after 1832, including Confederación Argentina, República de la Confederación Argentina, and Federación Argentina. Today Argentina's official name is República Argentina.

Bolivia chose its name in 1825, and Colombia in 1886, after experimenting with República de Nueva Grenada and then Estados Unidos de Colombia. In 1822, the kingdom of Quito renamed itself Ecuador. Mexico, formerly New Spain, considered calling itself Anahuac, then Imperio Mexicano, República Mexicana, and Estados Unidos Mexicanos, settling for the latter in 1867. Uruguay started as Provincia Oriental, then called itself República Cisplatina, then settled for República Oriental del Uruguay in 1918. The term *rioplatense*, still used today, refers to people on both sides of the río de la Plata, in Montevideo and Buenos Aires.

Border conflicts weren't the only challenge the new Latin American countries faced. The new nations of Central and South America quickly found themselves mired in conflicts over ideology, race, economic models, and relations with foreign powers like Britain, France, Spain, and the United States. These countries vacillated between becoming monarchies, republics, dictatorships, or empires. Centralists battled federalists, and conservatives fought liberals, while large segments of the clergy proclaimed their allegiance to the king, not the new republics. The conflicts were aggravated by rampant authoritarianism, low literacy rates, and intolerance, all of which stumped the continent's development for generations.

The meddling of foreign economic powers—namely Britain, the United States, France, the Netherlands, Spain, and Portugal—added pressure to an already explosive situation. They were all hustling to get or to keep a piece of Latin America's rubber, sugar, banana, coffee, and mining industries. On the Pacific side, foreign powers competed for control of the strategic guano industry. Guano (from the Quechua *wanu*) is a mix of bird, bat, and seal excrement. Exceptionally rich in saltpeter, it is an excellent fertilizer and an essential ingredient of gunpowder. Guano prompted Spain to wage war with Peru and Chile from 1864 to 1866.

The French and the Americans, meanwhile, were fighting for military control of Mexico and competing for the right to build a canal across Panama. The French, who had an important presence in the Lesser Antilles and French Guyana, were bluntly expansionist. In 1861, Napoleon III went as far as invading Mexico and attempting to install Maximilian I of Austria as the emperor. This move failed when French troops were badly defeated in Puebla on May 5, 1862—the famous Cinco de Mayo.

Yet, curiously, Latin American elites continued to emulate the French, no doubt in resistance to British and U.S. economic imperialism. French cultural diplomacy had always been effective in the Americas. In the 1840s, Latin American countries massively adopted the French metric system. It was the French who coined the name Latin America, to underline their shared heritage with

Spanish and Portuguese speakers everywhere. It appeared in the early years of the twentieth century when many members of the Latin American ruling classes were taking long sojourns in Paris.

In the continent's most populous country, Mexico, the situation went from bad to worse. Whereas the population of most new countries multiplied four to ten times during the nineteenth century, Mexico's only doubled, from 6.5 to 13.4 million, by 1900. After gaining independence, Mexico had to contend with secession movements on both its northern and southern borders, as well as two foreign invasions and almost permanent political instability. In the thirty-four years between 1824 and 1858, Mexico had forty-eight presidents—one ruled for a mere five days in 1829—and there were often two or three competing heads of state at the same time.

The Mexican name for its city squares—*zócalos*—was inspired by this instability. Zócalo means pedestal. Heads of state changed so fast that sculptors never had time to finish their statues before they had to make a new one. Inhabitants of Mexico City began referring to the Plaza Mayor as "the pedestal," a name that stuck and was eventually extended to all central squares in Mexico.

Mexico didn't gain even a semblance of stability until after 1867. Much of that was the result of Porfirio Díaz, who reigned as dictator for thirty-five years. In a way, Mexico owed its extreme instability to the fact that it had resisted dictators much longer. Most new Latin American countries turned to strongmen earlier in their history. Juan Manuel de Rosas, who ran Argentina between 1829 and 1852, was a typical Latin American tyrant: he put an end to anarchy, transformed Argentines into a united, patriotic populace, and boosted international trade—but only via a cruel and lawless reign of terror. When José Gaspar Rodríguez de Francia—*El Supremo*—ruled Paraguay from 1814 to 1840, he sealed the country from contact with the outside world, preventing external trade, travel, and even mail service. And of course Simón Bolívar, though he started out as a democrat, ended up as dictator of Colombia.

Every new country in Latin America had to contend with Bolívar's "tiger"—the possibility of slave and Indian uprisings. With the exception of Argentina, every country had to deal with large dissatisfied groups of mestizos, mulattos, and natives, or all three. In an effort to rally support from mestizos, blacks, and Indians, criollos offered undifferentiated citizenship. Mexico's name, Estados Unidos de México, was coined to portray Mexico as the continuation of the former Aztec Empire and a union of diverse ethnic communities. Mexico's instability during the nineteenth century was largely the result of jockeying among criollos, mestizos, and *Indios* for the upper hand.

Mexico would distinguish itself in embracing its mestizo identity—at least officially. When Jean-Benoît traveled in the Mexican countryside, he was always fascinated by the little shrines he saw tucked into corners of households. All had a candle of the Guadalupe, but many had an image of Benito Juárez next to them. Juárez, president of Mexico from 1858 to 1872, has a special place in Mexican political lore. He was Mexico's first native president— and the first in the entire western hemisphere. Born of Zapotec Indian stock and orphaned at age three, Juárez did not speak Spanish until he was twelve. He surmounted almost impossible odds to become Mexico's president, working as a domestic servant to pay his way through law school, then working his way up Mexico's social ladder. One hundred and forty years after his death, he is still a cult figure in Mexico—as well as other parts of Latin America. His birthday, March 21, is a national holiday in Mexico.

It is a bit of a miracle that Latin America is predominantly Spanish- and Portuguese-speaking today. The Spanish crown had done little to Hispanicize the masses during colonial times. And its successor states did not make much effort to teach Spanish during the entire nineteenth century—particularly in the areas with a strong native base, like Mexico, Central America, the Orinoco basin, Peru, and Bolivia.

Teaching Spanish to natives had never been Spanish colonialists' priority, and the best way to sum up the Bourbons' language policy in the eighteenth century is turning a deaf ear. By 1810, only half of Mexico's 6.5 million inhabitants spoke Spanish. The same was true in Peru, Bolivia, and Guatemala, whose large native populations make up the bulk of the total native population in Spanish America. Spanish made inroads in the native population mostly because of *mestisaje*: most offspring of mixed unions were raised speaking Spanish.

At first, Spanish teaching wasn't a high priority among Latin America's new countries either. Criollos were leery of introducing mass education because of the "tiger"—they knew it was easier to control an ignorant underclass. The result was that as late as 1939, 63 percent of Mexicans were still illiterate, a staggeringly high rate compared to Argentina's 25 percent. Countries with abundant native populations, like Peru, Ecuador, Bolivia, and Guatemala, struggled with teacher and school shortages well into the twentieth century. Some 12 percent of Mexicans still don't speak Spanish as a mother tongue and the proportions in Peru and Guatemala are even higher. Mexico, Peru, Guatemala, and Bolivia will probably never be 100 percent Spanish speaking.

The only reason that new nations with predominantly native populations—like Peru and Mexico—did not become Nahuatl or Quechua speaking was that neither of those tongues was a majority language in either country. Substantial proportions of the native populations rejected them in favor of a neutral language: Spanish. The few natives who, like Benito Juárez, rose up through society, owed their fortune to Spanish, not their native languages.

The only exception was Paraguay, where the criollo elite was fairly small, and native groups spoke a single language, Guaraní. Guaraní had benefited from extraordinary protection under the Jesuit missionaries. Its status increased when it was used as a secret tongue in the many wars Paraguay fought with Brazil, Argentina, and Bolivia. In 1996, 95 percent of Paraguayans declared themselves fluent in Guaraní.

Although lack of interest in teaching native Americans did slow the spread of Spanish, immigration didn't.

On the whole, Latin America's population was sparse. At the beginning of the nineteenth century, North and South America were practically empty. The total population was only 30 million, including 7 million in Brazil, 6.3 million in Mexico, and 5.3 million in the United States. This posed a problem for development. All the economies—excluding the United States—were based entirely on exporting primary resources, including agriculture and mining, and importing food and supplies. For the rest of the century, the former Spanish colonies suffered from underindustrialization and overreliance on exports.

Most Latin American countries tried to boost their populations by attracting immigrants. Yet only Argentina and tiny Uruguay across the río de la Plata were successful.

The Mexican writer Carlos Fuentes joked in his 1969 essay "*La nueva novela hispanoamericana*" that "Mexicans descend from the Aztecs, Peruvians from the Inca, and Argentines from the ship." Fuentes was referring to the massive immigration of Europeans to Argentina from the middle of the nineteenth century to the middle of the twentieth—while poking fun at Argentines' supercilious attitude toward the rest of the continent, itself largely a product of European immigration.

With a population of only 300,000 in 1856, Argentina attracted more than 6.5 million immigrants by 1936. More than half the total 11.5 million European immigrants who came to Latin America during that period went to Argentina. As an immigrant destination, Argentina was second only to the United States (34 million) and well ahead of Canada (5.5 million) and even Brazil (4.4 million).

Despite huge efforts, Peru and Mexico's attempts to encourage immigration fell flat. Political agitation in both countries was one deterrent, but another factor influenced European immigrants' decisions: they preferred empty countries with few natives (criollos did not have the monopoly on racism). Argentina was just such a country. So from 1800 to 1939, Argentina saw its population multiply forty-two times, to 14 million. That put it close to Mexico's population of 19 million.

Two other countries succeeded in attracting immigrants: Uruguay (700,000) and Cuba (1 million), although Cuba was not actually a country until 1903. Cuba was one of the few remaining Spanish colonies after the Latin American independence movement, and it became the control center of the Spanish Empire once again. Spain invested heavily in the island's economy and infrastructure. Cuba had South America's first railroad, finished in 1836—twelve years before Spain's—and received a slew of new technologies including a telegraph service. Such progress made the island attractive to Spanish immigrants as well as American investors. During the first half of the nineteenth century, 600,000 Spaniards flocked there, more than to any other country (another 800,000 arrived after 1898, when Cuba was no longer part of the empire).

In Argentina, even though immigrant arrivals outnumbered births for three generations, immigration had relatively little impact on the country's culture or language. Argentina is 100 percent Spanish speaking today, and its general pattern of speech—the use of *voseo*—has remained intact since independence, although Argentine slang developed interesting features, notably the famous *che* (man! or *eh!*) that Argentines drop into their speech.

What explains such linguistic continuity in a country that is so heavily dominated by European immigration? Some 80 percent of Argentina's 6.5 million immigrants came from Italy, Spain, and France, countries with Latin-based languages. French immigrants introduced wine production and revived the custom of drinking *yerba mate*, a tea that Argentines had stopped drinking in the eighteenth century. Three Argentine presidents had French origins. But

French immigrants assimilated quickly to Spanish. Argentina encouraged linguistic assimilation when it introduced mandatory schooling in 1884 and military service after 1902.

Yet the population movements in Argentina did affect the Spanish spoken there—albeit temporarily—by producing an Italian-Spanish pidgin called *Cocoliche*. Cocoliche comes from the name of a character in Argentine popular theater, Cocolicchio, an Italian peon. Between 1880 and 1930, 40 percent of people in Buenos Aires spoke Cocoliche and Argentine slang integrated Cocoliche expressions like *guarda* instead of *cuidado* (watch out) and *birra* instead of *cerveza* (beer). Most of these curious features have since disappeared.

Because of their country's high proportion of citizens of European origin, Argentines ended up identifying strongly with Europe. There is no doubt that the Argentine government set out to make Argentina a "white" country from the start. To this day, there are no official figures on the proportion of Argentines who have indigenous origins. Some sources claim that between 1 percent and 5 percent of the population is native and between 3 percent and 15 percent is mestizo. But it's anybody's guess, given the lack of enthusiasm for collecting reliable statistics on the subject.

Argentine revolutionary Ernesto Guevara (1928–1967)—nicknamed *El Che* for his frequent use of the trademark Argentine interjection—was one of the few individuals who tried to bridge the identity gap between Argentina and the rest of Latin America. Before fighting revolutions in Cuba and Bolivia, Guevara, in his twenties, explored the South American continent on a motorcycle, an episode of his life that inspired the beautiful film *The Motorcycle Diaries*. His Marxist ideology never erased the sympathy that most Latin Americans feel toward him for having reached out to what he called *nuestra mayúscula América*, meaning "our superlative America," an expression he coined to express the sense of pride and common destiny he hoped all Latin Americans would share, whether criollos, mestizos, Indios, or mulattos.

Argentines' attitude toward Latin America changed as a result of the Falklands war (1980–1981). The war started when Argentina took over the British-controlled archipelago, 290 miles off its coast. Argentines were surprised at the swift response of the British, who ended up regaining control. But what shocked Argentines even more was the fact that no European power supported them. Argentines had always considered themselves more European than Latin American. The only support they got came from other Latin American countries—and that was a bit surprising given how often Argentina had turned its back on the continent in the past.

In the rest of Spain's former colonies, the number and proportions of immigrants were a lot smaller than in Argentina, Cuba, and Uruguay, which together attracted eight million of the eleven million immigrants who went to Latin America before World War II. That left only three million to be divided up among sixteen other countries.

The impact of immigration would nonetheless be significant, for the simple reason that most other countries—except Mexico— were sparsely populated. There is a significant German and French presence in Chile and Nicaragua. Two Chilean presidents had French names—Pinochet and Bachelet. And the Mexican word *mariachi* came from the French word *marriage* (wedding). The famous Mexican painter Frida Kahlo was a descendant of German Jews. In Mexico and Colombia, two famously rich individuals, the Mexican billionaire Carlos Slim Helú and the pop singer Shakira are of Lebanese origin.

Despite the growing influence of Spain's language academy, the Real Academia, in the same period, Spanish in the New World was developing its own unique characteristics. And as the demographic center of Spanish shifted from Europe to the Americas, some of these features would go on to influence standard Spanish into the twenty-first century.

21. Standard Shift

VENEZUELA PRODUCED THE THIRD GIANT of Latin America's revolutionary period. In addition to El Precursor and El Libertador, there was El Escritor (the writer): Andrés Bello.

Unlike his famous revolutionary compatriots, Andrés Bello didn't wage wars or rally entire populations to take up arms in rebellion. Yet he spent his life fighting a battle akin to Bolívar's, albeit by different means. Whereas Bolívar struggled to unite the newly independent countries politically, Bello worked to maintain their bonds through a common tongue.

Bello had roughly the same background as Bolívar, who was an upper-class criollo. But that's where the similarities end. Bolívar was romantic, flamboyant, idealistic, and militaristic; Bello was shy, introverted, and bookish. An award-winning student, well versed in both the classics and vernacular Spanish, Bello became Bolívar's tutor when he was just twenty, instructing the eighteen-year-old Liberator-to-be in geography and literature. Bello, who obviously didn't see Bolívar's potential, famously characterized his young charge as "a talented but restless young man, deficient in application."

Bello went on to fight a quieter battle than Bolívar. Yet he fought longer. While Bolívar died prematurely at forty-seven, his great dream of a continental Colombia having failed, Bello lived to eighty-three, a renowned writer, scholar, philosopher, jurist, poet, and statesman. Bello had lived according to the belief that even if Miranda's idea of a continental Gran Columbia was politically untenable, Latin American could be united through language.

Independence threatened to split Spanish into separate dialects the way the continent split into separate political entities. Like King Alfonxo X of Castile and Antonio de Nebrija, Bello saw

Spanish as a tool of unification, and his accomplishments completely transformed Spanish as a national language—of not one but nineteen countries. In fact, Bello's work and influence changed attitudes in Spain. During the revolutionary period, Spain went from ignoring the Spanish spoken in the Americas to taking the first steps in defining Spanish as the language of a civilization that spanned two continents.

Bello started his professional life as a rising member of Venezuela's colonial administration, an administrator and secretary for three captains general translating French and English correspondence from the nearby Caribbean islands. In 1810, Bello produced the first book ever published in Venezuela, a *Handbook and Universal Guide for Visitors in Venezuela*, of which only three copies are known to have survived.

Bello's superiors recognized his immense potential. In 1810, when Venezuela's captaincy general was replaced by a junta, Bello was appointed first secretary of foreign affairs. The junta sent him, along with Simón Bolívar, to London to secure British support and funding for the nascent Venezuelan nation.

Venezuela's diplomatic campaign in London was an uphill battle. After Napoleon had invaded Spain in 1808, the British government had changed hats. Britain was no longer interested in weakening Spain's colonial empire; it supported Spain against Napoleon and refused to support any rebellious movements that threatened to weaken Spain's colonial empire. Bolívar returned to Venezuela to fight, but Bello decided to stay in London and keep on working as a diplomat.

Little did Bello know that he would be stranded in London, doing unsatisfactory work, for the next two decades. His situation was precarious: he was the representative of a revolutionary government that didn't always pay him. To support his family, he worked as a translator.

Yet being in London paid off. London in the 1820s was a global hub filled with Latin American exiles and expatriates seeking recognition for their nations, so Bello had a bird's-eye view of how change was unfolding in Latin America. He met every important Latin American who visited London, as well as intellectual figures including James Mill (the father of John Stuart) and Jeremy Bentham in 1820 and 1826. Bello also started two journals, *El Reperterio Americano* and *El Censor Americano*. He was one of the primary sources of news and information about independent Latin America. In 1823 he even coauthored the first volume of an encyclopedia, *La Biblioteca Americana o miscelánea de literatura, artes i cicencias* (The American Library, or Miscellaneous Literature, Arts, and Sciences). The result: Bello acquired a truly Pan-Hispanic perspective on the Latin American independence movement.

London also provided Bello with the academic opportunities he needed to pursue his work on the Spanish language. Bello had been writing about language since the 1810s and spent his time in London gathering material and developing his ideas. In 1823, he published an article proposing a thorough reform of Spanish spelling. His idea was simple: each letter should represent a single sound, for the sake of consistency but also to make it easier for children to learn to read Spanish. Bello intended to eliminate all inconsistencies of Spanish spelling, like the three spellings of the hard *c* (*c, k,* and *qu*), the three spellings for the sound *s* (*c, s, z*), the confusion between *ll* and *y,* between *y* and *i,* and between *g, x,* and *j*. He also began exploring the problem of verb tenses, whose names, adapted from Latin, varied widely from country to country.

Again like Antonio de Nebrija and Alfonso X before him, Bello considered language both a tool of communication and a tool of statecraft and believed that language and law went hand in hand. Bello was convinced that Latin American countries needed more law and working tribunals (actually, he thought this was more critical than democracy). But for laws to be effective, citizens needed to be able to understand them. The language had to be clear and unified.

Bello's other concern was that the Spanish spoken in the new countries of Latin America would explode into a multiplicity of distinct, possibly unintelligible dialects, the way Latin had splintered after the dissolution of the Roman Empire.

Bello wasn't the only one who feared this possibility. Wherever the literary scene was well developed, particularly in Argentina, Mexico, Cuba, Chile, and Colombia, authors were acutely conscious of how differences in grammar and vocabulary could hinder their ability to communicate with Spanish speakers in other regions.

Bello was often accused of being conservative, and that may have been true of his politics. But where language was concerned, he eludes categorization. Bello's position was that languages are always changing. In his mind, new phraseology and new words not only enrich the language but also make that language better able to convey the thoughts of a people in a changing society. New institutions, new inventions, new laws, and new customs require new words and new writing styles to express them. Yet Bello believed that language needed to be built on a solid structure. Like society, language needed rules that everyone observed, whether those rules were imposed from authority, arose through custom, or came about spontaneously.

Bello stood for this view, and his legacy has remained in Spanish to this day. In fact, most of his ideas about language were formed when, in 1829, at age forty-seven, Bello finally got out of London. But he didn't return to Venezuela. Bello knew he had to distance himself from Bolívar, who by then was dictator of Gran Colombia (which included Venezuela). Instead, he chose Chile, a relatively stable and comparatively well-managed country, where he had been offered a job as minister of foreign affairs.

In Chile, Bello quickly established himself as an essential intellectual and political figure. He also became a good friend of the regime's strongman, Diego Portales. In 1837, Bello became a senator. In 1842, he founded the University of Chile, one of the most significant events in the history of the early republic. Chile was also an excellent vantage point: like London, it was an important crossroads of literary expats and exiles, and Bello encountered many like-minded intellectuals concerned about the state of the Spanish language. During most of the 1830s and 1840s, Bello carried on a debate with the most famous Argentine expatriate of the time, the writer Domingo Faustino Sarmiento. Sarmiento belonged to the handful of undeniably great literary figures of nineteenth-century Latin America. A true man of his century, Sarmiento wrote vigorously about the epic challenges of building one's self through education and of building the nation. Sarmiento went on to be president of Argentina from 1868 to 1874. His greatest literary achievement was *Facundo: Civilización y Barbarie* in 1845. A work of creative nonfiction, it tells the story of a gaucho bandit, Juan Facundo Quiroga, who had been the terror of Argentina fifteen years earlier. In fact, it was an allegory of the dictatorship of Juan Manuel de Rosas, the incarnation of barbarianism. Sarmiento's idea that conflicts actually pit civilization against barbarianism remains at the core of political debates in Latin America to this day.

It was in Chile that Bello's work on both language and law would finally reach fruition. In 1832, Bello published *Principios de derecho de gentes* (Principles of the Laws of the People)—which established the equality of nations whatever their political systems. Twelve years later, he expanded it into *Principios de derecho internacional* (Principles of International Law)—the first text of international law in Latin America. In 1856, after twenty years of work, Bello finished his *Código civil* (Civil Code), which the Chilean congress adopted—his text also served as the basis for civil codes in Colombia, Ecuador, and Nicaragua.

Bello's prestige was such that he pushed the spelling reform he had imagined in 1823. The *Ortografía de Bello*—as it is often called—became the official standard of the government of Chile from 1844 to 1927. In the end, it was a "Bello-light" reform. The government did not adopt all of his ideas, but it did modify thousands of words. For the next century, official Chilean spelling was *rei* instead of *rey* (king), *jeneral* for *general,* and *testo* for *texto,* among others. The façade of the former School of Engineering, now at the University of Chile, still has *ingeniería* spelled *injeniería.*

Bello's spelling reform also spread to Argentina, Colombia, Ecuador, Nicaragua, and Venezuela, which adopted his system for a time. It even got a sympathetic reception in Madrid, particularly at the Academia Literaria y Científica de Profesores de Instrucción Primaria (Literary and Scientific Academy of Primary School Teachers). It came close to becoming universal, but the queen decided that Spain's official spelling standard would be that of the Real Academia, not Bello.

In the long run, Bello's system did not take root. Even Chile reverted to the Madrid Standard in 1927. But his spelling can be seen in the poetry written in the 1910s.

Bello's major work on language was *Gramática de la lengua castellana destinada al uso de los Americanos* (Grammar of the Castilian Language for the Use of Americans). First published in 1847, it would go on to be an immense success, appearing in six revised editions during his lifetime and more than seventy editions in the twentieth century.

Bello's motivation for writing the *Gramática* was to ensure that the emerging Latin American states would share a common language. Bello feared that if Latin American Spanish splintered into separate dialects, the continent would be left divided and powerless.

Twenty years earlier, Bello had decided that Spanish verbs had to be classified and systemized according to rules. In Chile, he set out to compile those rules. His approach was original, almost to the point of being revolutionary. Bello decided to describe Spanish grammar according to the intrinsic characteristics of the language itself and not using a Latin model. Bello felt that the entire grammar should be approached "as if there was no other language in the world but Spanish."

Andrés Bello has often been described as the Spanish-speaking world's version of Noah Webster, and indeed, like Webster, he linked language, education, law, and nationhood. The scholar Iván Jaksić, who wrote an extensive biography of Bello, says that the success of Bello's *Gramática* owes less to his "technical expertise" than to the "peculiar response it gave to political concerns about national, and supra-national identity."

The title of Bello's *Gramática* was deliberately chosen to announce its objective. Bello used the word *castellana* to show that he was bridging Spanish usage in Latin America *and* Spain. He deliberately avoided the term *lengua americana* (which would exclude Spain's), and *lengua española* (which would have alienated former colonials). But the examples he chose came mostly from the work of Spanish poets, perhaps to back up his contention that independence would not mean severing ties with Spanish culture. At the same time, Bello's title was meant to emphasize that his *Gramática* was conceived for *americanos*.

Bello's assessment of the situation and his call for a unified grammar of Spanish was at once realistic and ambitious—so ambitious, in fact, that it would be 150 years in the making.

The scale of the challenge dawned on Jean-Benoît when he traveled to Nicaragua to attend a friend's wedding. In the arrival concourse of Managua Airport, a huge red sign read: *Nicaragua se communica con vos.* It was a pun that meant both "Nicaragua is connecting with you" and "In Nicaragua, we say *vos*." The base of the joke is *vos* (you, singular), which Nicaraguans—as well as Argentinians and Uruguayans—prefer to the *tu* used almost everywhere else. This is one of the major grammatical differences in the Spanish-speaking world. Whereas most Spanish speakers say *tu tienes cara de triste* (you have a sad face), Nicaraguans—like Argentinians and Uruguayans—say *vos tenéis cara de triste*.

Like English, Spanish is spoken in a large number of countries each of which has its own standard but also its own slang and colloquialisms—a Panamanian will say *buena leche* (good milk) for good luck instead of *buena suerte,* and *peleo* for child instead of *niño.* Yet the notion of standards is so strong in Spanish-speaking cultures that the goal of education becomes, to some extent, teaching the "right way," or more precisely, the "right ways" to speak: both the national standard and the Spanish standard. It's as if American children were taught both American English and British English and how to use either in the right context.

These variations in Spanish have many roots, including the origin of the speaker, class relations, and contact with native languages. In Argentina, immigration played a large role in shaping the common variety of Spanish spoken by most Argentines. A good example is how they tend to express the future through a circumlocution: they say *voy a ver* (I am going to see) rather than *veré* (I will see). This is because, for immigrants, it was actually simpler to use the three-word future construction, formed with the verb "to go" and the infinitive of the verb. That way, they only had to learn to conjugate the irregular verb "to go" in the present, which is easy, rather than learning to conjugate Spanish verbs in the future.

Differences in pronunciation are also considerable among Latin Americans. Cubans tend to drop the final *s* almost universally: *estamos estupendos* (we're wonderful) sounds like *estamo' estupendo'* (or even *e'tamo' e'tupendo'*). Puerto Ricans also speak a distinctive brand of Spanish, where the trilled *rr* sounds like a single *r* or even *h,* whereas the regular *r* comes across as *l. Puerto Rico* can sound like *Puelto Hico,* especially in colloquial speech. In Colombia and Nicaragua, there is a softening of the *jota* (*j*), which makes the letter sound more like the English *h.*

On top of it all, it is not easy to generalize about national differences since few of them apply to entire countries, but rather specifically to cities or even neighborhoods.

In Mexico alone, linguists have identified ten variants of Spanish. Mexicans do not say *vos*: the standard is *tu* . . . except in the countryside and mountain areas, where twenty to thirty million Mexicans prefer the formal *usted* and *ustedes* over *tu* and *vosotros*. The same geographic and sociological differences exist in Colombia between *tu* and *usted*.

In view of all the variations in Spanish, the task of defining a Latin American standard was obviously well beyond the capabilities of any individual, even Andrés Bello, genius though he was. Fortunately, Bello would have reinforcements.

Of all international languages, Spanish is the only one that has clear national standards, as well as one international standard. This is a direct consequence of Andrés Bello's work. In the nineteenth century, the total population of Spanish Latin America had grown to twice the size of Spain's. Latin America's demographic weight alone forced the Real Academia Española to shake off its former indifference to Latin America. The Academia also noticed Bello, whose influence was growing as a result of his controversial spelling reform and grammar, and his other work on language.

These were not good times at the Academia. After its great achievements in the previous century, the nineteenth-century Academia suffered from both the political upheaval that followed the Napoleonic occupation and the aftermath of the wars of independence. The ranks of the *académicos* were depleted. Between 1808 and 1812, and again between 1823 and 1825, they hardly met at all.

Part of the Academia's problem was lack of funding, but it also relied too much on voluntary work. In the eighteenth century, most *académicos* were erudite aristocrats. Political tensions and the rise of the bourgeoisie reduced aristocratic influence in Spain, so the Academia sought out nonaristocrats with academic credentials as members. Unfortunately, this just added stress to an already bad situation. By 1837, things had gotten so bad that the Academia couldn't find a printer for its dictionary, let alone replace the *académicos* who were passing away. The Academia kept churning out dictionaries and grammars, but they were too Madrid-centered and out of sync with the times.

Spanish publishers did not capitalize quickly on the opportunity to produce better quality dictionaries than the Real Academia's. Rather, it was French publishers who moved in—particularly Larousse, still a common brand name in Spanish. Larousse began by translating their own dictionaries and encyclopedias into Spanish, and progressively adapted them into entirely Spanish editions. In Argentina, Larousse represents 60 percent of the dictionary market. Argentine singer Maria Elena Walsh even wrote a song "Vals del diccionario" (Waltz of the Dictionary), which is about the wonders of her *Pequeño Larousse Ilustrado* (Petit Larousse Illustré).

It was Bello's spelling reforms, new ideas about grammar, and astonishing productivity that shook the Academia out of its lethargy. Yet it took the meddling of an influential Spanish reformer—the Marquis of Molíns, aka Mariano Roca de Togores y Carrasco—to really change things.

Molíns was not an *académico* himself; he ran the Ministerio de Fomento (Ministry of Public Works). But he took language and learning to heart and was concerned about Spain's increasing self-centeredness. By 1847, he managed to reform not just the Real Academia Española but also the academies of history, of medicine, and of law.

Among its new statutes, the Real Academia was obliged to replace deceased academicians within two months of their death. The jobs of director, secretary, librarian, and treasurer became full-time paid positions. The number of *académicos* increased from twenty-three to forty-six, and half a dozen commissions were created to divide the work: for the dictionary, grammar and spelling, prosody (the rhythm, stress, and intonation of speech), etymology, history, awards, and the reedition of classics. All academicians had to reside in Madrid, to facilitate the Academia's work. But the reform also created a structure of twenty-four external correspondents, from designated areas outside Madrid to provide the point of view of Catalans, Basques, Latin Americans, and even foreigners like the French, Italians, and Americans.

Until then, the Academia had been only remotely interested in linguistic realities outside the peninsula. In the eighteenth century, the Academia made a small effort to include the colonies, appointing the Mexican-born jurist Manuel Miguel de Lardizábal y Uribe (who inherited the seat from his Spanish father-in-law). In 1845, the Argentine Ventura de la Vega was also accepted as a member. In 1826, following the revolutionary wars, the Academia considered expanding its mandate to encompass the entire Hispanic world. But in an age when steamships were the fastest mode of intercontinental communication, the idea was impracticable. There was also too much lingering acrimony between the Spanish and *Americanos* to make collaboration feasible at that point.

With Molíns's reforms, the Academia added foreign correspondents and increased the number of *académicos* from outside Spain, including the Peruvian Juan de la Pezuela (1847), the Mexican Fermín de la Puente Apezechea (1850), and the Venezuelan Rafael María Baralt (1853). Andrés Bello was made honorary member in 1850. Another reform, in 1858, created the status of *miembro asociado* (associate member), and six Latin Americans were appointed, including Bello in 1861.

Molíns became director of the Academia in 1865. He decided to take the reform of the Academy a step farther by fostering the creation of national *academias* in all the other Spanish-speaking countries in the world. The process was meant to be simple: three academicians were enough to start a national academy that would then be recognized by Madrid as a *corporación correspondiente* (corresponding corporation). This upped the ante.

These transformations were all the more desirable since the major developments in the Spanish language at the time were coming from the Americas. Bello had reinforcements and Latin American scholars were producing plentiful original work by this time. The Cuban Esteban Pichardo published the first dictionary of *americanismos* in 1836.

Lexicographers and grammarians were especially dynamic in Colombia, with Rufino José Cuervo being the most ambitious and original. His first major book, published in 1867, had the understated (though overdescriptive) title *Apuntaciones críticas sobre el lenguaje bogotano, con frecuente referencia al de los países de Hispano-América* (Critical Notes About the Bogotan Language with Frequent Reference to Those of Other Hispano-American Countries). It was so thorough that linguists studying the dialectal variations of Latin America still refer to it. Cuervo also updated Bello's grammar, but his life's work was the *Diccionario de construcción y régimen de la lengua castellana* (Dictionary of Castilian Language Construction and Rules). This general dictionary included notes on etymology, definitions, examples from authors, syntax, and comparison with synonyms. Cuervo had gotten only to the letter *D* when he died in 1911, but he left enough notes for his successors to produce the whole eight thousand pages he had planned by 1994.

Molíns's initiative got an enthusiastic response in Latin America. Not surprisingly, Colombians were the first to create an Academia: in 1871, Rufino José Cuervo established the Academia Colombiana with the writers Miguel Antonio Caro and Marco Fidel Suárez. Over the next two decades, seven countries followed suit: Mexico and Ecuador in 1875, El Salvador in 1880, Venezuela in 1881, Chile in 1886, Peru in 1887, and Guatemala in 1888.

Still, despite the Real Academia's new openness, Latin Americans were slow to get existing *academias* off the ground. Newly established ones in Chile, Peru, Ecuador, El Salvador, Guatemala, and Venezuela were stalled due to lack of commitment (these were voluntary organizations) and local quarrels. Chile had to restart its Academia in 1914, followed by Peru in 1918, Ecuador and El Salvador in 1923, then Guatemala and Venezuela in 1930. Meanwhile, starting with Bolivia in 1920, new countries started creating their own academies: Costa Rica in 1923, Cuba and Panama in 1926, the Dominican Republic and Paraguay in 1927, Argentina in 1931, Uruguay in 1943, and Honduras in 1948.

The American *academias* did not have immediate influence on the Real Academia in Madrid. As early as 1854, the Academia modified its approach to grammar to conform to Bello's ideas, but it took the Academy a century more to actually begin working on Pan-Hispanic dictionaries, grammars, and *ortografías*. In reality, the Academia didn't fully embrace Molíns's vision of Spanish until the 1970s.

Nevertheless, after Molíns, successive editions of the *Diccionario de autoridades* gradually included more and more American vocabulary. The 1726–1739 edition contained 127 American terms compared to 1,400 Spanish regionalisms.

Until 1884, the Academia's dictionary brought little nuance to the question of origin. The designation as *americanismo* was sufficient for all overseas terms. After 1884, it introduced country names. Here again, the evolution was striking: in 1916, the *Diccionario* had only 5 terms that were specifically from Puerto Rico; in 2001, it had 482. The fifteenth edition of the dictionary of the Real Academia, in 1925, marked a departure. The dictionary got a new title, which better reflected the Latin American influence: *Diccionario de la lengua española* (rather than *castellana*).

But then the Spanish language had also come into contact with a whole new type of external influence: that of the United States.

22. Enter the United States

We lived in Phoenix, Arizona, for six months in 2010. It turned out to be the perfect time and place to observe language dynamics in the United States. The spring after we arrived, Arizona's state legislature drafted Senate Bill 1070, which was to give the state extraordinary powers to control immigration. The bill sparked a nationwide debate about illegal immigration as opinions clashed over whether illegal immigration was rising or falling, whether border violence was climbing or abating. In Arizona, especially in the largely Hispanic school our daughters attended, SB 1070 created panic and despair. Rich or poor, established or newly arrived, all Spanish speakers in Arizona felt targeted and braced themselves to be hassled—at the very least.

In the middle of the controversy, we interviewed Carlos Vélez-Ibáñez, an anthropologist and director of Arizona State University's School of Transborder Studies. Vélez-Ibáñez proceeded to turn the entire question of "immigration" on its head. Both Mexican and American (he's a former Marine), he recoiled at the suggestion that he was an immigrant. "My family has lived in the Tucson area for centuries! My parents were born in Mexico but my father was raised by relatives in Tucson. I grew up with one foot in each country. I can't escape the idea that it's the border that crossed us, not the other way around," Vélez-Ibáñez told us.

The town of Nogales, located on the United States–Mexico border in Arizona, is a perfect example of Vélez-Ibáñez's point. It existed before the United States purchased southern Arizona from Mexico in 1854, and just happened to be located exactly where the border was drawn. Today, a fence made of metal plate recycled from the Korean War slices through the city, dividing it between the two countries.

Many Spanish-speaking groups in the United States today could say the same thing. Throughout the nineteenth century and the first half of the twentieth century, before massive waves of immigration brought Spanish speakers to the United States, it was the United States that crossed borders, annexing part of Mexico, Cuba, Puerto Rico, and the Philippines and taking over a section of Panama. In other words, the United States ventured into the Spanish-speaking world long before Spanish speakers started coming to the United States. This is one reason Spanish is so resilient in the United States to this day.

When the French writer Alexis de Tocqueville wrote *Democracy in America* in the 1830s, his observations about nineteenth-century American politics and society were so astute that many remain relevant today. Yet one topic is conspicuously absent from the Frenchman's observations: Spanish. That's because, prior to 1830, the United States had had only a few minor encounters with the Spanish-speaking universe.

One such case was General Bernardo de Gálvez, governor of Louisiana from 1777 to 1785, who supported the American Revolution before Spain officially declared war on Britain in 1779. He blocked British reinforcements from the south and, by taking Pensacola in 1781, deprived the British of their last base on the Gulf of Mexico. In spite of these successes, he never got anything close to the recognition Lafayette did—except for a port city in Texas, Galveston, named after him. (One year after Pensacola, Gálvez jailed a number of Spanish officers for seizing the Bahamas without his orders. One of these was the young captain Francisco de Miranda. This arrest made Miranda resent the Spanish Crown and this set him on his course to becoming *El Precusor* of the liberation of the Greater Colombia.)

The links between the young republic and the Hispanic world essentially started with Caribbean trade. The United States entered the Caribbean at the turn of the eighteenth century when the

Napoleonic Wars devastated Spain and its navy, and forced Spain to give up its trade monopoly with its colonies. American merchants traded gunpowder and grain for sugar, molasses, rum, coffee, tobacco, leather, and tropical products, and ramped up involvement in the businesses of rubber, bananas, coffee, sugar, mining, guano, farming, ranching, and railways. As a result, Spanish dollars poured into the United States.

It was in the nineteenth century that Americans first acquired the label *gringos*. This word is actually a deformation of *griego* (Greek). According to a Spanish dictionary published in 1786, the word was used in Málaga, Spain, to designate any "foreigner" with an accent—it was not pejorative. In Madrid slang, gringo specifically referred to the Irish. In 1840 Peru, the word applied to any European traveler. As the United States pushed the French and British out of Latin America, gringo came to be associated almost exclusively with Americans. (Curiously, in the Mexican countryside, we learned that gringo was also strongly associated with Protestantism. When we told the locals we met that we were French speaking and Catholic, they told us that that made us less gringos.)

Between the 1820s and the 1840s, American involvement in Latin America shifted from business to territorial expansion and strategic concerns. This change in stance coincided with both the Monroe Doctrine, formulated in 1823, which stated the western hemisphere was closed to European colonization, and with the notion of manifest destiny, formulated in 1845, that the United States had the mission of occupying the continent.

Mexico was the first Latin American country to feel the full impact of the United States' new calling. The object was Texas, which had declared its independence from Mexico in 1835. Texas was a republic for nine years, but during that time it had debated whether to stay independent or annex itself to the United States. The annexation party prevailed, and in 1845, shortly after taking office, President James Polk recognized the annexation of Texas to the United States. In Mexico, Polk's move was regarded as outright provocation.

In April 1846, the Mexicans attacked the American army stationed at the Nueces River, in Texas. Congress voted war credits of $10 million and called up sixty thousand volunteers. The Mexican-American War was under way.

The Americans had a surprise when they crossed the Rio Grande and marched into northern Mexico. Since 1818, the Comanche Indians had been pillaging and ransacking northern Mexico to sustain a brisk business of stealing horses, taking slaves, and reselling both to Americans. The few Mexicans left there put up little resistance. Given the legacy of the Comanche, they were as likely to see Americans as saviors rather than as a threat. In September 1847, sixteen months after declaring war, the U.S. army waved the American flag in Mexico City. By then, they had also seized New Mexico and California.

The U.S. victory left President Polk with a daunting decision: whether or not to carry on and annex all of Mexico. Congress debated the issue fiercely. In the end, South Carolina senator John C. Calhoun's arguments prevailed. The former vice president explained: "We have never dreamt of incorporating into our Union any but the Caucasian race—the free white race. To incorporate Mexico, would be the very first instance of the kind of incorporating an Indian race; for more than half of the Mexicans are Indians, and the other is composed chiefly of mixed tribes. I protest against such a union as that! Ours, sir, is the Government of a white race. The greatest misfortunes of Spanish America are to be traced to the fatal error of placing these colored races on an equality with the white race."

Consistent with this reasoning, Polk claimed only the most depopulated parts of Mexico for the United States. The new territory included all of today's California, Nevada, and Utah, plus chunks of Arizona, New Mexico, Colorado, and Wyoming. In 1853, the U.S. government paid $10 million to gain the southern chunks of Arizona and New Mexico to the present border.

The Mexican-American War allowed the United States to increase its territory by a third. As luck would have it, nine days before the signature of the 1848 Treaty of Guadalupe Hidalgo ending the war, James Marshall struck gold in California. The second gold rush of the modern era, after Brazil's in 1690, was about to get under way—the original conquistadores didn't mine gold; they stole it.

Even though the United States deliberately annexed the least populated parts of northern Mexico, the new territory still had a society with a mixed population of about one hundred thousand Mexicans, on which the United States built. Texas, New Mexico, and California all had missions and ranches, embryos of industry, and even some Spanish-language publications before they became part of the United States. Spanish-language newspapers had been operating in Texas since the 1820s. California and New Mexico had had printing presses since the 1830s. Félix Gutiérrez, professor of journalism and communication at the Annenberg School for Communication and Journalism, believes the first Hispanic newspaper on U.S. territory was *El Mississippi,* published in New Orleans in 1808. There were Spanish-language newspapers in Texas the next decade, and by the 1870s, they were spread all over the U.S. Southwest.

If it hadn't been for the colonial structures Spain built in California, the state could never have absorbed the quick population growth brought on by the gold rush. In 1849 alone, California's population quadrupled from fourteen thousand to sixty thousand. That was possible because there was already a food supply chain when the gold miners arrived. (Mines weren't the only source of wealth in California. Spanish ranchers jacked up the price of cattle fifty times, to as much as $75 per head in San Francisco. California's demand was so tremendous that ranchers organized cattle drives from Texas: this was when the vaquero (cowboy) cultures of the East and the West began to blend.)

Of course, the small Mexican population in California was quickly overwhelmed by the influx of Americans. The 1849 constitution of California made some concessions to Spanish-language rights, but by 1879, English was the state's only official language. Ranching and the church were the only remnants of Spanish colonial culture that endured.

Americans today automatically associate Hispanics with immigration. That reflex omits one fact: part of the reason Hispanic culture remains so influential in the United States is that America absorbed large sections of the former Spanish colonial empire and, by so doing, effectively entered the Spanish-speaking world, not the other way around. Until the 1910s, the border with Mexico was a vague concept and people circulated freely—to work in Arizona's mines, to dig in Texas's oil wells, or to pick California's fruit. In a landmark study, the historians Brian Gratton of Arizona State University and Myron P. Gutmann of the University of Texas at Austin found that the number of Hispanics in the United States had increased fivefold by 1900, to half a million, and to two million by 1940. The U.S. Border Patrol was created in 1924, then the Bracero Program, which set quotas for migrant workers, in 1942, but the border still remained a fiction.

The traces of this are still visible. In Phoenix, when we were walking our kids to school, we saw Mexican immigrants knocking at doors to ask owners if they could crop their hedges of nopal cactus, in order to cook *nopalitos,* a tangy dish of diced cactus leaves that is a common accompaniment for eggs, salads, and soups, Phoenix's landscape, its terroir, after all, is essentially the same as Mexico's in the Sonora desert. The border doesn't change anything.

Mexican cuisine is now known the world over, but everywhere we lived—in Montreal, Paris, Toronto, and Phoenix—we heard debates between Mexican food aficionados over the genuineness (or artificiality) of Mexican American cuisine. The varieties of Mexican cuisine, with its old indigenous roots, are mind-boggling, and all the more so since so much is a continuation of what people ate before the arrival of the Spaniards—except, of course, beef, pork, and chicken. Nevertheless, it does not make sense to think of

Mexican American food as an adulterated form of authentic cuisine, like Italian food, which was an import. In fact, it developed out of the same grassroots origins, with its own specialties, from Texan nachos, chile con carne, and fajitas to Arizonan chimichangas (deep-fried burritos), not to mention barbecue itself. When Americans put cheddar cheese and sour cream on their nachos, they aren't distorting an authentic custom. No one else eats nachos.

Though the idea of Tex-Mex cuisine entered popular vocabulary in the 1970s, Mexican food had already been part of the social makeup of the Southwest for two centuries. The words enchilada, guacamole, frijoles, and Tex-Mex itself entered basic English vocabulary beginning in the middle of the nineteenth century.

In addition to food terminology, American vocabulary absorbed many Spanish borrowings from the fusion of Spanish- and English-speaking cultures in the Southwest. The verb *vamoose* (deformation of *vámos,* let's go) means to "go away" or "decamp," as in "*vamoose* the ranch." In some cases, English spellings adapted Spanish spellings, like *canyon* from *cañón,* to avoid confusion with *cannon.* Other nineteenth-century borrowings included *bunco, cafeteria, fiesta, guerrilla, macho, mañana, marijuana, nada, poncho,* and *patio.* In the twentieth century, other terms became unrecognizable as English slang, like *hoosegow* (from *juzgado,* a panel of judges) and *reefer* (from *grifo,* smoker of marijuana).

Along with marijuana and machismo, chewing gum is another well-known American custom that grew out of the Mexican presence in the United States. In 1862, Thomas Adams, secretary to General Santa Anna, who was a U.S. refugee at the time, tried to find an industrial use for the gum from the chicle tree, native to Mexico (*chicle* means "gum" in Nahuatl). His attempts to commercialize chicle as a substitute for rubber failed. Then he recalled seeing his boss chewing chicle without swallowing, for hours on end. Adams went on to manufacture the product under the brand Chiclets.

* * *

Roughly at the same time the United States absorbed northern Mexico, it moved into Central America and the Caribbean.

Things started with the Panama Canal. As early as 1836, the United States began discussions with Colombia about building a railway across the Isthmus of Panama—a province of Colombia at the time. The Panama Railway was completed by 1855, but the United States' real goal was to dig a canal. Unfortunately, the French beat them to the chase and in 1878 secured the rights with Colombia to build a canal. When the French abandoned the project before it was complete because of yellow fever and bankruptcy, the United States went back to the negotiating table with Colombia. Colombia balked, so the United States encouraged the province of Panama to secede from it. That's how Latin America's nineteenth Spanish-speaking country appeared on the map in 1903. The Americans, who had found a cure for *fiebre amarilla* (yellow fever), took over the canal project: seventy-five thousand workers got the job done just in time for World War I. While they were at it, the Americans built half a dozen military bases and free-trade zones.

One of the United States' most famous "Panamanians" is Arizona senator John McCain. He was born in the naval air station of Coco Solo, one of the eight former U.S. military bases and forts in the Canal Zone. U.S. military bases employed many Panamanians, as did U.S. companies operating in Panama's free-trade zone. Colloquial Spanish in Panama has many Anglicisms that took on meanings very different from the original sense in English. *Eso está bien pretty* means "it's nice," and *pretty pretty* means "very nice." The word *yeyé* (derived from the yeah-yeah of 1960s pop music) came to describe a nouveau riche living above his means.

In 1909 and 1933, U.S. Marines occupied Nicaragua to prevent a competing Nicaragua canal scheme from materializing. The United States had been the first to propose building a canal in Nicaragua to compete with the French, but when the Americans took over the Panama project, Nicaragua unexpectedly vowed to keep building its own. To avoid this competing canal, Americans invaded Nicaragua in 1909 to put an end to the project.

Then in the 1930s, the U.S. military got involved in the so-called Banana Wars, which were meant to protect American interests—particularly those of the United Fruit Company—in Central America. After World War II, the U.S. army created, in Panama, the School of the Americas, which would train thirty-four thousand soldiers in anticommunist counterinsurgency. It would become infamous for its list of graduates, including the Panamanian dictator Manuel Noriega, the Argentine dictator Leopoldo Galtieri, and the Salvadoran death-squad leader Roberto D'Aubuisson.

Before World War II, the Panama Free Trade Zone, the U.S. military bases, and the considerable presence of U.S. companies were responsible for bringing the majority of Central American "immigrants" to the United States: they were already working for American interests and just followed the work. Although Panamanians would tend to be scattered all over the United States and not concentrated in one area, their presence would be felt in American sports—in boxing, but above all, in baseball.

The United States moved into the Caribbean at the end of the century, after the Spanish-American War of 1898. The war was really about Cuba.

Cuba, only ninety miles off the coast of Florida, was the largest and most populous of the Caribbean islands. One of the few territories the Spanish held on to after the wars of independence, "*La Siempre Fidelísima Isla*" (the ever most loyal island), as the Spanish government called it, had benefited from considerable Spanish investment in the nineteenth century. Not surprisingly, Thomas Jefferson dreamed of annexing the island: his secretary of state, John Quincy Adams, regarded Cuba and Puerto Rico as natural appendages of the United States. In 1848, James Polk tried to purchase Cuba for $100 million, but Spain refused to part with it on the basis that Cuba was more than just a colony. But the question never went away. Slave states in the United States dreamed of acquiring it (slavery wasn't abolished in Cuba until 1886). In 1854, a group of U.S. diplomats wrote a manifesto calling for outright annexation, but the remarkably undiplomatic Manifesto of Ostend (so named because it was written in Ostend, Belgium) created such a backlash in the United States that the issue was dropped for the next thirty years.

Meanwhile, the United States kept its eye on Cuba, if only to make sure that France or Britain didn't get the prize. Cuba produced 40 percent of the world's sugar, and a lot of Americans owned haciendas, or were involved in sugar, tobacco, mining, or railway businesses. Starting in the 1860s, anti-Spanish sentiment was on the rise in Cuba. Many Cuban students left the island to study at American universities. They brought baseball back to Cuba in the 1860s. As a result of U.S. involvement in the entire Caribbean basin, baseball became the most popular sport in the Dominican Republic, Panama, Venezuela, and Colombia. Cubans also took to it with a vengeance as an expression of Cuban nationalism.

Many Cuban nationalists also sought refuge in the United States, particularly in New York City. It was also in New York that a famous Cuban exile, the poet José Martí, founded the Partido Revolucionario Cubano (Cuban Revolutionary Party). Starting in the 1860s, American public opinion had strongly sided with insurgency movements in Cuba, but this sympathy became particularly intense during the Cuban revolutionary war of 1895–1898. Spain used especially heavy-handed tactics in Cuba. To contain the insurgency, the Spanish army invented a practice of confining populations to fortified towns and villages. They called it *reconcentrar* (reconcentrate). This is where the words, and the practice, of *concentration camps* come from.

The Spanish-American War began after the battleship *Maine* exploded in the port of Havana in February 1898. It had been stationed there to protect the eight thousand American nationals present on the island. Although the explosion's actual cause has never been established, the United States did not wait for the inquiry to interpret it as an act of war and declare war on Spain. The United States and Spain fought in Cuba, Puerto Rico, and the Philippines. In ten weeks, the United States had won what U.S. ambassador John Hay called a "splendid little war." Spain no longer had an empire, and the United States controlled Cuba, Puerto Rico, the Philippines, and the Mariana islands.

Formal control over Cuba lasted only three years. Nationalist sentiment was strong and the United States granted Cuba independence in 1902. But the U.S. government retained control over Cuba's finances and foreign policy, and Americans continued to intervene for the next sixty years. During that time, Cubans circulated in the United States, though they would become a significant presence only after Castro's revolution in 1959.

The Puerto Rican independence movement was never as strong as Cuba's, which may be one of the reasons why the United States never relinquished its hold on Puerto Rico. Slightly bigger than Delaware, but as populous as Connecticut, Puerto Rico is much, much smaller than either the Philippines, Cuba, or even Panama, yet its role in the building of the Hispanic presence in the United States was disproportionately great—if not tremendous. Nearly 2.7 million Puerto Ricans came to the United States during the twentieth century, a remarkable number for a country of 3.6 million inhabitants.

The root of Puerto Rican presence in the United States is Puerto Rico's status. The U.S. government has always been ambivalent about Puerto Rico, as reflected in the famously ambiguous 1901 Supreme Court ruling, which defined Puerto Rico as "foreign to the U.S. in a domestic sense." In 1917, Congress granted U.S. citizenship to all Puerto Ricans. However, the island never became a part of the Union but rather an Associated Free State (*Estado Libre Asociado*) with limited self-government in tax, education, and language. In spite of five referenda, the status quo prevails to this day.

Because Puerto Ricans are not immigrants properly speaking,

they move freely in and out of the continental United States. Their culture has remained dear to them. Between 1898 and 1944, forty thousand Puerto Ricans came to New York City. They formed structured communities there as early as the 1930s. The New York daily *El Diario-La Prensa* was founded in 1913. With Cubans, they were well established by the time of the great waves of Puerto Rican migrants in the 1950s. In 1964, 10 percent of the population of New York City was Puerto Rican.

Puerto Ricans would make their presence felt in all walks of American society. The list of famous Puerto Rican artists is stellar: Sammy Davis Jr., Luis Raul, Jennifer Lopez, Ricky Martin, Tito Puente, to name only the most famous. Puerto Ricans also climbed quickly up the ladder in American administration—including Antonia Novella, surgeon general from 1990 to 1993, and Supreme Court Justice Sonia Sotomayor, appointed in 2009.

Puerto Rico's influence is a study in contrast with that of the Philippines, whose effect on the future of Spanish in the United States was minimal. In fact, the Philippines, with Equatorial Guinea, are the only former Spanish colonies where the Spanish language declined. Contrary to Puerto Rico, Spanish was never solidly implanted there in the first place, and the Filipinos went along with U.S. colonial English-only policies. The 1903 census showed that no more than 11 percent of the Philippines population declared itself "Spanish." The 1918 census showed that 900,000 English speakers already outnumbered the 750,000 Spanish speakers. By 1945, 51 percent of the population spoke English. Because most Filipinos are strongly Catholic and maintained the custom of giving their children Spanish Christian names, Spanish seems more present than it ever was. Today, about three million Filipinos, in the total population of ninety-three million, speak Spanish.

All these actions—the Southwest takeover, the Puerto Rican colony, and the Panama Canal construction—created a strong domestic presence of Spanish in the United States by the time the big waves of Latin American immigration started in the 1960s. Curiously, the linguistic and cultural impact of the United States on its new territories was fairly shallow. This may well be because, like English speakers, Spanish speakers are not inclined to forfeit their language. The United States didn't erase Spanish where it took political control. It dislodged Spanish only in the Philippines, and not completely even there.

Elsewhere, Spanish remained resilient. The United States never succeeded in its policies to Anglicize Puerto Rico. Immediately after the conquest of the island in 1898, the American government tried to apply the same English-only education and government recipe that worked wonders in the Philippines. But Puerto Ricans' culture has remained important. They strongly asserted their right to be schooled and governed in Spanish, even if English does have a real presence there. Spanish remains the mother tongue of 95 percent of Puerto Ricans—a mere 5 percent are fully Anglicized, but they still need Spanish to function in Puerto Rican society.

On the whole, Spanish culture has proved itself not only resilient but also strong enough to fend off assimilation into American culture, even in the American Southwest. Spanish is an influential world language, after all. Like English-speaking cultures, Spanish-speaking cultures have repeatedly assimilated large numbers of new entrants—either immigrants or natives.

There's no doubt that this old domestic presence of Spanish primed Americans for what would happen next. Spain and Spanish were about to jump into American's living rooms—and in more ways than one.

23. The Spanish Renaissance

ERNEST HEMINGWAY: THE MERE EVOCATION of his name brings to mind hunting, fishing, and bullfighting. These motifs were already present in his first novel, *The Sun Also Rises,* about a group of friends who set out on an escapade to see the bullfight of Pamplona, Spain. Ernesto, as the Spanish are fond of calling him, was the first American writer whose entire body of work became deeply infused with Spain and Spanish culture.

In a way, Hemingway was dangerously bordering on the cliché. By the 1920s, the American public was steeped in Spain. What saved Hemingway from sounding commonplace was the sharpness of his point of view, or specifically his so-called iceberg theory, through which a character acquires weight by the fact that so much about him is left below the surface, unsaid. Like a character in his novels, Spain gained weight in Hemingway's work by omission. There really was more going on in Spain than bullfighting, and Hemingway knew it.

The world's interest in Spain had plummeted after the country's *Siglo de Oro.* Outside of Latin America, Spanish culture attracted little international attention during the eighteenth and most of the nineteenth century. Then, as the nineteenth century drew to a close, that changed. Suddenly Western Europe and the United States couldn't get enough of Spanish painting, flamenco dancing, guitar music, and *toreros* (bullfighters). Spain entered a kind of cultural renaissance. It was as if Spanish creators, inventors, and discoverers just woke up and realized there were advantages to sharing a common language with sixteen other countries. Spanish inventors and scientists paved the way to new discoveries, and Spanish philosophers began founding entirely new schools of thought. Hollywood directors made movies inspired by Spanish novels. The Spanish themselves embraced modern ideas as never before.

This renewed interest in Spain actually was kindled a century before Hemingway, when two authors, a king and a composer, suddenly saw Spain with new eyes. The first was the American Washington Irving (1783–1859). He developed an interest in Spain in 1826, when a U.S. ambassador lured him there with the promise that he could have full access to Spanish archives. It was a tempting offer for a writer always on the lookout for colorful new material and that's what Irving found. Two years later, he published the first of his "Spanish books," *Life and Voyages of Columbus*—the source of the extremely tenacious myth among schoolchildren that people before Columbus thought Earth was flat. In 1832, Irving published *Tales of the Alhambra,* a travelogue that portrayed Spain as a country caught in a time warp, both backward and picturesque, a mix of East and West, of Europe, America, and Africa, with abundant ruins of Christian and Islamic sites—in short, a cultural treasure trove that was still unmolested by modernity. Irving's romantic vision of Spain stuck, and even in Europe it helped shake off the *leyenda negra* (black legend) that had depicted Spain as a nation of tyrannical kings and malevolent inquisitors.

Around the same time, France's King Louis-Philippe (r. 1830–1848) decided it was time to rebuild relations with Spain's estranged Bourbon monarchy. Coincidentally, the king had decided to use Spanish art as an example that would steer French painters away from classicism and academism, toward realism. With that plan, he opened a "Spanish gallery" in the Louvre palace in 1838 and filled it with the work of Spanish masters like Diego Velázquez (1599–1660), the first to paint dwarfs and the common folk of Spain's court life. The initiative had exactly the effect the king had hoped for. French artists were deeply inspired by the realism of Velázquez's work.

Following Louis-Philippe's impetus, American art collectors became interested in Spanish art starting in the 1840s. It was as if

Americans suddenly became aware of a school of art that had been hidden from them for three centuries. *Siglo de Oro* painters like Velázquez and El Greco were suddenly regarded as among the greatest painters of all times. The public could not seem to get enough of Francisco de Goya (1746–1828). Goya's case is particularly interesting because he became immensely popular in the United States long after his death. Goya ushered in the modern age with his artistic freedom and personal views of the reality of his time: his political paintings of Spain's war of independence from France and the uncompromising realism he used to depict the Charge of the Mamelukes on May 2, 1808, are as stunning as the haunting Black Paintings he produced in his later years.

A few years after Louis-Philippe, a French novelist gave the growing craze for Spanish culture another push. In 1845, Prosper Mérimée (1803–1870) published his novella *Carmen,* which told the story of a beautiful Gypsy who fell in love with a soldier. Mérimée was the first to tie together the potent Spanish motifs of flamenco dancing, bold colors, bullfighting, Gypsies, and ruins. The images went on to make an impact internationally thanks to the French composer Georges Bizet (1838–1875), whose comic opera *Carmen,* based on Mérimée's novella, shot to planetary success shortly after the composer's death.

Today, Spain is so strongly associated with bolero, flamenco, and bullfighting that we tend to assume they are vestiges of ancient Spanish folklore. Yet when Spain came into fashion in the nineteenth century, all three were relatively new, at least in their modern forms.

Bolero, a musical style and dance form, was codified by Carlos III's dance master in 1780. Countless composers, including Maurice Ravel and Bizet, went on to write boleros, but the form would make its greatest impact on Cuban music, where it influenced the development of *contradanza* and *danzón*. Spanish bolero also inspired Mexican bolero, of which the most famous example is the

1941 song "Bésame mucho" and other successes like "Quízás, quízás, quízás" and "Dos gardenias."

Even though flamenco is now part of Unesco's Intangible World Heritage, like bolero it was quite new. Historians say it appeared in the last years of the eighteenth century. Essentially the blues of Spain, flamenco was a popular music and dance form that grew out of a mix of Arabic, Christian, Jewish, and Gypsy influences. It was born among the underclass of Gypsies living in Andalusia and saw the light of day after 1783, when King Carlos III passed a set of laws allowing Gypsies to practice their culture publicly. (Unfortunately, Carlos III's laws did not put an end to the persecution of Gypsies in Spain.)

Spaniards took up flamenco during and after the Napoleonic Wars, a time when they were rejecting everything foreign, particularly if it was French. After the wars, flamenco, which was originally exclusively Andalusian, became the embodiment of *hispanidad* (Spanishness) in the Spanish psyche. The vocabulary of flamenco quickly entered the Spanish mainstream, with words like *toque* (guitar playing), *palmas* (handclaps), *estilos* (melody and songs), and *palos* (various flamenco styles)—the most famous *palo* being *palo seco* (a cappella). By the end of the century, *cafés cantantes* (cabarets) were common in Spain, and Spanish society embraced *flamenquismo* (the affectation of flamenco customs).

In 1932, when Ernest Hemingway published his 517-page book on bullfighting, *Death in the Afternoon,* he was the first Western writer to explore bullfighting so deeply. Hemingway's last book, *The Dangerous Summer,* was also about bullfighting. In Spain, bullfighting is regarded more as an art form than a sport or a game. Spanish newspapers have *críticos taurinos* (bullfighting critics) who report on bullfighting in the cultural pages. It is called *tauromaquia, corrida* (for *correr,* to run) or more colloquially, *toros* (bulls), terms that describe very different bull games or bull runs. The man-to-bull struggle is only the best known and most spectacular of these forms in a country where every large city, and many small ones, has a *plaza de toros* (bullfighting arena), with the curious exception of Barcelona.

Bullfighting started in Spain with the Arabs and was originally done on horseback, not on foot. It was so common that in 1529, Cortés celebrated the anniversary of the taking of Mexico City with a bull run.

The big change in the art of the corrida took place in 1725 when the famous *matador* (killer) Francisco Romero got off his horse and stood waiting for the bull. After the bull charged through his cape several times, Romero killed it at close quarters with a stroke of his *estoque* (rapier). The technique of killing bulls by hand was common in slaughterhouses of the time, but Romero was the first to use it in the arena. In 1836, the famous matador Francisco Montes published a treatise on bullfighting called *Tauromaquia completa* (Complete Bullfighter) that formalized the modern ritual. Since then, the toreador has been at the center of the show, with the *picador* (lancer on horse) and *banderilleros* (lancers on foot) playing supporting roles in the killing.

Mexico, Peru, Colombia, Venezuela, Ecuador, Bolivia, Panama, and Costa Rica built their own *plazas de toro*. The corrida also made its way into southern France, thanks to Empress Eugenia, the Spanish wife of Napoleon III. The American poet Henry Wadsworth Longfellow studied Spanish in 1827, watching bullfights in Madrid. It was about that time that *aficionado* entered English vocabulary. The Spanish spoke of their passion for bullfighting as *la afición* (literally, the hobby). The word *aficionado* originally applied to bullfighting fans, but it, of course, later evolved to mean a knowledgeable fan of almost anything, from cigars to peppers and coffee.

When Jean-Benoît was growing up in the small town of Sherbrooke, Quebec, his family lived in a sprawling Tudor-style house built in 1914. The well-preserved interior of the house had one curious feature: the dining room was covered in austere wood paneling while the living room veered off into a totally different style: white walls, exposed beams, a stucco ceiling, wrought-iron gates, and alcoves with semicircular arches. We had always assumed this little irruption of Spanish-inspired features in the middle of a Tudor home was the product of a later owner's fancy, but Jean-Benoît's brother, who studied architecture, set us straight. The Spanish-style interior was part of the original 1914 design. The rage for Spanish architecture in North America in the first decades of the twentieth century was so strong it had made it all the way to Sherbrooke. The town even followed the interwar fad of giving cinemas Spanish or Italian names. It had a theater, built in 1929, called *Le Granada*.

When Hemingway began writing about Spain, the Spanish craze was already well under way. The Spanish-American War of 1898 had spelled the end of Spain's colonial empire, but it had an unexpected countercultural impact: right after the war, North Americans started loving everything Spanish. In the first years of the twentieth century, the New York–based sugar baron and art collector Henry Osborne Havemeyer joked that after winning the Spanish-American War, the United States should have gotten Spain's Prado Museum instead of the Philippines. In 1903, one of the main warmongers of the Spanish American War, the press tycoon William Randolph Hearst, attempted to purchase an entire Renaissance patio of the Casa de Miranda in Burgos, then have it dismantled, shipped, and reassembled in New York City. (The scheme was stymied by popular outcry in Burgos.) Later, Hearst imported a number of Spanish artifacts, including the elaborate *reja* (choir screen) from the cathedral of Valladolid, now on view on the main floor of the Metropolitan Museum in New York.

By the end of World War I, American Hispanophilia had evolved toward a taste for "Spanish kitsch," blending Andalusian motifs with ranch style. Stanford White's "Spanish flats"—a string of luxury apartment buildings on the southern edge of Central Park, each named after a different city in Spain—inspired copycat projects in San Francisco, Buffalo, Miami, Kansas City, and Cleveland. That also marked the beginning of the fashion of giving Spanish names such as the Alhambra or the Granada to theaters and entertainment venues.

Meanwhile, a more popular version of this Hispanophilia was taking shape, one that blended Spanish and Mexican influences. The trend was set off by the gigantic success of Helen Hunt Jackson's novel *Ramona,* published in 1884, depicting an idealized Mexican California before railroads were built. Around 1912, a Spanish Colonial Revival architectural style appeared in Florida and California, blending various Spanish Mission styles.

Another famous product of Spanish-Mexican kitsch was the legend of *El Zorro* (the Fox), created in 1920 by New York pulp-fiction writer Johnston McCulley. McCulley based his protagonist on California *bandidos* like Joaquín Murieta, Salómon Pico, Tiburcio Vázquez, and possibly William Lamport. The original story was set in California, but later films, whether they starred Douglas Fairbanks, Guy Williams, or Antonio Banderas, freely blended Spanish with Mexican Californian influences.

American fascination wasn't the sole factor driving this Spanish craze. Spanish culture had a lot more to offer than flamenco, bullfighting, and stucco ceilings. In fact, Spain had been experiencing an ongoing cultural renaissance since the 1850s, triggered by Napoleon's occupation of Spain between 1808 and 1812. Since the middle of the seventeenth century, Spain had been subjected to religious censorship that stifled the development of new ideas. In 1818, Spaniards decided to rid their country of some anachronisms, starting with the Inquisition. Although it had operated intermittently since 1808, the Spanish Inquisition executed its last victim in 1826. The event created such uproar in Europe that the Crown finally abolished the institution for good in 1834. The end of the Inquisition brought a breath of fresh air to Spanish society, and it transformed itself over the next two generations, culminating with a democratic revolution in 1868 called *La Gloriosa* (the Glorious One).

The spirit of modernization found a new expression in *panhispanismo* (Pan-Hispanism), formulated shortly after the Wars of Independence, when authors, merchants, and intellectuals from different parts of the Spanish-speaking world set out to build networks. Ernest Hemingway was the first Western writer to grasp what was going on, and then he became part of it, living in Cuba for twenty years, in a house called Finca Vigía (Lookout Farm) in San Francisco de Paula, near Havana. Cuba was the backdrop for the story of a poor Cuban fisherman that would become *The Old Man and the Sea*—and earn Hemingway a Nobel Prize.

This spirit of *panhispanismo* was already apparent in the way both Spain and the Americas had embraced Andrés Bello's work on language and grammar. But the Pan-Hispanists faced a major hurdle: the economies of Spain and Latin America were not complementary; neither had any industrial production to speak of, and both were primarily based on imports. As a result, Spain accounted for scarcely 4 percent of Latin America's international commerce. The United States' role in the economies of Latin America was much greater than Spain's. Still, even though intercontinental communications remained difficult, and although business interests clashed, during this period Spanish thinkers, writers, and businesspeople all endeavored to reach a broader, international audience and market, and this began with the former colonies

The development of encyclopedias was a sign that change was under way. Compared to the rest of Europe, Spain had been slow to start producing encyclopedias. The first one, published in thirty-four volumes between 1851 and 1855, was actually an adaptation of the French *Encyclopédie Moderne*. When Spain began producing its own encyclopedias, they were already infiltrated with the spirit of *panhispanismo*. Between 1887 and 1899, the Montaner i Simon publishing house launched the twenty-six-volume *Diccionario En-*

ciclopedico Hispano-Americano. But the genre reached its summit in 1908 with the *Enciclopedia universal ilustrada europeo-americana* (Universal Illustrated European-American Encyclopedia), pubished by Espasa in seventy volumes. Today's version, which has 110 volumes, 175,000 pages, and 200 million words, is even bigger than the *Britannica* and rivals it in the quality of its articles. And it has succeeded in appealing to Hispanics on both sides of the Atlantic.

This cultural and intellectual awakening quickly produced a generation of original thinkers, inventors, and creators. One of the most famous intellectuals of this period was the pathologist Santiago Ramón y Cajal, who received a Nobel Prize in Physiology or Medicine in 1906 for his seminal work on neuron theory. Ramón y Cajal was the first to demonstrate that neurons are not a continuous cable.

But he was not alone: a cohort of Spanish engineers and inventors made headway in a number of fields, attracting attention in Europe and the United States.

One of the most exemplary characters on this roster was the Catalan engineer Narcís Monturiol Estarriol, famous for designing and successfully testing the first engine-driven submarine in 1864— *el Ictíneo* (fish ship) *II.* His success inspired Jules Verne's *Nautilus* as the "setting" for his novel *20,000 Leagues Under the Sea.* Twenty-four years later, another Spaniard, the naval engineer Isaac Peral, designed the first true *submarino,* featuring electric motors, periscopes, and three torpedo-launching tubes.

The Spanish engineer and mathematician Leonardo Torres y Quevedo (1852–1936) created the first computer game and the first cableway, and pioneered the field of remote control, guiding a boat by radio in the port of Bilbao in 1906. This last achievement was not entirely surprising, since another Spaniard, Julio Cervera Baviera (1854–1929), was working with Guglielmo Marconi to develop wireless telegraphy. The Spanish engineer Juan de la Cierva (1895–1936) designed the first articulated rotor, making the first stationary flight possible in 1923, a critical step in the development of helicopter design. The filmmaker José Val del Omar was a pioneer in the use of stereophonic sound, with which he experimented in the 1940s.

During the same period of intellectual ferment, the Spanish philosopher José Ortega y Gasset (1883–1955) rose to prominence. In 1914, this Jesuit-educated thinker formulated a maxim that was the foundation of his philosophy: *Yo soy yo y mi circunstancia* (I am I and my circumstance), contradicting Descartes's "I think therefore I am," by stating that the self cannot exist on its own. In his readable writing style, Ortega y Gasset's numerous works represented breakthroughs in Western thought as well as popular successes. Ortega y Gasset was the first to state, "We have no nature, only history." He influenced existentialism, in particular Martin Heidegger's philosophy of being.

Another Spaniard of the period would become the most legendary painter of the twentieth century: Pablo Diego José Francisco de Paula Juan Nepomuceno María de los Remedios Cipriano de la Santísima Trinidad Ruiz y Picasso. Pablo Picasso (1881–1973), along with his friend Georges Braque, created a new painting school, cubism in 1907, when Picasso was an expatriate artist in Paris. Although Andalusian by birth, Picasso had spent his formative years in Catalonia. Barcelona had become the economic and industrial locomotive of Spain at the time, attracting many artists and architects. Picasso's father, himself a painter, took a job at the School of Fine Arts and moved the family to Barcelona when Picasso was fourteen. Picasso always regarded Barcelona as his home. And he paved the way for other Catalans, including Salvador Dalí (1904–1989) and Joan Miró (1893–1883), who matched Picasso in importance, if not reputation.

The architect Antoni Gaudí (1852–1926), born a generation before Picasso and two before Dalí and Miró, was also an inspiration to fellow Catalans. Part of the Catalan *modernista* movement, Gaudí developed a personal style that was organic and inspired by nature, placing him in direct opposition to the modernist Bauhaus movement in Germany. Gaudí's creations, landmarks in Barcelona, are immediately recognizable with their sinuous lines, round volumes, and combinations of materials like broken tiles and wrought iron. Gaudí even applied bridge-building techniques to buildings. Nothing like Gaudí's buildings had ever been constructed—although his chef d'oeuvre, the cathedral of Sagrada Família, remains unfinished after a century of work—but the link with Salvador Dalí's soft-hard structures is unmistakable.

This turn-of-the-century cohort of creators and thinkers were labeled the *Generación del 98*—it's a customary way of labeling groups of creators in the Spanish-speaking world. There's a *Generación del* 14, 27, 30, 36, 37, 50, and 80 (not all of which were Spanish in origin). Ninety-eight was highly significant: great changes were already under way in Spain by the time of the Spanish-American War of 1898, which Spaniards call *El Desastre.* More than the military rout itself, it was the catastrophic return of tens of thousands of malnourished and sick soldiers that provoked a sudden realization in Spain—even in the country's most conservative spheres—that the old ways would not work.

In its strictest sense, the *Generación del 98* refers to a school of modernist writers, mostly poets, who wanted to shake off a century of academism. Forming in the wake of *El Desastre,* the group crystallized into a kind of intellectual revolt that took multiple shapes, most markedly in literature. But the members didn't limit themselves to versifying. They examined many different ideas for saving their country, from practical reforms to new artistic concepts. Their contribution marked the opening of an important new chapter in the history of Spanish literature and political economy.

The model to emulate was José Echegaray (1832–1916), who in 1904 was the first Spaniard to win a Nobel Prize. Echegaray was not only a dramatist but also a civil engineer, mathematician, and politician, and he made significant contributions in all these fields. As a minister in successive governments, he was behind the development of railways in Spain and the creation of the Bank of Spain.

His writing and political work embodied the spirit of the *Generación del 98* even though he was a generation older than most other members of the movement.

One of the biggest names of the *Generación del 98* was Miguel de Unamuno (1864–1936), a poet, novelist, essayist, and philosopher. Unamuno regarded the *novelas* genre as fossilized and tried to distance himself from it with a new label: the *nivola*. Among his many pursuits, Unamuno created the personal novel, an existentialist novel before the word, whose characters are little more than incarnations of ideas. His 1914 *Niebla* (Mist) ends with a striking innovation: a philosophical dialogue between the creator and his creation, where the main character, Augusto, debates with the author as to whether or not he should kill himself.

The other renowned writer of the period was Vicente Blasco Ibáñez (1867–1928), in whose disturbing novels the elementary passions of greed, lust, and hate collide with the primitive forces of hunger, poverty, sickness, and death. His 1916 novel *Los cuatro jinetes del apocalipsis* (The Four Horsemen of the Apocalypse) was a best seller in the United States and was the basis for Rudolph Valentino's debut film. Between 1922 and 1926, five more of Blasco Ibáñez's novels became movies: *Blood and Sand, The Enemies of Woman, The Temptress, Mare Nostrum,* and *The Torrent* (the last featured Greta Garbo).

The famous tango scene of the *Four Horsemen of the Apocalypse,* with Rudolph Valentino in gaucho pants (the story begins in Buenos Aires), illustrates the other factor driving the renaissance of Spanish culture between 1850 and 1945: Latin America's coming of age.

24. The Latin Rage

TANGO IS TO ARGENTINE TOURISM what wine and food are to French tourism: inescapable. In Argentina's case, tango was also fortuitous. Tango went through a revival in the 1980s, so foreigners began flocking to Buenos Aires's tango schools and *milongas* (clubs and dance halls), bringing some relief to Argentina's economic slump between 1976 and 2003.

A century before that, cultivated Argentines would have balked at the idea of being associated with tango. At that time, tango wasn't even considered a dance style, let alone an art form. The origins of the name *tango* are obscure. It might have evolved from a traditional Andalusian dance called *tango flamenco,* but that dance was more like a rumba. In colonial times, tango was the name for a place where slaves were sold in the Americas. And generations of Spanish colonials used the word for any kind of music that slaves produced.

The name tango eventually became associated with the dance and music that was rising from the slums of Buenos Aires and Montevideo in the nineteenth century. The word was used by people who spoke *lunfardo,* the criminal jargon of Buenos Aires, which injected Italian, French, and English terms into Spanish, creating words like *jáilaif* for high life and using syllable inversion techniques like *gotán* (for tango) or *feca de chele* (for *café de leche*). Like tango culture, many *lunfardo* expressions are now part of mainstream speech in Argentina.

Tango music itself comes from Cuban habanera, a popular nineteenth-century dance played on European instruments, particularly the German *bandoneón* (concertina), now a mainstay of the *orquestra típica* (tango sextet). The dance originated in brothels, where it was a form of speed dating for hundreds of thousands of male immigrants stuck in the slums of Buenos Aires. One of Argentina's most famous tango composers, Enrique Santos Discépolo, coined a perfect metaphor to describe the genre, calling it *"un pensamiento triste que se baila"* (a sad thought that you dance). Tango fans use the expression *vivirse un tango* (to live, or to experience a tango), because the very close physical contact and the improvisation are as much an experience as a dance.

But it was the Parisians who really "discovered" tango at the end of the nineteenth century. Young Argentines sent to Paris to study brought it with them and sparked a trend. In 1912, a troupe of Argentine performers toured Paris. After that, Argentine dancers flocked there, setting off a veritable tango craze that then spread to London, Berlin, and most European capitals. The first tango show in the United States took place in New York City in 1913.

It was the Paris craze that pushed Argentines to accept that tango was not a form of lechery but a new dance with artistic merit. Tango's popularity shot up in the 1920s, slipped in the 1930s, then climbed again in 1943 with the election of Juan Perón, who adopted it as a national emblem under *peronismo* (Perón's personal movement). This was not an isolated case: in the same period, the Dominican Republic's dictator Rafael Trujillo declared merengue the national dance of the Dominican Republic for similar reasons. Tango went out of style after Perón was ousted in 1955 and the military dictatorships banned public gatherings. But another Parisian fad—the 1983 musical *Tango Argentino,* followed by the 1994 Broadway musical *Forever Tango* in 1994—revived tango once again.

Just as Argentine composers, dancers, and poets started attracting attention in the early twentieth century, Cuban musicians and Mexican filmmakers and painters were also gaining recognition. When tango took off in the 1910s, Latin America was joining Spain in the international resurgence of Spanish culture and language. This was partly coincidence. Spain happened to be entering a period of cultural rebirth just as Latin American cultural production was coming into its own. But the Spanish craze of the late nineteenth and early twentieth centuries had created more demand for Spanish culture than Spain could meet on its own. Thanks to *panhispanismo,* Latin American authors and intellectuals started to think of themselves not just as part of a large, Spanish-speaking international public but also as a large, international Spanish-speaking network of creators.

In the early twentieth century, Latin American creators who wanted to make it in the Spanish-speaking world had to make it in Buenos Aires first. Argentina had dispensed with the age of caudillos and dictators by the 1860s. By the 1920s, it was one of the wealthiest nations in the world. Buenos Aires, at the height of its splendor, was home of one of the richest artistic scenes of the era. It nearly surpassed Mexico in population, and its cultural production eclipsed every other center on the continent, aside from New York. It had a vigorous theater, concert, exhibition, and opera life, and a well-established book industry. The newspapers *La Nación* and *La Prensa* and the cultural review *Nosotros* were widely read throughout the Americas.

Although gauchos and the pampa were unifying national myths, Argentina's culture, like its population, was predominantly European. This Eurocentric view would be challenged later in the twentieth century when Mexico became more influential and other centers like Havana, Caracas, and Bogotá developed their own strong cultural industries. Yet Buenos Aires remained an important cultural center—its international book fair is twice as big and twice as old as Mexico's.

Education was an important factor that turned Argentina into Latin America's cultural locomotive. Wealth was fairly well distributed because the country had the most unionized working class in Latin America. By 1960, 40 percent of the country ranked as middle class, the highest proportion south of the Rio Grande.

Argentina continues to benefit from having a better education system than other Latin American countries. Five of Latin America's fifteen Nobel Prize winners are Argentine: Carlos Saavedra Lamas (Peace, 1936), Bernardo Houssay (Physiology, 1947), Luis Federico Leloir (Chemistry, 1970), Adolfo Pérez Esquivel (Peace, 1980), and César Milstein (Physiology, 1984). Argentines have always been strong in physiology: Juan Vucitech pioneered fingerprinting and scientific crime scene investigation in 1892, Domingo Liotta designed the first artificial heart, and René Favoloro perfected bypass surgery.

In short, Argentines have always taken excellence to heart.

Yet Argentina owed its tango and music largely to Cubans. Cuba was Latin America's first success story in exporting music. Rumba, salsa, cha-cha-cha, and mambo are the best-known examples of the music that gave Cuba its almost indecent hold on international ballroom dancing.

The roots of Cuban music are, of course, African, but with a Haitian twist. When slave rebellions broke out in French Saint-Domingue in 1791, estate owners and some of their slaves fled to eastern Cuba, bringing Afro-French culture with them. One musical genre that had evolved in Saint-Domingue was the *contredanse*, a fast-paced quadrille (the word came from the English "country dance"). In Cuba, the *contredanse* became popular as *contradanza*.

By 1836, the *contradanza* had evolved into the slower habanera. The habanera owed its success to two factors. The first was the use of *tresillo* (triplet), playing three notes in the time of two. The habanera's other virtue is that it is not just a musical genre or a dance, but also a song.

The habanera became Cuba's first contribution to world music. It was the basis for the famous aria in the opera *Carmen*, "*L'amour est un oiseau rebelle*" (Love is a rebellious bird), composed in 1874. Habanera also became very popular in Buenos Aires, where it evolved into tango. (The link between habanera and tango is so strong that people unfamiliar with tango mistakenly associate Carmen's aria with the Argentine dance.)

While the habanera was conquering the music world, Cubans wasted no time creating another genre out of it in the 1870s: *el danzón*. That set off a trend toward increased syncopation—notes played off-beat, a feature in the later evolution of Cuban music. *El danzón* became immensely popular in Mexico, and it is still played in Mexico City and Veracruz, which is why it is often confused with mariachi music. The unofficial anthem of Puerto Rico, "Verde Luz" (Green Light) by Antonio Cabán Vale, is a *danzón*.

By the 1910s, *danzón* had evolved into yet another type of music, Cuban *son* (sound), which was even more syncopated. The film *Buena Vista Social Club* is credited for introducing Cuban *son* to a world audience in 1997. Oddly, though, the Cubans did not embrace producer Ry Cooder's global hit because it was old news for them. Between 1920 and 1960, Cuban *son* had itself produced five new musical and dance genres: rumba, salsa, mambo, cha-cha-cha, and *pachanga*. These would go on to be even more popular internationally than Argentine tango.

The rumba craze began in the 1920s. Rumba was originally an outdoor dance performed by slum dwellers in Havana housing projects called *solares,* and by dockworkers in the western town of Matanzas. The style appeared at almost exactly the same time as the recording industry was born: the rumba's three-minute tunes turned out to be perfectly adapted to 78's (records with one song per side, which in turn shaped the standard of pop music). In the late 1920s, rumba and *son* spread throughout Cuba, then across the globe. They became even more popular among tourists in Cuba, especially Puerto Ricans. In the United States, the great popularizer of this genre was a Harlem-born Puerto Rican named Tito Puente, also known as *el rey del jazz latino* (the king of Latin jazz).

The names of Cuban music and dances are tied to Cuban musical slang spoken in *descargas* (jam sessions). Rumba is just the feminine form of *rumbo* (route). Salsa came from the title of a *son* song composed by Ignacio Piñeiro, originally as a crowd warmer, called "*Échale Salsita*" (literally "pour the little sauce," meaning "spice it up a bit"). The word *mambo,* the title of a song by Cachao López, has mixed origins but probably came from Haitian Creole, and more specifically from the Yoruba, where it means, "to talk." The origins of cha-cha-cha are better known: the violinist Enrique Jorrín coined the name as the onomatopoeia of the shuffling of feet and the ratchetlike sound of the *güiro,* the celebrated Latin American gourd-shaped percussion instrument that produces a scraping sound.

There was practically no limit to the international Latin music rage. One of the biggest stars of the 1940s was a French Canadian, Alys Robi (whose real name was Alice Robitaille), forerunner to Celine Dion. Robi produced a string of Latin-flavored hits despite the fact that she was a French speaker from a snowy province. A child prodigy, she was singing professionally at thirteen. By age twenty, she had learned enough English, Spanish, Portuguese, and Italian to translate from and compose songs in all four. Her biggest hit was "*Tico Tico*," adapted from a Brazilian *choro* (lament) called "*Tico-Tico No Fubá.*" Robi sang her Latin American repertoire on tours in London and in large venues in the United States and Latin America.

Over the same period, Latin American literature slowly starting coming into its own. Latin Americans earned six Nobel Prizes in Literature in the twentieth century, starting with the Chilean poet Gabriela Mistral in 1945.

The best adjective to describe the Latin American literary scene before the twentieth century is *convulsive.* Great works appeared, but nothing followed them. A distinctive criollo literary tradition had started emerging in the nineteenth century. But for the most part, literature of the century either followed classical models or veered into idealistic romanticism. Readers were fed a steady diet of heroic hymns, patriotic odes, elegies, madrigals, epigrams, fables, and comedies and tragedies.

The over-the-top idealism of most of the Latin American writing explains why the Mexican novelist José Joaquín Fernández de Lizardi's *El Periquillo Sarniento* (The Mangy Parrot) stood out so much when he published it in 1816. It was both a picaresque novel and a satirical look at opportunism and corruption in contemporary Mexican society. It was a great departure from the generic style of most novels of the period.

Andrés Bello had tried to forge a genre rooted in Latin America's realities in 1804, with his *"Oda a la vacuna"* (Ode to Vaccination), and in 1826, with *La agricultura de la zona tórrida* (Agriculture in the Torrid Zone). Although critics panned his poems, Bello had tapped into a theme that would mark Latin American writing to come: the land. Nineteenth-century Latin American authors followed nationalist agendas and sought emblematic images—the Indian, the gaucho, the Andes, the tropical forests. This spawned *Indianismo,* a type of romantic novel that exalted preconquest native life (and ignored contemporary natives). It took this long for Latin Americans to do what French novelists had done a century earlier: give natives heroic roles. And curiously, the genre emerged mostly in Latin American countries where natives weren't a social issue, like the Dominican Republic, where they had been wiped out. In contrast, few nineteenth-century Mexican or Peruvian authors went in for *Indianismo.*

The Romantic movement arrived late in Latin America, in the 1870s. One of the most distinguished writers was the Peruvian Ricardo Palma (1833–1919), creator of *Tradiciones peruanas* (Peruvian Traditions), a chronicle of stories that *combine* history and fiction—the style became known as *tradiciones.* Then the Cuban poet and revolutionary José Martí (1853–1895) brought Modernism to Latin America. Martí's style was a mix of simplicity, ingenuity, and vigor. Exiled in 1871 at the age of eighteen after spending a year in prison, he returned to Cuba only twice, for three years, over the next twenty-four years. Even though he was in exile for most of it, he devoted his entire life to the Cuban revolutionary cause wherever he lived, in Venezuela, Spain, and long periods in Mexico and Guatemala. Martí also spent fourteen years in the United States. That's where he published the first modernist novel in Spanish, *Amistad funesta* (Regrettable to Friendship), in 1885. Martí coined phrases that became common refrains in Spanish American culture, including *"Hay un solo niño bello en el mundo y cada madre lo tiene"* (The world has only one beautiful child, and it's the child of every mother) and *"Vale más un minuto de pie que una vida de rodillas"* (Better a minute standing than a life on your knees).

The absolute giant of the period was the Nicaraguan poet Félix Rubén García Sarmiento, better known as Rubén Darío (1867–1916). The interest in Darío's poetry today is mostly academic, but he played an enormous role in the development of Latin American literature. The world of Spanish poetry is divided into "before Darío" and "after Darío," and more precisely before and after *Azul* (Blue), his 1888 collection of poems and tales. Published in Chile (where Darío was despised by the upper society because of his mestizo roots), *Azul* was met with silence, until the famous literary critic Juan Valera realized that he was in the presence of something entirely original. He wrote in a tribute: *"Ni es Ud. romántico, ni naturalista, ni neurótico, ni decadente, ni simbólico, ni parnasiano. Usted lo ha revuelto todo."* (You're neither a romantic, nor naturalist, nor neurotic, nor decadent, nor symbolic, nor a Parnassian. You've scrambled them all.)

Rubén Darío became the biggest name in Spanish poetry since the *Siglo de Oro*. Critics had to head back four centuries, to the old rivalry between the poets Francisco de Quevedo and Luis de Góngora, to find Spanish poetry that was so personal and so perfectly tied together. Darío's poems, at once fluent, flexible, musical, and diaphanous, earned him the title of *Principe de las letras castellanas* (Prince of Castilian letters). In Darío's wake, Spanish poets began exploding conventions of meter, verse, and language, and started introducing foreign terms—the Mexican poet Manuel Gutiérrez Nájera went as far as rhyming the name "Job" with "Jockey Club" in one of his poems.

In an era of exiled literary figures, Darío was an itinerant writer. He couldn't settle anywhere for more than a couple of years. After living in El Salvador for a time, he moved to half a dozen countries before staying for a time in Argentina, where he published two important books: *Los raros* (the adjective means eccentric and strange, but it's about Darío's literary models) and *Prosas profanas* (Profane Prose). Then he traveled all over Central America, Cuba, Spain, and France. "Everywhere he enthused poets young and old, inspiring clubs and associations, and writing innumerable articles for newspapers in each country he visited," notes Leslie Bethell in his comprehensive *Cultural History of Latin America*. His connection with Argentina was particularly intense. He inspired Leopoldo Lugones (1874–1938), one of the most influential writers in Argentine literature. As a chronicler for the Argentine newspaper *La Nación,* Darío was welcomed everywhere. He was honorary consul for Colombia in Argentina. Later he was Nicaragua's ambassador to Spain. He was fêted everywhere he traveled, before dying of alcoholism at the young age of forty-nine.

In cultural terms, Mexico had been asleep during the period Buenos Aires dominated Latin American culture, between 1850 and 1920. But Mexico awoke between 1920 and 1940, and took the lead in entire new industries: cinema, recording, radio, and television. Other countries went on to become centers of their own, including Colombia, Venezuela, Chile, and Cuba, but none would match Mexico.

It took Mexico a long time to emerge from the century of cultural lethargy that culminated in the so-called Mexican Revolution of 1910–1920—so-called because it was actually a civil war. The war cost nine hundred thousand lives, a tremendous loss for a country of fifteen million, especially since it happened after a century of self-inflicted wounds. By the end of the Mexican Revolution, Mexicans realized that racial strife and divisions among the criollos, mestizos, and *Indios* had stifled their country during the previous century and the whole colonial period that preceded it.

The rise of Mexico also signaled the rise of a different sort of Latin American culture, less European and Belle Époque, like in Buenos Aires, and more endogenic and mestizo. Now Mexican culture would shift its focus from *hispanidad* (Hispanicity) to *americanismo*. In the 1920s, Mexico established itself as the most representative Spanish American republic, home of cultural nationalism and *latinoamericanismo,* with a resolutely "third-world" ideological orientation even before the concept was formalized by the French demographer Alfred Sauvy in 1952.

Only the Spanish Civil War and Cuban Revolution can compare with the impact of the Mexican Revolution on Hispanic art, culture, and thought since the 1920s. The shift was expressed in debates over language that focused on two questions: Could the true language of Mexico really be a colonial language from Spain? Would the Madrid Standard be the true standard of Spanish in Mexico, or should Mexico have its own national standard? These questions were tackled incrementally. In the end, the answers were yes, Mexico's language would be Spanish, and yes, it would also develop its own standard.

Mexican literature, the most abundant on the continent during the Spanish colonial period, had stalled during the nineteenth century. By 1900, it was entering a new phrase. Under the influence especially of the French writer Émile Zola, Mexican authors began treating daring themes like syphilis and alcoholism. One of the most emblematic writers of the revolutionary period was Mariano Azuela, a field doctor in one of the revolutionary armies. Azuela took refuge in El Paso in 1915, where he published a serial novel called *Los de Abajo* (The Underdogs), which inaugurated a fictional subgenre called the "novel of the Mexican Revolution." Mexican literature's maturation would be slow, but it developed a particularly strong bond with Mexican cinema and, later, television.

By 1920, language was a central pillar of Mexican identity. That was partly thanks to the revolution, when the government began investing massively in libraries, theaters, museums, and radio programs and put in place a vast education system with the hope of creating a single Mexican identity out of Mexico's mixed population of criollos, Indios, and mestizos. This gigantic educational machine, hungry for content, fed not only on Mexican cultural production but on everything the Spanish-speaking world was producing, including rumba, salsa, Argentine literature, and Spanish poetry. While Argentines were rallying to the French artistic tradition and embracing other European vogues, Mexicans embraced the mystical exaltation of the Indian peasant and the urban proletariat. In the process, Mexico started generating material in visual arts and cinema that was entirely original.

The intellectual figure who captured the essence of this quest— and, in fact, created most of its institutional impact—was José Vasconcelos (1882–1959), rector of the National University in 1919, minister of education in 1921, and presidential candidate in 1929. As a statesman, Vasconcelos was responsible for initiating the revolution that created the Mexican education system and established its public libraries. His strong *americanista* point of view was articulated in his major work, *La Raza Cósmica* (The Cosmic Race), published in 1925. Contrary to what the title suggests, Vasconcelos's work was not science fiction; it was the cornerstone of *indigenismo* (the celebration of ancient indigenous cultural heritage). Vasconcelos's purpose in writing *La Raza Cósmica* was to give the oppressed (the mestizo and the Indians) a reason to be proud and move beyond racism, a process begun, somewhat inadvertently, during the Latin American independence movement between 1810 and 1830. The early revolutionaries, he wrote, "formulated the transcendental mission assigned to that region of the globe: the mission of fusing the peoples ethnically and spiritually." In his introduction, he explained what his title meant: "*Llegaremos en América, antes que en parte alguna del globo, a la creación de una raza hecha con el tesoro de todas las anteriores, la raza final, la raza cósmica*" (We will come, in the Americas before anywhere else in the world, to the creation of a race made from the treasures of all of those of a final race, a cosmic race). That was the impetus for the motto he coined for Mexico's National University: "*Por mi raza hablará el Espíritu*" (Through my race the spirit will speak).

The original intention of his essay was fundamentally universalist and antiracist. It went on to inspire generations of young creators in Mexico, Peru, and Guatemala. Unfortunately, in the 1930s, Vasconcelos veered toward a more stridently nationalist and reactionary idea of *hispanidad,* which is why his theory of *la raza* is often wrongly decried as antiwhite racism, especially in the United States. Fortunately, Vasconcelos was by then out of power and could neither influence the course of things nor put his Fascist sympathies into practice.

Octavio Paz (1914–1998), who won the Nobel Prize for Literature in 1990, is probably the best product of Vasconcelos's efforts to boost cultural production and create an authentic Mexican national identity. Paz was a prolific writer and poet. He was also an intellectual heir to Vasconcelos—the good side of him—because much of his work is a reflection on what it means to be Mexican. One of his masterpieces was a collection of nine essays, written in Paris, titled *El Laberinto de la soledad* (The Labyrinth of Solitude). Published in 1950, the essays constitute a biting, extremely penetrating analysis of the Mexican personality. Paz presents Mexicans as lost in an existential labyrinth of all the identities they carry. He pushes deeply his reflections on themes like death, the fiesta, and *la Malinche.*

Mexico's awakening was also felt in its visual arts—especially with *muralismo* (mural art), for which Vasconcelos himself had a particular fascination.

Muralismo was a direct product of the Mexican Revolution's goal of educating the masses. In its simplest sense, it glorified everyday occupations in colorful settings. Since most Mexicans were illiterate, this public art was meant to serve as a kind of book of common history. It made instant celebrities out of *los tres grandes* (the three great ones): José Clemente Orozco, David Alfaro Siqueiros, and—the best known of the three—Diego Rivera.

Rivera had been living in Paris for fourteen years when Vasconcelos called him back to Mexico in 1921 to participate in a government-sponsored mural program. Rivera painted a series of 235 vibrantly colored panels at the Secretariat of Public Education that glorified all things Mexican: workers, festivals, markets, landscapes, arts and sciences, religion and, of course, the Mexican Revolution. His best-known and most spectacular fresco is in the staircase of the Palacio Nacional in Mexico City, which portrays the entire history of Mexico.

Rivera's larger-than-life personality matched his brilliance in mural painting. Rivera was tall for a Mexican—six feet two—and he weighed around three hundred pounds. An avowed Communist, he produced work that even Mexican Communists considered too controversial. He hosted the exiled Leon Trotsky in his home in Mexico City from 1933 to 1935. In spite of his views, Rivera was invited to make murals in the United States, in San Francisco and for the Detroit Institute of Arts. But his work for Rockefeller Center in New York, which included a figure of Lenin, provoked such outrage that it was painted over and never shown.

And then there was Mexican cinema. The industry began in 1898—two years after the Lumière brothers introduced cinema in Paris—with a primitive fiction film by Salvador Toscano Barragán. Latin America quickly developed thriving national film industries and one of the largest audiences in the world. Until 1914, the French Pathé film company dominated the Latin American market, with branch offices in Mexico City, Buenos Aires, Havana, and Rio de Janeiro. But World War I paralyzed European filmmakers and Hollywood quickly moved in and captured some 95 percent of the Latin American market.

The talkies gave Mexican cinema a second life. In the 1930s, the Mexican public was tired of the Hollywood cliché of the wild-eyed, dangerous, and uncontrollable Mexican revolutionary. With the introduction of sound, the Mexican public grew positively in-dignant hearing so-called Mexican characters speak with Spanish or Argentine accents. The Mexicans' outrage, supported by the nationalist policies of Lázaro Cárdenas, fueled the Golden Age of Mexican cinema, which started in 1935 with the success of *¡Vá-monos con Pancho Villa!* (Let's Go with Pancho Villa!) and lasted until 1969.

World War II was another boost to the Mexican film industry. Because Mexico had sided with the Allies, the U.S. government encouraged Mexico to build up its national film industry while it slapped restrictions on films from Argentina, which had refused to go to war.

In the 1940s, Mexico was producing an average of 70 films per year, with a peak of 107 in 1949, for a share of 24 percent of the domestic Mexican domestic market. Films tended to be extremely patriotic, yet some attracted international audiences. *María Can-deleria,* directed by Emilio "El Indio" Fernández and starring the Hollywood actress Dolores del Rio, won the Palme d'Or in 1946. (Fernandez is also famous in Hollywood lore for having been the physical model for the Oscar design.) Mexican cinema was always very popular at the box office and developed its own subgenres, from *rumberas* (cabaret films) to *rancheras* (ranching or rural) and *churros* (B-movies). The great star Pedro Infante was known as *El ídolo del pueblo* (the idol of the people). Chano Urueta directed no fewer than 116 films during his career. Domingo Soler shot more than 150. Raul de Anda played in only 36 films, but he produced 140. Eduardo Arozamena was involved in 97 films. The Golden Age of Mexican cinema cast a shadow on other Latin American cinema industries, notably Argentina's, which wouldn't undergo a revival until the 1980s (when Mexican cinema collapsed).

Given Mexico's bourgeoning cultural scene, Cuba's effervescent music world, and the Hispanic world's general brilliance, it's no wonder that people in *El Norte* developed a sudden interest in learning Spanish.

25. Learning Curve

PUEBLA, MEXICO, IS A PICTURE-PERFECT place to learn Spanish. A slow-paced, medium-sized city a couple of hours from Mexico City, it has a beautiful historical center, a zócalo lined with restaurants and shops, lots of bookstores, cafés, and museums, and a friendly, educated population. With its 1.6 million inhabitants, Mexico's fourth-biggest city has the greatest concentration of universities outside of the capital. In fact, Puebla has all the advantages of Mexico City but on a smaller scale—and without the smog.

We visited one of Puebla's Spanish schools to talk to students about their motivations for studying Spanish. The students we met were mostly middle-aged Americans, including an entrepreneur, some evangelical Christian missionaries, a dentist, a recent divorcée, and a priest, all of whom had taken time off from work specifically to learn Spanish.

Naturally, we wondered, with English being hailed as the international language of business, why would so many Americans think they had to learn Spanish to get ahead in their jobs? Their answer: they needed Spanish for their work.

Among the students, Ken Vialpando was an interesting case. Ken passed for a local in Puebla. He was the son of a Mexican mother and Spanish father, and had grown up in Tooele, a small town thirty-four miles southwest of Salt Lake City. "When I was growing up, Utah was predominantly Mormon, blond haired and blue eyed," he explained. "My parents refused to teach me or my brother Spanish. They wanted us to have a heads-up in life. And we would only fit in if we spoke English."

But Ken hadn't come to Puebla to reconnect with his roots. Just like everyone else, he said he needed Spanish for his job. Since his ordination as a Catholic priest in 1991, the ethnic composition of

Catholic congregations in Utah had shifted from predominantly blond-haired and blue-eyed to majority Latino. Today, 70 percent of Ken's congregation is Hispanic. "I had to learn Spanish. Otherwise, I knew I would lose them," he said.

Evidently, Ken's superiors knew too. They happily paid for him to spend a month in Mexico to build his vocabulary (because, curiously, like many re-acculturating Mexicans, Ken spoke with a perfect accent). Ken told us, with a wink, "Thanks be to God and to our Blessed Mother that she appeared to the people of Mexico. Their faith is strong and they pack the churches!"

Most Americans view the interest in learning Spanish as a relatively recent affair sparked by Hispanic immigration over the previous decades. There is some truth to this. Yet American attitudes about Spanish shifted considerably during the twentieth century, particularly in the first half, as the attitude about learning all languages changed.

Despite its deep Hispanic roots and the proximity of a Spanish-speaking continent, there was barely any Spanish teaching in the United States prior to the nineteenth century. In Philadelphia, in 1749, the trustees of the city's Public Academy (now the University of Pennsylvania) expressed the desire to hire teachers of French, Spanish, and German. The records don't show whether they actually found teachers to fill the positions. At Harvard College, Paul Fooks started teaching French and Spanish in 1766. A decade later, he was still teaching French, but Spanish had vanished from the curriculum.

The American Revolution sparked a bit of interest in Spanish, mostly because Spain, like France, supported it. After the revolution, a teacher from Bordeaux, Benjamin Nones, became the first official Spanish interpreter of the embryonic U.S. government.

Thomas Jefferson was the first person to claim that Spanish was an "important language" for Americans. Jefferson was an avid reader with a huge personal library that included works in Spanish. In

1787, fourteen years before he became president, Jefferson instructed his nephew, Peter Carr, to "bestow great attention to the Spanish language," predicting that future relations with Spain and Latin America would make Spanish "a valuable acquisition." Jefferson knew enough Spanish himself to write letters in Spanish about the pronunciation of Greek poetry. He convinced the University of Virginia to adopt a modern language studies program offering French, Italian, Spanish, and German.

The problem was that no one in nineteenth-century scholarly and educational circles was interested in Spanish. The students who attended college preferred French or German. France was experiencing a century of cultural glory, and French was still the world's diplomatic tongue, while German was the language of the United States' largest ethnic minority and was making inroads as a language of technology. In the nineteenth century, bilingual German-English instruction was common in elementary schools, particularly in the Midwest.

In his short history of Spanish teaching in United States, the renowned American Hispanicist Sturgis Leavitt wrote, with almost comical understatement, that the story of Spanish teaching in nineteenth-century United States was "not one of continuous growth."

Interest in Spanish started to grow as the century progressed. But there were so few teachers that it was difficult to structure programs, so Spanish teaching had trouble getting off the ground. Harvard, a trailblazer in teaching Spanish literature, had struggled to find qualified scholars fluent in Spanish to start a Spanish department. In 1816, Harvard hired George Ticknor, a well-traveled Boston lawyer with an interest in the humanities and European culture, to teach Spanish. Ticknor had just one flaw: he didn't know Spanish. Harvard solved that by sending him to Madrid to learn it. Ticknor was an earnest student, commencing his studies every morning at 6 A.M., attending class at 10 A.M., then engaging in extensive discussions of Spanish literature in the afternoon. While in

Spain, he traveled to Córdoba, Seville, Cádiz, Málaga, and Gibraltar. He went on to become a renowned expert on Spanish literature.

When Ticknor retired in 1835, Harvard still had trouble finding a scholar fluent in Spanish to fill his shoes. The college hired the poet Henry Wadsworth Longfellow. Longfellow's father, acting against common practices, had sent his son to Spain for eight months in 1827. He was one of the few who believed that Spanish would be more important to Americans than German or Italian. His son reportedly spent his days watching bullfighting. Consequently, he came home fluent in Spanish but with a "rather slight" knowledge of literature, as Leavitt put it.

When Longfellow began teaching at Harvard in 1836, there still wasn't much demand for Spanish, but Longfellow didn't turn out to be much of a professor anyway. He preferred writing—he even translated *Rip Van Winkle* into Spanish, renaming it *Andrés Gazul*.

One of the problems Spanish faced in the nineteenth century was that universities still favored teaching Latin and Greek over modern languages. Spanish was handicapped even more by the fact that Spain was thought to be a dangerous place to travel. Outside of the Ivy League, Spanish departments sprung up in colleges in Alabama, New Jersey, and New York. But teachers were rare and usually taught more than one language, or entirely different subjects in perplexing combinations, like Rev. W. J. Moore, of Granbury College in Texas, who taught "English, Mental and Moral Science, and Spanish."

Before the twentieth century, few elementary and high schools taught Spanish. There were, however, a couple of exceptions. In Massachusetts, the Round Hill School, founded in 1823, offered Spanish classes. Salem High School also started teaching Spanish in 1830. Spanish was taught in Central High School in New Orleans in 1829, and continued to be included in the curricula of the public schools of New Orleans until the Civil War. By 1860, four schools in Massachusetts were teaching Spanish.

Still, Americans were a long way from thinking there was any-thing "useful" about Spanish. The goal of studying Spanish in the nineteenth century was to be able to read the great works of Span-ish literature, notably from the Golden Age. Despite the proximity of Latin America, and the fact that it was producing its own litera-ture, Latin America had no place in the U.S. curriculum. Accord-ing to Sturgis Leavitt, when the Argentine author Domingo Faustino Sarmiento visited the United States in 1845 and again in 1865–1868 as ambassador (shortly before becoming president), American scholars like Ticknor and Longfellow were surprised to hear that Latin America had *any* writers of stature. In 1902, *The Literary World* of Boston published some statistics on Cuba, Puerto Rico, the Philippines, and Mexico, and remarked: "It is no exaggeration to say that this mass of our fellow beings have no common litera-ture worthy of the name."

In 1902, the scholar and dilettante Archer Milton Huntington (1870–1955) purchased one of Spain's finest private libraries, that of the Marquis de Jerez de los Caballeros, and shipped it to New York City. In 1904, he founded the Hispanic Society of America to promote Hispanic culture in the United States.

Spanish technically became a language of the United States in 1848, following the Mexican-American War. But even after the United States seized Spanish possessions in the Caribbean and the Pacific, there was still no interest in Spanish American literature.

The one exception was the military. For strategic reasons, the military has always paid more attention to modern language than to classical languages. U.S. military colleges had started teaching conversational Spanish long before the Great War. Spanish was introduced at West Point in 1856, after the Mexican War. The Na-val Academy at Annapolis opened a Modern Languages Depart-ment in 1850, which included French and Spanish.

World War I would definitively change Americans' ideas about Spanish, as it did about all modern languages. By bringing the reality of foreign lands home to Americans, the war raised interest in languages among the general population. And the case of Spanish was special. The Spanish craze and the Latin rage were both in full gear during the war, and growing U.S. involvement in the Caribbean— culminating with the opening of the Panama Canal in 1914—raised Americans' awareness of the strategic and economic value of being able to communicate with their Spanish-speaking neighbors. As prospects of increased trade in Latin America grew, the concept of Spanish as a "commercial" language suddenly appeared.

In 1910, only 1 percent of high school students in the United States were studying Spanish compared to 11.3 percent studying French and 23.6 percent studying German. By 1915, enrollment and rates had gone up for all languages, but mostly Spanish: Spanish had increased to 2.72 percent, French went to 11.70 percent, and German to 24.19 percent. After that, Spanish teaching, like French, grew 50 percent every year, and German teaching took a dive from which it never recovered. After World War I, Spanish grammar books and readers multiplied.

The focus on Spanish was also starting to shift toward Latin America. In 1916, Columbia University established a Department of Hispanic Studies, later called Instituto de las Españas. And in the same year, the great scholar Alfred Coester—who at the time taught Spanish at Commercial High School in Brooklyn—published his landmark *Literary History of Spanish America,* a classic to this day that, by its very existence, boosted the reputation of American Spanish.

The first master's thesis on Spanish American folklore, "Puerto Rican Folklore," was presented in 1915 at the University of Washington. The first Ph.D. thesis on Spanish American literature was defended at Columbia University in 1923 by Henry Alfred Holmes. His topic was "Martín Fierro: An Epic of the Argentine."

In 1917, a group of professors founded the Association of American Teachers of Spanish and Portuguese (AATSP). They sent a notice to 2,850 Spanish teachers, and 600 applied for membership.

The AATSP organized teacher exchanges, field trips, and study tours—but mostly to Spain. The AATSP's first president, Lawrence A. Wilkins, was decorated as *Comendador con placa* (Knight commander) of the *Real Americana Orden* (Royal Order) *de Isabel la Católica*. Today, the AATSP is the biggest language teachers' association in the United States, with seventeen thousand members.

By 1922, the picture of Spanish teaching in the United States had shifted dramatically. Enrollment in German had almost vanished (from 325,000 to 14,000). Spanish still wasn't as popular as French, but in less than a decade it had grown beyond all expectations, from 36,000 to 252,000 students.

Attitudes about Spanish were changing rapidly. In 1930, more than two hundred American colleges and universities were offering courses in Latin American studies. Teachers had begun shifting from the Madrid to the Mexican Standard (though the transformation wasn't complete until the 1970s).

In 1934, the Pan-American Union (later the Organization of American States) released a document called *On the Importance of the Study of Spanish*, in which influential Americans argued for the usefulness of Spanish in business, culture, arts, and science. Victor M. Cutter, president of United Fruit Company, said, "Year by year, we do more business with South and Central America, and we know that the greatest obstacle to transacting that business is lack of familiarity with the Spanish language." Nicholas Murray Butler, president of Colombia University, claimed, "We must know Spanish, as Americans, because Spanish—quite as much as English—is *the* American language."

But it was Paul U. Kellogg, of the journal *The Survey*, who made the best case for learning Spanish. After summarizing the "notable contributions to world progress" made by Spain and Spanish America, Kellogg declared that Spanish was simply the language of the future: "It has been suggested repeatedly that Spanish, because of the number now speaking it and its relative ease of acquisition, will become the world medium of communication rather than either French or English."

In the 1930s, another novel idea appeared: teachers began suggesting that Americans should speak Spanish to understand their Spanish-speaking minority and, ultimately, to make sense of their own country.

In a 1934 article published in the journal *Hispania,* New Mexico professor Francis M. Kercheville, famous for his book *Practical Spoken Spanish,* went even farther. According to him, "A working, a practical, knowledge of the Spanish language [would be] a genuine aid in the solution of the problems of social adjustment in the Southwest." Noting that the history of Southwest is "basically Spanish," he argued that "[although] no one in his right mind would advocate its being taught at the expense of English or even as a substitute for English, [Spanish] should be taught and studied for its very real value in a better understanding of community, state, and interstate problems in the Southwest." Another teacher at the time went as far as arguing that the Southwest had a "vocation" of providing "interpreters between the Republic of the north and the republics to the south."

Like the previous world war, World War II made Americans acutely aware of foreign realities and of how critical foreign languages were to national security. As Zaina Glass, an Oklahoma high school teacher, wrote in the *Modern Language Journal* in 1948, "Before the war, many of our pupils with no cultural background shunned a foreign language course; it appeared remote to their needs and interests. But during the war years there was an increase of the enrollment in foreign languages."

But the war did more than raise awareness. It also changed how languages were taught. Faced with a sudden need for interpreters for European and lesser-known Asian languages, the U.S. Army hired the linguist Mortimer Graves, then secretary of the American

Council of Learned Societies, to develop a method that would enable people to communicate quickly in new languages. Graves's method, dubbed the "Army Method," shifted the focus from reading to communicating. Originally developed to teach rare languages like Turkish, Russian, Arabic, Japanese, Chinese, and Burmese, it was later used to teach French, Spanish, German, and Italian. For the first time, the American public began to think it was more important to *speak* a foreign language than to *read* it.

In the Southwest, this new approach to teaching coincided with a new attitude toward the Spanish language itself. In 1948, schools in Tuscon, Arizona, introduced Spanish in the first grade with the objective of teaching children to be bilingual. The supervisor of elementary schools, Jonathan Booth, said that Spanish teaching was "part of a movement in the southwestern states to acquaint English-speaking students with the Spanish languages and to create a better understanding between English- and Spanish-speaking peoples."

The idea that Spanish was "useful" was making headway by the 1950s. As the applied linguist Claire Kramsch of the University of California at Berkeley wrote, "A great incentive to the enrollment in Spanish was the prospect of increased trade with Latin America . . . *Commercial Spanish* became a magic word that was supposed to open the way to new careers."

In the 1950s, a new medium also provided impetus for learning Spanish: television, which allowed people to hear foreign languages. Teaching now focused on what was called the "audio-lingual method." One elementary school in Portland, Oregon, developed a half-hour program called *Hola Amigos!* to "acquaint" children with the sounds of Spanish and common expressions. It was so popular that parents started watching the show too.

At the same time, Spanish teachers shifted away from Castilian pronunciation. This was partly the result of growing immigration from all parts of Latin America.

This trend has lasted. At Arizona State University, we met

Carmen García-Fernández, a professor of Peruvian origin, who taught English in Peru and then taught Spanish at Johns Hopkins University before coming to ASU in 2002. ASU has one of the biggest Spanish departments in the country, with about two thousand undergraduates and seven hundred graduate students. "It doesn't matter if you teach with a Peruvian accent or a Bolivian accent or a Nicaraguan accent," she told Julie. "Spanish speakers are not bothered by accents probably because there are so many countries. We are more interested in communication. We don't consider one accent better than the others."

But even before the massive waves of immigration would start to change the demographic makeup of the United States, a series of events in Spain was about to topple the hierarchy that had always placed the Castilian above the Latin American accent.

Something was going horribly wrong in Spain.

26. The Franco Years

ONE WEEKEND WHEN WE WERE visiting Alicante, near Valencia, our friend Celia Vara was having a reunion with some old university friends. To make things simpler for us, she didn't bother introducing everyone and just called the whole group her *chicas y chicos* (girls and boys). We first met them at the Cafetería Damasol—or, more precisely, on the sidewalk in front of it, since the café was so packed its owners had to send tapas, beer, and wine out to the street through a hole in one of the walls.

By midnight, the group had migrated to a fusion restaurant owned by one of the *chicos,* serving Galician dishes eaten with chopsticks. But before that, they stopped at El Bar de Eric, one of Alicante's most famous hangouts. Even though it was no bigger than a large RV, and could legally seat only about thirty, at least sixty people were packed inside, most of them boldly ignoring Spain's recently passed antismoking laws. There were musicians playing, but the crowd sang so loudly they almost drowned them out. One of the *chicos* explained, "That's the spirit of *La Movida.*"

Movida literally, means, "the scene" or "the happening." When it's written with a capital *M,* it refers to the vast and rich counterculture that erupted in Madrid immediately after the death of *El Caudillo* (the chief) Francisco Franco in 1975. Not only did *la Movida madrileña* withstand the test of time, it spread to many other towns. Barcelona and Bilbao have their own variations of it today, though the ambience of *La Movida* is still the strongest in Madrid, especially in the Malasaña neighborhood.

But then again, much of Spain's cultural production and language development in the last forty years has been a reaction to the end of the Franco era, in one way or another.

* * *

Franco arrived at the end of a difficult century for Spain. After Napoleon's occupation of Spain in 1808, then the loss of its last colonies in 1830, Spain slowly disintegrated. The country was marked by political and social trauma, class struggles, and dynastic quarrels over the Spanish throne. Not a decade passed without a coup, countercoup, revolution, civil war, or *pronunciamiento* (a military declaration of nonconfidence) by a new junta. Guerrilla war by one extremist faction or another was almost constant.

Things looked promising with the arrival of Spain's Second Republic in 1931, when the Spanish restored democracy to their country after ousting both the king, Alfonso XIII, and the military dictator he supported, Miguel Primo de Rivera. The first governments of the republic were center-left. They gave substantial autonomy to the Basque country and Catalonia, granted women the right to vote, and pushed hard to educate the rural population. Unfortunately, coalition governments changed rapidly and were too unstable to cope with the revival of anarchist movements, armed uprising of workers, reactionary activism, and quarrels between different branches of the Bourbon dynasty.

In 1936, civil war broke out for the fourth time since Napoleon, pitting Republicans (who held legitimate power and had support from the Soviet Union) against the Nationalists (who had the support of Germany and Italy). The war lasted until 1939, leaving some 900,000 Spanish dead and turning another 2.3 million into refugees.

As the filmmaker Luis Buñuel wrote in his autobiography, in civil war Spain "you couldn't so much as lift your hand to signal your car was turning, or it would be interpreted as a fascist salute." A staggering number of great artists died during the war, including Miguel de Unamuno, who had invented the personal novel but was stripped of all his titles (he had been head of the University of Salamanca) after arguing with one of Franco's generals. The death of Federico García Lorca was even more emblematic. A brilliant young poet, playwright, and folklorist, García Lorca's 1930 *Poeta en Nueva York* (Poet in New York) is probably the best-known book written by a Spaniard about New York City. He was executed for being a Republican and a homosexual.

Normally, history is written by the winners. But in the case of the Spanish Civil War, the Republicans' side of the story endured even though they lost. It certainly helped that their cause was supported by a vast international artistic community that included the French poet and novelist André Malraux, Pablo Picasso, Ernest Hemingway, and the photographer Robert Capa. One of Picasso's masterpieces, *Guernica,* now hangs in Madrid's Reina Sophia Museum. A wall-size painting showing men, women, and children crying out in anguish, eyes raised to the sky, depicts the air bombing—the first of its kind—of the Basque city of Guernica. Picasso produced the work for the 1937 World's Fair in Paris, specifically to garner support for Republican Spain. Hemingway's *For Whom the Bell Tolls* tells the story of a soldier in the International Brigades (volunteers from different countries who fought for the Republicans). Robert Capa's *Falling Soldier,* taken during the Civil War, became one of the most famous war photographs of all time.

In short, the losers won the war of propaganda.

Curiously, when the Civil War broke out, Francisco Franco (1892–1975) was not the dominant figure among the so-called Nationalists. He was a competent officer and a hero of the Rif War in Morocco who had become Europe's youngest general in 1926, at age thirty-three. When Spanish Nationalists rebelled against the republic in 1936, Franco was one of the few generals who supported them. He became part of the junta, then rose in its ranks after winning battles against Republicans and brokering alliances with Italy and Germany.

Franco became Spain's de facto dictator in 1937, and its official ruler when the Civil War ended in 1939. The first years of his regime were particularly brutal. Between 1939 and 1943, 115,000 Republicans were executed at gunpoint. There were a staggering 114,000 to 143,000 *desaparecidos* (missing) during the Franco

regime. Franco ran things with an iron hand—minus the prover-
bial velvet glove. Spain had one political party: the Falange Española de las Juntas de Ofensiva Nacional-Sindicalista (Spanish
Phalanx of the Committees for the National-Syndicalist Offen-
sive), the Falange (Phalanx) for short.

Franco and his *falangistas* had a tremendous impact on Spanish
culture and language, both during and after the Franco dictatorship.

Franco's economic policy was autarky. Essentially, he cut the
country off from foreign influence of any kind. Foreign films were
systematically dubbed; the works of foreign authors—those the
regime deemed acceptable—had to be translated. The religious
control of behavior was so stifling that people could not even kiss
in the street. No unmarried couples were represented in works of
art. State control was everywhere, and criticism had to be very
subtle to make it past the censorship laws.

When we visited the Real Academia Española, we met with
Carlos Domínguez, head of the Instituto de datos léxicos (Institute
of Lexical Data). During our long discussion, Domínguez told us
that linguists who study language in Spain generally divide the
second half of the twentieth century into two periods: before and
after Franco.

The reason is simple. The effect of *franquismo* was to freeze the
Spanish language.

One of the first things Franco did when he took power was
centralize all decision making in Madrid. Regional languages were
perceived as a threat to centralized power, so Franco forbade them,
pure and simple. The move was meant to knock the wind out of
Spain's three main regional tongues: Basque, Galician, and Catalan.
Each had experienced a *renaixença*, *rexurdimento*, or *euskaltzaindia*
("renaissance" in Catalan, Galician, and Basque) in the nineteenth
century and even had their own *academias*.

Under Franco, only Castilian could be used for official purposes. All government, notary, legal, and commercial documents
had to be written in Castilian; documents in any other languages

were deemed null and void. Road signs and store signs had to be in Castilian, and schools could teach only in Castilian. Franco went as far as forbidding non-Castilian names. A mother in Catalonia could not name her newborn Jordi (George); he had to be Jorge. In 1968, Joan Manuel Serrat was not allowed to sing "*La La La*" in Catalan at the Eurovision Song Contest. He refused to sing in Spanish. Even after dropping out of the contest, Serrat went on to become the most popular Spanish and Catalan singer of his day— comparable to Charles Aznavour in the French-speaking world.

Despite his efforts, Franco failed to eradicate Spain's regional languages. The Basque kept unofficial Basque schools running. Galician literature survived thanks to exiles—so many Galicians immigrated to Argentina that Argentines ended up referring to all Spaniards as "Gallegos."

Languages evolve largely through contact with other cultures. By isolating Spain from the outside world and suppressing Spain's regional languages, Franco's regime cut Spanish off from its main sources of renewal. The Academia nearly stopped including vocabulary from other Latin American sources in its dictionary. In 1925, it accepted 177 new words from Venezuela. But in the 1947 edition, the number of new Venezuelan terms was down to 6. The dictionary's renewal, begun in 1925, totally lost momentum.

The Real Academia was in a sorry state under Franco. And among writers, linguists, and lexicographers, there was a joke that each new edition of the dictionary was worse than the last. Many of the Real Academia's members fled into exile and the Academia pointedly refused to replace them. A famous case was Salvador de Madariaga, who fled Spain immediately after being elected a member in 1936. He didn't read his acceptance speech until he returned to Spain after Franco died, forty years later. Madariaga was ninety by that time.

Under Franco's regime, where the Spanish language became a victim of state repression, dictionary writing turned into a veritable act of resistance.

While the Real Academia floundered, a number of lexicographers wrote impressive works. Julio Casares (1877–1964), a polyglot genius who could write in and translate eighteen languages, published the *Diccionario ideológico de la lengua castellana* (Ideological Dictionary of the Castilian Language) in 1942. It was in fact a whole new type of dictionary that allowed readers to locate words starting from their definitions.

Another star was Joan Corominas, who wrote the four-volume *Diccionario crítico etimológico* (Critical Etymological Dictionary) from exile. A Catalan nationalist and leftist, Corominas (1905–1997) fled to the University of Chicago in 1946. His dictionary, published in 1957, turned out to be so influential that the Franco regime tried to offer Corominas perks and awards, but he refused them all on principle.

Another Spanish genius of lexicography, Vicente García de Diego (1878–1978), spent his entire life working on dictionaries, and in 1968—at the age of ninety—published the unique *Diccionario de voces naturales* (Dictionary of Native Words). The work was a slap in the face to the Franco regime, since it included the very regionalisms Franco was trying to eradicate.

But the figure who stands out in the period was María Moliner (1900–1981). A librarian under the Second Republic, Moliner had established a groundbreaking network of rural libraries in Spain in the 1930s, part of the Second Republic's short but intense period of educational reform. At the time, only four million of the twenty-three million Spaniards had access to books and newspapers. By 1934, she had already opened 5,000 libraries, and had plans for 5,500 more in primary schools and small towns.

Unlike other left-wing intellectuals, María Moliner, a mother of four, did not run away from Franco. She and her family suffered for the decision. Her husband, a professor of physics and left-wing activist, was suspended from his job for three years. Moliner stayed on the government's payroll but was demoted eighteen ranks. By 1946, she was working way below her abilities, as head librarian at the Higher Technical School of Industrial Engineers.

The idea to write a dictionary was born in 1952, when Moliner's son, who was living in Paris, sent her a copy of *The Oxford Learner's Dictionary of Current English*. Conscious of the decline of the Real Academia's dictionary under Franco, Moliner began taking notes to write a small Spanish dictionary similar to the *Oxford Learner's Dictionary*. She understood the methodology. Thirty years earlier, while she was studying at the University of Zaragoza, Moliner had been part of a team working on a dictionary of Aragonese. She thought she could write it in two years.

In 1966, after fifteen years of solitary work, Moliner finally published her landmark *Diccionario de Uso del Español* (Dictionary of Spanish Usage). It was an immediate success: since 1967, it has sold almost two hundred thousand copies. Gabriel García Márquez called it "the most complete, useful, diligent and entertaining dictionary of the Castilian language."

Moliner based her corpus on the Academia's dictionary, augmented with what she gleaned from newspapers. The Academia had accepted words such as *record, test*, and *film* but it ignored technical terms that were becoming common, including *cibernética, entropía* (entropy), *reactor,* and *transistor*. Striving to be clear and up-to-date, Moliner included foreign words, colloquialisms, slang, and acronyms that were part of common usage. Moliner also refused to treat *ch* and *ll* as separate letters (the Academia followed her example in 1994).

When Moliner died in 1981, Gabriel García Márquez wrote her obituary. He said her dictionary was "twice as big as the Academia's and, in my opinion, twice as good." Its only drawback, he declared, was the absence of profanities, "the words Spaniards have used the most since time immemorial." In 1972, the great philologists Rafael Lapesa and Dámaso Alonso nominated Moliner for membership in the Real Academia and it was widely believed she would become Spain's first female academician. The Academia instead chose the philologist Emilio Alarcos Llorach, even though his best work

(*Gramática de la lengua española*) was still twenty-two years in the making. Moliner's biographer, Inmaculada de la Fuente, wrote, "Her work questioned the dictionary of the Real Academia. She was admired, but not valued."

On learning that her candidacy was rejected, María Moliner commented ironically, "What could I have said? I spent my life darning socks."

María Moliner, like Joan Corominas, was one of the few writers and creators in Franco's Spain who managed to maneuver around censorship laws to produce their work. The Franco regime extolled and encouraged the so-called literature of the winner. Franco's own novel, *Raza* (Race), published in 1942 under the pseudonym Jaime de Andrade, was a perfect example of this, glorifying the principles of the Franco regime and depicting its opponents as losers. Not surprisingly, "Jaime de Andráde" had no trouble finding a producer and the financing to make the novel into a film.

Most novelists suffered some form of censorship. The psychiatrist Luis Martin-Santos, who published one of the most important Spanish novels of the century in 1961, *Tiempo de silencio* (Time of Silence), had twenty pages cut from his manuscript, which were restored only in 1980. His compatriot, Juan Goytisolo, a corrosive and antipatriotic writer, published all his work from Paris. Goytisolo, who now lives in Marrakesh, rejected the "official" history under Franco, which was unforgivable in the eyes of the *falangistas*. The protagonist of his Don Julian series was the legendary traitor who aided the Arab invasion of Spain in 711.

The case of Camilo José Cela (1916–2002) is even more interesting, and not just because he won the Nobel Prize for Literature in 1989. His debut novel, *La Familia de Pascual Duarte* in 1942, was said to have had a thousand critics and only three hundred buyers. It is the hyperviolent story of an Extremaduran for whom violence is the only recourse for anything he wants or against anything that stands in the way. Both excessive and satirical, the book was censored a year after publication. It went on to spark a new brand of Spanish existentialism called *tremendismo*.

Cela in fact collaborated with the Franco regime as a spy, denouncing other writers, but he remained a loose cannon. His most famous novel, *La colmena* (The Hive), published in Buenos Aires in 1951, portrays a gallery of three hundred grotesque characters living in bleak conditions in Madrid. Cela also collaborated with the Venezuelan dictator Marco Pérez Jiménez on a project of five propaganda novels, but the first novel in 1955 created such an uproar in Venezuela that the dictator canceled his contract.

Cela was a first-class provocateur who dedicated some of his books to his critics, "who did so much for his career," but his writing became increasingly experimental with the years. In 1968 and 1972, he wrote two volumes of his *Diccionario secreto* (Secret Dictionary) of dirty words, in which he analyzes slang words and euphemisms for penis and testicles—this morphed in 1976 into a *Diccionario de erotismo*. In 1988, one year before winning the Nobel Prize, he published the novel *Cristo versus Arizona* (Christ versus Arizona), an interior monologue written in a single sentence of 230 pages, which takes place during the shootout in the O.K. Corral.

Censorship under Franco had the same effect on cinema. Those who could get around it continued to produce work of surprisingly good quality in spite of limiting rules. Official censorship was strict. Films couldn't portray unmarried men and women living together, regional languages, or the Republican side in the civil war. Foreign films, if accepted, had to be dubbed. To see uncensored films, Spaniards traveled en masse to the French border town of Perpignan, where they also loaded up with forbidden French books, among other things.

Yet Spanish cinema did not do too badly under Franco. One of the pillars of the period is Juan Antonio Bardem, whose 1955 *Muerte de un ciclista* (Death of a Cyclist) portrays Spanish society as corrupt and complacent. Two years earlier, Bardem wrote the script for a film directed by Luis García Berlanga, *Bienvenido Mister Marshall* (Welcome Mr. Marshall). This delicious comedy tells the story of a town that goes to great lengths to seduce American representatives of the Marshall Plan. It's so well made that it gets laughs even sixty years after it was released. The saloon scene, in fake English, is irresistible.

Spanish film got a surprise boost in the 1950s with Franco's progressive liberalization, which allowed hundreds of coproductions with France, Italy, and the United States. Hundreds of spaghetti westerns were actually shot in Spain, as well as many of the great sword-and-sandal films like *King of Kings, The Pride and the Passion, Lawrence of Arabia,* and *Doctor Zhivago,* as well as contemporary science fiction films, including *Star Wars II.*

And then there was the film director Luis Buñuel (1900–1983), who belonged to a category all his own. Buñuel grew up in the small village of Aragón that he dubbed "the Middle Ages," in a family of *indianos*. His father had made a small fortune in the Americas before returning to Spain in 1898. Buñuel was already well known before the Civil War, although he had more success in Paris, where he hung around the Surrealists. Buñuel became famous in 1929 when he and Salvador Dalí made the avant-garde film *Un chien andalou* (An Andalusian Dog). Charlie Chaplin watched *Un chien andalou* twelve times and showed it to his daughter Geraldine to scare her.

After living in Paris, Buñuel returned to Spain in April 1931, two days before the proclamation of the Second Republic. In 1933, he released the documentary *País sin pan* (Land Without Bread), portraying the miserable life in a backward region of Extremadura, Las Jurdes. Buñuel's film was the first "mockumentary," with kids dipping bread in water (because there was no fresh bread) and people throwing goats down a cliff (the goats had died of starvation). Even the progressive Second Republic banned it.

Buñuel didn't have any illusions about working after the outbreak of the Civil War, and he fled to Mexico, where he produced or co-produced twenty of his thirty-two films. His films remained pro-vocative—*Los Olvidados* (The Young and the Damned) portrays juvenile delinquents festering in the slums of Mexico City—and generated the same violent reaction as they had in Spain. Buñuel's reputation in Mexico was saved by an article of support from the writer Octavio Paz. *Los Olvidados* won the best director award at the Cannes Film Festival in 1951. It was only after this success in France that the Mexicans embraced him.

Ever the misfit, Buñuel got into trouble in the United States as well. In 1955, his anti-*franquista* past got him blacklisted for "anti-American" activity—as if the link were obvious. He made only two films in English, financed by U.S. companies: *The Adventures of Robinson Crusoe* (1952) and *The Young One* (1960). In his autobi-ography, he explains that he had trouble making a film that fit America's "moral system" (good versus evil).

Buñuel was also an early returning exile. Back in Spain in 1960 for the first time in twenty-three years, he directed a Spanish-Mexican production *Viridiana,* a sharp criticism of Franco's Spain. It was too much even for the French, who thought that Buñuel's portrayal of an ex-nun seeking redemption was blasphemous, raw, and cruel. But the film won the 1961 Palme d'Or in Cannes anyway, and in spite of Spain's protest. Buñuel was subsequently blacklisted and had to leave Spain.

Franco's regime probably owes its longevity to El Caudillo's reptil-ian talent for survival. Though Germany and Italy had supported him, and although Franco personally supported Nazism and fas-cism, he refused to become their formal ally during World War II. *Franquista* Spain was excluded from the United Nations between 1946 and 1950, but Franco successfully used the cold war to garner U.S. support and to strike a formal alliance in 1953, where Spain got financial aid in exchange for allowing the United States to establish military bases and film sets in Spain.

This financial support came just in time, because the Spanish economy was in the dumps. Franco's Nazi-inspired policy of economic autarky resulted in hunger, epidemics, and high infant mortality. Spain under Franco was so retrograde that even the reactionary religious order Opus Dei became a progressive force, urging Franco to open the regime to non-Spanish technology and liberalize the economy. In 1957, Franco grudgingly introduced Opus Dei's program of economic liberalization. It brought such a sudden change in the country's economy that the period between 1959 and 1974 is dubbed the *Milagro español* (Spanish Miracle).

And indeed, in a very short period, Spain was transformed from an agrarian to a modern urban society. Economic prospects improved so much that between 1965 and 1980 some 1.5 million expatriates returned to Spain.

One of the linchpins of Franco's reforms was the car industry, based in Madrid—a capital city that had been virtually devoid of industry until then. The other objective was to build an "industry without smokestacks": tourism. Indeed, in one generation Spain turned itself into Europe's second tourist destination, after France. Between 1950 and 1975, the number of visitors multiplied by twenty-five to reach a staggering 25 million per year. Spain is still the world's fourth tourist destination, with 57 million visitors a year, after France with 75 million, the United States with 62 million, and China with 58 million.

Nonetheless, in 1975, the country breathed a sigh of relief when Franco finally took his last breath and King Juan Carlos I assumed the transition to democracy. *Transición* and *mitin* (meeting) finally became acceptable words.

Yet although it was much desired, *la transición democrática* was not simple. Spaniards were fortunate that their king played such an active role in balancing popular desire for change with powerful reactionary forces—Franco's party, the Falange, still exists. In order to facilitate transition, a general amnesty was extended to all crimes under Franco, which cannot even be investigated.

From 1977 to 1982, Spain had to contend with three attempted coups d'état and conspiracies. The most dramatic episode occurred on February 23, 1981—a coup known in Spanish lingo as 23-F. Two hundred soldiers rushed into the Congress of Deputies (the lower house of Spain's legislature) just as it was voting in the new prime minister. The deputies and entire government were held hostage for most of the day. Juan Carlos denounced the coup and it collapsed the next day, but it was a close call.

This volatile political climate added powerful fodder to the counterculture *La Movida madrileña*.

Before Franco, no Spaniard would have believed that Madrid, of all the cities in Spain, would one day become the center of an edgy and spirited counterculture. Until the 1920s, Madrid had been a city of civil servants. In the 1950s, Franco industrialized the capital, sparking a rural exodus that brought masses to Madrid from all parts of the country in the 1950s and 1960s. These transformations spawned an underground art scene in Madrid, which started to take shape even before Franco's death.

The death of Franco is akin to the fall of the Berlin Wall in Germany: it unleashed political, economic, and social energies in a wide array of forms, including a nightlife and gay culture. One of its most emblematic figures is the filmmaker Pedro Almodóvar, who is known as *El chantre* (bard) of *La Movida*.

Born in 1949, Almodóvar was working as an administrative assistant for Spain's national phone company, Telefónica, when he began producing very short films for the underground art scene in 1974. Being an amateur, Almovódar started out using super 8 film with no sound. He became famous for voicing-over the entire film himself during presentations. His early experimental films were high in sexual content and had crude titles such as *Sexo va: sexo viene* (Sex Comes and Goes) and *Folle, folle, fólleme, Tim* (Fuck Me, Fuck Me, Fuck Me, Tim).

Even before his first real 35-mm film in 1980 (this one had a sound track), Almovódar had mastered the campy melodramatic comedies for which he would become famous. In 1987, *La Ley del Deseo* (Law of Desire) was nominated for an Academy Award (Best Foreign Film). In 1999, *Todo sobre mi madre* (All About My Mother) won an Academy Award and a Palme d'Or at the Cannes festival.

But Pedro Almodóvar is just the best-known figure in the very rich art scene of *La Movida,* which affected all art forms in Spain, from music to film, fashion, and literature. Some creators crossed genres, like Olvido Gara Jova, aka Alaska, a Mexican-Cuban punk bass guitarist who appeared in Almodóvar's first real film in 1980 and then hosted an edgy children's TV show *La Bola de Cristal* (The Crystal Ball) between 1984 and 1988.

La Movida also brought Madrid's secret argot, *Cheli,* into the mainstream. Sociologically, *Cheli* is close to London Cockney: *Cheli* means "bloke." It blends extreme vulgarity with preciousness. A typical sentence might be, *Tienes el cerebro carcomido por el microbio de la idiotez* ('Your brain has been worm-eaten by the microbes of idiocy'), a long and windy way of saying, "You're stupid." Like all argots, *Cheli* harvests slang from the underworld: *pipa* (gun; instead of *revólver*), *chocolate* (hash), *chirla* (knife, instead of *navaja*).

Many *Cheli* terms have become so common they have entered the Academia's dictionary, such as the vulgar *gachó, gachí* (guy, girl), which is a borrowing from *Caló* (Gypsy language). Another accepted *Cheli* term is *pasota* (marginals, dropouts). It derives from *yo paso* (I pass), and it refers to an attitude of indifference to the great social debates.

Cheli terms taint the colloquial conversation of many Spaniards. *El gusto es mío* (The pleasure is mine) becomes *El gustazo es mío* in *Cheli.* ¡*Qué gafas tan bonitas!* (What nice glasses!) becomes ¡*Vaya gafas máximas! Buen coche* (a good car) becomes *carro gay* (a gay car).

Cheli has a peculiar catchall word, *mogollón* (a lot, too much). According to Margarita de Hoyos González, "It can mean whatever is good, bad, pleasant, horrible, heavy, boring, electrifying, beautiful, complicated, crowded, easy, hard, rich, happy, sad. And it can apply to work, lodging, a wedding, a boyfriend, Marlon Brando, a bus pass, a concert." *Cheli* being decidedly subversive, its written form tends to simplify spelling by multiplying the *k*, like the famous punk rock band called Kaka de Luxe.

The death of Franco signaled a revival of regional languages as well as regional autonomy in Spain, which is now more of a federation than the centralized nation Franco dreamed of creating.

Four languages in Spain have "co-official status" with Spanish: Catalan, Basque, Galician, and Aranese, each of which is the main language in its region. Three other tongues are "recognized" languages: Aragonese, Catalan (in Aragón), and Leonese (also called Asturian and Bable). "Recognized" means the regions can take certain measures to protect their languages—the languages do not need to be declared official. An unspecified number of lesser languages, including Astur-Leonese, Eonavian, Fala, Riffian, Berber, and Caló, have no official status and are not even recognized.

Some of these languages, particularly Catalan and Galician, are widely spoken. Catalan is spoken by some 10 million Spaniards, or about 21 percent of the population. Galician has roughly three million speakers. Basque has 660,000 speakers, or a quarter of all residents in the Basque country. But even though Basque is not as widely used as the other two languages, it is doing much better than any other regional languages in Spain. The next one after it on the list is Leonese, with about 35,000 speakers. All of the main regional languages even have their own academy, and the government of Catalonia has successfully applied Quebec-inspired language laws to protect Catalan.

Franco's efforts to stamp out the influence of Spain's regions had the opposite effect. They triggered extremely brutal Basque terrorism, starting in 1968, and provoked a strong nationalist response in Catalonia. In 1958, Catalan exiles in Mexico created a Catalan government in exile, five years after Basque nationalists had done the same. Strong Catalan nationalism is the reason Valencians (who speak a variety of Catalan called Valenciano) insisted, until the 1990s, that Valenciano was not Catalan: they did not want to be associated with Catalan nationalism, which they regarded as anti-Spanish. Valencians recognized they spoke a dialect of Catalan in the 1990s when the European Union unofficially recognized Catalan as a European language and as Catalan cultural production in television and the press became increasingly present.

Even though it is common to hear that Spanish is floundering in some of Spain's autonomous communities, the number of unilingual Catalans, Basques, and Galicians is small. Less than 10 percent of Spain's population speaks no Spanish at all. In other words, no region of Spain has stepped out of the story of Spanish yet, like Portugal did in the twelfth century, to evolve into a national language of its own.

Each of the main co-official languages—Catalan, Galician, and Basque—have their own academies fashioned after the Real Academia Española. In 2012, the *Real academia de la lengua vasca* published a twenty-thousand-word dictionary of Basque. There is also an official dictionary of Catalan. Its first edition came out in 1932, and the 2005 edition has seventy thousand words.

One result of the Spanish recession has been an increasingly strident separatist movement in Catalonia. But whether or not it will be successful would have little impact on the future of Spanish, for the simple reason that Spain itself is only one-tenth of the Spanish speakers in the world. For the last two centuries, the language's destiny has not depended on Spain alone.

Nothing demonstrated that better than the rise of Latin American authors in the 1960s.

27. The Secret Agent of the Boom

Gabriel García Márquez. Mario Vargas Llosa. Miguel Ángel Asturias. Julio Cortázar. Carlos Fuentes. The "Big Five" of the Latin American Boom took the global publishing world by storm in the 1960s. The first three went on to earn Nobel Prizes in 1982, 2010, and 1967, respectively. The two still living—Vargas Llosa and García Márquez—are literary rock stars whose influence stretches far beyond the Spanish-speaking world. With his mustachioed face, Gabriel García Márquez is a globally recognized brand, and his unusual nickname, *El Gabo,* is familiar across Latin America.

The Latin American Boom was such a huge phenomenon that it is hard to define who its members are, not to mention what united them, or why the Boom happened when it did. Actually, it's hard to pinpoint exactly when it happened, since many authors now considered part of the Boom, including Argentina's Jorge Luis Borges, Chile's Pablo Neruda, and Cuba's Alejo Carpentier, wrote decades before the 1960s and became associated with the Boom only because they influenced its main writers.

Born in 1899, the same year as Borges, Miguel Angel Asturías is ample proof that the actual boom did not begin in the 1960s. He owes his 1967 Nobel Prize to a series of work begun in the 1930s, including *Leyendas de Guatemala* (1930), *El señor president* (1946), *Men of Maize* (1949), the Banana trilogy, and *Mulata de tal* (1963).

Yet despite their differences, there is one thing that unquestionably united Fuentes, Cortázar, Asturias, Vargas Llosa, García Márquez, and many others: they all had the same Catalan literary agent.

Before retiring at sixty-nine, in 2000, Carmen Balcells (b. 1930) represented every author who mattered in the Spanish language.

El Gabo called her *la Mama Grande* (Big Mama) of Latin American literature. Others spoke of her as the Super Agent 007, *Santa Carmen de las Letras* (Saint Carmen of the letters) or, just familiarly, *la Balcells*. She can boast having represented six Nobel Prize winners: in addition to the first three, there were Pablo Neruda, Camilo José Cela, and Vicente Aleixandre. Among the Latin Americans, Balcells now represents Isabel Allende, Juan Carlos Onetti, and Alfredo Bryce Echenique. The writers on her Spanish client list—including Miguel Delibes, Gonzalo Torrente Ballester, Terenci Moix, Jaime Gil de Biedma, Carlos Barral, Josep Maria Castellet, Juan Goytisolo, Juan Marsé, Eduardo Mendoza, Rosa Regàs, Gustavo Martín Garzo—have won most of the prestigious Spanish-language literary awards.

Balcells opened her agency at age thirty, in 1960, in Barcelona, after working for six years as a secretary at the agency of Romanian exile Vintilă Horia. In those years, Europe's few literary agents didn't represent authors vis-à-vis publishers; they brokered deals between publishing houses. Carmen Balcells was the first to represent authors instead of publishing houses.

Carmen Balcells, whom some publishers called *la Terrorista*, pioneered true professional relationships between authors and publishers. A sharp negotiator, she demanded that contracts include time limits, that publishers pay advances and royalties to authors in full, and she put an end to the customary thinking that authors "belonged" to their publisher. As the writer Manuel Vázquez Montalbán put it in a tribute to Balcells on her retirement: "Up until Carmen Balcells, publishers signed authors up for life contracts and paid them a pittance. From time to time authors were paid in kind with gifts of sweaters or Stilton cheese."

Carmen Balcells no doubt had a sixth sense for detecting which Latin American writers would be important, but she also had help from the great poet and Barcelona-based publisher Carlos Barral, of Seix Barral Publishing. Balcells met Barral in Barcelona in the early 1960s, when he was already working hard to raise the profile of Spanish-language literature. She soon took an interest in the Colombian writer and journalist Gabriel García Márquez. In 1964, Balcells did the rounds of New York publishing houses peddling his book ideas, including one called *Cien años de soledad* (One Hundred Years of Solitude). She managed to get a four-book contract with Harper & Row with a one-thousand-dollar advance. "Your contract is shit," said Gabriel García Márquez, when he met her for the first time in Mexico.

Such a small amount seems incredible to us in retrospect, but in the mid-1960s, Márquez was known only to a couple hundred aficionados of Latin American literature. French publisher Julliard had acquired the French rights to *A Hundred Years of Solitude* for an undisclosed amount but actually relinquished the contract, so Fayard snatched them up for five thousand francs (about one thousand dollars). Even the original Argentine publisher, Sudamericana, had paid only five hundred dollars for the Spanish rights. As the story goes, Márquez was so poor when he finished writing the manuscript in Mexico in 1966 that he had to sell his last wedding present, a blender, to be able to mail to Buenos Aires.

Carmen Balcells would do better for him next time. *Cien años de soledad* sold thirty million copies in thirty-five languages. In 1985, *El amor en los tiempos del cólera* (Love in the Time of Cholera) earned a $1 million advance. Then four years later, Carmen Balcells garnered advances totaling $10 million for *El general en su laberinto* (The General in His Labyrinth). By then, la Balcells and El Gabo were fast friends—she even asked his permission before she moved her agency's office.

The Chilean poet Pablo Neruda famously described Carmen Balcells as having the *pellejo de rinoceronte* (skin of a rhino). But for her authors, she was more of a mother hen than a rhino. In 1968, Balcells paid $500 a month as a stipend to a certain "young Peruvian author" stuck in London in the hopes that he would be able to finish his book. Six years earlier, the young author in question, Mario Vargas Llosa, had had tremendous success with his first novel, *La ciudad y los perros* (The Time of the Hero), which was translated into two dozen languages. But his contract was so bad he ended up not earning much from it. The book for which Balcells supported Vargas Llosa—and which he nearly lost in an airplane—would be his chef d'oeuvre, *Conversación en la catedral* (Conversation in the Cathedral), which went on to be a milestone in world literature.

In spite of its notoriety, it's hard to nail down exactly what the 1960s Latin American Boom was all about. The five emblematic Boom authors were all Latin Americans, all were popular in Europe, and all had the same agent. Otherwise, they didn't have much in common. Neither did their precursors, or their successors, for that matter. Asturias had a strong folklorist bias. Cortázar was experimental. Carlos Fuentes has spent much of his career as a script and essay writer, and Vargas Llosa's writing is realistic compared to that of García Márquez, which is almost dreamlike.

One thing they undoubtedly share is a debt to the Argentine writer Jorge Luis Borges (1899–1986). The Latin America scholar Leslie Bethell went as far as saying that without Borges, none of the new novelists, including García Márquez, would have emerged. Borges wrote mostly short stories, but he also translated James Joyce's *Ulysses* into Spanish. Although his star never shone as brightly as that of his successors, Borges's brilliant short stories influenced them all. His 1936 *Historia universal de la infamia* (A Universal History of Infamy) was completely original, at once European and truly Latin American. Borges was a courageous and opinionated writer who fought blindness but never let an opportunity to criticize Juan Perón's regime slip by. He refused to flee into exile and went as far as calling Eva Perón a prostitute.

The other influential trend that preceded the Boom was the rise of a new generation of poets, most notably Chilean, including Gabriela Mistral (Nobel Prize, 1945) and Pablo Neruda (Nobel Prize, 1971). Neruda (1904–1973) was so famous he was invited to read his poems in soccer stadiums. During a rally in honor of a Brazilian Communist leader in 1945, some one hundred thousand people listened to one reading. In his twenties, Neruda traveled extensively in Burma, Ceylon, and Java, and occupied a number of diplomatic posts, before being forced into exile in the 1940s for being a Communist. He was a dogged writer who held many topics. His *Veinte poemas de amor* (Twenty Love Poems), though they appeared in 1924, have never lost their popularity. Even today, the poems have a fresh and youthful quality. Neruda's 1935 *Residencia en la tierra* (Residence on Earth) remains a key work in the history of Latin American lyrical poetry.

The renown of Borges, Neruda, and many others spawned *tertulias* and *veladas* (informal gatherings and social evenings) of writers who read and commented on each other's work in every major city in Latin America. These brought Latin American writers into intense contact, allowing them to create cultural networks between different American capitals and Paris, capital of them all. One of these, Grupo de Barranquilla, in Colombia, was an informal gathering of writers and journalists to which El Gabo belonged.

The other thing the Latin American Boom authors inherited from their predecessors, particularly from Borges, was common goals for the Spanish language. They consciously set out to abolish the gulf between "high" and "popular" culture. They wanted to write in a Spanish language that was urban, modern, and nonacademic. The second sentence of Mario Vargas Llosa's most famous work, *Conversación en la catedral,* reads: "*¿En qué momento se había jodido el Perú*" (At what precise moment had Peru fucked itself up?).

The Boom authors also undeniably brought one new literary invention to an international audience: *el realismo mágico.*

Magic realism merges the fantastic with the ordinary. In a typical scene in *Cien años de soledad,* a young woman, Remedios the Beauty, rises to heaven while she's hanging out her laundry. In magic realism, neither the narrator nor the characters find this extraordinary. Such events are portrayed as the normal course of events. In García Márquez's short story *"Un señor muy viejo con unas alas enormes"* (A Very Old Man with Enormous Wings), characters treat the discovery of an unconscious angel casually. One character simply says, "He must have been coming for the child, but the poor fellow is so old that the rain knocked him down." García Márquez mastered the technique of magic realism so thoroughly that he used it to write the first half of his own autobiography.

According to Valentín Pérez Venzalá, editor of the cultural review *Cuadernos del Minotoro,* the Surrealist scene in Paris in the 1920s was the source of *realismo mágico*. Americans initially paid little attention to the Surrealists, but the Latin Americans followed them closely. The German art critic Franz Roh coined the term *magischer Realismus* in 1925. At the time, it was strictly associated with visual arts. The term entered Spanish in 1927 when it was translated by José Ortega y Gasset. In 1947, the Venezuelan art critic Arturo Uslar Pietri introduced it in his analysis of a Venezuelan short story. In the 1940s, two authors were already using magic realism: Miguel Ángel Asturias in *El Señor Presidente* (The President) and the Cuban writer Alejo Carpentier in *El Reino de este mundo* (The Kingdom of this World). Carpentier called it *lo real maravilloso* (marvelous realism).

Even though magic realism is now almost automatically associated with Spanish-language literature, writers in other languages have been influenced by it, including Italo Calvino, Salman Rushdie, Umberto Eco, and even John Updike. There are also two very early cases of magic realism being used in French literature, in Marcel Aymé's 1943 collection of short stories, *Le Passe-Muraille* (The Man Who Passed through Walls), as well as in most novels of Boris Vian.

Yet if magic realism now embodies the Latin American style—exotic and tropical, overblown and unrestrained, phantasmagorical and hallucinatory—this is precisely what magic realism is *not* about.

What does magic realism try to achieve? In an essay on what he calls *magical* realism, the American short fiction author Bruce Holland Rogers claims that it is neither escapism nor a synonym for fantasy stories. "It is trying to convey the reality of one or several worldviews that actually exist, or have existed." In other words, a ghost is not a fantasy element but the manifestation of the reality of people who believe in, or have "real" experiences of, ghosts. He writes, "Magical realist fiction depicts the real world of people whose reality is different from ours. It's not a thought experiment. It's not speculation. Magical realism endeavors to show us the world through other eyes."

One reason magic realism became so influential in Latin American literature was that it coincided with the quest for a new identity, which united the many dichotomies of society: urban and rural, American and Spanish, modern and old, native and European, colonial and neocolonial. Magic realism is an effective tool for expressing all these conflicting elements. As Carlos Fuentes said to Frederick Nunn in *Collisions With History: Latin American Fiction and Social Science from El Boom to the New World Order*, "The so-called Boom, in reality, is the result of four centuries that, literarily, reached a moment of urgency in which fiction became the way to organize lessons from the past."

Although many authors, including Asturias, Cortázar, and Fuentes, use elements of magic realism in their work, the master of the practice is, of course, Gabriel García Márquez (b. 1927). *One Hundred Years of Solitude* is one of the most important works of the twentieth century. It makes full use of all the devices of magic realism, from first page to last. Even its structure is built on a succession of hallucinatory flashbacks. The book recounts the history of the village of Macondo, inspired by García Márquez's Colombian birthplace, Aracateca. It explores the impenetrable mysteries of life yet reads like a fantasy.

Although Latin American authors widely adopted *realismo mágico,* there are exceptions, most notably Mario Vargas Llosa (b. 1936). Vargas Llosa never used the techniques beyond a few elements here and there. Though very experimental, his writing is hyperrealistic. Yet it was Vargas Llosa who really kick-started the Latin American Boom in 1963 with *The Time of the Hero.* This scathing depiction of a fictional crime at Lima's military academy had a first printing of one thousand copies. Peru's generals accused Vargas Llosa of being unpatriotic and a Communist, and allegedly burned one hundred copies of the book in a formal ceremony. But this modern-day auto-da-fé backfired. The publicity it generated turned Vargas Llosa's first book into a smash hit, although his contract was so bad that he did not earn a living as a writer until the end of the decade.

The momentum of the Latin American Boom carried on after the 1960s with the arrival of a new generation of Spanish and Latin America authors. Isabel Allende (b. 1942), a cousin of Chilean president Salvador Allende, is by far the most successful Latin American female writer with an international audience. Elena Poniatowska (b. 1935) is probably the most important writer in Mexico today, after Octavio Paz and Carlos Fuentes. Another Mexican, Laura Esquivel (b. 1950), inspired the most significant box office success for a Spanish-language film in the United States with her *Como agua para chocolate,* which earned $21 million. The Argentine writer Manuel Puig (1932–1990) made history with books that appeared frivolous but were deadly serious, like *El beso de la mujer araña* (Kiss of the Spider Woman).

One other notable Latin American editorial success story, though not exactly literary, is the work of Joaquín Salvador Lavado, aka Quino. The Argentine illustrator created the comic strip *Mafalda,* about a six-year-old perpetual rebel, sort of a Latin American version of Charlie Brown. Mafalda appeared in various Buenos Aires dailies between 1964 and 1973 and was translated into many languages. A huge success in Europe and in Quebec, *Mafalda* inspired two animated series and a film.

Given the mountain of successful literature in the Boom, it is no surprise that the Spanish-speaking world started organizing

world-class international book expos in its wake. Yet the most successful among them have been held not in Madrid or Barcelona
but at the extremities of Latin America. The Feria Internacional del
Libro de Buenos Aires was inaugurated in 1972 and today attracts
1.2 million visitors. Though smaller, Mexico's Feria Internacional
del Libro de Guadalajara is more influential. Founded in 1987,
roughly half a million people attend it each year, including 100,000
students, but it draws thousands of agents and publishers from all
over the Spanish-speaking world and beyond, and awards half a
dozen prizes. The book fair, which honors a different country each
year, gathered 1,935 publishers from forty-three countries in 2011.
New Mexico was honored in 1994, Canada in 1996, Brazil in 2001,
Quebec in 2003, Italy in 2008, Los Angeles in 2009, and Germany
in 2011.

In many ways, the Latin American Boom was the product of one
of the Spanish-speaking world's most fascinating yet least known
features: *high entropy*.

Entropy is a concept from thermodynamics that refers to disorder. Applied to languages, it refers to the degree to which they are
spread out geographically. The French linguist Louis-Jean Calvet, a
specialist in Latin languages, runs a Web site called Le Poids des
langues (The Weight of Languages), where he ranks 137 tongues
with more than five million speakers according to ten criteria to
determine their influence. Entropy is one of these categories. The
world's most spoken language, Mandarin—with more than 850
million native speakers—ranks near the bottom of the entropy
scale, at ninety-seventh, because most Mandarin speakers live in
the same country. English has much higher entropy—it ranks as
number eleven. But on this scale, Spanish ranks first.

What does a high degree of entropy do to a language? Its speakers move around more. In other words, high entropy means high
mobility for Spanish writers, entrepreneurs, artists, exiles, and ex-

pats. A Spanish-speaking creator can seek audiences in twenty-two countries that have an average of twenty million inhabitants each and share the same language and general culture. High entropy generates a great variety of political-economic systems, choice and opportunity within the same cultural environment.

Although the political instability that shook Latin America throughout the twentieth century forced many writers and creators into exile, thanks to high entropy, there was always a haven somewhere where Spanish-language cultural production could continue. In the nineteenth century, Chile and Argentina were these havens. But Argentina progressively spiraled into dictatorship in the mid-1920s. After 1920, Mexico was at peace when most of the rest of the continent was wracked by political chaos. Four countries—Mexico, Colombia, Spain, and Argentina—account for 60 percent of the population of the Hispanic world. And fortunately, since the revolutionary era, they have never been in upheaval at the same time.

The high degree of entropy in the Spanish-speaking world has resulted in the oddest acquaintances being struck. In his autobiography, *Vivir para contarla* (Living to Tell the Tale), Gabriel García Márquez tells a fascinating anecdote about befriending a Cuban student activist named Fidel Castro during a particularly brutal riot. Even after he became president of Cuba, Castro regularly invited his friend Gabo to literary discussions there. Mario Vargas Llosa wrote a doctoral thesis on Gabriel García Márquez, and the two remained friends until 1976, when Vargas Llosa gave García Márquez a black eye for the way he had "consoled" Vargas Llosa's estranged wife.

The high entropy of Spanish also intensifies the writers' political involvement. The political chaos of the Cuban Revolution and the Chilean coup d'état gave Latin America high international visibility at the same time as a generation of young writers was emerging. In 1990, twenty years before winning the Nobel Prize for Literature,

Vargas Llosa ran for the Peruvian presidency. Sarmiento, Bello, Darío, Neruda, and Octavio Paz were all either diplomats or statesmen.

The fact that Latin America produced five Nobel Peace Prize winners, compared to six Nobel Prizes for literature, points to the fact that, magic realism notwithstanding, literary genius and political chaos went hand in hand in Latin America. The earliest work by a Latin Boom author was the avant-garde *El Señor Presidente* published in 1946. With this novel, Miguel Ángel Asturias initiated the prolific Latin American subgenre of "dictator novels." Another work, published in 1974 by the exiled Paraguayan Augusto Roa Bastos, *Yo el Supremo* (I, the Supreme), shows how language and power linked the reign of José Gaspar Rodríguez de Francia, Latin America's first nineteenth-century despot in Paraguay. García Márquez wrote not just one, but two such "dictator novels": *El otoño del patriarca* (The Autumn of the Patriarch) and *El general en su laberinto* about Simón Bolívar's last journey toward his premature death. Because of high entropy in Spanish-language writing, the same political themes cut across national literatures in remarkably similar ways.

The extent to which foreign powers—including Spain, Britain, France, the USSR, and the United States—have meddled in Latin America also increased the entropy of Spanish. Until a decade ago in Latin America, *el 11 del septiembre* referred to the 1973 coup against Chilean president Salvador Allende, which was supported by the CIA. The renowned Latin America specialist Pat M. Holt, chief of staff of the Foreign Relations Committee of the U.S. Senate in the late 1970s, was famous in Washington circles for a joke he made about American interventionism: "Why is Washington the only capital in the Americas where there hasn't been a coup?" he would ask rhetorically, before answering: "Because Washington doesn't have a U.S. embassy."

There's no doubt that the international interest in Boom authors also came from the way they expressed feelings about a cold war in which they refused to be pawns. Many critics argue that it was the Cuban revolution of 1959 that triggered the Latin American Boom. It's probably fair to say that no other single event since the Mexican Revolution had as great an impact on Latin American politics and culture. When Fidel Castro overthrew the Batista regime in 1959, at the height of the cold war, he sent shockwaves throughout Latin America and beyond. The Cuban revolution was a rare case where a Latin American dictator was deposed by a true rebellion and not a political coup like the overthrow of Juan Perón in 1955 or of the Venezuelan dictator Marcos Pérez Jimenez in 1958. Latin Americans saw that change did not have to come from the top; it could build from the bottom up. Since 1930, the entire continent had been progressively falling into the hands of dictators and becoming dominated by foreign powers—mostly the United States. Castro's victory created an immense wave of hope in Latin America, showing that it was possible to overthrow a dictator. Revolutionary movements flared up everywhere.

But the Latin American Boom authors would get much more material for reflection when the Cuban revolution slipped into a totalitarian dictatorship. In 1971, the Cuban poet Heberto Padilla, previously a supporter of Castro and his regime, was arrested on vague charges of anti-Castro activities. After a mock trial, he was released from prison—after publicly reading his *Autocrítica* (Self-criticism), admitting to errors in judgment and confessing to "counterrevolutionary" ideas and activities. After Cuba and Chile, Latin America got a savage dictatorship in Argentina, Argentina's Dirty War, the Sandinista revolution in Nicaragua, civil war and drug lords in Colombia, Peruvian militarism and democracy, the Salvadoran revolution, the Falklands War, the urban guerrillas of the Tupamaros in Montevideo, the Peruvian guerrillas of *Sendero Luminoso* (Shining Path), Subcomandante Marcos's Zapatista rebellion in Mexico, the rise of drug lords in Mexico. . . . It did not seem to stop.

Such phenomenal chaos produced massive movements of refugees, fueling the age-old tradition of exiled literary figures in the Spanish-speaking world, whether Spaniards in Mexico, Colombians in Argentina, or Cubans in Florida. Mexico, El Salvador, Ecuador, Colombia, and the Dominican Republic all have 10 percent or more of their population living abroad. The proportion for Mexico is 25 percent, a world record. In Chile, the military coup of September 11, 1973, forced two hundred thousand Chileans (2 percent of the population) into exile. Thanks to Chile's high-quality education system, most of its immigrants were skilled. Most went to Venezuela, Mexico, Cuba, Costa Rica, Brazil, and Canada.

Chilean refugees, for political reasons, were never welcome in the United States. Instead, Mexican and Cuban immigrants would play the greatest role in the burgeoning Latin American community.

28. From Ketchup to Salsa

We headed to Arizona for six months in 2010 to see how Spanish and English coexisted in that part of the United States. Things started on an optimistic note. While we were looking for a school for our six-year-old twins, we happened to phone Holdeman Elementary School, in Tempe where the school secretary answered, "Holdeman School, *buenos* días!" We thought we had accidentally stepped into *Dora the Explorer,* the TV show about a peppy bilingual Latina cartoon heroine.

Indeed, when we got settled in Tempe, we saw lots of friendly goodwill toward Spanish speakers around us. Although Arizona is one of the thirty-one U.S. states that declared English their (only) official language, everything in Arizona is translated. Every errand to the grocery store, the doctor, or the bank was a little dip into the Spanish-speaking world. Our local hardware store sold "Spanish for construction" dictionaries. The Arizona Department of Transportation, we discovered, published a Spanish version of its Highway Code (although driving tests are administered in English).

Of course, language politics in Arizona did not turn out to be as simple as they first appeared. Arizona, with its quickly growing Hispanic population and increasingly Hispanic culture, is emblematic of the transformations going on right now all over the United States. Those changes, in turn, are shaping the role the United States is playing in the larger story of Spanish—and, in turn, transform the story of Spanish itself.

Statistics are one part of the story. The United States is home to about 11 percent of the world's 460 million *hispanohablantes* (Spanish speakers). According to the 2010 census, 52 million Americans—or 16.3 percent of the U.S. population—are Hispanic. Of these, an estimated 70 percent (37 million) speak Spanish. This raw number of Spanish speakers puts the United States fifth among Hispanic nations, after Mexico, Spain, Colombia, and Argentina, and before Peru and Venezuela.

The growth of Spanish in the United States is often portrayed as a recent phenomenon. In fact, Spanish is the oldest European language continually spoken on U.S. territory. Deeds, oaths, and contracts written in Spanish date from the founding of St. Augustine, Florida, in 1565. According to a landmark study published by historians Brian Gratton and Myron P. Gutmann, between 1850 and 1900 the number of Mexicans living in the United States multiplied fivefold to reach half a million. During this period, Hispanics represented roughly 0.6 percent of the U.S. population, and their numbers increased at the same rate as the overall population.

Things started to change in 1940, when the 2.1 million Hispanics in the United States—now Mexicans, Puerto Ricans, Cubans, and Panamanians—represented 1.6 percent of the population. Since 1900, the Hispanic population has multiplied one hundred–fold, while its proportion of the total U.S. population increased twenty-five-fold. In the first decade of 2000, the growth rate of Hispanics was four times that of the general population and ten times that of non-Hispanics.

In fact, over the last century, the Hispanic population in the United States increased faster than the population of any other Spanish-speaking country in the world, and almost as fast as Argentina's during the massive wave of European immigration from 1850 to 1950.

Spanish began entering mainstream American culture with the sharp rise in Hispanic immigration after the 1960s. In 1960, Spanish was the language of a small and quiet minority that accounted for less than 3 percent of the total population. Only Americans in the Southwest, New York City, and Chicago were really aware of the Spanish presence in the United States. Hispanic culture was visible—or rather, audible—to the general population only when it popped up in cowboy films, Disney comics, and musicals like *West Side Story*. (And on the whole, the image these media fostered was rarely flattering.) By 1970, the increase was important enough for the United States to start including "Hispanic" as a category on the national census. After that, the number of Hispanics doubled every twenty years: from 4.5 percent of the population in 1970, to 8.7 percent in 1990, to 16.3 percent in 2010. In the United States, Hispanics have now overtaken African Americans as the largest minority group.

This change in the social makeup of the United States took everyone by surprise. Starting in the 1970s, a number of different labels popped up for the ensemble of the Hispanic population. The Nixon administration coined the term *Hispanic* for the 1970 census; *Latino* is more commonly used by Hispanics themselves, and can include Brazilians. *Chicano* refers specifically to the political identity of Mexican Americans. *Mexicano* has a derogatory sense since it is used for Hispanic manual workers *Hispano* is reserved for old-stock Mexicans of New Mexico. Since 2009, a new label, *hispanounidenses* (Hispanic Americans), has been gaining currency. When they are filling out the census, roughly 50 percent of Hispanics check the box "some other race."

Until the end of the 1950s, Hispanic immigrants settled mostly in California, New Mexico, Texas, New York City, and Chicago. But since the 1990s, immigrants have been going to all states, even the smallest towns. West Virginia has the lowest proportion of Hispanics, 1.2 percent. Arizona's proportion of Hispanics climbed from 5 to 30 percent of the population in fewer than twenty years. But the Hispanic populations of Alabama, Arkansas, Georgia, Kentucky, Maryland, Mississippi, North Carolina, South Carolina, South Dakota, and Tennessee grew by at least 100 percent in the first decade of the twenty-first century, with Alabama topping them at 144 percent.

Immigrants go where there are established communities, which take root where there is work. We saw one such place, quite off the traditional route of Latin American immigrants, on our way from Arizona back to Canada: Postville, Iowa. A cute town of roughly 2,200 inhabitants, it is surrounded by cornfields with a quiet main street and neat parks where Hassidic Jewish and Hispanic mothers stroll their babies. Postville became famous in 2009 when U.S. Immigration and Customs Enforcement agents raided the local kosher slaughterhouse and meat-packing plant, arresting 390 of its 1,100 employees who were illegal immigrants. Postville's Catholic and Jewish community leaders jumped to the defense of the workers, demanding special legislation to grant them legal status. The town's main employer, which provided a living to many citizens, depended on Hispanic laborers. "Things were going well here before the *razzia*," said our server at the Mexican restaurant where we stopped for lunch. Today, Postville's main street is full of empty storefronts.

The truth is, no matter what obstacles they face, Latin American immigrants will keep coming to the United States, although the numbers will fluctuate according to economic and political circumstances. When we joined a tour of the Arizona-Mexico frontier in the city of Nogales organized by scholars from Arizona State University, we learned that in 2009, the U.S. Border Patrol dismantled twenty-two do-it-yourself tunnels in Nogales alone. Every day the Mexican city of Nogales receives three hundred illegal immigrants who have been expelled from the United States, including an average of fifteen children. This is a fraction of the four thousand illegal immigrants who enter the United States daily, in addition to those who migrate legally, which is a fraction, in turn, of the sixty thousand Mexicans who visit the United States daily to conduct business, work, or visit—legally.

This mass migration to the United States is opening a new chapter in the story of Spanish. Since Spain expelled its Jewish population in 1492, and the Moriscos in 1608, this is the first time Hispanics have migrated in such large numbers and to a zone outside the control of either Spain or any other Hispanic country.

This gigantic movement is transforming both the immigrants and the welcoming society. Although soccer is far from being as popular as American football, baseball, and basketball, salsa sales in the United States almost match ketchup sales today. The list of popular Hispanic artists in the United States is so long it would be tedious to go into detail. Because Hispanics' purchasing power is rising faster than that of the general population, companies are looking for ways to reach them. Credit card companies have even started offering "workshops" on credit in Spanish to lure traditionally credit-resistant Latinos. U.S. employees who take the trouble to learn Spanish can earn up to 30 percent more, according to a study done in Spain.

The impact of the increased Hispanic presence is apparent in English. Spanish terms first appeared in the *Dictionary of American Regional English* in 1972. Some Spanish calques (loan translations) are gaining currency. "She puts him breakfast on the couch!" or even "Put it the juice" (turn on the power) are calques from the Spanish verbs *poner* (to put) and *meter* (to put in). One also hears people say "get down" from the car instead of "get out" of it—from the Spanish *bajarse* (to descend, to dismount from a vehicle).

Immigrants, of course, end up assimilating, yet the scale of Hispanic immigration in some places in the United States is changing the dynamics of that process. As James Garcia, a middle-aged Phoenix playwright who handles media relations for the Arizona Hispanic Chamber of Commerce, explained, "I am typical of a generation of children who assimilated. We define ourselves as American and speak English fluently. But today, immigration has reached such proportions that people can maintain their language easily."

We witnessed this phenomenon at an *intercambio*, a Spanish-language exchange group, at Rio Salado Community College in downtown Phoenix. Contrary to what we expected, few of the Spanish speakers in the group were recent immigrants. Most had lived in the United States for a decade or more before deciding to learn English. Sandra, a thirty-five-year-old immigrant from Puebla, Mexico, had been working in hamburger restaurants for fifteen years. She was worn down from speaking only Spanish, she said. *"Estoy aburrida"* (I am bored). José, a sixty-year-old trained mechanic told Julie English wouldn't help him in his career at this point in his life, but he wanted to speak English so he could better understand his English-speaking children.

Most of the Spanish speakers we met admitted that it was easy to live, and even work, as a unilingual Spanish speaker in Phoenix—in fact, they said, it was *too* easy. Indeed, Arizona has Spanish-language TV, radio, and newspapers. And if this is not enough, Spanish-speaking employees everywhere can bridge the linguistic gap. The reason Spanish speakers decide to learn English is that they get tired of relying on interpreters, especially when they venture beyond the Hispanic community.

Before the large wave of Hispanic immigration started in the 1970s, two things boosted the presence and status of Spanish in the United States: the arrival of Cubans and the civil rights movement.

After fleeing Fidel Castro's revolution in 1959, Cuban refugees organized into a prosperous community in the United States, and in doing so created an entirely new Hispanic center in Florida. One million Cubans migrated to the United States in two large waves, in the 1960s and the 1980s.

Cuban culture was distinct from that of the other three main groups of Hispanics in the United States: the Mexicans, the Puerto Ricans, and the Panamanians. The influence of Cubans also grew at a rate disproportionate to the size of their community, mostly because so many Cuban immigrants came from the middle and upper classes. When they arrived they instantly became the darlings of the U.S. government, benefiting from special laws that entitled them to automatic refugee status and public assistance, Medicare, free English courses, scholarships, and low-interest college loans. Some U.S. banks even pioneered special business loans for Cuban exiles who had no collateral or credit, which enabled them to quickly secure funds to start businesses.

And Cubans started hundreds of businesses. The most successful was Univision, now the main Hispanic TV channel in the United States, which celebrated its fiftieth anniversary in 2012. In 1998, Univision became the most-watched station in Miami, a first for a Spanish-language station in American history. In 2003, 5 percent of the total Hispanic population in the United States lived in Miami, but Miami had half of the forty largest Latino-owned industrial and commercial firms in the country. Because of their business acumen and education, and the anti-Castro solidarity that united them, Cubans went on to form a powerful political lobby that now represents the swing vote in Florida and New Jersey.

At the same time the Cubans were making their presence felt, Hispanics, and particularly Mexicans, made their first political breakthroughs with the civil rights movement.

A couple weeks after we arrived in Phoenix, in January 2010, our daughters asked if we could attend a Martin Luther King Day parade. Civic parades being rare events in Canada, the experience was one of cultural immersion for us (our daughters were enthralled and spent the rest of that day marching around our house clashing imaginary cymbals). There were a number of parades in the greater Phoenix area, but we chose the event in Mesa, one of the area's Hispanic centers. Yet one element truly surprised us. Among the sixty groups that participated in the parade, there were almost no Hispanics. Our Hispanic friends later explained that the Hispanic community, at least in Arizona, considers MLK Day as an exclusive African American celebration.

Hispanics have their own version of the civil rights movement, which they see through the lens of their own history in the United States. That political history starts with the creation of the League of United Latin American Citizens (LULAC) in 1929, followed by the Chicano movement of the 1940s. San Diego was the scene of an early cause célèbre in 1931, when seventy-five Mexican children were banned from entering Lemon Grove Grammar School. Parents sued to desegregate the school and won. (This took place twenty-three years prior to the *Brown* decision, which required the desegregation of public schools.)

The movement got new life in the 1960s with the arrival of César Chávez (1927–1993), a charismatic leader who fought to improve working conditions of migrant agricultural workers in California. Born in Yuma, Arizona, his own family was forced to resort to pea and tomato picking after losing their grocery store and ranch in a foreclosure. Despite completing only eighth grade, Chávez managed to lead farmworkers to victory after protracted strikes. With Dolores Huerta, he cofounded the National Farm Workers Association, which later became the United Farm Workers. His main tools were slogans—"*Si, se puede*" (Yes, it's possible)—and active nonviolent resistance, including Gandhi-like fasts, the last of which killed him. California, Arizona, and Georgia celebrate César Chávez Day on March 31, although it's a civic holiday only in California.

In the early 1970s, Hispanics created the influential civil rights and advocacy organization the National Council of La Raza. That's when the Hispanic civil rights movement entered mainstream American culture. Spanish-language newspapers, television, and radio started to multiply. The Bilingual Education Act, originally passed in 1968, was amended in 1974 to make it compulsory for schools to provide education in languages other than English. This new wave of self-affirmation materialized in a number of new groups, the most extreme perhaps being Aztlán, a fringe nationalist movement that claims that the U.S. Southwest is the historical center of Aztec culture.

Despite this history, and the contribution of leaders like César Chávez, Hispanics in the United States have always punched below their weight politically. One obvious reason is that a large proportion of Hispanic immigrants are not citizens, or do not have legal status, which relegates a sizable chunk of the community to silence. According to the National Association for Latino Elected and Appointed Officials (NALEO), more than six thousand Hispanic appointed officials and elected politicians in the country sit on school boards, boards of utility districts, or other branches of local government. It sounds good, except, as NALEO points out, these positions constitute only the "first rung of the political ladder."

Political divisions have always prevented Hispanics from gaining political power in proportion to their numbers. Contrary to African Americans, the national representation of Hispanics is splintered among many organizations (the same is true in Canada). Low voter turnout has also been detrimental to Hispanic politicians. The turnaround in California in the 1990s, when frustrated Hispanics flocked en masse to the Democratic Party, showed that the Hispanic vote is a sleeping giant with huge potential. During the 2012 presidential elections the Republicans paid the price for this when over ten million Latinos showed up at the polls and gave 75 percent of their support to the Democrats.

Two months after we arrived, the Arizona legislature voted Senate bill 1070, to give the state's police forces exceptional powers in controlling immigration. Arizona was suddenly the focus of a national debate. It was the strongest case of a state challenging federal powers since the repeal of the Jim Crow laws in 1966.

In 2012, in a unanimous judgment, the U.S. Supreme Court validated the "show me your papers" provision in SB 1070 but rejected most of the measures in the law that criminalized illegal status. Yet during the months the law was debated, the lives of illegal immigrants in Arizona were thrown into gut-wrenching limbo. Even American citizens of Mexican origin felt singled out, sometimes even humiliated by the fallout of SB 1070.

At Holdeman School, where our daughters were enrolled in first grade, SB 1070 hung over the school like a dark cloud all spring. Roughly half the pupils at Holdeman were Hispanic, many the offspring of recent immigrants. The proportion of Hispanic immigrants at Holdeman was pretty representative of demographics in Arizona as a whole, where Hispanics account for 30 percent of the population, but nearly 50 percent of people under the age of forty-five. Teachers told us that many of the parents at Holdeman were illegal immigrants, though no one officially asked them for their immigration status.

We had befriended a number of Hispanic mothers we met at the school's special Spanish-language parents' meetings. In April, when Arizona governor Jan Brewer signed SB 1070 into law, we learned most of them were undocumented. The law was scheduled to go into effect on July 29, but its constitutionality was being challenged. That put many lives into limbo. As the school year drew to a close, our friends were frantically making and unmaking contingency plans in case the law was passed.

The mothers faced an awful dilemma. No matter what they did, their children's futures would be jeopardized. If they stayed in Arizona, they risked being deported, in many cases, splitting up the family. Moving to another state was a possibility many considered, but even that would come at a cost to their children—and they might end up in the same situation if other states followed Arizona. Returning to Mexico was not a simple solution: experience had shown that children educated in English were often lost in Mexico's education system. Indeed, none of the immigrant mothers Julie met at Holdeman had taught their children to read or write in Spanish. There was an overwhelming sense among them that this would hinder their children's chances in life: whatever time they spent learning Spanish would be lost learning English.

The controversy over SB 1070 also brought to the surface an issue on everyone's mind: Exactly what is the place of Spanish culture and language in the United States?

The conversation between the English-speaking majority and growing Hispanic minority is not an easy one. Many Americans have yet to come to terms with massive Hispanic migration and possibly never will. On the extreme end of the scale, there are organizations that aim to stop the flow of illegal immigrants, like the Minuteman Civil Defense Corps, but also self-appointed, personal anti-immigration crusaders like Joe Arpaio, who has been trying to "smoke out" immigrants in Phoenix since he became sheriff of Maricopa County in 1992. Arizona state representative John Kavanagh, who cosponsored SB 1070, told us, "Our goal is to make Arizona so uncomfortable to illegal immigrants that they will go away on their own."

From everything we saw, the Hispanic community in Phoenix got the message. At our daughters' school, many families were planning to leave the state when the school year ended. Our daughters' teacher told us that five hundred children had registered for Holdeman's summer school, but two hundred did not show up. She assumed they had either left Arizona or were too afraid to come back to school.

In the same vein as these anti-immigrant initiatives, there has been a wave of activism directed specifically to the Spanish language. In Palo Alto, California, we met billionaire Ron Unz. In 1998, Unz had sponsored Proposition 227, which was passed; it essentially put an end to bilingual education in California by forcing parents to "request" it at their schools (immigrant parents aren't likely to know the option is available, let alone request it). The son of a Russian immigrant, Unz didn't see himself as someone trying to roll back the civil rights movement. Instead, he argued that he was trying to help immigrants by forcing them to learn English. "Bilingual education was a misnomer. It was Spanish education." He admitted, however, that the move had had no measurable results in improving school performance.

We had visited one of the remaining bilingual schools in the area earlier that day, where our friend Nuria Godcharles, a confident, experienced, and perfectly bilingual teacher originally from El Salvador, read her kindergarden class a story about baby owls,

"Las Lechucitas," in Spanish. After the story, she quizzed the kids in Spanish, throwing in the odd question in English. About a third of the kids understood the English. "Sharing the culture and language is key to helping these kids make the transition from Spanish to English," Nuria told Julie. "More importantly, you have to understand the Latin American culture to be able to help the parents. They don't question teachers' decisions, let alone demand anything," she said. "It's cultural."

The influential American political scientist Samuel Huntington stoked the fire of language debate in his 2004 article in *Foreign Policy*, "The Hispanic Challenge." In the same vein as his famous clash-of-civilizations thesis, Huntington warned that Hispanic immigration risked dividing the United States into "two peoples with two cultures and two languages." Huntington's argument was built on the debatable premise that there was some kind of "pure" or "authentic" American culture, which predated Hispanics.

Huntington also alluded to an alleged *reconquista* by Mexican immigrants in the Southwest United States—a popular theme in anti-immigrant circles. But if nearly a quarter of Mexicans moved to the United States, it was not to reconquer it but to benefit from a prolific job market that has been profoundly deregulated. The wave of labor deregulations since Ronald Reagan nearly matches the exponential growth of Hispanic immigration—and these deregulations were not brought about by Mexicans.

But the perception that Spanish is "taking over" persists in some circles. We visited a community organization founded in Phoenix in 1967 to improve living conditions of "Mexicanos," Chicanos Por La Causa (Chicanos for the Cause), to see what they had to say about Huntington's argument. The organization's CEO, Edmundo Hidalgo, told us, "Salsa, *cocina* [cuisine], music, street names, the fiestas—that's the fun part of the transformation. But whenever we reach a critical mass capable of influencing politics and economics, red flags are raised."

Yet a lot of old-stock Hispanics themselves have mixed feelings about uncontrolled Latin American immigration. In Phoenix we met Hispanics who thought that this phenomenon, especially in California and Texas, could threaten those states' competitiveness. One of them, Lydia Aranda, is the granddaughter of the city's first Hispanic city counselor, Adam Díaz, and is active in community development. She expressed concern about young Hispanics' 30 percent dropout rate. "The typical Mexican immigrant is more educated than the Mexican average, but they are much less so than the American average. A grade-eight education may be good in Mexico, but it's just not enough here," she said.

While visiting a few parishes in Phoenix, we realized that although Hispanics account for more than half of—and often the whole—parish, Hispanic priests are rare. "This is because we have trouble finding Hispanic candidates with the academic credentials," one priest, of Polish origin, explained.

The group U.S. English describes itself as "the nation's oldest, largest citizens' action group dedicated to preserving the unifying role of the English language in the United States." U.S. English was founded in 1983 by Senator S. I. Hayakawa, who was born in Canada of Japanese parents. The group calls for "uniform language testing standards" to ensure that citizens can read and understand the Declaration of Independence, the Constitution, and the laws of the United States. The group's president, Mauro E. Mujica, is a Chilean immigrant. Mujica maintains that Hispanic ghettoes foster linguistic isolation, a strange position when you consider that almost all adults of Hispanic origin who were born in the United States are fluent in English.

Yet despite these extreme positions, and overreporting about social and political tensions regarding the Hispanic community, Americans remain remarkably keen on learning Spanish. Although there is no way to estimate the percentage of the American population that is effectively bilingual, some 6.4 million Americans attend Spanish classes, including 850,000 college students. (The proportion of those students who are Hispanics, however, is anyone's guess.) In all, more Americans learn Spanish than all other "foreign" languages combined. But, in more ways than one, Spanish is not a foreign language in the United States.

Americans' massive interest in learning Spanish is unusual for a number of reasons. Historically, languages attract learners either because of the social dominance of their speakers or because their speakers have made systematic efforts to promote their language. French, for instance, made more progress in Africa after decolonization than it had during the colonial period. The reason: the upper classes of the newly independent nations made it a language of government and education, so it quickly became a tool of social promotion. In Canada, the official bilingualism policy gives an unqualified advantage to those who master French and English, at least for public-sector jobs.

None of this applies to Spanish in the United States, where Hispanics tend to occupy the lower rungs of society. Their wealth, education, and prestige are well below the average, and their language is not protected by legal or official status of any kind.

Yet Americans flock to Spanish classes. Part of the attraction of Spanish may simply be the very allure of low culture, which is particularly seductive in the United States, where the culture is fundamentally anti-elitist. Since most Hispanic immigrants come from humble origins, the part of Hispanic culture that is projected in the United States tends to be more "popular" than Hispanic culture is on the whole.

But that's not the whole explanation. Over the course of our research, we asked dozens of Americans why they were studying Spanish. We talked to nurses, restaurant workers, politicians, social workers, police officers, retirees, entrepreneurs, a range of businesspeople, university employees, a hotel owner, a computer programmer, and more—all busy people who were devoting an evening or two a week to practicing their Spanish. Most were barely fluent and had a long road ahead of them before becoming conversational.

What was motivating them? Americans always have a heightened interest in language in times of war, and some people were motivated by the feeling that Americans had made themselves vulnerable by not speaking enough foreign languages. But most people's motives were a mix of pragmatism, careerism, and plain humanity. Our neighbor in Tempe, a thirty-year-old fireman, was a typical case. "The Fire Department isn't making me take Spanish," Billy Miller explained. "But in an emergency, you don't have the time to look for a translator."

In Phoenix, we joined a Spanish meetup group called Phoenix Amigos. (Meetups work from an Internet-based system to organize meetings and group communications: there are groups like this for all languages, almost everywhere.) The interesting thing about Phoenix Amigos was that membership was split evenly between Spanish and English speakers, which made the language exchange fruitful for everyone. The founder of the group, Gantry York, is an engineer who grew up in the Midwest and moved to Arizona in 1996. "Opportunity to practice is the reason most adult learners choose Spanish, and then comes travel and business," he explained. "A lot of people in the group started off learning or studying French and switched to Spanish because there's no opportunity to practice French."

But one member, Jim Thompson, probably nailed down the most fundamental motivation of the group's members. "Whatever they do, people learn Spanish because they want to be independent. They don't want to rely on translators." This was also true of the Spanish speakers we had met, who had decided to learn English after a decade or more of living in Phoenix.

Few stories illustrated this mix of motives as well as June Laraway's. A former spa director in her fifties, Laraway had switched careers to become chaplain for a hospice organization in Phoenix. In 2009, she found herself in a two-bedroom apartment in Phoenix counseling a ninety-two-year-old woman whose son was dying of stomach cancer. The mother only spoke *un poco inglés*. June was rocked by the realization that she couldn't communicate with the mother during one of the saddest moments of her life. In broken English, the mother asked, "Is my son going to die?" But June didn't even know the word for "dying" in Spanish. She had to ask the dying son to translate for his mother. "I felt devastated and fearful, really fearful, not knowing the words. My role is to comfort. And I just didn't have the words." A week after the son died, June enrolled in Spanish classes at a seniors' center. She has a private tutor she meets and talks to by Skype, and she listens to Spanish CDs in the car while she's driving. "My goal is to learn enough Spanish to be able to counsel in Spanish."

For all these efforts, not everyone is capable of bridging or dares to bridge the language gap. As a family, we were considered a bit of an oddity at a Friday morning coffee group for parents of Holdeman School. The common thread uniting the immigrant parents was a feeling of isolation. Although the school offered a few services to help new immigrants adjust to life in the United States, an invisible wall seemed to divide the Spanish-speaking parents from the English speakers. A member of the group, Irma García, had become remarkably fluent in English and served as a kind of bridge between the two communities. But on the whole, even though many English speakers in Arizona wanted to learn Spanish, surprisingly few actually ventured out to speak and interact with Spanish speakers, even the ones who live next door—an odd phenomenon when so many Americans say they want to learn Spanish because they can practice it so easily.

And for all the enthusiasm about learning Spanish in the United States, employers still have a hard time finding workers who speak good Spanish. In Louisiana, for instance, the New Orleans police department has had an official translator only since September

2007, and the force reported having an "acute shortage of officers who can take an accurate police report from a Spanish speaker." In a force of sixteen hundred, only a dozen officers fit this description.

Today, there's a new twist in Spanish learning in the United States Particularly at the college level, teachers sometimes have classes that are split evenly between students starting from scratch in Spanish and trying to gain fluency, and students who learned Spanish at home and are fluent native speakers but cannot read or write it. As Emily Spinelli, director of the American Association of Teachers of Spanish and Portuguese, explained, "this often forces us to divide groups and create a different pedagogy."

The split between two kinds of learners is part of another trend under way in the United States, called "retro-acculturation." This refers to totally or partly acculturated Hispanics who decide to re-learn Spanish in order to get a better contact with their family and cultural practice (and also because they see the advantages of speaking Spanish). Our friend Erik Lee, associate director the North American Center for Transborder Studies at Arizona State University, is a perfect example of this. Though tall, fair, and blue eyed, Erik, we discovered, was the grandson of a Mexican immigrant. His mother and aunts spoke Spanish to their father but had failed to transmit the language to their own children. The result was that neither Erik, nor his sister, Alison, nor any of their cousins were raised in Spanish.

As adults, all the cousins, including Erik and his sister, relearned Spanish for personal or professional reasons. Alison learned Spanish while working at a restaurant in Washington, and she is now married to a Mexican student. Erik, now fluent in Spanish, is married to a Mexican engineer, Karla, a native of Sonora. "On the 2012 census, I declared myself Hispanic, but it really depends on my mood," Erik told us.

In Puebla, we learned that a Spanish-language school we visited had hosted many students like Erik, Hispanics who had not learned

Spanish from their parents but decided to learn it as a second language. A number of U.S. Hispanic celebrities have done the same,
including Jennifer Lopez, Jessica Alba, and America Ferrera, the
star of the TV series *Ugly Betty*.

But that raises the question: What Spanish does the United
States speak?

29. I Say Spanglish, You Say Spanish

IN 2010, WE CELEBRATED Cinco de Mayo in what felt like a truly authentic fashion: we drank $5 margaritas from plastic glasses and ate *carnitas* with the regular crowd at Macayo's Mexican Kitchen, a famous eatery near Arizona State University that touted itself as "the headquarters of Cinco de Mayo." The entrance of the restaurant, principally a student hangout, was appropriately decorated with a gigantic inflatable bottle of vodka—it wasn't even tequila.

In other words, even in a city of Mexican immigrants like Phoenix, there is hardly anything Mexican about Cinco de Mayo. As one of our friends, the Spanish meetup group organizer Gantry York, put it, "It's just one long happy hour."

In fact, there never has been anything exactly "Mexican" about Cinco de Mayo, at least the way it is celebrated in the United States. In Mexico, Cinco de Mayo is a minor celebration in the state of Puebla commemorating the victory of the Mexican army over the French in a battle fought there on May 5, 1862. California Mexicans began celebrating it at the end of the 1860s to commemorate the victory of an army of mestizos and Indians over powerful, well-equipped European forces. In the 1940s, the Chicano movement gave Cinco de Mayo political significance in the United States. But it remained an obscure Mexican American holiday for decades.

That changed in the 1970s, when the Latin American community in San Francisco turned Cinco de Mayo into a panethnic U.S. celebration for Hispanic immigrants of all national origins. It was a savvy choice: most Latin Americans, even Mexicans, had never heard of it, so it didn't pit different nationalities against one another. In the long run, the popularity of Cinco de Mayo was also secured by the fact that it has no religious association, a handy feature since 15 percent of Hispanics in the United States today are evangelical Christians, not Catholics.

Over the last decade, beer and alcohol companies have capitalized on this new American "tradition," making Cinco de Mayo a mainstay of American popular culture. Some 150 official Cinco de Mayo celebrations take place throughout the country. In 2005, both houses of Congress issued a joint resolution calling for the president to make Cinco de Mayo an official U.S. celebration, although it is not a federal holiday—yet. The White House throws an annual Cinco de Mayo party.

But in Phoenix, where Cinco de Mayo parties abound, middle-class Mexicans are curiously absent from the festivities. "It's not a Mexican holiday," our friend Erik Lee flatly told us. We had the feeling that other assimilated Latinos were also distancing themselves from the festival. Ten years ago, a Salvadoran friend in California used to spend days preparing a Cinco de Mayo feast for her friends. The custom seems to have waned.

Whatever is happening to Cinco de Mayo, its story highlights one of the greatest attributes of the Latino population of the United States: the melting pot is creating a novel Hispanic identity. U.S. Hispanics are splintered politically but not in conflict, at least not in any way comparable to the extreme division that is still the norm in the Hispanic world. There are 420 million Spanish speakers living in twenty-one Hispanic countries. Some of these countries have been at war; others have tense diplomatic relations. Yet while Hispanic immigrants could easily carry these conflicts with them to the United States, they generally don't. In the United States, Guatemalans and Salvadorans don't get along well with Mexicans. Miami Cubans are known to deride their Nicaraguan neighbors as *tira flechas* (arrow throwers). But even though they are far from being "united," U.S. Hispanics have mostly managed to overcome two centuries of deep divisions in the Hispanic world to live in relative peace together, with their leaders generally searching for common ground. Professor Gonzalo Navajas at the University of California at Irvine refers to this as a "transnational culture."

One linguistic product of the Hispanic melting pot in the United States is, of course, Spanglish.

Spanglish is actually a blanket term for a variety of different Spanish slangs, including *Cubonics* (from Miami Cubans), *Nuyorican* (from New York Puerto Ricans), and *Domincanish* (from New York Dominicans). The Spanglish of Mexicans is roughly divided among *Pocho, Pachuco, Chicano,* and *Tex-Mex*. But a number of scholars believe that an evolution toward standardization of its variants may be under way. A Miami Cuban, a New York Puerto Rican, a Chicano from Texas, and a Mexican from California will tend to seek a middle ground between the slangs, creating a more standard version—which is not to say that Spanish slang is anywhere near becoming the standard.

Ilan Stavans, professor of Latino Culture at Amherst College, is one of the most vocal defenders of Spanglish. Although Stavans acknowledges that the use of Spanglish in the United States varies with the age, social class, and nationality of speakers, and how long they have been in the United States—like the slang of any language, really—he argues that Spanglish is a language, not just corrupted Spanish or a slang, and that people should start thinking of it that way.

Stavans often uses the following sentences as examples of this new language: *Bajate al baismen y checa el boiler* (Get down the basement and check the boiler), *Vamos a la mareketa en mi troca y la parquiamos un bloque adelante* (Let's go to the market in my truck and park it down the block), and *Wáchale, carnal. No pierdas el focus porque viene la migra* (Watch out, brother. Don't lose focus when the immigration agents show up).

Stavans even claims that there is a *"Codex Espanglesis"* (Spanglish Standard). He cites one hundred or so words that demonstrate that writers are reflecting on oral and written Spanglish, a phenomenon that historically has led to efforts to define and standardize a language. Some of the works Stavans identifies go back forty years or more, including *Canto y grito mi liberación* (I Sing and Cry My Liberation) by Ricardo Sánchez, (1971), in which he coined the term *La Loisaida* (Lower East Side). Stavans also mentions Giannina Braschi's *Yo-Yo Boing!* a novel published in 1998 that was written entirely in Spanglish, the result of a decade of experiments. There are other names and titles: Luis Valdez's *Zoot Suit* (1979), Susana Chávez-Silverman's *Killer crónicas* (2004), Ana Lydia Vega's *Pollito Chicken* (1994), and *The Brief Wondrous Life of Oscar Wao,* which earned its author, Junot Díaz, a Pulitzer Prize in 2007.

Contrary to Stavans, most scholars dismiss Spanglish as a bastard tongue born of ignorance, or some variation on that. They characterize it as a scourge. But the growing use of Spanglish is also forcing scholars to question that position. We attended a panel discussion of a group of Spanish professors at the conference of the American Association of Teachers of Spanish and Portuguese in 2011. The scholars debated carefully before agreeing that it was impossible to really define what Spanglish is. The only thing they did agree on was that Spanglish was doing more damage than good. Yet the scholars gave the question serious consideration.

It's easy to understand why Spanglish irks scholars. Like all slangs, it is anti-academic by nature, and it can sound jerry-rigged. In a McDonald's in Anaheim, California, we listened to a young Hispanic who evidently didn't speak a word of English and was trying to figure out what comes in a Happy Meal (he could say that much). Another young Hispanic, behind the counter, answered the customer in fluent Spanglish, "*Viene con ketchup, mustard, onions, and pickles.*" The unilingual customer just stared at the server, confounded. He will get it eventually, but does that mean his mastery of Spanish will suffer?

For scholars, that's the question. As Domnita Dumitrescu, a professor at California State University at Los Angeles, said, "It doesn't help Hispanics to repudiate their knowledge of a major world language." But on the other hand, colloquial speech and slang are by definition always local and cannot be academic.

In short, Spanglish is a loaded term. When the New York Academia Norteamericana de la lengua española sent a list of terms typical of U.S. Spanish for inclusion in the new edition of the Real Academia's dictionary, one of the terms was *Spanglish*. The intention was misunderstood. U.S. Hispanic journalists wrongly criticize the ANLE for lobbying the RAE to have Spanglish accepted as a language of the United States. The ANLE had to organize a press conference to clarify that it was just recommending that the word *Spanglish* be included in the RAE's dictionary!

Spanglish is not a recent phenomenon, as people generally assume it is. The term *Spanglish* was coined in 1948 by Salvador Tió, a Puerto Rican columnist who later became a member of the Puerto Rican Academy of Spanish. In 1971, he recoined it *El Inglañol,* but the Spanglish label stuck.

The process that spawned Spanglish had started a century earlier. At the end of the nineteenth century, Mexicans coined the term *pochas* for *Californios* who were heavily influenced by Anglo-American lifestyle and language. The language they spoke was dubbed *mocho* (literally, mutilated or even amputated). The term *pocho* was widespread by 1920. By World War II, it had morphed into *pachuco* and referred to second-generation Mexicans in Los Angeles who wore zoot suits and spoke their own dialect, by this time called *Caló* or *pachuquismo.* The speech migrated to San Diego and became influential along the border as far as Ciudad Juárez. A similar process took place among Puerto Ricans in New York City and Cubans in Miami.

Like today's Spanglish, *pachuquismo* was built primarily out of Anglicisms. The Mexican comedy genius Tin-Tan (Germán Váldes) bases a lot of his humor on *pachuquismo,* including the famous line: *¿Óyeme vato, como se dice window en Inglés?* (Hey man, how do you say window in English?). *Vato* was a typical *pachuco* term derived from *chavato* (meaning goat, but used in the sense of *man*).

Spanglish is the normal result of the contact between two cultures, which produces large numbers of bilingual speakers. Spanglish syntax and grammar can be influenced by either Spanish or English. On one end of the spectrum, that produces what sounds like bastardized English—for example, "I washed the floor *de rodillas y le daba* wax" (literally, "I washed the floor on my knees and gave it wax"). At the other end of the spectrum, it's just dialectal Spanish with a number of Hispanicized Anglicisms, neologisms, or calques thrown in. In other words, Spanglish has either English words or phrases used in a Spanish context, or Hispanicized versions of English terms, like *Riders Daiyest* (Reader's Digest). Another class case of this kind of Hispanicization of English is *chíngar* (with the accent, not to be confounded with the Spanish obscenity *chingar*), a deformation of "shin guard." Another feature of Spanglish is what are called loan translations (calques), like the use of *actualmente* to mean "actually," when its true sense in Spanish is "at present" or "nowadays."

The main thing Spanglish speakers strive for is concision. The search for succinct ways of saying things is by no means exclusive to Spanglish, or to English, for that matter. People are naturally inclined to take shortcuts in their speech, seeking more synthetic ways to express ideas: oral language universally complies with the law of least effort. That's why words erode over generations. Code switching follows the same pattern: when a bilingual or unilingual speaker alternates languages in a single sentence, he or she chooses the language that expresses an idea most concisely. A good example is the Puerto Rican habit of substituting the English *so* for *entonces* (then, so), as in *Tengo clases ahora, so me voy* (I've got class now, so I'm leaving).

Many examples are so Hispanicized that English speakers unfamiliar with Spanish would never recognize them. That's because Spanglish terms remain phonetically and grammatically Spanish. Spanglish verbs are also conjugated according to the Spanish, not the English, rules. In Spanglish, speakers say *chatearemos* (we chat), not *nosotros will chat*. Spanglish turned *acceder* (to accede) into *accesar*, but "we accede" is *accesamos*.

When commentators dismiss Spanglish as a product of lack of education and acculturation, they might be missing a new development: Spanglish is gentrifying. Some Spanglish speakers say *carpeta,* for instance, because they don't know that the proper Spanish term for "carpet" is *alfombra* (in Spanish, *carpeta* means portfolio). Spanglish speakers say *troca, forma, aseguranza* instead of the proper Spanish terms: *camioneta* (truck), *solicitud* (application), *planilla* (form), and *seguro* (insurance). But even the best-educated Hispanics in Miami or Los Angeles have said, at least once in their lives, *tengo un appointment* (I've got an appointment), or *vamos a lonchear* (let's go have lunch). This kind of fusion is natural wherever languages coexist. It happens among English speakers of all educational levels in the majority French-speaking province of Quebec, who regularly say, "I'm going to the *depanneur*" (corner store).

Barbarisms are not necessarily a sign of ignorance. They are a natural result of bilingualism. Spanglish, can be seen as the badge of a special American identity—the way Franglais is for English speakers in Quebec. Indeed, some Spanglish words demonstrate great linguistic ingenuity and verbal inventiveness. *Cuora* or *cora* (quarter of a dollar) is word creation for a concept that doesn't exist elsewhere—it would have been simpler to say *cuarto*. The same can be said for *janguear* (to enjoy oneself, but derived from the verb *to hang out*).

And Spanglish is not an exclusively American phenomenon. In Gibraltar, the local Spanglish is called *Llanito*. In the Panama Canal Zone, it's *Zonian*. Brazil has *Portuñol* and France has *Fragnol,* while Peru has *Quechuañol* and *Japoñol* (Spanish slang among second-generation Japanese immigrants). Though never documented, the historical contact between Spanish and native languages like Guaraní, Quechua, and Nahuatl certainly produced their own "fusion" languages.

In his famous essay *"El llamado espanglish"* (The So-called

Spanglish), the linguist Ricardo Otheguy compared the popular Spanish of the United States with that spoken in other countries and found that American Spanish does not contain markedly more English words than popular Spanish spoken elsewhere. In his opinion, it does not even deserve the unique label of Spanglish.

A lot of the discussion about Spanish in the United States—but also in Madrid, Buenos Aires, and Bogotá—is really about the influence of English. Hispanics living in the United States aren't the only ones whose language is inflected with Anglicisms. Some of these words are so Hispanicized that they have become unrecognizable, like Central American *chinchibi* for "ginger beer," or the Cuban *yip* or *yipi* for "jeep," or *siol,* which somehow evolved from "shortstop." Some Anglicisms have even taken on different meanings in different countries. *Friqui* (from *freaky*) to a Peruvian refers to someone who is too affectionate, while to an Ecuadorian it means "hare-brained." To a Honduran, *frikiado* means "annoying."

And while Anglicisms are often derided as products of undereducation, curiously, the Web site of the Academia Argentina de Letras—the country's authority on language—offers *packs de libros* (book packs). And the books are about Spanish terminology! Spain's Real Academia Española has repeatedly condemned Spanglish in the past, yet it recently admitted the words *chatear* (to chat) and *tuitear* (to tweet) into standard Spanish vocabulary on the grounds that such words are neologisms.

In short, there's no clear line between what is Spanglish and what are Anglicisms. Nor is there any consensus that either is bad. José Moreno de Alba, former director of the Academia Mexicana de la Lengua, says, "Spanglish doesn't exist. What exists [in the United States] is a variety of Spanish that deserves respect." His American counterpart, Gerardo Piña-Rosales (a Spaniard), director of the Academia Norteamericana de la Lengua Española (ANLE) is more nuanced: "Spanglish exists, but it's getting smaller and smaller as the Hispanic middle class grows." Antonio Muñoz Molina, a novelist, academician, and former director of the Cervantes

Institute in New York City, says, "The enemy of Spanish is not English, but poverty."

Spanglish is not the only part of the story of Spanish that's unfolding in the United States. There are strong signs that U.S. Spanish might be developing its own standard. This is happening under the formal guidance of ANLE but also under the influence of thousands of translators, journalists, and scriptwriters across the country.

Few people are actually aware that the United States has its own Spanish-language academy. ANLE was created in 1973 by seven scholars, including three Spaniards, and was officially recognized by the Real Academia in Madrid in 1980. Its peculiarity among the twenty-one other Spanish-language academies is that Spanish is not an official language in the United States, nor was the United States ever part of the Spanish Empire (though some of its territory was). That's why ANLE is not called the United States Academy of Spanish. Officials opted against including "U.S." in its name because they feared that would make the academy sound official, and it's not.

At the moment, ANLE is something of a shoestring operation. It has no office and relies entirely on volunteers: thirty-nine full members, forty-two U.S. correspondents, sixty-one foreign correspondents, and seventy contributors. ANLE receives private donations but has no major funding. Yet that might change.

The Academia Norteamericana de la Lengua Española made the news in 2009 when the U.S. government formally recognized it as the top authority on Spanish in the United States. Laura Godfrey, comanager of GobiernoUSA.gov, the official Spanish-language portal of the General Services Administration, explained that GobiernoUSA.gov would consult ANLE on the appropriate translation of technical and nontechnical terminology, as well as on questions of grammar and style. The goal was to standardize Spanish usage in governmental documents and improve communication with the widespread Hispanic public constantly making use of Spanish-language services.

The catalyst for change was Bill Clinton's Executive Order 13166, which he signed in 2000 (it was reratified in February 2011). The policy requires all federal administrations and agencies to provide access to services for persons with limited English proficiency. On the heels of this, the U.S. government inaugurated a Spanish-language version of its Web portal in 2003 to help Spanish speakers find information about government programs and services, immigration, employment, education, and more. GobiernoUSA.gov is not a strict translation of USA.gov. It's an adaptation designed to address the specific needs of Spanish speakers, and it has more than twenty-four million users.

But the U.S. government quickly discovered it faced a conundrum: what *kind* of Spanish to use. Some writers want the standard second-person pronoun to be *tu*, but those familiar with Mexican rural Spanish prefer *usted*, and some even favor *vos*, common in the Southern Cone countries and Central America. So in 2003, Laura Godfrey took the problem to ANLE to set standard guidelines for all U.S. government agencies.

"When the Academia was created in 1973, everyone spoke of Spanish *in* the United States, a bit like a foreign element. Today, the true project of the ANLE is to identify what the Spanish *of* the United States is," explained Leticia Molinero, a translator who has been involved with the Academy since 1996 and has been a full-fledged member since 2011.

Even if ANLE were not involved, writers and translators would eventually have to define a written standard for American Spanish. That's because in the United States, a full 98 percent of written material in Spanish comes though translations from English, whether this is material from publishers, or used in banks, schools, universities, government agencies, or companies. Even when newspapers produce copy directly in Spanish, the stories largely translate realities that unfold in English. So the problem of referring to a standard crops up all the time. Oral media like television and radio are mostly scripted, so writers in these industries face the same challenges. In the absence of a local standard, writers and translators have resorted to the Iberian or Mexican standards. But these don't always apply.

The 2008 financial crisis cast light on another problem of U.S. Spanish: the names of large numbers in Spanish and American English are deceptive cognates. "One million" in American English is the same as *un millón* in Spanish. After that, the numbers don't match: a billion in American English has nine zeros, but a *billón* in Spanish has twelve zeros. A trillion in the United States has twelve zeros; a *trillón* in Spanish has eighteen zeros. To prevent confusion and make Hispanics' lives easier, ANLE decided to break away from standard Spanish and just use the American standard for large numbers.

There are many similar cases in the language guidelines of GoviernoUSA.com. ANLE recommended the use of *departamento* for "department" over *ministerio* or *secretaría,* standard Spanish words used with some variation in the rest of the Hispanic world. ANLE also recommended *agencia* for "agency" instead of *organismo, entidad, dependencia,* and so on.

Why? For many Hispanics in the United States, English vocabulary is familiar and recognizable.

But that doesn't mean that ANLE always favors English-influenced words over standard Spanish. The same year it was recognized by GobiernoUSA.com, ANLE published a small book titled *Hablando bien se entiende la gente* (Speaking Well Makes the World Go 'Round) that included three hundred tips on proper Spanish use. The work is prescriptive, proposing correct Spanish terms in many cases where usage is tending toward Anglicisms. ANLE recommends *solicitud* for a job application, even though *aplicación* is a very common. Another example is *seguro* (insurance), which ANLE recommends over the common Anglicism *aseguranza*. Why does ANLE depart from General Spanish in some cases and enforce it in others?

Leticia Molinero describes the philosophy guiding ANLE's choices as *funcionalidad operativa* (operational functionality). Basically, ANLE looks at how useful words or expressions are in their specific context of life in the United States. The use of *departamento, agencia,* and *trillón* make life a lot easier. Using their standard Spanish equivalents would create confusion.

In the absence of this confusion factor, ANLE favors "correct" words like *solicitud* and *seguro* because of another socioeconomic characteristic of U.S. Hispanics: they are highly mobile, constantly circulating between their country of origin and the United States. When they go to their countries of origin, Hispanics need to understand and be understood. To avoid being cut off from the rest of the Spanish-speaking world, they need to know the correct Spanish terms, whether or not they use them in the United States.

Another cultural factor guides ANLE's decisions. In the Spanish tradition, people expect *lo correcto* (the correct way). They want to know that *solicitud* and *refrigerador* are correct, not *aplicación* or *frigo* (or even *friga*). Even the least educated Spanish speakers expect a certain elevation in the speech used in public discourse, and they resent being talked down to. This is a major sociological difference between Spanish speakers and English speakers. Even if Spanish speakers use Spanglish themselves, they expect to hear better from their government, their radio, their television, or their doctor.

ANLE recommended the use of *solicitud* on the basis that native speakers would still recognize it as the correct word. The logic is that people's passive understanding of a language is always a lot better than their ability actually to speak it.

Will ANLE one day follow the example of other language academies, like those in Mexico and Argentina, and write a full dictionary of U.S. Spanish? The idea of defining a written standard for American Spanish is still controversial, particularly among sociolinguists, who have identified half a dozen brands of oral Spanish in the United States—Californian, Texan, Florida, New York, Chicago, and Puerto Rican. But Leticia Molinero, who earns her living as a translator, is convinced that a standard of the Spanish of the United States exists, somehow. For instance, at the end of 2012, the Associated Press produced its own 486-page style manual in Spanish with 4,900 entries—including some *hispanounidismos* like *tuitear* (to tweet). Every day, writers and translators make decisions on the basis of what they think or imagine American Spanish to be.

The truth is, Hispanics in the United States have long suffered from an inferiority complex. As Rafael Prieto, a Colombian-born journalist living in the United States, pointed out at the 2009 convention of the National Association of Hispanic Journalists, "Spanish was the first European language spoken in the United States but the dictionary of the *Real Academia* doesn't contain a single *estadounidismo* [U.S. Spanish]."

That's why ANLE's first step in creating an American standard was to assemble a glossary of *estadounidismos*. As we write, two years before the publication of this new edition in 2014, ANLE still has not determined exactly how many words they will recommend for inclusion in the RAE's dictionary, but the list will include words like *egibilidad, rentar, paralegal, van, hispanounidense, parade* and *bagel.*

Yet Leticia Molinero admits she is unlikely to see a finished dictionary of U.S. Spanish in her lifetime. For one, ANLE still has no resources, no staff, no budget, and no office of its own. Molinero recently created a public relations committee to attract support. "GobiernoUSA doesn't even give us money. We think we may get money from Spanish banks and American corporations who have an interest in the Hispanic market."

As Leticia Molinero knows, demographics and politics shape a language's destiny. But so do economics.

30. Spanish Dollars

THE STORY IS ALWAYS ABOUT a woman. She's usually poor and normally in love with a rich, handsome, unattainable man. But she's never hopeless—mostly because she's almost always stunningly beautiful herself.

Welcome to the world of *telenovelas*: over-the-top prime-time melodramas that glue families, barrios, and entire nations to TV screens night after night, all across the Spanish-speaking world and as far as Croatia, Sarajevo, Jerusalem, Moscow, and New Delhi. Though their plot twists tend to get more far-fetched the longer the series lasts, viewers happily suspend their disbelief for 100, 150, sometimes even 300 episodes. And the more people watch them, the longer they last. As the Venezuelan *telenovela* scriptwriter Alberto Barrera Tyszka put it in his book *Rating*, "*Amor sin rating no dura*" (Love doesn't last without ratings).

Telenovelas always revolve around a heroine who has been thrown into some kind of existential dilemma, usually poverty, often twinned with a love triangle, or some other kind of impossible love, with jealous relatives, disinheritances, and the like. Absolutely anything can happen along the heroine's road to happiness: couples split, lovers turn out to be fathers or brothers, characters are struck down by accidents or fatal diseases, or they end up in timely comas, then amazingly recover. Reversals of fortune are a nightly occurrence, whether in the form of a deathbed confession, miraculous return of a long-lost lover or relative, identical twins who discover each other, hit men who fall in love with their targets, or— the best—old men who die, then return to life in the body of a young servant only to win back their widow. No matter what happens, the drama unfolds in a beautiful setting: a sumptuous villa, chic office, sprawling ranch, quaint village, or stupendous beach.

Condensed versions of the most popular *telenovelas* can be easily purchased on the Internet and they are great for learning because the level of language is relatively good, even if the standard vocabulary—*¡te odio!* (I hate you), *¡sueltame!* (let me go), *¡éres un desgraciado!* (you're disgusting), or *¡largate!* (get out!)—isn't the most practical in the classroom.

Yet as we discovered, watching *telenovelas* has another advantage: everywhere in the Hispanic world, they are great conversation starters. Unlike U.S. soap operas, *telenovelas* were not designed for daytime escape; they are broadcast on prime-time television. Everyone watches them, even men, and if they don't watch them, they hear about them.

Their magic comes from the melodrama, a great Hispanic forte since the days of Lope de Vega. We asked Pablo Boullosa, the host of the Mexican TV show *La dichosa palabra* (The Happy Word) who edits scripts for *telenovelas*, what people are looking for. "Mexicans aren't interested in American television series. They want stories with people exactly like them," said Boullosa, who admitted he loves *telenovelas*, too.

Telenovelas first aired on Brazilian TV in 1950. Cuba, a big producer of *radionovelas*, immediately started adapting them for TV. They became immensely popular in the Hispanic world soon after. Mexico entered the game relatively late, with a first *telenovela* in 1958. But Mexico quickly snatched the lion's share of the industry, though Venezuela, Colombia, Argentina, and the United States all have thriving industries of their own. By 1979, Mexico had completely mastered the art (and business) of *telenovelas* and began to tap into global markets with the first worldwide success, *Los Ricos También Lloran* (The Rich Also Cry). The show was translated into twenty-five languages and broadcast in 150 countries, and turned the actress Verónica Castro into an international Mexiwood star, which she remains to this day.

Since this breakthrough, *telenovelas* have continued to cross both language and national barriers. Stories from Colombia are remade in Mexico, and vice versa. Productions are shot in Argentina with Mexican actors imitating Argentine accents. *Telenovelas* from everywhere are resold and dubbed and watched the world over—Mexican actors have fan clubs in Greece, China, and Indonesia. The Israeli television station Viva specializes in *telenovelas,* broadcasting thirty per day.

Needless to say, *telenovelas* are huge moneymakers. They account for a large proportion of the revenue of the main Hispanic TV networks like Mexico's Azteca, and the United States' Univision and Telemundo. One adaptation even made it into the *Guinness Book of Records*: Colombia's *Yo soy Betty, la fea* (I am Betty, the Ugly Girl), which aired between 1999 and 2001, with 339 installments, to glorious success. The crucial character was so atypical—the heroine was smart but homely—that Colombian producers had ignored the script for twenty years before deciding to make it. They regarded it as experimental, but the topic turned out to be so universal that it became one of the biggest successes of global TV. Not only was the show dubbed in fifteen languages, it was also reformatted in no fewer than twenty different franchises—including one in English for the United States: *Ugly Betty*. Mexicans liked it so much they made two remakes of it: *La Fea más bella* (The Prettiest Ugly Girl) and *El Amor no es como lo pintan* (Love Is Not as They Depict It).

The global success of *telenovelas* is perhaps the best example of what has been going on in the economics of the Hispanic world over the last thirty years. Despite the many hardships the Spanish-speaking world has suffered since the end of the colonial period—wars, coups, revolutions, and general instability—things have been looking up since the middle of the 1990s. Since 2000, the number of middle-class families in the Americas has more than doubled. The entire area resisted the 2008 global economic downturn and maintained healthy economic growth despite the crippling impact of drug-related violence in Mexico, the only true dark spot in Latin

America as we write this book. This resilience should not come as a surprise: globally speaking, more trade happens between Spanish-speaking countries than between English-speaking countries today. The purchasing power of the world's 450 million Spanish speakers amounts to 9 percent of global GDP.

This is a stunning turnaround from a century ago, at the end of Spanish colonial rule, when Britain and the United States dominated trade in Latin America and Spain only represented 4 percent of its former colonies' overall trade. The change accelerated when Spain entered the European Common Market (1986), Mexico signed the North American Free Trade Agreement (1994), and most South American countries organized into trade zones like the Mercosur (1991) and the Andean Community (1969). Among the world's top two thousand publicly traded companies, sixty-one are from a Hispanic country, including twenty-seven Spanish and eighteen Mexican. Some of the world's richest individuals are Hispanics, starting with number 1, the Mexican telecom magnate Carlos Slim Helú, who has a net worth of $69 billion. Number 5 on the *Forbes* ranking of billionaires is a Spaniard, Amancio Ortega, the fashion entrepreneur who owns the Zara chain. In all, the Hispanic world has at least forty-three billionaires, including eleven from Mexico and sixteen from Spain.

Yet since 2008, news about Spain's economy has being going from bad to worse. As we wrote, Spain was in the grip of a debt crisis, grappling with 25 percent unemployment. The European Union had decided to bail Spain out with a $125 billion aid package, but the Spanish knew that further budget cuts were on the horizon. This was a turnaround. Between 2000 and 2008, Spain's economy had experienced strong growth and was considered one of the economic bright spots in the EU. The growth turned out to be mostly the product of a real estate bubble that burst in 2008, sending Spain into a downward spiral of rising debt and unemployment. In 2011, for the first time in fifty years, more Spanish emigrated from Spain than immigrants came to Spain.

Yet as dramatic as Spain's economic problems are, they haven't sent Spain back to anything close to the state it was at the lowest point of the Franco era, in the 1950s. We visited Spain in October 2010 and again in June 2012. In 2012, there were regular protests going on—the Occupy Wall Street movement was inspired by Spanish *indignados* who were protesting unemployment, cuts in social services, and the political elite in general. But the economic situation had certainly not returned the country to the Spain of the 1930s that Luis Buñuel called "the Middle Ages"—let alone to Spain in the early decades of Franco.

At the moment, Spain and Mexico are still the economic leaders of the Hispanic world. Language has played no small part in this and will also influence the shape of things to come.

Even in the middle of an economic crisis, dynamism is obvious on a stroll down Madrid's Gran Vía, a bustling boulevard lined with offices, cinemas, plazas, and a century of public art (though there a more than a few For Rent signs). This is the location of one of the oldest *rascacielos* (skyscrapers) in Europe, the Edificio Telefónica, whose neobaroque penthouse would fit in perfectly in Chicago. Formerly a telephone monopoly, Telefónica is now the world's third-largest broadband and telecommunication provider, generating $81 billion in business and employing 270,000 workers in two dozen countries. Spain's Banco Santander is the world's thirteenth-largest publicly traded company, with $1.7 trillion in assets. Other Spanish companies—BBVA (a bank), Repsol (petrol), Iberdrola (Basque utility company), Caixa (a Catalan bank)—are familiar names to global investors. This is a radical change from fifty years ago.

After Franco, Spain's telephone, banking, and media companies capitalized heavily on the Spanish language, entering Latin America as a first step in global expansion. Since the end of the 1950s, Spanish companies have benefited from a remarkably stable business environment, a great departure after centuries of political agitation that created an adverse business climate. Today Spanish companies sell high-speed trains, airplane wings, a surprisingly diverse number of medical products, and account for a significant proportion of the global car industry.

The Spanish daily *El País*, founded in 1976 just a few months after Franco's death, epitomizes Spain's transformation. In just a year, *El País* became the nation's newspaper of record, and it has remained so mostly thanks to its strong commitment to democratic values and high-quality journalism. Now a part of the Grupo Prisa, *El País* is a source of global information in Spanish, along with Spanish-language EFE, the world's fourth-largest news agency. *El País's* excellent coverage of business, culture, politics, and international affairs is a response to what Spanish consumers, voters, and businesspeople have demanded over the last thirty-six years—and had no doubt been craving for since 1939.

El País's coverage of international affairs is all the more impressive since so many events in Spain's history cut the country off from outside influences. The paper concentrates on news from the entire Hispanic world—including the United States—as well as North Africa and Haiti. *El País's* coverage of news in Haiti is among the most thorough in the world, which isn't surprising, since Haiti's history is closely linked to that of Hispanic republics: Haiti offered military and financial support to early revolutionaries like Bolívar.

This globalization of Spanish culture started with the rumba rage of the 1920s, gained momentum with the Latin Boom of the 1960s, and is now carrying on in business and technology via the Internet and the global circulation of ideas through social media. Hispanics lead the pack in demanding social media tools in their own language. Spanish ranks second for the number of Internet users and is the second language in which users access Facebook, well behind English but way ahead of French.

Spain's economic renaissance over the last fifty years reversed historic emigration patterns, turning Spain into a country of immigration. In the 1960s, for the first time in its history, Spain became a destination for immigration, a fortunate change, since Spain's birthrate is now as low as Japan's. Between 1960 and 1980, 1.5 million Spanish émigrés returned to Spain after fleeing the civil war and Franco's regime.

Since the 1990s, foreign immigration to Spain has increased from a trickle to a flood. The number of immigrants multiplied tenfold between 1998 and 2008, from 630,000 to 6.4 million, with a quarter coming from Latin American countries.

The economic downtown in 2008 was so severe that migration trends have reversed since 2012. For the first time in decades, Spanish refugees were spotted off the coast of Algeria!

Yet despite the economic downturn, Spain continues to drive the economy of the Spanish-speaking world. It is by far the richest Hispanic country. Although Spaniards account for only 10 percent of the global Hispanic population, they produce 30 percent of its wealth. Their per capita income is three times higher than Mexicans' and five times higher than Argentines'.

But this will inevitably change.

As other Hispanic countries' economies improve—and *if* they continue to improve—Spain's relative wealth with respect to the rest of the Hispanic world will decline. And Spain's relative weight will decrease regardless of the state of its economy. Mexico, Colombia, and Argentina could surpass Spain in GDP and per capita income in the next two or three decades. A fourth rising economic power is the Hispanic community of the United States, which is quickly becoming an economic locomotive with a strong contingent of wealthy consumers and investors. In fact, the overall per capita wealth of Hispanics in the United States is superior to that of the Spanish.

While Spain's businesses were coming into their own and expanding abroad, Hispanic mom-and-pop *taquerías,* grocery stores, and small garages in the United States were also hitting their stride. In the last fifteen years, a dozen Hispanics have appeared among the billionaires on *Forbes's* U.S. tally. These include acculturated Hispanics such as Amazon's Jeff Bezos, but others have deeper Hispanic roots, including Christopher Reyes (food and beverages) and John Arrillaga (real estate).

There are definitely more Hispanic billionaires in the making. When we lived in Phoenix in 2010, Hispanic *empresarios* (entrepreneurs) were running fifty thousand small and medium-sized businesses in the state. "And not all of them are Mexican restaurants," joked Armando Contreras, then president and CEO of the Arizona Hispanic Chamber of Commerce. The businesses included publicity companies, solar panel makers, and software designers. They have good examples to follow, such as Arte Moreno, who became a billionaire in 1998 when he cashed in his $8 billion billboard business. In 2003, Moreno bought a major league baseball team, the Anaheim Angels.

The U.S. Hispanic market is growing so quickly, both in raw numbers and per capita income, that non-Hispanic businesses (and the U.S. government) are beginning to cater to them in their own language. American companies push to get the best stands at the business fair held during the annual conference of the National Council of La Raza.

The sudden multiplication of media since the 1980s—by the hundreds in radio, TV, newspapers and magazines, and Web sites—has created an entire parallel U.S. media industry that runs strictly in the language of Cervantes. The oldest Spanish-language network, Univision, celebrated its fiftieth anniversary on September 29, 2012. The New York and Miami–based network now ranks on the short list of major national channels, along with ABC, CBS, NBC, and Fox. An interview with Anchorman Jorge Ramos has become a mandatory stop for presidential candidates. Another important important Hispanic channel, Telemundo, began in Puerto Rico in 1954 and was sold to NBCUniversal in 2002 for $2.7 billion. The combined activity of Univision's Miami studio and Telemundo's studio in Hialeah is such that Florida now rivals Mexico City's Mexiwood as the epicenter of Hispanic TV and film production.

The press group ImpreMedia, with its seven dailies, has 72 percent of the Hispanic market in California, New York, Illinois, and Florida. The group owns the top Hispanic paper and second overall in L.A. (*La Opinión*) as well as the main Hispanic paper in New York City, *El Diario-La Prensa*—also the oldest; it celebrates its centennial in 2013.

Mexican immigrants are not the only ones who see opportunities in the U.S. Spanish-language market. Mexican businesses themselves are moving into the United States, including Grupo Azteca (TV) and the ice cream company Paleteria La Michoacana. Competition for U.S. market share among TV giants Univision, Televisa, and Telemundo Azteca is particularly intense. Televisa and Univision fought for control of electronic rights over *telenovelas* in the United States for four years. Televisa won, and the companies now form an alliance against Telemundo. Since 2008, Univision has had the rights for *Dora the Explorer,* a language-teaching show whose ratings are higher than those of *Sesame Street.* In fact, the story of this epic rivalry between TV giants would be great background for a *telenovela*!

Meanwhile, Hispanic businesses in the United States are expanding abroad, using the Latin American market as a springboard the way Spaniards traditionally have. The Los Angeles–based Lozano family, which owns ImpreMedia, broadened the coverage of its newspapers from community papers to news sources for all Latin Americans and Hispanics. In the words of the former publisher, Ignacio E. Lozano Jr., "Our mission was no longer to be a Mexican newspaper published in Los Angeles, but an American newspaper that happens to be published in Spanish."

The success of Univision, like that of the press group ImpreMedia, is a direct product of the growing Hispanic community in the United States. Aside from entertainment, Univision's programming does two things: it gives U.S. news in Spanish to Hispanics and brings them news from the Hispanic world. Network news programs have correspondents in U.S. cities and all over Latin America. And some of Univision's most popular programs come from abroad, like Chile's *Sábado Gigante* (Giant Saturday), an over-the-top variety show, now produced from Miami, hosted by the outrageous Don Francisco, that has been running for more than fifty years—the world's longest running TV show.

Americans, whether Hispanic or not, are starting to see what Spaniards, Argentines, Mexicans, and Colombians saw long ago: the Spanish language is a valuable asset in itself.

But exactly how much is it worth? At the turn of the millennium, the Spanish foundations of the Santander Bank and Telefónica set out to calculate the exact monetary value of Spanish. The initiative turned out to be a major intellectual endeavor, but it yielded results.

Santander hired Ángel Martín Municio, a chemist and author of dozens of studies, who was president of the Royal Academy of Exact, Physical, and Natural Sciences and member of the Real Academia Española. Municio was not an economist, so he applied a simple method to the problem: using a percentage, he rated how much various sectors of the economy owed their existence to the Spanish language itself, and then added them up. He gauged that language accounted for 100 percent of the value of the communications, media, and telecom businesses, but close to zero for industries like mining and agriculture.

Using this relatively simple approach, in 2003 he concluded that Spanish was worth exactly 15 percent of Spain's GDP.

This study, underwritten by Banco Santander's foundation, was a good start, but it needed to be refined since its author was not an economist (many economists criticized his methodology). Municio died a year before the study was published and no one picked up the torch until 2006. That year, the Fundación Telefónica went back to the drawing board and hired three economists with impeccable credentials to launch a new study.

The results filled nine books.

We met one of the economists, Professor José Antonio Alonso. In his office at the University of Madrid in Alcalá de Henares, he explained the new team's methodology. They just decided which sectors of the economies relied on language and which didn't: a total of twenty-eight language-related activities, including media and information technology, were in. The rest were out.

Logically, the team's result should have been lower than Municio's. But the economists ended up with a higher figure: 16 percent of Spain's GDP. The reason? They had considered one aspect of the question that their predecessor had not. Namely, Poland.

Though Poland is slightly poorer, its size and wealth are comparable to Spain's. The big difference is that the Polish language is hardly spoken outside of Poland and the Polish diaspora. All things being equal, the economists tried to evaluate what Spain gained from having a global language rather than a national one, like Poland. They proceeded by applying the principle of what economists call "club goods," meaning they evaluated to what extent being part of the "club" of Spanish language accrued benefits to Spain, the Spanish club obviously having more value than the Polish club.

So what were these benefits? The Telefónica team examined fields such as immigration, Internet communication, scientific study, and business decision making. They discovered that Hispanic immigrants were twice as likely to choose a Spanish-speaking destination over another. And when they chose Spain, it cost Spain half as much to integrate them as non-Spanish speakers cost. When it came to investing, Spanish-speaking businesspeople were almost six times more likely to choose a Spanish-speaking country than another, all things being equal.

However, membership in the Spanish-speaking club doesn't always pay off. The researchers discovered that a lot of things worked against Spanish, notably in diplomacy, science, and anything related to the Internet. Spanish amounted to 5.8 percent of all Internet pages in 2000, but this fell to 4.2 percent a decade later. The Web is a hotly debated topic, because the Spanish-speaking world scores high if you consider other data. There are 80 million Spanish-speaking Internet users compared to 50 million French-speaking. And the market penetration of smartphones is higher in the Spanish-speaking world than anywhere else. Regarding diplomacy, the picture is clearer, as the number of international forums where Spanish is the dominant language is very small except for the ones that include Spanish-speaking countries exclusively.

Yet Telefónica's study did underscore one very peculiar feature of the Hispanic business world: the commitment of corporate leaders to the Spanish language itself and their interest in turning it into a more efficient tool.

And when they are looking for help with language, Spanish-speaking business leaders go straight to the experts: Spanish-language academies.

31. The Department of Urgent Spanish

WHAT WOULD YOU DO if you had to write a text in Spanish that people in twenty different Spanish-speaking countries could read, but you didn't have a dictionary or an editor to tell you what was right and what was wrong? How would you know if an expression was used in one country but not in another? And even if you did know, how would you decide which one to use?

This is the conundrum Spanish-language journalists, writers, poets, linguists, scholars, and scriptwriters have faced since the wars of independence in Latin America. The absence of a common linguistic reference work has been painful to broadcasters, publishers, and producers alike. Unlike English or Portuguese, Spanish does not have one or two very powerful countries whose language sets the standard for everyone else. The Spanish-speaking world is divided among twenty countries with a top tier of six that are comparable in size and wealth, each with its own media, culture, education system, and national language standards, set by its own language academy and educated class.

Throughout the twentieth century, the problem got even worse because of increases in the number of English words and the amount of technical vocabulary being used in Spanish. It became clear to Spanish-speaking business and media that if they wanted to expand into other Spanish-speaking markets, they needed to solve this problem. In short, they needed some kind of "international Spanish."

But solving the problem was not as easy as *coger el toro por los cuernos* (seizing the bull by the horns). The word *coger* itself illustrates the scale of the challenge. *Coger* is a perfectly harmless word in Spain, where it means "to take," but on the other side of the Atlantic, it means, "to fornicate." Meanwhile, different countries have their own renderings of the expression "to take the bull by the horns." Most Latin Americans say *tomar el toro por los cuernos,* but Uruguayans say *tomar el toro por las guampas,* while Argentines, Paraguayans, Bolivians, Chileans, and Peruvians say *tomar el toro por las astas.*

In 1959, the Cuban edition of *Reader's Digest, Selecciones del Reader's Digest,* really did try to take the bull by the horns. The magazine was looking for a way to write stories-for-the-world in Spanish without having to rewrite them for each Spanish market. The solution: a rudimentary stylebook that laid out the acceptable vocabulary and spelling for all *Selecciones* editions.

Then in 1975, the Madrid-based news agency EFE went a step further. Like *Selecciones del Reader's Digest,* EFE was looking for ways to expand into the Hispanic world. To do so, it had to find a way to break into national markets without having to rewrite the same dispatch twenty-two times in twenty-two varieties of Spanish. So EFE hired a couple of in-house philologists to put some order in the morass of the agency's contradictory editorial policies and to come up with quick alternatives to Anglicisms. The philologists ended up putting together a 144-page stylebook that was very similar to the one *Reader's Digest* developed in Cuba. Then in 1978, EFE went still farther and asked the linguist Fernando Lázaro Carreter, a member of Spain's Real Academia, to write a new edition of the stylebook.

The links between EFE and the Real Academia grew stronger over the years. In 1980, EFE created a mini–language academy, Departamento de español urgente (Department of "Urgent" or "Immediate" Spanish). The name sounds slightly arcane, but it described the exact mandate of the department: to find a quick fix to the most pressing vocabulary discrepancies in the Spanish language. EFE managed to lure a dozen members of the Real Academia to its advisory board.

By that point, many academicians were *frustrated* with the conservatism of the Academia itself. The Academia had refused to include even common terms like *frigo* and *bici* (fridge, bike) for *refrigerador* or *bicicleta* in its dictionary. One of the academicians, Manuel Seco, became so exasperated with the Academia that he began writing his own dictionary of contemporary Spanish, even before he was an Academy member. In 1989, Manuel Alvar López, a member of the advisory council of the Department of Urgent Spanish, became head of the Real Academia. EFE and the Academia joined forces.

EFE wasn't alone. In 1978, the Madrid daily *El País* and the Catalan daily *La Vanguardia* each produced a stylebook of its own. But EFE's *Manual de estilo* (Style Manual) became the reference in the Hispanic world. Eighteen new editions of it have been published since. A new version, titled *Estilo. Manual para los nuevos medias* (Manual for the New Media) is currently in the works through an open source blog.

As an unofficial authority on standard Spanish, EFE was soon fielding questions from the public. In 1985, it published a new edition of the manual under a new title, *Manual de español urgente,* which became an instant reference among press groups, book publishers, producers, broadcasters, students, and public relations firms throughout the Spanish-speaking world. The idea also spawned imitators. No fewer than 163 different style manuals appeared between the 1970s and 2000, most of them copies of either the EFE or the *El País* manual.

By then, Spanish-language businesses were also pushing for the development of international standards. The problem was strategic. In the 1980s and 1990s, Spanish banks, telephone companies, and utilities were expanding into overseas markets, but language inconsistencies turned out to be a bigger problem than anticipated. Language discrepancies were creating communications problems and misunderstandings. Spanish CEOs turned to the Real Academia for help. The Spanish corporations Telefónica, BBVA, Santander, Repsol, and IBM Spain even offered financial support to the Real Academia to help it advance its work on language standards. IBM Spain developed special software to handle lexical data.

The Department of Urgent Spanish, which is now a private foundation underwritten by the BBVA Bank called Fundéu, works closely with the Real Academia. Fundéu's job is to answer vocabulary problems quickly—in a matter of days, and sometimes hours. It has come up with a number of successful technological terms in Spanish to replace English terms: Internet (*la Red*), browser (*navegador*), link (*enlace*), and surf (*navegar*). When Fundéu's terms become widely adopted—as was the case for these—the Real Academia adds them to its dictionary. Fundéu helps keep the Academia's dictionary up to date, and the Academia helps boost Fundéu's credibility.

Though it sounds contradictory, much of the story of Spanish over the last two centuries has been about finding a way to get separate national language academies to collaborate and to create an international, Pan-Hispanic standard for Spanish. The term *panhispanismo* was coined at the onset of the revolutionary movement in the soon-to-be-former colonies. Originally, it referred to a social or economic union between newly independent Latin American countries and Spain. That union never happened, but the idea of linguistic *panhispanismo* remained alive. In the 1850s, the idea of establishing a formal, Pan-Hispanic standard for Spanish appeared, but work was slow and it was hampered by political instability in Spain.

Then in 1951, Mexico's president, Miguel Alemán, himself a member of the Academia Mexicana de la Lengua, called for the creation of an association of *academias*. Every *academia* agreed, and that year they joined under the umbrella of the Asociación de Academias de la lengua española (ASALE), now housed in Madrid in the same building as the Real Academia.

ASALE's goal, from the start, was to establish a new, unified international norm of Spanish, called *español general* (General Spanish). But to do this, ASALE first had to overcome a number of obstacles. Even if all twenty-two *academias* were theoretically equal, not all had the same savoir faire, weight, or status in their own population. Because of their literary tradition and population, the *academias* of Argentina, Colombia, and Mexico had gained enough confidence to challenge Spain on language points. But many countries, like Guatemala and Nicaragua, did not even have undergraduate courses in lexicography. In New York City, ANLE didn't have an office (and it still doesn't). Many *academias* were underfunded. According to Humberto López Morales, the Academy of Mayan Languages in Guatemala receives two hundred times more funding than the Guatemalan Academy of Spanish.

Although the Real Academia had many progressive academicians, generations of benign neglect and decades of official censorship under Franco had left their traces. Attitudes and traditions changed slowly. Dámaso Alonso, the Real Academia's director from 1968 to 1982 and ASALE's first president, fervently supported collaboration between academies, but his work didn't pay off until the twentieth edition of its dictionary was published in 1984. Needless to say, the dictionary was considerably fresher than previous editions published during the Franco years but not nearly as much as the public expected.

In the early years of collaboration, money was also a problem. In 1993, the Academia's director, Fernando Lázaro Carreter, created a foundation specifically to finance work on "unifying Spanish." IBM Spain, Santander Bank, and BBVA Bank, and even the Spanish petrol company Repsol all supported this Fundación pro Real Academia. Their donations have doubled the annual budget of the Real Academia, which is now about $9 million.

Yet by far the single biggest hurdle the academies had to overcome to create a Pan-Hispanic standard of Spanish was technology.

The problem: the twenty-two *academias* could not coordinate their work using index cards. Only computers would make a true scientific study of language possible through sampling and statistical analysis of occurrences of words and by matching current uses with old uses and definitions.

But computers are expensive, and all the more so because of yet another obstacle: the twenty-nine-letter Spanish alphabet. Since 1803, the official Spanish alphabet had the same twenty-six letters as English, plus three more: *ch, ll,* and *ñ,* which appeared separately apart after *c* and *l* and *n* (imagine if the English *th* was a distinct letter between *t* and *u*). English language–based computers and dated software had difficulty handling this twenty-nine-letter alphabet, especially *ch* and *ll,* which are "letters" made of two letters. In 1994, ASALE made the sensible but polemical decision to eliminate these two letters and restore the more familiar alphabetical order. The only exception was *ñ,* which is now the fifteenth letter of a twenty-seven-letter alphabet, but its occurrence is a lot rarer than that of the other two and its rendition involves only one character instead of two, which was more suitable to old-school programming.

When Jean-Benoît visited the Real Academia in 2010, the first thing he noticed was an enormous custom-made filing cabinet for index cards. The massive wooden structure, with more than one hundred drawers, filled an entire wall from floor to ceiling. As the director of database management explained, the Academia once had dozens of filing cabinets exactly like this one, holding a total of fourteen million index cards he called *papelitos.* Each contained word definitions written in different handwriting from over the centuries. Some of the index cards were actual postcards containing circled images to illustrate obscure concepts. Jean-Benoît was shown a PDF sample of a *papelito:* it was a postcard from the late nineteenth century with a picture of two peasants on it. There was a circle around their breeches with the word *zájon* scribbled beside it, but no mention of the author's name. Until 1995, this card filing system was the actual "brains" of the Academia. When it came time to update the Academy's dictionary, lexicographers literally mined the drawers for words. Fortunately, the remaining filing cabinet is just memorabilia.

Since 1995, the memory of the Academia is stored in a row of computers located in a beautiful art deco building a few miles from the Academia on calle (street) Serrano. There, seventy lexicographers and computer specialists work on the Pan-Hispanic project. Between 1995 and 2000, lexicographers at the Academy scanned all 14 million *papelitos* plus another 450 million terms from historical sources.

The result was that in 2001, the Real Academia Española and ASALE finally issued the much anticipated and totally revamped twenty-second edition of its dictionary after a gestation of more than five decades. The dictionary was even available as a CD-Rom and an online edition.

Technology does more than just make it possible to create and update a truly Pan-Hispanic dictionary. Technology is affecting the very nature of the Spanish language. That's because lexicographers can sample usage across the Spanish-speaking world. And that information can be used to make recommendations for usage. Lexicographers now have very clear statistical information of actual usage and which terms to prioritize. Just fifteen years ago, this would have been guesswork.

Consequently, Spanish is becoming less Ibero-centric. The number and proportion of *americanismos* (vocabulary proper to the Americas) is increasing dramatically. By 2011, the total number of words in the dictionary doubled, to 88,000. Fifteen percent, or 13,500 words, are *americanismos,* double the number in the dictionary's previous edition. The number of definitions to differentiate Spanish and American meanings of words increased 150 percent. References to countries like El Salvador increased 17 times, from 100 to 1,700, and Honduras, from 300 to 2,400. According to Darío Villanueva, the secretary of the Real Academia, the Spanish are adopting more and more *americanismos* into their own vocabulary.

Simply put, this change is happening because the Academia expanded the sources it uses for vocabulary. In the database prior to 1974, 75 percent of sources were Spanish and 25 percent were

Latin American. From 1974 to 2000, there was a half-and-half split between Spain and Latin America. Since 2001, the sources have been 75 percent Latin American, and this will be the case for all future dictionaries.

The treatment of the word *computer* is a good illustration of how Latin America is now influencing standard Spanish. The common term in Spain is *ordenador* (from French, *ordinateur*). Latin Americans say *computador* (borrowed from English). Yet the Academia's database showed that 15 percent of the time, the word *computador* is also used in Spain. Older versions of the dictionary would have automatically given priority to the Iberian term and either ignored *computador* or presented it as an Anglicism or an Americanism. From now on, it will be the other way around. Global usage—not Iberian usage—will dictate standards. As a consequence, it's the Latin American *computador* that is presented as the standard and *ordenador* as a regionalism.

But though the numbers will speak, they don't solve everything. As the Academia is realizing, defining standards sometimes requires compromise and creative negotiation. Some words are loaded with conflicting moral underpinnings—like *matrimonio* (marriage, wedlock), for instance. In 2005, Spain legalized same-sex marriage, but most Latin American countries do not tolerate it. How do you work out a Pan-Hispanic definition?

When we met Darío Villanueva, he was just coming out of the fifth and last meeting on the issue of *matrimonio*. In the end, the academicians settled for three definitions. The first is about the union of man and woman in the form of a ritual or legal procedure. A second definition says that in some legislation, it applies to same-sex union. And third, it speaks of a religious union. "I don't anticipate problems because we really considered their point of view from the onset," says Villanueva. "If we hadn't, the first and second definitions might have been reversed." And indeed, this new definition will be the one used in the twenty-third edition of the dictionary.

In 2009, ASALE also published a 4,032-page *Nueva gramática*, and in 2010 an 864-page *Ortografía,* both strongly Pan-Hispanic in orientation. For the Real Academia's tricentennial in 2013, ASALE has been working on a highly anticipated twenty-third edition of the dictionary. It will be even less Ibero-centric and more Pan-Hispanic. In particular, there will be fewer Spanish regionalisms and more *americanismos.* "We will get rid of the regionalisms that are not part of General Spanish," says Villanueva.

These important transformations in the dictionary, grammar, and *ortografía* have had a tremendous impact. Since 2001, 5 million copies of the various reference books have been sold, which is more than the Real Academia sold during the previous two centuries. ASALE receives 3.5 million online dictionary requests a month. When the new edition of the dictionary comes out in 2014, the number of online requests will increase.

This stance has not gone over well with everyone. Since the creation of EFE's manual, ASALE's and now Fundéu's efforts at defining General Spanish, many Hispanics have complained that General Spanish is overleveling the Spanish language. They wonder if people will be expected to *speak* General Spanish.

The short answer is no. General Spanish applies mainly to written Spanish, which is only a small part of overall communications. Its creators have no designs on colloquial Spanish. Spanish speakers are proud of the diversity of their language, and rightly so. The beauty of Spanish is its immense variety and humor. A U.S. dollar is almost universally referred to as a *verde* (green). Spanish speakers in the Southern Cone call a million dollars, or any large sum of money, a *palo verde* (green tree). Elsewhere they speak of a *melón.* Cubans call a dollar a *hoja de lechuga* (lettuce leaf), but Puerto Ricans say a *washington.* The national currency of Honduras, the *lempira,* has been dubbed *desplumado* (plucked or spoiled): one thousand *desplumados* make a *milagro* (miracle).

Many Spanish speakers resist the idea of General Spanish because they think its objective is to homogenize Spanish. The catchphrase associated with this thinking is *español neutro* (neutral Spanish), which evokes a simplified, flavorless newspeak, devoid of any color. Jean-Benoît met an Argentine translator who complained bitterly about the fact that publishers were asking for translations in neutral Spanish. "It doesn't exist any more than neutral English or neutral French does," she said.

But the goal of General Spanish is not to neutralize all the varieties of Spanish or to simplify the language. It is to produce a standard, unified dictionary that can be used as a reference in international written communications. This standard was not invented; it was identified by recording the common words people write. Studies going back to the 1980s already showed that basic vocabulary used by cultivated Hispanics in Mexico and Madrid in written communication was the same in 98.5 percent of cases. International corporations that need to be able to communicate easily with anyone in the Hispanic world have asked for this "common" vocabulary to be written down so they can refer to it.

In a way, it's simply a codification of what people already do. Raúl Ávila, a linguistics professor at the Colegio de México, has determined in his studies that articles or oral communications directed to local audiences contain many more local expressions than communications that target a broader audience.

One important criterion for selecting the content of the dictionary was "comprehension." It is well known among linguists that native speakers' "passive understanding" includes more vocabulary than that which they actually use, either in speech or writing. Even the best-educated Hispanics understand more words than they use.

Defining General Spanish is about what the largest number of speakers in international or cultivated exchanges will understand. It is not about what all people should use in all contexts.

Yet the Academia is taking complaints about neutral Spanish seriously, to the point of developing its own antidote: the *Diccionario de americanismos*. Contrary to what the title may suggest to English readers, this is not a book on Spanglish or U.S. Anglicisms but a celebration of the dialectal Spanish of Latin America. The seventy-thousand-word dictionary was eight years in the making. It required software that could match all words and definitions of all 150 dictionaries published between Patagonia and the Rio Grande between 1975 and 2001! All twenty sister *academias* (the Philippines were not included) were involved in revising every single word that was reportedly used in their country.

In essence, the *Diccionario de americanismos* was meant to be differential. It focuses on words or definitions that are in neither General Spanish nor Iberian Spanish. This means that the oldest *americanismo* of all, *canoa* (canoe), adopted by Nebrija in 1495, is not defined as "a boat" in this new dictionary. Instead, the *Diccionario de americanismos* provides the fourteen American-specific definitions of *canoa*: depending on the country, it can mean either drawer, canal, coconut seed, gutter, neon light cover, dish, or oversized shoe!

It seems like a fascinating contradiction: the same people who work on defining General Spanish also produce a differential work that celebrates Spanish diversity. But this double desire to keep Spanish united and at the same time encourage its diversity goes to the heart of Spanish speakers' relationship to their language. It was the reason Andrés Bello published his famous grammar a century and a half ago.

We visited the Academia on the day that ASALE was releasing the *Diccionario de americanismos*. All representatives of the twenty sister *academias* (Spain and the Philippines were not involved) were present for the occasion, which offered the opportunity for fascinating discussions. But it was Alfredo Matus Olivier, the director of the Chilean Academy, who best summed up their objective. "Our goal is to create unity in diversity, not uniformity," he said. "Our language remains diverse, it is polycentric, but we work on defining what we have in common."

32. The Language of the Cervantes

WHEN MARIO VARGAS LLOSA LEARNED that he had won the Nobel Prize for Literature in October 2010, he happened to be teaching a class in New York City. A former Peruvian presidential candidate and a literary star of the Latin American Boom, Vargas Llosa cannot travel incognito and journalists quickly tracked him down in New York. That left him with a dilemma: whether to hold a press conference at the Peruvian or the Spanish consulate. He is a citizen of both countries.

In the end, Vargas Llosa held the press conference on neutral territory: the Instituto Cervantes. A cultural center and language school with an art gallery, an eighty-five thousand-document library, and a large auditorium, the Instituto Cervantes had the added benefit of a reliable videoconferencing system, which was important because in addition to the 150 giddy journalists listening to Vargas Llosa inside the auditorium, there were another 150 listening in Madrid.

There are seventy-seven Cervantes Institutes in forty-four countries, and they are not merely language schools. Together, they form a government agency that promotes the Spanish language and culture abroad, similar to the way the British Council, the Alliance française, and the Goethe Institute promote English, French, and German. Concretely, the Cervantes Institute network serves as a window on everything going on in Spanish in the world. Connected by an in-house media system—Cervantes TV and Cervantes radio—it is the admiral ship of Spanish cultural diplomacy.

Yet one thing distinguishes the Cervantes Institute from the cultural diplomacy organizations in other countries: its young age. It was founded only in 1991, more than a century after the French created the Alliance française.

Spanish may be the world's second or third language for the

number of speakers and number of Web sites, but until very recently it had no international window through which to promote itself. This is odd, because all other developed countries have at least one agency, or tool, that carries out cultural diplomacy. The United States has the Fulbright program, the Voice of America, and a dozen other official or semiofficial programs. The world leaders are still the French, whose cultural diplomacy machine remains unmatched, even today.

Why is cultural diplomacy so important?

Western countries understood two centuries ago that hard power (military and economic strength) was not enough to promote a nation's interests. Diplomacy is the art of getting countries to play on your field and establishing the rules of the game. Without diplomacy, neither peace treaties nor economic conventions ever see the light of day. In the long run, as much goodwill and influence, if not more, is gained by exerting what's known as soft power—the exchange of ideas. Religion and ideology are two traditional tools of soft power. Language is another one.

That's why the British, the Americans, and the French each developed a toolbox for cultural diplomacy. The French started the trend, reasoning that if people spoke French, they would be more likely to buy French products, ideas, art, and way of life, or just be loyal to France. The mere aura of culture was not enough to achieve this, nor were market forces and private initiatives, at least not on their own. The French understood that language teaching, through classes or other means, has strategic value. To sell their culture, diplomats had to promote university programs, put French classes in place, and organize social and cultural events and conferences in a concerted manner. The British and Americans do the same.

Throughout the twentieth century, Spain, Mexico, and Argentina made some timid forays in the field, but until 1990 their efforts were directed almost exclusively to other Spanish- or Portuguese-speaking countries, not to the outside world, with two exceptions: Brazil and the United States.

* * *

The best way to gauge the success of a country's cultural diplomacy efforts is to count how many foreigners study its language and see where they live. If they live in a neighboring country, chances are there are learning the language for purely practical reasons, not because cultural forces have convinced them the language is important. Sure enough, the map of Spanish learners confirms how laissez-faire Spanish speakers have been in cultural diplomacy.

Who in the world learns Spanish? The best estimates are published by the Cervantes Institute itself. There are 18 million people learning Spanish in the world. Of these, 13.5 million learners are concentrated in the United States, Brazil, and France, which are, respectively, the world's third, fifth, and twenty-first most populous countries. And they are influential nations, which bodes well for Spanish.

In Brazil, where half the population of South America lives, Spanish is making the most progress in terms of both raw numbers of learners and government policies that promote Spanish. Between 2005 and 2021, the number of learners of Spanish in Brazil is expected to multiply tenfold, to fifteen million.

The reason for this sudden rise in interest is a 2005 Brazilian law that made Spanish learning mandatory, known as *la Ley del español*, although its official name is actually Lei No. 11.161/2005. Teacher shortages have prevented Brazil from fully implementing the program. In 2010, for instance, only six thousand Brazilian teachers of Spanish graduated—a quarter of the number needed.

As Fernando Henrique Cardoso, Brazil's president from 1995 to 2002 put it, "Brazil is a country located between the ocean and Spanish." The witticism points to the main reason Brazil decided to make Spanish learning mandatory: the country is surrounded by Spanish. But that doesn't explain everything: Portugal is surrounded by Spain, and only 12,312 Portuguese study Spanish (this very precise tally comes from the Cervantes Institute's *Enciclopedia del español en el mundo*).

In fact, there's something else going on. Brazil is the B of the so-called BRIC countries (with Russia, India, and China), all of which are no longer considered underdeveloped and are expanding rapidly. Brazil is part of the Mercosur, the free-trade zone of the Southern Cone, where it trades with all its Hispanic neighbors. Spain is the second-largest foreign investor in Brazil, after the United States—the Spanish-Brazilian chamber of commerce reports $30 billion of investments during the first decade of the millennium, and the number of Spanish companies doing business in Brazil multiplied fivefold, to 250. Brazil will host soccer's World Cup in 2014 and the Olympics two years later.

The intensity of trade with the rest of South America is driving Brazilian interest in Spanish to new heights. In 2005, the Brazilian government estimated that twelve million Brazilians spoke at least some Spanish. By 2012, that estimate had risen to thirty million. This is all the more remarkable given the relatively low presence of Hispanics in Brazil—fewer than half a million. An estimated 50 percent of Brazilian businesspeople have a command of Spanish. The contact between Spanish and Portuguese has been so intense over the last 250 years that linguists have documented a belt of Portuñol around the country—Brazil's version of Spanglish, which combines Spanish and Portuguese (90 percent of the vocabulary in Portuguese and Spanish is so similar it can easily be recognized by speakers of either language).

On the border with Uruguay, in the sister cities of Rivera and Santana do Livramento, Portuñol has evolved into a new dialect that linguists call Brazilero or Fronteiriço (Fronterizo). Moreover, due to a complicated set of historical and sociological factors, Spanish ended up being more prestigious than Portuguese, with the result that a lot more Portuguese speakers are bilingual in Spanish than the other way around.

The case of the United States is exactly the opposite of Brazil. North of the Rio Grande, Spanish is driven by the growth of the Hispanic population. The Spanish language has never been officially recognized in any capacity, nor does it have support of any kind in the United States. Until recently, the United States was the first "market" of Spanish teaching, with six million learners. But when Brazil's new Spanish-learning policies come into force, the United States will slip to second.

Among the six million Americans learning Spanish, who is Hispanic and who isn't? From the perspective of cultural diplomacy, the question is important. The large number of Hispanics means that the United States is both a home market for Spanish and a "foreign" market. An estimated 70 percent of the fifty million Hispanics in the United States are reported to have a command of Spanish. As far as we know, it is impossible to assess how many Spanish students are Hispanics and how many are not. The Cervantes Institutes estimate that about 6.4 million Americans have a command of Spanish as a second language, and 9 million more have either "limited capacity" or "second language proficiency" (see appendixes Spanish Speakers by Country and Spanish Speakers, Other Countries), but no official study has been done to substantiate this.

In France, there are 2.1 million people learning Spanish. This is more than the rest of Europe combined, where there are a total of 1.4 million Spanish students. In 2006, 15 million Europeans outside of Spain said they spoke some Spanish. Seven million of these were in France. These numbers are remarkable because they mean that, with all proportions considered, France is nearly as bilingual as Brazil and proportionately three or four times more bilingual than the United States.

Why are so many French interested in learning Spanish? The French travel a lot in Spain—eight million in 2010—yet the British travel there even more, and the number of British learning Spanish is one-twentieth that of the French. Proximity seems to be a factor. But France's education system also requires students to learn two foreign languages. Naturally, given its historical similarities as a Romance language, Spanish is perceived as easy. And roughly half a million French have Spanish ancestry, so that might be a factor.

The popularity of Spanish in Brazil, the United States, and France sets them apart from the eighty-six other countries on the Cervantes list (see the appendix, Spanish Speakers, Other Countries). In the second tier, there are seven countries with more than 100,000 people studying Spanish: Germany (450,000), Italy (300,000), the Ivory Coast (235,000), Sweden (163,000), and Canada, the United Kingdom, and Senegal (each 100,000). The remaining countries listed account for 765,000 learners of Spanish, with an average of 10,000 learners per country.

These numbers illustrate what is working in the promotion of Spanish, but they also show what is *not* working. The three countries where Spanish is making the most spectacular inroads— Brazil, the United States, and France—all share borders with the Hispanic world. Their interest in the language is primarily the result of socioeconomic and demographic forces. (Second-tier countries like Germany and Italy have far fewer learners.)

Hispanic countries have made some limited efforts at cultural diplomacy. Starting in the 1930s, Spanish embassies and consulates opened three dozen cultural centers and *Casas de España* in various countries, but these never followed a plan. At least fifteen of the *Casas de España* were nothing more than Spanish restaurants catering to expatriates and exiles (most of their employees were waiters and cooks). Mexico created a Cultural Institute in Washington in 1989, and it is respected as a dynamic and influential center today.

But on the whole, until the 1990s, hardly anyone made a concerted effort to sell Spanish.

Then, in 1991, the government of Felipe González created the Instituto Cervantes. The original idea was to establish a network of high-quality schools that would also serve as a window on Hispanic culture. Originally, the Instituto Cervantes was just a new label for a haphazard collection of thirty-five cultural centers and *Casas de España*. It took time to shape these cultural venues into a system. A dozen had to be closed because they were too decrepit or because the communities that patronized them refused to let their restaurants be transformed into schools. Still, the journalist, writer, and academician Antonio Muñoz Molina hailed the creation of the Instituto Cervantes as "the best cultural idea Spanish democracy has ever produced."

There are now seventy-seven Institutos Cervantes operating in forty-four countries: eight in Brazil, five in the United States, and four each in France, Germany, and Britain, plus a large number spread throughout the rest of Europe and North Africa. The entire system runs on a shoestring budget of $150 million, a tenth of the British Council's budget. However, the young and energetic staff at the Madrid head office quite possibly compensates for Instituto Cervantes' limited means—namely, they come up with a lot of new ideas. The Cervantes Institute was the first international network of cultural centers to create its own TV and radio stations, as well as an online center that provides services to the entire network and has acted like a virtual seventy-eighth institute since 1998.

In all, Instituto Cervantes organizes or coordinates six thousand activities a year, including exhibitions by leading artists, lectures by prominent thinkers, and various events and festivals. When the head office moved to its present location in the beautiful building of Madrid's Banco Español del Río de la Plata, someone had the brilliant idea of transforming the bank's two thousand safety-deposit boxes into a *Caja de las Letras* (Vault of Letters), to hold manuscripts of great Hispanic authors, artists, and thinkers. When Jean-Benoît saw this vault in October 2010, the poet José Manuel Caballero had just locked his archives, in box 1543, not to be opened until 2051. And the great Mexican poet José Emilio Pacheco has locked box 1525 until 2110.

"Our work is not directed toward Spanish-speaking countries, but elsewhere," said Carmen Caffarel, director of the Cervantes Institute from 2007 to 2011, whom we met at her office before her tenure ended. "And the Cervantes Institute is not about Spain. It's about Spanish." Cervantes's teachers come from everywhere, as do guest artists and writers featured in its events. The Instituto Cervantes organizes international events like the Día del español (Spanish Day), held on June 23, and the Congresos international de la lengua española, large international forums that gather the who's who of Spanish lexicographers, academics, linguists, translators, and wordsmiths from all Hispanic countries.

The big get-togethers are always controversial. In Zacatecas, Mexico, in 1997, Gabriel García Márquez gave a famous lecture titled "*Botella al mar para el dios de las palabras*" (A Bottle to the Sea for the God of Words), during which the orthographically challenged genius ranted about the complexities of Spanish spelling (never his forte) and called for the "*la jubilación de la ortografía*" (the retirement of complicated spelling). At a convention in Rosario, Argentina, in 2004, the organizers were not too pleased when the Nobel Peace Prize winner Adolfo Pérez Esquivel took it upon himself to inaugurate the third Congreso de las lenguas "in honor of the American natives who were victims of Spanish colonialism."

Though the Instituto Cervantes is clearly a trailblazer, to be fair, it hasn't shouldered cultural diplomacy in Spanish all on its own. Mexico has the largest consular representation in the United States with forty-five consulates, and is very active in cultural diplomacy. According to an article by Laureen Laglagaron of the Washington, D.C.–based Migration Policy Institute, these consulates are ramping up the social and cultural services they provide to Mexican nationals in the United States and organizing teacher exchanges and partnerships with museums, including the Smithsonian in 2007.

Cuba has been famous for its medical diplomacy since 1960, when it sent a team of fifty-six doctors to Algeria for fourteen months during the brutal war of liberation of the French colony. In her book about Cuban medical diplomacy, *Healing the Masses,* the American sociologist Julie M. Feinsilver estimates that thirty thousand Cuban doctors and nurses were working in seventy countries in 2008. The Bolivian soldier who shot and killed Che Guevara in 1967 had had his eyesight saved by a Cuban doctor. This was part of a large operation by which Cuban doctors performed more than six hundred thousand eye operations throughout Latin America. Since 2000, at least fifteen thousand Cuban medical personnel have been working in Venezuela in an oil-for-doctors trade agreement between the two countries. As part of the deal, Venezuela threw in an undersea cable to give Cuba better Internet access.

Good cultural diplomacy always has a domestic angle. It celebrates a nation's greatness, an important feature of any official propaganda, at home. Spanish has never been a linguistic monopoly, even in Spain, and Madrid still feels it's important to make the case for Spanish to its own population, especially to the Basques, Galicians, and Catalans. The self-assertiveness of Catalans, never as violent as that of the Basques, is nonetheless a major concern of the Spanish government, all the more so because they represent 25 percent of Spain's population and the most prosperous part of the country, at that. Spanish cultural diplomacy, for that matter, strives to "remind" Catalans that Spanish is a lot more "useful" than is Catalan.

Prior to the 1990s, cultural diplomacy was mostly directed to other Hispanic countries and the United States, or unfolded within multilateral organizations of Iberian (Spanish and Portuguese) countries. So the initiatives were generally inward looking. The creation of the Association of Spanish Language Academies in 1951 was a perfect example of this, as is the Organization of American States, which has existed in about a dozen forms since 1826. Meanwhile, as early as 1926, Mexico City hosted the First Central American and Caribbean Games, though these included a grand total of only 269 athletes from three countries (Mexico, Cuba, and Guatemala). The Pan American Games grew out of these and were first held in Buenos Aires in 1951 with 2,513 participants from fourteen countries. The 2011 edition attracted 6,000 athletes from forty-two countries in Guadalajara.

It was also through these organizations that the *carretera pana-mericana* (Pan-American Highway System) was created. The idea came up at the fifth Conference of American States held in Santiago in 1923, during which member states had resolved to link their nascent road systems. The project acquired sudden strategic importance during World War II when the United States sought supply routes free of German submarines, between Panama and the Rio Grande. The nineteen-thousand-mile system now links the Americas from Alaska to Tierra del Fuego.

The Organización de Televisión Iberoamericana is another influential multilateral organization. Founded in 1971, its mandate is to foster relations among Spain, Portugal, Brazil, and other Hispanic countries. Hispanic countries have even ironed out a system of mutual recognition of diplomas with an international system of linguistic certification that applies to all participating universities.

In a way, cultural diplomacy is about salesmanship. The limits of cultural diplomacy are the limits of any seller: the sale can be only as good as the product. Unfortunately, in the case of Spanish, the product has posed a challenge. One obvious historical limit to cultural diplomacy in the Spanish language has been the serious challenges the Hispanic world has faced in developing functioning, durable democracies with rule of law and free-market economies. This has seriously hampered the "sales potential" of Spanish, the way the legacies of fascism and Nazism have hampered cultural diplomacy efforts by Italy and Germany.

For the last four hundred years, Spanish credibility in critical fields like science and technology has also been low. The situation started to change only three or four decades ago. And to this day, there are still fewer patent requests made in Spanish than in French, English, or German. Between 1997 and 2010, Spain obtained 7,196 U.S. patents; the total for the rest of the Hispanic world was 5,237. The sum of both is less than what Texas or Quebec normally registers. During that period, fewer patents were granted in Spain than in the states of Vermont, New Mexico, and Nevada, which each had more than 8,000. France and the European Union obtained 15 times more than Spain; Germany, 30 times more; Japan 115 times more; and the United States, 321 times more. So it's not surprising that the European Union rejected Spanish as one of the three languages in which individuals can apply for patents.

But things are improving. Between 1990 and 2011, Spain quadrupled its output of scientific papers and increased the number of scientific journals in the country by 50 percent. In the last ten years, the number of Spanish-language journals referenced by ISI-Thomson has increased by 66 percent, but there are still only 73 Spanish-language journals among the 8,605 journals published in all languages. As José María Martínez, editor in chief at the Instituto Cervantes, put it, "The Spanish product that has the most international demand is . . . Spanish."

Yet it's clear that whenever Hispanic countries decide to throw their weight around, they succeed. Eleven of the twenty-three Nobel Prizes won by members of the Hispanic world are for literature. A third of these twenty-three are Spanish, and Argentina accounts for another five winners. In short, if Latin America had gambled on education centuries ago, the situation in the Hispanic world would be much different today.

As the success of *telenovelas* and Hispanic media show, the Hispanic world is more than capable of pioneering innovations. The example raises the question of whether the only measure of the success of cultural diplomacy is number of learners.

Spain has consistently been one of the world's main tourist destinations for the last forty years. But it only just woke up to the phenomenal potential of this window when it is properly exploited. Spain's government recently created the Proyecto Marca España (Spanish Brand Project). Before that, creators like Pedro Almodóvar, Amancio Ortega Gaona (owner of Zara), and star chef Ferran Adrià did a better job turning the spotlight on Spain through their individual efforts.

It is of course possible to gauge the influence of a culture by considering factors other than the number of people who want to learn its language. This is what the linguist Louis-Jean Calvet does on his Web site Le Poids des langues, where he rates the 137 world languages with five million speakers according to ten criteria, including the number of Nobel Prizes won, or Wiki pages that appear in a specific language, as well as human life index and how many translations are done to or from a language (see appendixes, Influence of Spanish by Absolute Numbers and Influence of Spanish by Rank). In this ranking, Spanish comes third after English and French. To be fair, Calvet himself recognizes that such rankings have built-in biases. Indeed, Spanish would rank higher if he had used smartphone penetration rates rather than Wiki pages, or television production rather than translation. Interestingly, though, a similar ranking done in 1997 by the anthropologist George Weber using a different methodology had similar results, as did the Bloomberg ranking "The Languages of Business."

The goal of cultural diplomacy is to promote what is already working, but also to make inroads into new fields. Spain produces airplanes, telephones, high-speed trains, and medical products, but there is a huge gap between how outsiders view Spain and the Hispanic world, and how Spain and the Hispanic world would like to be perceived.

Nicholas J. Cull, an American specialist of cultural diplomacy and nation branding, asked a group of students in Mexico City what they thought could be a new source of Mexican soft power. "They answered, 'our friendliness, Corona Beer, our painters, our cuisine.' But then they ran out of steam." According to Cull, people such as the great comic actor Cantinflas and contemporary star Salma Hayek were also raised. (Frida Kahlo was not a favorite choice since Mexican art lovers consider her to be a creation of the New York art market.) Cull continued, "British English associated the term 'Mexican' with an odd array of concepts, including everything from the 'Mexican wave,' also known as the 'stadium wave,' which came to attention in the soccer's 1986 World Cup, to the "Mexican" standoff, that action film cliché where three or more antagonists are locked in a stalemate with their weapons drawn, and the self-propelled seedpod so beloved of schoolchildren: the Mexican jumping bean."

This is exactly what the editor of the Instituto Cervantes, José María Martínez, meant when he told Jean-Benoît: "We are trying to sell high-speed trains and new airplane designs but Spain is still so strongly associated with nineteenth-century Romanticism, and Hemingway, and the idea that we are a world of passion, inconstancy, a quasi-medieval world, the myth of Carmen. Spaniards don't recognize themselves in that vision. There are very passionate Spanish writers and artists, but what about Borges? We are not a stereotype. Look at flamenco: it's about sensuality and passion, but it's also about control, hard work, and discipline."

For the salesmen and -women of Hispanic cultural diplomacy, it will probably take years, if not generations, to overcome this branding problem. In addition to spreading the facts about the Hispanic world, it will take a lot of Almodóvars, Vargas Llosas, García Márquezes, and Ramón y Cajals to change outside perceptions of the Spanish-speaking world.

33. Traces of the Future

MOST OF THE WORLD'S five hundred million Spanish speakers would be surprised to learn that the name of their language derives from "land of the rabbits" in Phoenician. Which is to say, even in the history of a language that spanned three thousand years, crossed five empires—Phoenician, Roman, Visigothic, Arabic, and Spanish—and picked up words from Greek, Basque, French, West African, and Native American languages, there are some humorous notes.

Though empires rise and fall, the languages they leave behind preserve artifacts of their cultures and carry them into the future. The all-powerful Roman Empire was slipping from European memory when remote tribes living in hill forts in northern Spain started expanding their reach over the entire Iberian Peninsula. The Castilians' language, at first an obscure version of popular Latin, would evolve and eventually spread across a maritime empire the likes of which the world had never seen. The collapse of *that* empire then spawned two dozen new countries that share the Spanish language.

Spain's empire was indeed critical to Spanish. But the real force driving Spanish over the last one thousand years has been the spirit of its speakers, at once ingenious and sensitive, cruel and caring, coarse and highly spiritual.

How will this spirit shape the Spanish of the future? It's impossible to say. But there have been many surprises.

For instance, no twelfth-century Muslim in Córdoba would have predicted that Al-Andalus—epicenter of the most brilliant culture in Europe at the time—would one day be the scene of a massive witch hunt against false converts, where hundreds of thousands of people would be expelled from its borders because of

their religion, and religious zeal would foster intellectual obscurantism.

Nor would a thirteenth-century cleric in Burgos have believed
that the Castilian tongue, so crude it wasn't considered fit for writing, would be the first European vernacular language to have a full
dictionary and a systematized grammar with clear spelling rules.

And not even the most literate among Columbus's crew could
have imagined that their voyage would trigger the largest genocide
in history. The Spanish explorer Juan Ponce de León, who landed
on the shores of Florida on Easter Day five hundred years ago,
would have been surprised to learn that his country would one day
forfeit chunks of its empire to anti-British insurgents. James Polk
and Theodore Roosevelt didn't know that annexing northern Mexico to the United States would set off one of the largest human migrations in history.

And who would have imagined the rise of *telenovelas,* or magic
realism, or Facebook, or *La Movida,* not to mention cowboy sad-
dles, cannon powder, and tango? Armies, navies, gold, diplomacy,
ideas, and good luck were all key elements in the story of Spanish.

Since so much of the story of Spanish has been about events no
one could have predicted, it seems futile to predict its future. However, the past does reveal some deeply embedded features of Spanish that withstood the centuries. And these will probably shape its
future.

What are the enduring features of Spanish?

The first is its "culture of language." The personality or culture
of Spanish is very orderly and neat, in complete contrast to the life
of the Spanish language itself, which has been disorderly and ad-
venturous. King Alfonso X began defining *lo correcto* (what is correct) in Castilian in the thirteenth century. Generations of writers,
grammarians, lexicographers, and philologists after him upheld
the principles he established. The result? Without dismissing colloquial or popular Spanish, or striving to attain an idealized language the way the French do with their doctrine of purism, Spanish

speakers over the centuries have grown to expect their language to be used correctly. So even Hispanics in the United States—who form a large minority in a country that is definitely not Spanish speaking—are working to establish their own set of standards. The effort to identify an international standard, called General Spanish, is also the product of the "culture of language" that Spanish speakers have shared for centuries. And Spanish could gain a lot from being the only international language with a very clear international standard.

The second consistent feature of Spanish is its tendency to spread. Spanish is a very entropic, centrifugal language. Born in one empire, it spread, and is still spreading, as if it requires disorder to stay alive. Already present when Castile became an organized force, this quality was an essential ingredient of the Reconquista and of Spanish colonialism after that. But after the collapse of the colonial empire, when Spanish countries found themselves distanced by competing powers, Spanish kept spreading. Yet this feature carried disadvantages: although Spanish is the world's second or third language for its number of speakers, no single Spanish-speaking country is very big. On the other hand, this spread or geographic diversity means that Hispanics who faced severe problems in their home country have always been able to find a Spanish-speaking haven somewhere in the world.

"Depth" is the third lasting feature of Spanish. French is more widely spread but is deeply implanted in only a few places. Spanish has a deep presence wherever it is spoken. The large number and density of native speakers produce a rich and prolific cultural market in Spanish, a market that has demonstrated its potential repeatedly, with a great number and variety of cultural products entering global culture. Yet oddly, Spanish doesn't seem to spread by any means other than close contact, which is why it expands only in neighboring territories like the United States, Brazil, and France. This inability to reach out may have its roots in Spain's early rejection of the Enlightenment ideals. Today, this inward-looking tendency is rearing its head in the form of undereducation of the masses and a chronic struggle to sustain functioning democracies—both of which, whatever their exact causes, diminish the attractiveness of Spanish.

There are a few things in the future of Spanish that seem quite certain. They can all be summarized in the oft-repeated formula, *El futuro del español es América* (The future of Spanish is America)— *América* here referring to the entire continent and not a single country.

Spanish will continue to be an international language dominated by a large number of native speakers, 90 percent of whom live on the west side of the Atlantic Ocean. Short of a massive global catastrophe or epidemic, this will not change, except perhaps in Bolivia and Paraguay, where there are native languages that still rival Spanish. Linguistically speaking, Spanish will be driven by Latin American dialectal influence. That tendency will keep increasing as (and *if*) the economies and standard of living of Latin America countries continue to improve.

Spain is a different story. While Spanish is solidly entrenched in most Hispanic countries, in Spain it is still competing with Catalan, and on Catalan's home turf. Although nothing in the foreseeable future suggests that Catalan will erase Spanish, the idea that Catalan might break away from the story of Spanish, the way Portuguese did nine centuries ago, is not inconceivable.

The two main non-Hispanic countries where Spanish is making serious inroads, Brazil and the United States, constitute big chunks of *América*. The reasons Spanish is making progress in each country are very different: in Brazil, it's trade; in the United States, it's migration. Theoretically, either country could reverse the trend with laws or policies, but this would come at a price, and in both cases is unlikely.

Hispanic migration—or migratory pressure—will last as long as the standard of living in the United States remains so much higher than that of the rest of the continent. Demographics also reveal another certainty: Mexico's birthrate is dropping. According to Jim Peach of New Mexico State University, the aging of the border population will slow migration but not bring it to a halt.

As we were writing, Hispanic immigration to the United States had slowed to historically low levels. Most experts believe that high unemployment in the United States, especially in the construction industry, explains the trend. If that's the case, migration is likely to pick up again as the economy improves. The other explanation is Mexico's economy, which is growing, as its birthrate is falling. If that's the real explanation, then migration rates to the United States will slow, though no one can predict how much.

But in either case, the United States is bound to weigh much more heavily than Brazil in the predictable future of Spanish. This is clear from the numbers. Brazil is pushing to spread Spanish as a second language, and its efforts are aided by the fact that 90 percent of the vocabulary of Portuguese is similar to Spanish. Yet only half a million Hispanics live in Brazil. There are already a hundred times more Spanish speakers living in the United States. The relative weight of the United States on Spanish is also phenomenal. In the 1960s, Hispanics in the United States amounted to no more than 2 percent of the global Hispanic population. They now represent 16 percent and might reach almost 25 percent by 2050.

In the U.S. counties where Hispanics form the majority, or close to it, Spanish shows signs of competing with English as an assimilating force. This massive demographic shift will leave traces on the language. The United States has is own academy of Spanish, which works in collaboration with all the other Spanish-language academies in the world in defining General Spanish. The academy in the United States is even striving to define the Spanish *of* the United States, since American media and translators are progressively doing that anyway.

As a result, the tastes and inclinations of American Hispanics count more and more to Spanish-language countries trying to reach global markets. This is true of *telenovelas* and of music. The Lebanese Colombian singer Shakira was already an international Spanish-speaking star before she made her foray into the American market around 2000. Ten years later, when she reverted to Spanish, she was an entirely different type of artist, and Hispanics bought it.

Writing is another example. Hispanics in the United States are culturally distinct from Hispanics elsewhere. Linguists have noticed that Spanish writing in the United States tends to use more concise sentences and paragraphs. Exactly how this will modify or influence Hispanic writing around the world remains to be seen, but the more Hispanics there are in the United States, the stronger their influence will be.

Miguel Abad, the cultural attaché of the Spanish consulate in Los Angeles, told us that every Hispanic country in the world is trying to get into the U.S. cultural markets. Spain, Mexico, Colombia, and Argentina are all working actively to boost their cultural links with the United States. This may or may not influence U.S. society as a whole, but it will certainly affect U.S. Hispanics as well as all the world's *hispanohablantes* (Spanish speakers).

Beyond these few certainties, much of the future of Spanish should be written in the subjunctive tense—for what's hypothetical, uncertain, or desired.

What policy and politics will do to Hispanics—in the United States, Latin America, or Spain—is anybody's guess. Historians and sociologists have often observed that intolerance rises when a minority's population reaches 5 to 25 percent of the general population. Hispanics in the United States crossed the 5 percent line in 1973. Today, they account for 16 percent of the population and are expected to reach 25 percent in thirty or so years. That means that, over merely three generations, they could have moved in and out of the danger zone.

In the meantime, will political intolerance stunt the growth of the Hispanic population? Immigration could be stopped, immigrants could be sent back, assimilation could be forced. It's unlikely, but it's possible.

It's also possible that Hispanics will go on to create a new political reality in the United States, including official bilingualism in some states, more federal support for Spanish, or deeper ties with Mexico. If 22 percent of Mexicans live in the United States today, what will the proportion be in thirty years, and what will that mean for the United States when it comes to managing retirement, labor relations, and trade? These are speculations. And if the U.S. Congress some day agrees to incorporate Puerto Rico into the Union, Spanish will enter the U.S. Congress. These again are speculations, but also possibilities.

And in either of these scenarios, what will happen to the Spanish spoken in the United States? Will it vanish as Hispanics assimilate? Will it adapt to the rules of General Spanish? Or will Spanglish evolve into a whole new language? Speculations, again.

The politics of the rest of the Hispanic world are equally impossible to predict. If lessons from the past can be used to predict the future, then the Americas will not grow as fast as the rest of the world, and massive migration toward neighboring countries will continue north of the Rio Grande. If Brazil succeeds in its passage from third-world to first-world country, this will certainly induce more Hispanic migration there.

Will Latin America overcome chronic undereducation, underdevelopment, and its authoritarian tendencies as Spain managed to? Spain had the help of the European Union, but no one will underwrite Latin America's transformation.

Yet the recent past may signal a promising new trend. Latin America is richer, more democratic, and better educated that it has ever been. Even Mexico's economy and democracy, despite the brutal drug war going on, are not on a downward spiral, largely because the growing Mexican middle class is holding the country together out of sheer willpower.

What will these political trends do to the language? Impossible to say.

The Spanish language, meanwhile, is unquestionably the unifying force of the Hispanic world and its greatest cultural export. Two centuries of centrifugal politics on two continents have not resulted in any country pulling away from General Spanish. There is always a risk it may happen, but neither Fidel Castro in Cuba nor Hugo Chávez in Venezuela—to name recent examples—has dared do that. And even if one country were to splinter from General Spanish—and one of the small countries could—this would probably not affect the future of Spanish in the least.

The more significant question about the future of Spanish is whether Hispanics will meet the educational challenges they face and overcome the heritage of colonialism, conservatism, and inquisitorial obscurantism. Global artistic and cultural success shows that the Hispanic world can achieve a lot when it wants to. But it still faces an uphill battle to overcome its deficit in scientific and technological output.

H. G. Wells, in his novel *The Shape of Things to Come,* predicted—among other things—that Spanish and English would one day "become interchangeable languages." He predicted that in 2059, a so-called Dictatorship of the Air would create a global lingua franca called Basic English, which would mix English and Spanish.

His utopia is totally off the mark, and based on what we know of linguistics, next to impossible. Still, it is fascinating to think that this great visionary saw the future of English linked with that of Spanish—as they undoubtedly will be in the future chapters of the story of Spanish.

Appendixes

SPANISH SPEAKERS BY COUNTRY

COUNTRY	RANK	POPULATION (MILLIONS)	YEAR OF INDEPENDENCE (DECLARED)
Mexico*	1	112.3	1810
Colombia*	2	46.5	1810
Spain*	3	46.2	–
Argentina*	4	40.1	1816
Peru*	5	28.2	1821
Venezuela*	6	27.2	1811
Chile*	7	17.4	1818
Guatemala*	8	14.7	1821
Ecuador*	9	14.6	1809
Cuba*	10	11.2	1902
Bolivia*	11	10.4	1825
Dominican Republic*	12	9.4	1821
Honduras*	13	8.4	1821
Paraguay*	14	6.3	1811
El Salvador*	15	6.2	1821
Nicaragua*	16	5.8	1821
Costa Rica*	17	4.3	1821
Puerto Rico*	18	3.7	–
Panama*	19	3.4	1903
Uruguay*	20	3.3	1825
Equatorial Guinea†	21	0.7	1968
Total		**420.3**	

Source: Cervantes Institute, 2012.

* Countries with an official Spanish-language academy.

† Country where Spanish is a minority language.

SPANISH SPEAKERS, OTHER COUNTRIES

COUNTRY	NATIVE LANGUAGE	SECOND LANGUAGE, OR LIMITED PROFICIENCY
Algeria	300	223,000
Andorra	33,300	21,600
Aruba	6,800	68,600
Australia	106,500	374,600
Belize	173,600	22,000
Brazil	460,000	12,000,000
Cayman Islands	2,000	–
Canada	909,000	92,900
Dutch Indies (Bonair, Curaçao)	107,000	114,800
European Union (excluding Spain)	2,397,000	15,600,000
Guam	19,900	–
Iceland	700	–
Israel	130,000	45,200
Jamaica	8,000	–
Morocco	6,600	3,408,900
Norway	12,600	23,700
Philippines*	439,000	2,557,800
Russia	3,300	20,000
Switzerland	86,000	25,000
Trinidad and Tobago	4,100	61,800
Turkey	1,100	12,300
United States*	37,000,000	15,000,000
Virgin Islands	16,800	–
Western Sahara	–	22,000
Total	**41,923,600**	**49,694,200**

Source: Cervantes Institute, 2012. Compiled from national censuses and UN estimates.

* Countries with an official Spanish-language academy.

LEARNERS OF SPANISH AS A FOREIGN LANGUAGE

COUNTRY	LEARNERS
Belgium	41,000
Brazil	5,000,000
Cameroon	64,000
Canada	93,000
Denmark	40,000
France	2,100,000
Germany	453,000
Italy	302,000
Ivory Coast	236,000
Japan	60,000
Morocco	58,000
Senegal	101,000
Sweden	163,000
United Kingdom	102,000
United States	6,000,000
Subtotal Top 15	**14,813,000**
Next 71 countries*	630,000
Rest of the world[†]	2,557,000
Total	**18,000,000**

Sources: *Enciclopedia del Español en el mundo* and Cervantes Institute, 2012.

* The list compiled in 2007 had 86 countries.

[†] To account for the rest of the world, the Cervantes Institute projected an extra 15 percent.

INFLUENCE OF LANGUAGE BY ABSOLUTE NUMBERS

Professors Louis-Jean Calvet and Alain Calvet created an index that ranks languages. The list compiles data for the 137 languages spoken by more than five million people. Ten criteria are used and the Calvets' Web site contains a very detailed explanation of how they converted numbers into a system of points that would allow for comparison.

CRITERION	SPANISH	ENGLISH	FRENCH	ARABIC	MANDARIN
Overall score	**4.465**	7.238	4.587	2.660	2.303
Number of native speakers*	**329 million**	328 million	68 million	222 million	845 million
Entropy[†]	**2.52**	1.18	0.87	2.39	0.04
Human Dev. Index (%)	**0.84**	0.95	0.96	0.64	0.77
Fertility rate (%)	**2.2**	2	1.9	3.2	1.8
Internet penetration index	**38%**	74%	70%	16%	27%
Wikipedia articles	**402,400**	2.6 million	709,000	77,400	205,000
Official status[‡]	**21**	63	36	21	3
Nobel Prizes literature	**10**	27	12	1	1
Translation from	**43,900**	1 million	189,100	10,100	7,700
Translation to	**207,800**	116,600	203,600	10,300	11,200

Source: Le baromètre Calvet des langues du monde, 2012, www.portalingua.info/fr/poids-des-langues/.

* Based on statistics by Ethnologue. Compiles speakers according to first language only. Second-language speakers are excluded.

† Measures the degree of dispersion of language.

‡ Countries where the language has official status.

INFLUENCE OF SPANISH BY RANK

CRITERION	SPANISH	ENGLISH	FRENCH	ARABIC	MANDARIN
Overall rank	3	1	2	8	13
Number of native speakers*	2	3	15	4	1
Entropy†	1	11	21	2	97
Human Dev. Index	23	12	3	74	47
Fertility rate	77	87	92	27	101
Internet penetration	29	7	11	67	43
Wikipedia articles	9	1	3	23	12
Official status‡	3	1	2	4	10
Nobel Prizes literature	4	1	2	12	14
Translation from	6	1	2	14	17
Translation to	2	5	3	27	25

Source: Le baromètre Calvet des langues du monde, 2012, www.portalingua.info/fr/poids-des-langues/.

*Based on statistics by Ethnologue. Compiles speakers according to first language only. Second-language speakers are excluded.

† Measures the degree of dispersion of language.

‡ Countries where the language has official status.

Hispanic Nobel Prizes by Country

Argentina
Carlos Saavedra Lamas, Peace, 1936
Bernardo Houssay, Physiology or Medicine, 1947
Luis Federico Leloir (born in France), Chemistry, 1970
Adolfo Pérez Esquivel, Peace, 1980
César Milstein, Physiology or Medicine, 1984

Chile
Gabriela Mistral, Literature, 1945
Pablo Neruda, Literature, 1971

Colombia
Gabriel García Márquez, Literature, 1982

Costa Rica
Óscar Arias Sánchez, Peace, 1987

Guatemala
Miguel Ángel Asturias, Literature, 1967
Rigoberta Menchú, Peace, 1992

Mexico
Alfonso García Robles, Peace, 1982
Octavio Paz, Literature, 1990
Mario J. Molina,* Chemistry, 1995

Peru
Mario Vargas Llosa,* Literature, 2010

Spain

José Echegaray, Literature, 1904
Santiago Ramón y Cajal, Physiology or Medicine, 1906
Jacinto Benavente, Literature, 1922
Juan Ramón Jiménez, Literature, 1956
Severo Ochoa,* Physiology or Medicine, 1959
Vicente Aleixandre, Literature, 1977
Camilo José Cela, Literature, 1989

Venezuela

Baruj Benacerraf, Physiology or Medicine, 1980

*Country of birth

Select Bibliography

General Spanish and Linguistics

Alatorre, Antonio. *Los 1,001 años de la lengua española.* 3rd ed. Mexico, D.F.: Colegio de México, Fondo de Cultura Económica, 2003.

Antonio Alonso, José, and Rodolfo Gutiérrez. *Emigración y lengua: El papel des español en las migraciones internacionales.* Madrid: Fundación Telefónica, 2010.

Calvet, Louis-Jean, and Alain Calvet. *Baromètre Calvet des langues du monde.* http://www.portalingua.info/fr/poids-des-langues/.

Carrera Troyano, Miguel, and José J. Gómez Asencio. *La Economía de la enseñanza del español como lengua extranjera: Oportunidades y retos.* Madrid: Fundación Telefónica, 2009.

Constenla, Tereixa. "Una sola voz hacia el mundo." *El País,* April 7, 2011.

———. "Medio siglo de lupa sobre el español." *El País,* October 21, 2011.

Corominas, J., and J. A. Pascual. *Diccionario crítico etimológico castellano e hispanánico.* Madrid: Editorial Gredos, 2006.

García Delgado, José Luis, José Antonio Alonso, and Juan Carlos Jiménez. *Economía del español: una introducción.* 2nd ed. Barcelona: Ariel, 2008.

García Márquez, Gabriel. "Botella al mar para el Dios de las palabras." Inaugural speech, First International Latin Language Congress, Zacatecas, Mexico, 1997.

González Ollé, F. "Defensa y modernización del castellano: Salazar y Castro frente a la Academia Española." In M. Ariza et al., eds., *Actas del II Congreso Internacional de Historia de la Lengua Española.* Madrid: Pabellón de España, 1992.

Iannuzzi, Isabella. "Talavera y Nebrija: Lenguaje para convencer, gramática para pensar." *Hispania: Revista Española de Historia* 68 (2008): 37–62.

Javier Girón, Francisco, and Agustín Cañada. *Las cuentas del español*. Barcelona: Ariel, 2009.

Jiménez-Ríos, Enrique. "Algunas Críticas Tempranas al Diccionario de la Academia." *Thesaurus* 54, no. 3 (1999): 1071–1101.

"Languages of Business." Bloomberg Rankings, August 5, 2011.

Lapesa, Rafael. *Historia de la lengua española*. 9th ed. Madrid: Editorial Gredos, 1991.

Leclerc, Jacques. "L' Aménagement linguistique dans le monde." http://www.tlfq.ulaval.ca/AXL/.

Lipski, John M. "Spanish Linguistics: The Past 100 Years: Retrospective and Bibliography." *Hispania* 81, no. 2 (May 1998): 248–60.

López Morales, Humberto. *La globalización del léxico hispánico*. Madrid: Espasa Calpe, 2007.

Maltby, Robert. "Hispanisms in the Language of Isidore of Seville." In G. Urso, ed., *Hispania Terris Omnibus Felicior: Atti del 2001 convegno internazionale, Cividale del Friuli*. Pisa: 2002.

Marcos-Marín, Francisco A. "Spanish Lexicography: A Short Report." Workgroup for Lexicography, Thematic Network Project, European Language Council. Berlin, 1999.

Martínez, José María, ed. *Enciclopedia del español en el mundo*. Barcelona: Círculo de lectores, 2006.

Medina López, Javier. "Elías Zerolo (1848–1900) y la labor de la Real Academia Española." *Revista de Filología Española* 87, no. 2 (2007): 351–71.

Menéndez Pidal, Ramón. *Orígenes del español*. Madrid: Espasa Calpe, 1968 [1926].

Moliner, María. *Diccionario de uso del español*. 2 vols. 3rd ed. Madrid: Gredos, 2007.

Moreno Fernández, Francisco, ed. *El español, una lengua viva*. Madrid: Instituto Cervantes, 2012.

Moreno Fernández, Francisco, and Jaime Otero Roth. *Atlas de la lengua española en el mundo.* Barcelona: Ariel, 2008.

Penny, Ralph. *Variation and Change in Spanish.* New York: Cambridge University Press, 2000.

———. *A History of the Spanish Language.* New York: Cambridge University Press, 2002.

Pezzi, Elena. *Arabismo:. Estudio etimológicos.* Almería: Universidad de Almería, 1995.

Pharies, David A. *A Brief History of the Spanish Language.* Chicago: University of Chicago Press, 2007.

Prieto, Carlos. *Cinco mil años de palabras: Comentarios sobre el origen, evolución, muerte y resurrección de algunas lenguas.* Mexico D.F.: Fondo de Cultura Económica, 2007.

Real Academia Española. *Diccionario de la lengua española.* 22nd ed. Madrid: Espasa Calpe, 2001.

Rodríguez Marcos, Javier. "En ningún sitio se habla el mejor español del mundo." *El País,* December 15, 2011.

Rojo, Guillermo, and Mercedes Sánchez. *El español en la red.* Madrid: Fundación Telefónica, 2007.

Sarmiento, Ramón, and Fernando Vilches. *La calidad del español en la red: Nuevos usos de la lengua en los medios digitales.* Barcelona; Ariel, 2009.

Vaquero, Antonio. "El español y la tecnología." *El País*, April 21, 2011.

Wilkinson, Hugh E. "The Latinity of Ibero-Romance." *Ronshu,* 1967.

Wright, Roger. *Early Ibero-Romance: Twenty-one Studies on Language and Texts from the Iberian Peninsula Between the Roman Empire and the Thirteenth Century.* Newark, DE: Juan de la Cuesta, 1994.

Zamora Vicente, Alonso. *Historia de la Real Academia Española.* Madrid: Espasa Calpe, 1999.

———. "Real Academia Española." *Las Reales Academias del Instituto de España.* Madrid: Collective Alianza Editorial, 1999.

Spanish in Spain and Portugal

Anderson, Robert R. "Alfonso X el Sabio and the Renaissance in Spain." *Hispania* 44, no. 3 (September 1961).

Chabás, José, and Bernard R. Goldstein. *The Alfonsine Tables of Toledo.* Norwell, MA: Kluwer Academic Publishers, 2003.

"Catalan, Language of Europe." Barcelona: Generalitat de Catalunya, Secretaria de Política Lingüística, 2008.

De Hoyos González, Margarita. "Una variedad en el habla coloquial: La jerga 'cheli.'" *CAUCE* 4 (1981): 31–39.

Douglass, R. Thomas. "The Letter *H* in Spanish." *Hispania* 70, no. 4 (December 1987).

Elliot van Liere, Katherine. "After Nebrija: Academic Reformers and the Teaching of Latin in Sixteenth-Century Salamanca Authors." *Sixteenth Century Journal* 34, no. 4 (Winter 2003): 1065–1105.

Gómez Font, Alberto. "Los libros de estilo de los medios de comunicación en español: Necesidad de un acuerdo." Universidad Complutense de Madrid, 1998.

Hartman, Steven Lee. "Alfonso el Sabio and the Varieties of Verb Grammar." *Hispania* 57, no. 1 (March 1974).

Kanellos, Nicolás. *Hispanic Firsts: 500 Years of Extraordinary Achievement.* Canton, MI: Visible Ink Press, 1997.

Landeira, Ricardo. *The Modern Spanish Novel: 1898–1936.* Boston: Twayne Publishers, 1985.

Lope Blanch, Juan M. *Nebrija: Cinco Siglos Después.* Mexico, D.F.: Universidad Nacional Autónoma de México, 1994.

Martín Municio, Ángel. *El valor económico de la lengua española.* Madrid: Espasa Calpe, 2003.

Noceda, Miguel Ángel. "El valor económico de un idioma redondo." *El País,* February 27, 2010.

O'Callaghan, Jospeh F. *The Learned King: The Reign of Alfonso X of Castile.* Philadelphia: University of Pennsylvania Press, 1993.

Rodríguez Marcos, Javier. "Hay que volver a enseñar a leer y a escribir." *El País,* December 5, 2010.

Smith, Colin. *The Making of the "Poema de mio Cid."* New York: Cambridge University Press, 1983.

Van Scoy, Herbert A. "Alfonso X as a Lexicographer." *Hispanic Review* 8, no. 4 (October 1940): 277–84.

———. "Alfonso X, Educator." *South Atlantic Bulletin* 24 (May 1958): 4–6.

Spanish in Latin America

Ávila, Raúl. "Los medios de comunicación masiva y el español internacional." Paper presented at Congresos internacionales de la lengua española, Valladolid, 2011.

Bono López, María. "La Política lingüística en Nueva España." *Anuario mexicano de Historia del Derecho* 9 (1997): 11–45.

Canfield, D. Lincoln. *Spanish Pronunciation in the Americas.* Chicago: University of Chicago Press, 1981.

Clements, J. Clancy. *The Linguistic Legacy of Spanish and Portuguese: Colonial Expansion and Language Change.* Cambridge: Cambridge University Press, 2009.

D'amore, Anna Maria. "La influencia mutua entre lenguas: Anglicismos, hispanismos y otros préstamos." *Revista Digital Universitaria* 10, no. 3 (March 10, 2009).

Lopéz Morales, Humberto. *La aventura del español en América.* Madrid: Espasa Calpe, 2005.

Luque Alcaide, Elisa. "¿Proyecto educativo de Carlos III para la Nueva España?" In Manuel Casado Arboniés and Pedro Manuel Alonso Marañón, coords., *Temas de Historia de la Educación en América.* Madrid: Asociación Española de Americanistas, 2007.

McWhorter, John H. "The Scarcity of Spanish-Based Creoles Explained." *Language in Society* 24, no. 2 (June 1995): 213–44.

Moreno de Alba, José G. *El español en América.* 3rd ed. Mexico, D.F: Fondo de Cultura Económica, 2005.

Ostler, Nicholas. *Empires of the World: A Language History of the World.* New York: HarperCollins, 2005.

Real Academia Española. *Diccionario de americanismos.* Madrid: Santillana Ediciones Generales, 2010.

Wagner, Claudio. "Andrés Bello y la Gramática Castellana latinoamericana." Santiago de Chile: Universidad de Chile, Documentos Lingüísticos y Literarios, 2006.

Spanish in the United States

Alvarez, Robert R., Jr. "The Lemon Grove Incident: The Nation's First Successful Desegregation Court Case." *San Diego Historical Society Quarterly* 32, no. 2 (Spring 1986).

Aparicio, Frances R. "Teaching Spanish to the Native Speaker at the College Level." *Hispania* 66, no. 2 (May 1983): 232–39.

Butler, Nicholas Murray, Victor M. Cutter, and William R. Shepherd. "The Importance of the Study of Spanish." *Hispania* 17, no. 4 (December 1934): 370–72.

"Courses in Spanish Language and Literature in Madrid: The Eleventh Summer Session for Foreigners 1922." *Hispania* 5, no. 1 (February 1922).

Duany, Jorge. "Puerto Ricans in the United States." In Melvin Ember, Carol R. Ember, and Ian Skoggard, eds., *Encyclopedia of Diasporas.* New York: Springer, 2005.

Earley, Helen C. "An Optimistic View of Spanish in the Elementary School." *Hispania* 27, no. 1 (February 1944).

"Emerging Communities: A Snapshot of a Growing Hispanic America." Presented by the League of United Latin American Citizens. Washington, D.C., June 2003.

Fierros, Aurelia, ed. *Spanglish, el Suplemento.* 17 article series, hispanicLA.com, April 19, 2010.

Glass, Zaina. "Teaching Spanish in a Small High School." *Modern Language Journal* 32, no. 3 (March 1948).

Harvey, William C. *Spanish for the Construction Trade.* Hauppauge, NY: Barron's, 2007.

Helman, Edith F. "Early Interest in Spanish in New England (1815–1835)." *Hispania* 29, no. 3 (August 1946).

Kercheville, F. M. "Fitting the Teaching of Spanish to Community Needs." *Hispania* 17, no. 2 (May 1934).

Kramsch, Claire. "Post 9/11: Foreign Languages between Knowledge and Power." *Applied Linguistics* 26, no. 4 (December 2005): 545–67.

Leavitt, Sturgis E. "The Teaching of Spanish in the United States." *Hispania* 44, no. 4 (December 1961).

McCuaig, W. D. "A Reconsideration of the Teaching of Spanish on the Undergraduate Level." *Modern Language Journal* 25, no. 2 (November 1940): 108–12.

Molinero, Leticia. "La traducción al español en los Estados Unidos." Paper presented at the 5th Congreso Latinoamericano de Traducción e Interpretación, Buenos Aires, May 2010.

———. "El español de los Estados Unidos, un nuevo punto de partida." Speech presented at Academia Norteamericana de la lengua española, New York, October 2011.

Pedalino Porter, Rosalie. "The Case Against Bilingual Education." *Atlantic Monthly*, May 1998.

Piña-Rosales, Gerardo, Jorge I. Covarrubias, Joaquín Segura, and Daniel Fernández, eds. *Hablando bien se entiende la gente.* Miami: Santillana USA, 2010.

"Power in Numbers: Hispanics, Long Under-Represented as Voters, Are Becoming Political Kingmakers." Editorial. *The Economist,* January 7, 2010.

Rusciolelli, Judith. "Teaching a Course on United States Hispanic Cultures: A Multicultural Approach." *Hispania* 77, no. 1 (March 1994).

Sinclair, Murray. "Tucson Tots Talk Spanish." *Hispania* 31, no. 4 (November 1948).

Sommers, Laurie Kay. "Inventing Latinismo: The Creation of 'Hispanic' Panethnicity in the United States." *Journal of American Folklore* 104, no. 411 (Winter 1991).

Spell, J. R. "Spanish Teaching in the United States." *Hispania* 10, no. 3 (May 1927): 141–59.

Stavans, Ilan. *Spanglish: The Making of a New American Language.* New York: HarperCollins, 2003.

———. Codex Espanglesis. HispanicLA.com., April 19, 2010.

Tió, Salvador. "Teoría del Espanglish." *Diario de Puerto Rico*, October 28, 1948.

Tucker, E. Bernice "¡Hola, Amigos!—In-School Television Spanish Classes." *Hispania* 41, no. 4 (December 1958).

Weise, Julie M. "Mexican Nationalisms, Southern Racisms: Mexicans and Mexican Americans in the U.S. South, 1908–1939." *American Quarterly* 60, no. 3 (September 2008): 749–77.

Withers, A. M. "Spanish and, Not Versus, French." *Modern Language Journal* 29, no. 2 (February 1945).

History of Spain and Portugal

Al-Hassani, Salim. "Islamic Coins during the Umayyad, Abbasid, Andalusian and Fatimid Dynasties." Foundation for Science Technology and Civilisation, 2004.

Bennassar, Bartolomé. *Brève Histoire de l'Inquisition: L'intolérance au service du pouvoir.* Monsempron-Libos: Éditions Fragile, 1999.

———. *La España del Siglo de Oro.* Barcelona: Crítica, 2010.

Buñuel, Luis. *My Last Sigh.* Minneapolis: University of Minnesota Press, 2003.

Carr, Raymond. *Spain: A History.* New York: Oxford University Press, 2000.

Cazorla Sánchez, Antonio. *Fear and Progress: Ordinary Lives in Franco's Spain, 1939–1975.* Malden, MA: Wiley-Blackwell, 2010.

Constenla, Tereixa. "El archivo de la 'superagente.'" *El País,* November 18, 2011.

Corral, José Luis. *El Cid.* Barcelona: Edhasa, 2001.

Cruz, Juan. "La Balcells." *El País,* May 27, 2000.

Defourneaux, Marcelin. *Daily Life in Spain in the Golden Age.* Palo Alto: Stanford University Press, 1971.

De Gennaro, Angelo A. "Américo Castro Interprets Spain." *Hispania* 43, no. 2 (May 1960).

Diamond, Jared. *Collapse: How Societies Choose to Fail or Succeed.* New York: Viking, 2005.

Disney, A. R. *A History of Portugal and the Portuguese Empire.* 2 vols. New York: Cambridge University Press, 2009.

Elbl, Ivana. "Man of His Time (and Peers): A New Look at Henry the Navigator." *Luso-Brazilian Review* 28, no. 2 (Winter 1991).

Fierro, Maribel. *Al-Andalus: Savoirs et Échanges Culturels.* Aix-en-Provence: Edisud, 2001.

García Márquez, Gabriel. "La mujer que escribió un diccionario." *El País,* February 10, 1981.

Geli, Carles. "El arquero del siglo: Seix Barral refleja en sus 100 años de vida la evolución del sector editorial." *El País,* July 5, 2011.

Hämel, Adalbert. "The Spanish Movement in Germany." *Modern Language Journal* 12, no. 4 (January 1928): 261–71.

Higginbotham, Virginia. *Spanish Film Under Franco.* Austin: University of Texas Press, 1987.

Hitti, Philip K. *History of the Arabs.* 10th ed. New York: Palgrave Macmillan, 2002.

Jordan, Barry. *Writing and Politics in Franco's Spain.* New York: Routledge, 1990.

Labanyi, Jo. *Myth and History in the Contemporary Spanish Novel.* New York: Cambridge University Press, 1989.

Lacroix, Paul, Édouard Fournier, and Fernand Seré. *Histoire de l'imprimerie: Du manuscrit au livre imprimé.* Paris: Adolphe Delahays Publisher, n.d. [19th century].

Legendre, Bertrand. "La dame aux trois Nobel." *Le Monde,* January 27, 1989.

Markham, James M. "Hemingway's Spain." *New York Times,* November 24, 1985.

Navarro, Vicente. "How Secretary of State Cordell Hull and Nobel Laureate Camilo José Cela Collaborated with Spain's Fascist Regime." *Counterpunch,* October 30, 2004.

Nourry, Philippe. "Par la magie de Carmen." *Le Point,* February 4, 1995.

O'Callaghan, Joseph F. "The Interior Life of the Military Religious Orders of Medieval Spain." Malta Study Center Lecture Series. Presented at St. John's University, Collegeville, MN, October 2001.

————. *Reconquest and Crusade in Medieval Spain.* Philadelphia: University of Pennsylvania Press, 2003.

Osuna Alarcón, María R. "María Moliner and Her Contribution to the History of Spain's Public Libraries." *Libraries & the Cultural Record* 44, no. 2 (2009): 220–33.

"La España de los Visigodos." *Muy Historia* 39 (January/February 2012).

"La UE aprueba el sistema de patentes que deja fuera a España." Editorial. *El País,* June 28, 2011.

"Les européens et leurs langues." *Eurobaromètre,* February 2006.

"Patents By Country, State, and Year—All Patent Types Granted: 01/01/1977–12/31/2010," U.S. Patent and Trademark Office, December 2010. www.uspto.gov.

Rubio, Fanny, and Jorge Urrutia. "La debilidad actual del español." *El País,* March 3, 2011.

Sureda, Joan. *The Golden Age of Spain: Painting, Sculpture, Architecture.* New York: Vendome Press, 2008.

Tolan, Sandy. *The Lemon Tree: An Arab, a Jew, and the Heart of the Middle East.* New York: Bloomsbury, 2006.

Villanueva, Darío, and Pere Gimferrer. *El Quijote antes del cinema.* Madrid: Villena Artes Gráficas, 2008.

Watt, W. Montgomery, and Pierre Cachia. *A History of Islamic Spain.* Piscataway, NJ: Aldine Transaction, 2007.

History: Latin America and the United States

Acosta, Yesenia D., and G. Patricia de la Cruz. *The Foreign Born From Latin America and the Caribbean: 2010.* Washington, D.C.: U.S. Census Bureau, September 2011.

Aguila, Jaime R. "Mexican/U.S. Immigration Policy Prior to the Great Depression." *Diplomatic History* 31, no 2 (April 2007): 207–25.

Alvarez, Robert R., Jr. "The Lemon Grove Incident." *Journal of San Diego History* 32, no. 2 (Spring 1986).

Bersentes, John, and Mark Havard. "Why the Federal Government Can't Recruit and Retain Hispanic-Americans." ERE. net, January 27, 2010.

Bethell, Leslie, ed. *A Cultural History of Latin America: Literature, Music and the Visual Arts in the 19th and 20th Centuries.* New York: Cambridge University Press, 1998.

Boyd-Bowman, Peter. *Patterns of Spanish Emigration to the New World (1493–1580).* Buffalo: State University of New York, Council on International Studies, 1973.

Bulmer-Thomas, Victor. "British Trade with Latin America in the Nineteenth and Twentieth Centuries." University of London, Institute of Latin American Studies, 1992.

Bushnell, David, and Neil Macaulay. *The Emergence of Latin America in the Nineteenth Century.* 2nd ed. New York: Oxford University Press, 1994.

Chávez, Thomas E. "The Cuartocentenario of Juan de Oñate." Santa Fe: *The Museum of New Mexico Magazine, El Palacio,* 1998.

Chavez y Gilbert, Donald A. "New Mexico's First Thanksgiving." *El Defensor Chieftain Reports,* November 23, 2010.

Chiaramonte, José Carlos, Carlos Marichal, and Aimer Granados. "Las Invenciones de los nombres de las naciones latinoamericanas." 12-article series. *El País,* August 8, 2010.

Cohen, Noam. "García Márquez's Shiner Ends Its 31 Years of Quietude." *New York Times,* March 29, 2007.

Columbus, Christopher. *The Four Voyages*. Trans. J. M. Cohen. New York: Penguin, 1969.

Constenla, Tereixa. "En el epicentro del 'boom.'" *El País,* November 17, 2011.

Coonrod Martínez, Elizabeth. "The Latin American Innovative Novel of the 1920s: A Comparative Reassessment." *CLCWeb* 4, no. 2 (June 2002).

Cormier, Jean. *Che Guevara*. Monaco: Éditions du Rocher, 1995

Dary, David. *Cowboy Culture: A Saga of Five Centuries*. Lawrence: University Press of Kansas, 1989.

Díaz del Castilo, Bernal. *Historia verdadera de la conquista de Nueva España*. Mexico City: Editorial Porrúa, 1980.

Eakin, Marshall C. *The History of Latin America: Collision of Cultures*. New York: Palgrave Macmillan, 2007.

Feinsilver, Julie M. *Healing the Masses: Cuban Health Politics at Home and Abroad*. Berkeley: University of California Press, 1993.

———. "Cuba's Medical Diplomacy." In Mauricio A. Font, comp., *Changing Cuba/Changing World*. New York: Bildner Center for Western Hemisphere Studies, Graduate Center, City University of New York, 2008.

Fuentes, Carlos. *The Buried Mirror: Reflections on Spain and the New World*. New York: Houghton Mifflin, 1999.

Gratton, Brian, and Myron P. Gutmann. "Hispanics in the United States, 1850–1990: Estimates of Population Size and National Origin." *Historical Methods* 33, no. 3 (Summer 2000).

Hämäläinen, Pekka. *The Comanche Empire*. New Haven: Yale University Press, 2008.

Harris, Michael D. "Art of the African Diaspora." In Melvin Ember, Carol R. Ember, and Ian Skoggard, eds., *Encyclopedia of Diasporas*. New York: Springer, 2005.

Huhn, Wilson. "The Effect of Hispanic Demographic Growth on the Interpretation of the Constitution." *Akron Law Café,* February 24, 2011.

Humes, Karen R., Nicholas A. Jones, and Roberto R. Ramirez. "Overview of Race and Hispanic Origin: 2010." Washington, D.C.: U.S. Census Bureau, 2011.

Huntington, Samuel P. "The Hispanic Challenge." *Foreign Policy*, March 1, 2004.

Jaksić, Iván. *Andrés Bello, la pasión por el orden*. Santiago: Editorial Universitaria, 2001.

Kiser, Margaret. "What the Pan American Union Is Doing to Foster the Study of the Spanish Language and of Spanish American Literature and Culture." *Hispania* 30, no. 1 (February 1947).

Laglagaron, Laureen. *Protection through Integration: The Mexican Government's Efforts to Aid Migrants in the United States*. Washington, D.C.: Migration Policy Institute, January 29, 2010.

Las Casas, Bartolomé de. *A Short Account of the Destruction of the Indies*. Ed. and trans. Nigel Griffin. New York: Penguin, 1992.

Liptak, Adam. "Blocking Parts of Arizona Law, Justices Allow Its Centerpiece." *New York Times,* June 25, 2012.

Lynch, John. *Simón Bolívar: A Life*. New Haven: Yale University Press, 2006.

McCaa, Robert. "The Peopling of Mexico from Origins to Revolution," in Michael R. Haines and Richard H. Steckel, eds., *A Population History of North America*. New York: Cambridge University Press, 2000.

Meneses, Nacho. "El (lento) avance del español en brasil." *El País,* February 25, 2011.

Neruda, Pablo. *Memoirs*. Trans. Hardie St. Martin. New York: Farrar, Straus, 1977.

Owens, Anna M. *Hispanics in the United States*. Washington, D.C.: U.S. Census Bureau, 2006.

Passel, Jeffrey S., and D'Vera Cohn. "Unauthorized Immigrant Population: National and State Trends, 2010." Washington, D.C.: Pew Hispanic Center, 2011.

Payne, Stanley G., et al. *When Spain Fascinated America*. Madrid: Fundación Zuloaga, 2010.

Pérez Venzalá, Valentín. "Notas sobre el realismo mágico." Madrid: *Cuadernos del Minotauro,* February 2002.

Pleitez Vela, Tania. *Ramón Vinyes, "el sabio catalán" de* Cien años de soledad, *un escriptor a cavall de Catalunya y el Carib Colombia.* Barcelona: Universidad Autónoma, 2005.

Rodriguez, Marc Simon. "A Movement Made of 'Young Mexican Americans Seeking Change': Critical Citizenship, Migration, and the Chicano Movement in Texas and Wisconsin, 1960–1975." *Western Historical Quarterly* 34, no. 3 (Autumn 2003).

Ruiz Mantilla, Jesús. "García de la Concha: 'El eje del Cervantes será América.'" *El País,* January 27, 2012.

Rytina, Nancy. "Estimates of the Legal Permanent Resident Population in 2010." Department of Homeland Security, Office of Immigration Statistics, October 2011.

Saenz, Rogelio. "Latinos and the Changing Face of America." Washington, D.C.: Population Reference Bureau, 2012.

Sánchez-Alonso, Blanca. "European Immigration into Latin America, 1870–1930." *Journal of Iberian and Latin American Economic History* 3 (2007).

Suro, Roberto. *Changing Faiths: Latinos and the Transformation of American Religion.* Washington, D.C.: Pew Hispanic Center, April 25, 2007.

Tavernise, Sabrina. "Whites Account for Under Half of Births in U.S." *New York Times,* May 17, 2012.

Toral, Pablo. "Spanish Investment in Latin America." Canadian Foundation for the Americas, 2001.

Vega, Dr. Santos C., and Barrios, Frank. *Reflections from a Community.* Phoenix: Chicanos Por La Causa Inc., 2009.

Vélez-Ibáñez, Carlos G. *Border Visions: Mexican Cultures of the Southwest United States.* Tucson: University of Arizona Press, 1996.

Vogely, Nancy. *Lizardi and the Birth of the Novel in Spanish America.* Gainesville: University Press of Florida, 2001.

Volpi, Jorge. "La pesadilla de Bolívar." *El País,* July 1, 2009.

Index